Partnership within Hierarchy

Partnership within Hierarchy

The Evolving East Asian Security Triangle

SUNG CHULL KIM

SUNY PRESS

Cover photo of United States President George W. Bush, South Korean President Kim Dae-jung, and Japanese Prime Minister Junichiro Koizumi at the Asia-Pacific Economic Cooperation summit in Los Cabos, Mexico, October 26, 2002. Courtesy of Yonhap News. All Rights Reserved.

Published by State University of New York Press, Albany

For information, contact State University of New York Press, Albany, NY
www.sunypress.edu

Production, Ryan Morris
Marketing, Michael Campochiaro

Library of Congress Cataloging-in-Publication Data

Names: Kim, Sung Chull, 1956– author.
Title: Partnership within hierarchy : the evolving East Asian security triangle /
  Sung Chull Kim.
Description: Albany : State University of New York Press, 2017. | Includes
  bibliographical references and index.
Identifiers: LCCN 2016031443 (print) | LCCN 2016050246 (ebook) | ISBN
  9781438463933 (hardcover : alk. paper) | ISBN 9781438463940 (pbk. : alk.
  paper) | ISBN 9781438463957 (e-book)
Subjects: LCSH: Security, International—East Asia. | East Asia—Foreign relations |
  Japan—Foreign relations—Korea (North) | Korea (North)—Foreign relations—
  Japan. | Japan—Foreign relations—Korea (South) | Korea (South)—Foreign
  relations—Japan. | Korea (North)—Foreign relations—Korea (South) | Korea
  (South)—Foreign relations—Norea (North)
Classification: LCC JZ6009.E18 K56 2017 (print) | LCC JZ6009.E18 (ebook) |
  DDC 355/.03305—dc23
LC record available at https://lccn.loc.gov/2016031443

10 9 8 7 6 5 4 3 2 1

For my mother Lee Gwang-duk,
who gave me inspiration, wisdom, and the spirit of endurance

Contents

Contents

Tables

Acknowledgments

Since I conceived the idea of this project nine years ago, I have benefited from the insight, guidance, suggestions, and kindness of many people, and from the generous support and assistance at various institutions. Inasmuch as I used a voluminous amount of archives declassified in the United States, Korea, and Japan, I relied on the guidance of archivists and specialists in that respect: Jim Leyerzapf and David A. Langbart at the National Archives and Records Administration; Mary Curry and Robert Wampler at the National Security Archive at the George Washington University; Yu Bong-hyun at the Office of Diplomatic History Archives of the Ministry of Foreign Affairs in Korea; Park Jin-hee, Kim Jeom-sook, and Kang In-goo at the National Institute of Korean History. Also, I received kind assistance of librarians at the Jangseogak of the Academy of Korea Studies in Seongnam in Korea, the Institute of Developing Economics in Chiba and the National Diet Library-Kansaikan in Kyoto in Japan. Park Jung-jin, Choi Kyungwon, and Hong Seuk-ryule provided helpful suggestions for locating Japanese or U.S. sources. Paul Midford was kind to immediately send me his works that I needed urgently.

On this particular topic, I have received more penetrating insights from David Kang than from any others; in particular, his conception of hierarchy in international relations in Asia greatly attracted my attention. Because I presented parts of this work at some annual conferences including the Association for Asian Studies and the International Studies Association, I had wonderful chances to either receive specific comments from or learn through discussions with many scholars. They are Gilbert Rozman, Huiyun Feng, Kim Ji Young, Walter Hatch, Mark Caprio, Charles Armstrong, Tae-Hwan Kwak, Heon-joo Jung, Min-hyung Kim, Togo Kazuhiko, Kimura Kan, Asano Toyomi, Tsuneo Akaha, Kei Koga, Michael Cohen, Justin Hastings, Wade Huntley, Choi Youngho, and Kim Tae-ki. Those whom I met at workshops or conferences held in Japan, Korea, China, Hong Kong, Singapore, and Taiwan during my research on this topic contributed to broadening my views on regional dynamics between powers of differing capability: they are Lowell Dittmer, Etel Solingen, Stephen Haggard, Kenneth Quinones, Dae-sook Suh, Chae-jin Lee, Young C. Kim, Im Hyug-baeg, Lee Guen, Victor Teo, Kim Soung-chul, Shin Bong-gil, Sheen Seong-ho, Ahn Byung-woo, Bong Youngshik Daniel, Youn Hwang, Kim Keun-sik, Lee Jung-chul, Choi Sang-oh, Park Pilho, Kim Young-jak, Nakanishi Hiroshi, Kimijima Akihiko, Takahara Takao, Yamane Kazuyo, Moon Chung-in, Yi Ki-ho, Umebayashi Hiromichi, Morton H. Halperin, Yoon Tae-ryong, Zhe Sun, Jingdong Yuan, Chung Hunsup, Takesada Hideshi, Choo Jaewoo, Kim Bong-jin, Suh Seung-won, Miyamoto Satoru, Komaki Teruo, Nakagawa Masahiko, Hoshino Toshiya, Chang Dal-joong, Chun Chaesung, Kim Eun-mi, Kim Chang-su, Son Key-young, Chung Yousun, Sorpong Peou, and Van Jackson.

Hiro Katsumata, who always makes humorous but critical and helpful comments at conferences, read the two opening chapters of the manuscript and made valuable suggestions to clarify my analytic framing. My old friends Lam Peng Er and Yangmo Ku, with their colossal knowledge on details of events, did not hesitate to read chapters and help me improve them. The Korean experts on Japan studies such as Nam Ki-jeong, Park Cheol Hee, and Lee Won-deog either gave me invaluable suggestions on the manuscript or connected me to the academics in Japan. Through critical debates, Park Dong-jun, Lee Sang-hoon, Kwon Hee-young helped to refine my views on the troubling issues in Korea-Japan relations. Ku Nan-hee helped my collection of the data on disputes on the Japanese textbook issue and gave me further insights on the historical issues.

Through my attendance at the annual forum organized by the National University of Singapore East Asian Institute under the leadership of Zheng Yongnian, I have had the valuable opportunity to learn about China and Southeast Asia that otherwise I might have missed. I really appreciate the advice from those great scholars on China and the world such as Edward Friedman, Dorothy Solinger, T. J. Cheng, Chienmin Chao, and Fei-Ling Wang. Also the meeting with Patrick Morgan, T. V. Paul, and Terence Roehrig was a precious chance to widen my scope on deterrence, an increasingly important integral part in the topic of this book.

My former colleagues at the Hiroshima Peace Institute–Hiroshima City University provided me with a warm environment that enabled me to concentrate on this topic until I left there in 2012. Fukui Haruhiro read the entire manuscript and gave me specific comments for clarification. Asai Motofumi told me of old U.S.-Japan relationship, a narrative that was based on his diplomat experience. Numerous discussions with Kikkawa Gen, Mizumoto Kazumi, Yuki Tanaka, Christian Scherrer, Narayanan Ganesan, and Robert Jacobs enriched my ideas on this topic. Nagai Hitoshi, Takemoto Makiko, Takahashi Hiroko, Kawakami Akihiro, and Kim Tae-wook did not hesitate to help me access diverse Japanese materials and made my time in Hiroshima most exciting and productive. Inoue Yoshitaka, Tatebe Kenji, Tsumura Hiroshi, Yodono Takeshi, Santoh Tadahiro, Yamashita Yoshie, Nomura Miki, Yoshihara Yukiko, Yoshimoto Michiko, Kajihama Jun, Takahashi Yuko, and Kuramoto Tomoko all made efforts for my success with their administrative assistance and library work, including locating microfiches and microfilms. Also, I was fortunate to have met many great scholars during my time in Hiroshima: Wada Haruki, Kang Sang-jung, Tessa Morris-Suzuki, Gavan McCormack, Lee Jong-won, Kimiya Tadashi, Carol Gluck, Mark Seldon, Marie Soederberg, Okonogi Masao, Lee Aeliah, and Akiba Tadatoshi. They became a source of inspiration and nuanced interpretation of old subjects of Japan.

I am grateful to my current colleagues at Seoul National University Institute for Peace and Unification Studies. The institute pursuing excellence in research and my colleagues here have nurtured and stimulated inspirations on related topics on humanities and peace studies; thus, I would like to extend thanks to Jung Keun-sik, Park Myoung-kyu, Kim Byung-yeon, Lim Hong-bae, Kim Philo, Lee Moon-young, Baik Jiwoon, Kim Cheon-sik, Kim Taewoo, Yi Chan-su, Chang Yong-seok, Suh Bo-hyuk, Jeong Eun-mee, Choi Gyu-bin, and Song Young-hoon.

In conducting the research on this topic, I have received generous support from three grant sources: Grants-in-Aid for Scientific Research (kakenhi) funded by the Japan Society for the Promotion of Science (21510265), from 2009 to 2012; the Academy of Korean Studies Grant (AKS-09, 10-R59); and the National Research Foundation of Korea Grant funded by the Korean Government (NRF-2010-361-A00017), from 2012 to the completion of this writing. Travel, collecting materials, and hiring part-time workers were financed by these grants.

My deep gratitude goes to the two anonymous reviewers for their critical comments for my clarification of the notions in the frame and improvement of the chapters on the recent period. I would like to extend my thanks to Michael Rinella and Ryan Morris at SUNY Press for excellent editorial guidance and also to Edward Reed, Judith Fletcher, and Carol Agrimson for their hard work to make the manuscript more readable. Heartfelt support from Lee Byoung-yong, who was the institution builder of the Korea Institute for National Unification, sustained my interest on this topic. Finally but not the least, my wife Hyun-suk has inspired me and imparted to me the spirit of endurance in coping with all kinds of difficulty in life. My older son's family, Dalin and Soojin and their newborn daughter Taeri, has given me a new joy at the final stage of this work. My younger son Joshua read four chapters of the manu-script and suggested important points for clarification. All their hearts are embedded in this book, but any errors are my own.

Romanization

For the Japanese sources and names, the Hepburn system is used. In the Korean case, the standard ministry of culture system is adopted. Exceptions are some already commonly used spellings. Following the traditions of the countries, the family name appears first with the given name following. But the spellings of personal names that appear in works written in English are used as in the originals.

Abbreviations

ACSA	Acquisition and Cross-Servicing Agreement
ASEAN	Association of Southeast Asian Nations
CoCom	Coordinating Committee for Multilateral Export Controls
DLF	Development Loan Fund
DPJ	Democratic Party of Japan
DPRK	Democratic People's Republic of Korea
DRP	Democratic Republican Party
EDPC	Extended Deterrence Policy Committee (between ROK and the United States)
EXIM Bank	Export-Import Bank
FMS	Foreign Military Sales
FRUS	Foreign Relations of the United States
GARIOA	Government Aid and Relief in Occupied Areas
GHQ	General Headquarters (Supreme Commander of the Allied Powers)
GSOMIA	General Security of Military Information Agreement
HR	House of Representatives
IAEA	International Atomic Energy Agency
ICJ	International Court of Justice
ICRC	International Committee of the Red Cross

JRC	Japanese Red Cross Society
KCIA	Korean Central Intelligence Agency
KEDO	Korean Peninsula Energy Development Organization
KEPCO	Korea Electric Power Corporation
KTO	Korean Theater of Operations
LDP	Liberal Democratic Party
MITI	Ministry of International Trade and Industry
MSDF	Maritime Self-Defense Force
NATO	North Atlantic Treaty Organization
NEATO	Northeast Asia Treaty Organization
NKRC	North Korean Red Cross Society
NSAM	National Security Action Memorandum
NSC	National Security Council
NSDM	National Security Decision Memorandum
NSS	National Security Strategy (of the United States)
NSSD	National Security Study Directive
NSSM	National Security Study Memorandum
ODA	Official Development Assistance
OECD	Organization for Economic Co-operation and Development
PD	Presidential Directive
POSCO	Pohang Iron and Steel Company
PRC	People's Republic of China
ROC	Republic of China
ROK	Republic of Korea
SCAPIN	Supreme Commander of the Allied Powers Instruction
SCM	Security Consultative Meeting (between South Korea and the United States)
SCNR	Supreme Council for National Reconstruction

SDF	Self-Defense Forces
TCS	Trilateral Cooperation Secretariat
THAAD	Terminal High Altitude Area Defense
TISA	Trilateral Information Sharing Arrangement
UNC	United Nations Command
UNCURK	United Nations Commission for the Unification and Rehabilitation of Korea
UNGA	United Nations General Assembly
UNHCR	United Nations High Commissioner for Refugees
UNICEF	United Nations Children's Fund
UNSC	United Nations Security Council
VAWW-NET Japan	Violence Against Women in War Network Japan

1

Introduction

This book examines a unique security framework that joins the United States, Japan, and South Korea (Republic of Korea: ROK). This security framework is unique for two reasons: first, it is triangular, and second, it is hierarchical. The aim of this book is to show how the unique framework shapes the interactions between the three states with regard to two contentious issues—burden sharing and commitment.

From the Cold War era to the post–Cold War period, the United States has led two separate alliances: one is the Security Treaty between the United States and Japan, which was signed in 1952 (amended and renamed in 1960 as the Treaty of Mutual Cooperation and Security between the United States and Japan), and other is the Mutual Defense Treaty between the United States and the Republic of Korea, signed in 1953. Relations between Japan and South Korea until normalization in 1965 were anchored by the United States and consisted of modest trade relations only. The Japan-ROK normalization per se was not directly related to security cooperation; indeed, the most important component of the normalization treaty was economic cooperation, as stipulated in the "Agreement on the Settlement of Problems Concerning Property and Claims and on Economic Cooperation." With the Japan-ROK normalization, a triangular hierarchy was institutionalized among the United States, Japan, and South Korea in that order.[1] Although the nature of the hierarchy was informal and no one dared speak of it, each state's status was created by the power that it possessed and by its capability for maintaining its own national interests. Certainly there was tension between South Korea's official relations with the two others, on the one hand, and its unofficial rank in the hierarchy, on the other.

The particularly problematic part of the security triangle was the relationship between Japan and South Korea, which was marked by differing references regarding security and the resultant competing expectations, particularly on the burden sharing and commitment issues. To

Japan, the South Korean concern about bellicose North Korea was a secondary, if not trivial, concern. Japan's scope of security was broader than that of South Korea. The absence of rules or channels to resolve differences easily resulted in discord between the two on important security concerns. Japan, located in the middle of the hierarchy, had the upper hand since it could use its strategic importance in dealing with the two Koreas, as well as with China and other Asian states.

As the Cold War thawed, the security triangle in general and Japan-ROK relations in particular entered a new phase. The weakest power in the triangle, South Korea, benefited most from the grand change. South Korea opened normalized relations with the Soviet Union and China in 1990 and 1992, respectively. Furthermore, it became an OECD member country in 1996, graduating from aid-recipient status. North Korea was most disadvantaged by the change, and thus became an aggressive and destabilizing actor. In the post-9/11 era, changes in the U.S. security strategy and the rise of China have contributed to continued evolution of the security triangle. One of the most distinctive features is that the controversy over historical issues surfaced in Japan-ROK relations during the second half of the 2000s decade, despite increasing economic interdependence and cultural exchanges.

What has tied the three states together through friendly and troubling times? What has been the role of the United States? By addressing these questions, this book sheds new light on the internal dynamics surrounding the burden-sharing and commitment issues, and in doing so contributes to illuminating the intra-alliance politics in general. In the security triangle, the two U.S.-led security treaties have clearly stipulated the rules, whereas Japan-ROK relations have remained undefined and contentious. This situation has frequently invited U.S. intervention. The United States' dominant position and its binding role in the security triangle are important points in this book, whereas Japan's behavior in the middle is another point of nuanced analysis. During the Cold War era in particular, the policies and tactics of the three states were subsumed under the U.S. strategy of containing the Soviet Union. But there was room in which Japan was able to set its own policy preferences and indeed to pursue and achieve them even under this constraint. Japan adroitly used its strategic significance in order to take advantage of this space and maintain its interests and policy preferences. What led to Japan being established in the middle of the hierarchical order, even if informally? First, Japan had material power, and thus it could contribute substantially to burden sharing for assisting strategic areas around the world, including South Korea, during the Cold War. Second, Japan's scope of security increasingly converged with that of the United States toward the end of the Cold War period. After the thawing of the Cold War the two have become even closer in dealing with important global issues, as well as in coping with the rise of China.

Argument in Brief

The U.S.-Japan-ROK security triangle has retained hierarchical relations in that order. Here Japan and South Korea, the allies of the United States, are partners with each other. I call the Japan-ROK relations a partnership. Asymmetrical, uneven relations, not only between the United States and its allies but also between the U.S. allies, are undeniable facts that originated from the formative stage of the trilateral relations. The hierarchy has been an unofficial but virtual governing rule whereby the individual states have interacted with one another. Considering their different positions in the hierarchy, it is fair to call the relationship between Japan and South Korea an asymmetrical partnership. This was particularly true during the Cold War. The hierarchy was established in the context of the staging of the U.S.-led postwar order in the Asia Pacific region. At the heart of the hierarchy, there were the two U.S.-led treaties that shaped the two hub-and-spoke alliances. With the 1952 U.S.-Japan security treaty, the United States completed its policy of transforming a wartime enemy into an ally.[2] With the 1953 U.S.-ROK defense treaty, the United States committed itself to the defense of war-torn South Korea. In return, the two alliances incorporated Japan and South Korea into the U.S. strategy of containing the Soviet Union. Later, in 1965, Japan-ROK normalization supplemented the two U.S.-led treaties to complete the security triangle, although the normalization treaty did not explicitly mention security.

The security triangle has been a hybrid composed of two alliances and one partnership. And thus it has not operated as a single unified system. Particularly during the Cold War, the two U.S.-led security treaties and related agreements clearly stipulated constraints, obligations, and duties that each ally should bear. But the relations between Japan and South Korea, despite their shared value of anticommunism, suffered from an absence of rules for resolving differing interests and conflicting expectations. For example, South Korea considered North Korea the primary enemy and believed itself to stand on the front line, paying an extra cost that Japan should share. Japan, however, considered the expansion of the Soviet influence its primary concern, arguably without any indebtedness to South Korea. In relation to the Korean peninsula, Japan had its own policy preference, that is, maintenance of stability even with continuing division, and tried to exert it regardless of South Korean demands and preferences. Such differences between the two developed into disputes, which in turn invited U.S. intervention. In other words, dispute was built into this partnership.

Just as in other intra-alliance politics, there are two important but contentious issues at the heart of the security triangle, particularly in the eyes of the dominant power—burden sharing and partnership commitment. Creation and maintenance of a security mechanism necessitates a financial burden, and individual participants should share it; otherwise, meaningful cooperation for security of the entirety cannot be expected. Commitment is another important element of the security mechanism. Commitment in general, or partnership commitment in this particular case of Japan-ROK relations, involves declarations of the linkage of one's security to the other's and explicit statements of the will to cooperate on the security front. Burden sharing and commitment are the core elements that bind the security mechanism, and the two are closely interconnected.[3] Without burden sharing, it is difficult to say that a state is committed to the entirety to which it belongs; likewise, without commitment, a state is not likely to contribute to sharing the burden needed for the entirety. In the case of the triangle under investigation, burden sharing means that within the dominant power's (the United States') frame, a capable partner (Japan) provides aid to a less capable partner (ROK). Commitment means the dominant power's assurance vis-à-vis its allies' (Japan's and ROK's) cooperation with the dominant power to maintain the red line framed by the dominant power; it means also diplomatic and military cooperation between partners (Japan and ROK) in the triangle. The dominant power regards contention or dispute between the partners surrounding burden sharing and commitment as damaging its own interests and the security triangle as a whole.

In partnership within the hierarchy, owing to the absence of rules between the partners, the burden sharing issue, particularly the aid issue, becomes contentious. Against the dominant power's and the less capable state's expectations, the middle power (i.e., a capable state) is reluctant to take on a share of the dominant power's burden needed for the entirety. Whereas treaties normally stipulate the division of labor about burden sharing between allies, there is no clear or shared definition about it between partners. Likewise, the commitment issue is likely to remain contentious. The extent of fear of both abandonment and entrapment is not equal among the states of different capabilities. The more capable state worries about entrapment into a conflict in which the less capable partner state is involved, whereas the less capable state is afraid of the capable state's abandonment. This difference makes the states act differently. The less capable one demands the capable state's expressed commitment, whereas the capable one tries to avoid such commitment. Consequently, partnership commitment remains contentious until the dominant power intervenes between the partners. The Japan-ROK disputes have taken place in this way, and the United States has intervened in them.

U.S. intervention has taken various forms: superpower coercive pressure, a legalistic approach, moralistic preaching, businesslike intermediation, and nonintervention. In some cases the United States has remained mute or ambivalent, believing it useful for the management of the alliances. During the Cold War, U.S. behavior normally exhibited a combination of these forms. The more the United States considered disputes to be directly related to burden sharing and partnership commitment, the more likely it intervened assertively (e.g., the United States' intervention in the Japan-ROK normalization talks, its drawing of a red line on Japan's approach to North Korea, its close cooperation with Japan in protecting the ROK's legal standing in the UN, its encouragement of Japan's economic aid to South Korea, and its mediation of the Japan-ROK negotiations over the comfort women issue). The more the United States perceived a situation to be detracting from its influence, the more likely it was to rely on superpower coercive pressure (e.g., the ROK's use of delaying tactics on the repatriation issue, Japan's and the ROK's foot dragging in normalization negotiations, and the ROK government's mismanagement of a domestic scandal during the normalization negotiations). Japan's legalistic and moralistic approaches toward Korea-related issues were by and large aligned with the United States, thus its position usually prevailed (e.g., Japan's and the United States' reference to international law on maritime borders, and their reference to the humanitarian principle of free choice of residence). In the post–Cold War era, U.S. intervention in the differences between Japan and South Korea has become by and large businesslike, and has taken more ambivalent forms, for example, in the case of such sensitive issues as the comfort women and Dokdo/Takeshima.

The security triangle has persisted for more than six decades, even though relations among the three states in the post–Cold War era differ from those of the Cold War. In the Cold War period, despite frequent disputes between Japan and South Korea over burden sharing and partnership commitment, the security triangle produced a feedback effect to the system itself and to all three states. The feedback effect here means that a cooperative relation between states yields benefits, albeit in varying degrees and in asymmetrical ways, and in turn makes exiting the relation extremely costly. (Here I do not use such terms as *positive* and *negative* in order to avoid confusion in the adjectival connotations. Some proponents of historical institutionalism view positive feedback as the process of producing gains to the institution. In contrast, systems scientists have long held the view that positive feedback "alters variables and destroys their steady states," while negative feedback controls deviation and maintains homeostasis. Certainly there has been no serious communication between different disciplines on the notion of feedback.)[4] The United States has succeeded in shifting to Japan a part of its burden for sustaining strategically important states around the world, including South Korea. The burden sharing between the United States and Japan, for South Korea's defense and economy, was legitimized by their declared statements on the close relevance of the defense of Seoul to Tokyo's security—the Korea clause or the new Korea clause that frequently appeared in the U.S.-Japan joint statements. The declaration of relevance was certainly a U.S.-framed expression of Japan's security commitment to its partner South Korea. The United States and South Korea earnestly wanted it, although Japan was halfhearted on it.

On the flip side of the persistence, there has been internal dynamics of the security triangle. Since the thawing of the Cold War, the rank between the U.S. allies has been substantially relaxed because of South Korea's graduation from Japanese aid and its expanded diplomatic scope beyond the security triangle—that is, the opening of normalized relations with Russia and China. Also, Japan's activist security policy, aligned with U.S. strategy especially in coping with China, has contributed to an overall change in the security triangle. Despite above-mentioned changes, the security triangle has continued to yield a certain degree of feedback effect. The increasing North Korean threat has remained a common denominator that has continued to demonstrate the utility of the security triangle, although Japan's and the U.S.-Japan alliance's global roles reach far beyond East Asia.

Whereas burden sharing (specifically Tokyo's aid to Seoul), even if contentiously, has sustained the Japan-ROK partnership within the hierarchy during the Cold War, the absence of it in the post–Cold War era has markedly relaxed the asymmetrical relations. Given this, the escalating dispute over historical issues is not a surprise. With U.S. intervention, the partners reached an agreement in December 2015 over the long-contentious comfort women issue, but the historical enmity continues to reverberate in both societies. It is worth noting that the U.S. alliances and its intervention continue to sustain the Japan-ROK partnership and the security triangle as an entirety.

Six Cases

For this book, I select six contentious cases of Japan-South Korea relations—four during the Cold War and two in the post–Cold War period. Concentrating on burden sharing and commitment, I analyze those cases from the Cold War era by using primary sources: U.S. State Department archives, South Korean diplomatic archives, and some Japanese archives. These cases disclose details of Japan-South Korea differences, negotiations, disputes, U.S. interventions, and solutions (Table 1.1, page 8). The degree of animosity and acrimony differed from case to case. The four cases during the Cold War commonly show that Japan's policy toward the Korean peninsula subscribed to hierarchy, and they also shed light on how the United States as the dominant power intervened in the disputes involving Japan and South Korea and utilized different combinations of interventions, depending on the nature of the dispute. The two cases from the post–Cold War period illustrate new features of interstate relations owing to both the internal changes within the security triangle and the changing international environment in which the triangle is embedded.

Repatriation of Korean Residents from Japan to North Korea in 1959 (Chapter 3)

Japan's repatriation of Korean residents to North Korea started in 1959. Following Japan's achievement of de jure independence in 1951 as a result of the San Francisco Peace Treaty, the repatriation marked the first major Japanese policy in relation to the Korean peninsula. Despite the tense Cold War divide, Japan struck a deal with North Korea on the repatriation issue, and obtained the ICRC's support in carrying out the project. Japan's repatriation project was fiercely resisted by South Korea, which considered it a threat to its own legitimacy. However, the U.S. position relied on a legalistic interpretation based on the free-will principle, thus releasing Japan to implement the mass repatriation. That is, the United States sustained the Japanese position while sacrificing South Korea's interest. At this particular juncture, during U.S.-Japan negotia-

Table 1.1. U.S. Interventions in Japan-ROK Discords and Disputes

	Repatriation of Korean Residents to the North	Japan-ROK Normalization	Japan's Two Koreas Policy	"Security-based Economic Cooperation"	Comfort women, Dokdo/Takeshima	North Korean Nuclear Program
Japanese Government's Position	Political support for ICRC and JRC-NKRC deal	"Economic cooperation," not compensation	Proactive approach toward the North	No aid-defense link; calling it "economic cooperation"	Reexamination of Kono statement; Passage of screening of textbooks	Sanctions; Activist security policy
Japanese Domestic Politics	Chongryon's mobilization; Domestic consensus	Opposition by socialists, but convergence on national interests	China fever, and North Korea fever	Avoidance of entrapment	Revisionist rise	Politicization of abduction issue; Bashing North Korea
ROK Government's Position	Call for stopping repatriation; Request for compensated return to the South	Maximizing compensation	Questioning partnership commitment; Request for ban on plant exports	Aid-defense link; "security-based economic cooperation"	Diplomatic protest	Engagement and sanctions
ROK Domestic Politics	Criticism of and protest against Japan	Demonstrations weakening the government's negotiation	No particular protest	No particular response	Criticism of Japan; Request for government action	No particular difference from the government's position

U.S. Concern	Kishi cabinet's stability; Minimizing impact on Japan-ROK talks	Burden sharing; Establishment of a triangular tie	Red line (no recognition of the North); Military balance on the peninsula	Burden sharing; Framework of strategic aid	Concern about the partnership; Avoidance of mixed-in between Japan and ROK	Commitment to nonproliferation
U.S. Intervention	Legalistic and moral call for "free will" principle; Businesslike mediation for Japan-ROK talks; Pressure on ICRC and ROK	Coercive pressure on both for early conclusion; Businesslike mediation for claims issue; Legalistic fishery solution	Moralistic and businesslike intervention in Japan-ROK; Legalistic no-recognition of the North	Businesslike mediation for strategic aid regardless of title	Ambivalence between Japan and South Korea; Businesslike mediation	Businesslike mediation

tions on the revision of their security treaty, the United States wanted the Kishi cabinet to successfully carry out the domestically popular repatriation project. The dispute, particularly the South Korean protest, was centered on the question of Japan's commitment or noncommitment to anticommunist partnership, although burden sharing was another hidden agenda, as seen at the later stage.

Japan-ROK Normalization Talks in the First Half of the 1960s (Chapter 4)

These talks, which dragged on from 1951 to 1965, might be regarded as one of the most protracted negotiations in the history of postwar international diplomacy. Earnest negotiations started only after the Kennedy administration put pressure on the Ikeda cabinet to have talks with the military regime in 1961 in South Korea. And the United States facilitated its intervention through its embassies in Tokyo and Seoul. Here the United States' strategic aim was to ensure Japan's burden sharing for the South Korean economy. When serious disturbances in South Korea—caused by protests against the government going ahead with the talks—brought about a standoff in the negotiations, the United States increased its direct coercive pressure on the ROK government. As Washington, instead of Tokyo, became the driving force of the negotiations, Japan's alignment with the U.S. legalistic viewpoint negatively affected the outcome for South Korea, particularly in the fishery issue. The normalization brought about a formalized U.S.-Japan-ROK security triangle, although it did not explicitly refer to security but instead to "economic cooperation" between the two U.S. allies.

Japan's Two Koreas Policy in the 1970s (Chapter 5)

Japan's normalization with South Korea in 1965 and its Okinawa reversion negotiations with the United States in 1969 significantly contributed to expanding Japan's diplomatic scope. Indeed, Japan's approach to North Korea, following the 1972 Sino-Japanese normalization, took place relatively independently of the U.S. viewpoint. Taiwan's abandonment was the price of Sino-Japanese normalization, and Japan's approach to North Korea was basically a two Koreas policy, both steps rendering South Korea nervous and North Korea emboldened. South Korea protested Japan's approach to the North, claiming that Japan-North Korea economic cooperation would increase Pyongyang's war potential. South Korea's protest focused on the issue of Tokyo's commitment to the partnership between the two. The United States' main concern was the red line at Tokyo's diplomatic recognition of Pyongyang, but otherwise it remained neutral between its allies as far as Japan-North Korea economic relations were concerned.

"Security-based Economic Cooperation" in the First Half of the 1980s (Chapter 6)

In 1983, Japan provided South Korea with an aid package, the largest since economic cooperation had begun at the time of 1965 normalization. The aid was a microcosm of Japan's role in the U.S.-framed strategic burden sharing. There were differing views and interpretations on the nature of the aid relationship between the two U.S. allies. South Korea saw it as economic cooperation for strengthening security, whereas Japan argued that there would be no aid-defense linkage, using plain terms such as "economic cooperation." Japan's 1983 aid was certainly strategic in nature, and this was confirmed by the new Korea clause that appeared in the 1981 joint U.S.-Japan summit statement as well as in the 1983 Japan-ROK summit statement. That clause formally stipulated the connection between stability on the Korean peninsula and the security of East Asia as a whole, including Japan. The Japan-ROK contention was basically focused on burden sharing, that is, the aid issue, but this aid was legitimated by the declared security commitment between the partners.

Controversy over Historical Issues since the 1990s (Chapter 7)

This chapter sheds light on the historical setting and undercurrents of the controversies surrounding the "comfort women" issue and the Dokdo/Takeshima dispute. Because of its hasty, strategic handling of Japan's wartime responsibility in the early years of the Cold War—in order to transform an enemy to an ally—the United States is not immune from involvement in these disputes. The revisionist rise in Japanese society is the main driving force for the continued disputes in the post–Cold War era. This revisionism is not simply a reactive backlash against Tokyo's apology diplomacy in the first half of the 1990s, but is also a reflection of domestic political changes that have gained new momentum in the age of Japan's perceived vulnerability. For the South Korean side, the disputes over historical issues reflect both its economic and diplomatic rise as well as the substantial balancing of the Japan-South Korea asymmetry (particularly the end of the donor-recipient relationship) in the post–Cold War era. After sustaining an ambivalent attitude for an extended time, the United

States intervened in the comfort women issue and guided its allies to an agreement on December 28, 2015, whereby Japan stated its apology over the comfort women issue and pledged financial support for the victims, and in return South Korea accepted the solution as final and irreversible. The United States felt that its intervention was strategically necessary in order to cope with a rising China and a nuclearizing North Korea.

North Korea Factor in the Security Triangle in the Post–Cold War Era (Chapter 8)

North Korea's pursuit of nuclear arms has produced a certain feedback effect underpinning the persistence of the security triangle even after the end of the Cold War. That is, the increasing threat posed by North Korea helps the three to bind together, maintaining the security triangle in place. However, this does not mean that all three perceive the North Korean threat equally, nor that the benefits of the security triangle are of equal value for the three. For the United States and Japan, and for the U.S.-Japan alliance, a rising China is the most important reference point for their security policies. In contrast, South Korea perceives the North Korean threat most seriously and thus frames its security policy accordingly. North Korea, as seen in its fourth and fifth nuclear tests in 2016 and its continued defiance, has taken advantage of the diverging interests between the United States and China. The United States, in response, exerts more efforts to strengthen the U.S.-Japan-ROK military cooperation.

Implications for Scholarship and Policy

This book sheds new light not only on the hierarchical relations in the security triangle in general but also on the asymmetrical partnership between the two U.S. allies. Remaining dominant in the hierarchy, the United States has controlled boundaries and red lines with regard to security of the three and increasingly institutionalized the triangular security and military cooperation. Notably, its instrumental pursuance of burden sharing has actually empowered Japan. While acknowledging the quasi alliance theory on the asymmetry in alliance politics,[5] my book highlights the point that hierarchical rank and the absence of rules regarding security between Japan and South Korea have been the sources of bilateral disputes that have resulted in U.S. interventions.

This book contributes to the existing literature on intra-alliance politics by showing the ways in which burden sharing and partnership commitment may become contentious in the hierarchical order. Hierarchy produces a variant form of security dilemma between abandonment and entrapment, a dilemma that Glenn Snyder has elaborated.[6] That is, a hierarchical security order provides the states that possess different capabilities with different settings of the dilemma. The less capable state is mostly afraid of abandonment, whereas the more capable state fears entrapment. Given this, the less capable one tries to obtain expressed commitment to common security from the more capable state, but the latter does not want such commitment. Between them, this differing commitment is closely associated with their different expectation of the burden sharing. The dominant power is likely to worry that any disputes between its allies may give an advantage to the enemy eventually. The case studies in this book show such internal politics within the security mechanism—contentions and disputes between asymmetric partners, as well as the dominant power's interventions.

In addition, this book examines underexplored aspects of the East Asian security triangle, as follows. First, it illuminates the position of Japan, the middle power in the security triangle, while highlighting the United States as the dominant power. Because of Japan's relative power and broader scope, the two U.S.-led alliances have differed from one another in capacity and role. Particularly during the Cold War, Japan became a significant burden-sharing partner for the U.S. policy of strategic aid around the world, including aid for South Korea, and in turn, Japan had the upper hand in dealing with the Korean peninsula issue. Second, the book illustrates the ways in which the United States took into account domestic politics when it intervened in the various disputes between its allies. The form of U.S. intervention depended not only on its allies' approaches toward the issue that Washington was concerned about but also on its assessment of the sensitivity of the issue in the domestic politics of the allies. Thus, each ally government needed to employ triple-edged diplomacy. Third, the book explains the Japan-ROK disputes over historical issues as not simply stemming from different views of history per se, but emerging from internal dynamics in the security triangle.[7] Chapter 7 shows that the historical issues developed into bilateral disputes at the thawing of the Cold War, owing to both domestic changes in Japan and South Korea and substantial balancing in the Japan-South Korea asymmetry. Fourth, the book deals with the reasons why the security triangle has persisted for so long.[8] U.S.

intervention has not simply maintained its own strategic interest but also continued to produce a feedback effect advantageous to the three member states. The intervention has brought about mostly balancing outcomes to the entirety. Today, the perceived North Korean threat sustains and increasingly strengthens the security triangle.

For policymakers, this book suggests that, first, there needs to be a new outlook on the relations between the three, particularly on the role of South Korea in the region. The present security triangle is not same as the old one that existed in the Cold War era. Significant changes have occurred in each bilateral relationship. More broadly, with the rise of China, power dynamics in the Asia Pacific has shifted dramatically. China today is not a replacement for the Soviet Union, and thus South Korea's engagement with China may contribute to absorbing shock that may arise from the contention between the powers in the Asia Pacific. South Korea may play a pivotal role in easing differences and frictions among the contenders.[9] This role is now symbolized by South Korea's status in the Trilateral Cooperation Secretariat (TCS), which was established in Seoul in 2011 as an arena of cooperation among China, the ROK, and Japan. The TCS's capacity, and the trilateral cooperation, is limited in promoting cooperation in traditional security affairs; however, South Korea is in a position to balance the different preferences of China and Japan and to expand the scope of trilateral cooperation from nontraditional security issues to traditional security affairs.[10]

Second, the U.S. rebalancing of the Asia Pacific, particularly in coping with assertive China, brings about emergence of new partnerships surrounding territorial disputes in Southeast Asia. Analytically, the U.S.-Japan-ROK triangle is a model case of partnership within hierarchy embedded in hub-and-spoke alliances. Between the United States and ASEAN states, Japan and Australia as U.S. allies are engaging in the security affairs in the South China Sea. Various combinations of security cooperation—such as U.S.-Japan-Australia, U.S.-Japan-Philippines, and their linkages with ASEAN as a whole—include different capabilities and roles of the partner states, and thus discords and disputes surrounding burden sharing and commitment will be natural consequences. Just as the question of who pays how much is an emerging burden-sharing issue, so who commits to what kind of security will become a thorny commitment issue.

2

Partnership within Hierarchy

An Analytic Frame

The U.S.-Japan-ROK security triangle has seen gradual changes but has persisted over the last six decades. During the intensification of Cold War tensions the United States assigned Japan the role of expanding its economic contribution to Western Pacific security in general, and to South Korean development specifically. Japan, as the strategically significant middle power in the security triangle, while remaining cooperative with the dominant power, became independent in dealing with issues relevant to the weakest power, South Korea, in particular and to the Korean peninsula in general. Within this hierarchy, the absence of rules regarding security between Japan and South Korea, at times of competing expectations, particularly about burden sharing and commitment, brought about a series of bilateral disputes. By the time of the critical juncture, that is, the thawing of the Cold War, the asymmetry between Japan and South Korea had notably dissipated due particularly to the latter's empowerment on both economic and diplomatic fronts. In the post–Cold War era, while military cooperation has been strengthened in the two U.S.-led alliances, a new form of tension has arisen between Japan and South Korea, as seen in the historical disputes. This chapter defines some notions and develops propositions about the security triangle, and then it traces its important developments during the Cold War and the post–Cold War periods.

Hierarchy, Partnership, and Disputes

Two Forms of Rank

According to Waltzian neorealism, each state is sovereign, and each should be functionally equal to others. At the same time, it is true that the resources each state possesses and uses differ. Unequal distribution of resources internationally creates differences in power among states and division of labor between states.[1] These relations consequently produce hierarchy in international politics. In examining hierarchical relations in the U.S.-Japan-ROK security triangle, I identify the United States as the dominant power of this hierarchy, and Japan—and its policy toward the two Koreas—in the middle.

More than any other discipline, systems science seriously delves into the concept of hierarchy. Therein hierarchy is defined by first identifying the rankings, which normally consist of more than two entities. Rank in hierarchy automatically implies another notion: controlling power. In this respect, Kenneth D. Bailey regards hierarchy as "a system which has two or more internal echelons of control or command."[2] Hierarchy is best exemplified by the military or by a bureaucracy. But rank and commanding power are not the only properties of hierarchy. Hierarchy is also associated with the controlling of boundaries. Division of labor, for instance, may produce conflict over boundaries among the states within the hierarchy, or with states bordering the system. The dominant power in the hierarchy manages controversial issues and discourages the rise of conflict. As Niklas Luhmann notes, "The hierarchy's top must be able to control the system's boundary relations."[3] A hierarchy demonstrates its individuality and distinctiveness from the surrounding environment and involves asymmetrical relations among the units within it. Also, it retains rules that define the mode of outward behavior of its member units.

Unlike in systems science, the definition of hierarchy is not straightforward in the study of international relations, particularly in that of alliance politics. Rank is associated with a state's capability to maneuver using the means and resources at its disposal. A state with high rank may have many available options; a low-ranking state is limited in its choices, either because of a lack of resources or due to limited means. Additionally, a state's rank is closely related to its status and honor. While recognizing the existence of rank in reality, proponents of hierarchy in international relations are divided on the legitimacy of rank. David Lake identifies hierarchical relations by the extent of the legitimate authority that exists between the dominant and the subordinate, positing that "the greater the number of possible actions by the ruled that the ruler can legitimately regulate, the more hierarchical is the relationship."[4] In reality, however, legitimacy is not always clear enough to exclude disputable points in regard to rank, boundaries, and the use of power. David Kang, for instance, leaves room for the possibility of disagreements over legitimacy between the ruled and the ruler, stating that "hierarchy itself can be imposed, or it can be accepted. That is, it can be seen as legitimate or not by actors."[5]

Hierarchy, to be clear, differs from hegemony. A hegemonic state may dominate hierarchy, but hierarchy is not always hegemonic. Hegemony pursues the control of raw materials, capital, and markets, and this pursuit provides "a traditional justification for territorial expansion and imperialism, as well as for the extension of informal influence."[6] A hegemonic state prevents subordinates and potential rivals from challenging its status; it creates a structure of relations that allows subordinates no option of acting independently.[7] In contrast, to secure long-term survival, hierarchy—particularly in alliances—maintains certain rules that bind the member states together. Whereas relations between the dominant power and weak states are asymmetrical, the dominant power does not rely exclusively on coercive pressure. In addition to such pressure, the dominant power uses various forms of engagement. Also, there is an exchange of benefits: protection of weaker states for recognition of the dominant power's sphere of influence. To use Glenn Snyder's term, there is reciprocity "at the heart of" alliances that have to be hierarchical.[8] Furthermore, the dominant power does not deprive member states of their independence. This rule of reciprocity guarantees the maintenance of relations in the long run. The Imperial Chinese tributary system probably represented the best example of this kind of hierarchy in international relations.[9]

At the core of the U.S.-Japan-ROK security triangle are the two U.S.-led treaties that originally shaped the hub-and-spoke alliance system: the Treaty of Mutual Cooperation and Security between the United States and Japan, which was first signed in 1951 and amended in 1960; and the Mutual Defense Treaty between the United States and the Republic of Korea, signed in 1953. With the Japan-ROK normalization in 1965, two forms of ranking emerged within this postwar East Asia security triangle: one between the United States and its two allies, and the other between Japan and South Korea. These forms of ranking continued to exist throughout the Cold War period.[10]

The ranking between the United States and its two allies was a historical outcome that has remained the foundation of the security triangle. In an attempt to solve the puzzle of the formation of alliances, Stephen Walt stresses the balance of threats, altering the existing theory of balance of power. According to Walt, states evaluate the threat posed by other states in terms of geographical proximity, offensive capability, and perceived intention, and seek alliances to balance against the perceived threat.[11] This theory posits anarchy in international relations and regards alliance formation as a strategic choice. However, the U.S.-led alliances were both what history at that time required and what the dominant power led to create. The United States established the treaty with Japan as part of the postwar negotiations, and with South Korea immediately following the Korean War. Since then, as the dominant power, the United States has led overall interstate relations. The relationship between the dominant power and its allies has been asymmetrical. The United States instituted what Lake identified as the two indicators of hierarchy: the dominant state's military presence and the weak state's lack of outside options.[12] The United States exercised its commanding power with both its military presence and a guarantee of security, offering its nuclear umbrella over Japan and South Korea. The United States was careful to ensure that its two treaty allies were committed to the containment strategy it was forging. It did not allow Japan or South Korea to create conditions that might favor Soviet expansion. A red line drawn by the dominant power served as a controlling mechanism in the hierarchy's boundary relations. Furthermore, the United States recognized and facilitated a broader strategic and economic role for Japan than for South Korea in relation to the containment strategy.

The relationship between the two U.S. allies also remained ranked and asymmetrical. The United States took into consideration the different capabilities and roles that each of its allies retained, thus acknowledging a distinctive, expanded role for Japan in the Western Pacific during the Cold War. This made the relationship between Japan and South Korea interdependent but asymmetrical, just as could be observed in the asymmetrical interdependence of the U.S.-Japan relationship.[13] On the one hand, Japan provided South Korea with economic aid in the form of grants and loans. At the same time, South Korea became an invaluable market for Japan that produced huge profits throughout the Cold War period.[14] Answering the question of who benefited more from Japanese aid and the trade imbalance still remains controversial. On the other hand, on both the security front and the economic front, Japan sought a greater stake in mainland China than in the Korean peninsula.

Within the hierarchy, Japan was located in the middle. There was some leeway in this middle-power ranking. While not crossing the boundary drawn by the dominant power, Japan came to exert its own policy toward the Korean peninsula, regardless of South Korea's preferences (e.g., despite the heightened anticommunist alert, Japan's repatriation of Korean residents in Japan to North Korea from 1959, and its two Koreas policy during the 1970s).

Burden Sharing and Partnership Commitment at the Core

The asymmetrical partnership between Japan and South Korea was not officially defined. Absence of rules yielded ambiguity, whereby differing interests and expectations developed into bilateral disputes. If ambiguity is not a temporary phenomenon but remains a permanent feature, "actors with different interests contest the openings this ambiguity provides."[15] Indeed, ambiguity, competing expectations, and resultant bilateral disputes became normal between Japan and South Korea. Also, the rank embedded in the partnership, which was not expressed officially, easily fostered discontent on the part of the weak power, South Korea, and frustrated its challenge to the middle power. To be more explicit, an asymmetrical partnership in the absence of rules is more controversial than any other partnership combination, such as asymmetry with official rules, symmetry with official rules, or symmetry in the absence of rules.

The U.S.-Japan-ROK security triangle, which was seemingly simpler in structure than NATO, retained nonetheless complex relations because of ample ambiguity. Conflicting expectations about roles, responsibilities, and rewards arose, even though all three countries shared the aim of containing communism. The United States, the dominant power, in an effort to manage each alliance separately, informally recognized the differentiated roles of Japan and South Korea, while acknowledging each ally's sovereignty. Japan and South Korea not only had different expectations of each other, but interpreted containment strategies in differing ways. The differences were amplified when the weaker state, South Korea, interpreted the partnership as disadvantageous to itself relative to Japan. The differences also widened when Japan took it for granted that the policy it pursued—for instance, the abandonment of Taiwan and the proactive approach toward North Korea in the early 1970s—did not need to be compatible with South Korean interests and preferences. The differences often rendered the bilateral relations extremely confrontational.

Victor Cha's account of the asymmetry in the security triangle is an exceptional contribution to analyzing alliance politics in East Asia. In examining the cause of contention in the quasi alliance, Cha traces compatibility of the two quasi allies' concerns of abandonment and entrapment.[16] While recognizing the importance of the abandonment and entrapment issues, I delve into the ways in which the United States acknowledged the power disparity between its two allies, and how the disparity produced constant asymmetry between their views of abandonment and entrapment. Among the three states, there arose conflicting expectations with regard to who should pay and what to commit.

I show that at the heart of the security triangle, there are two con-
tending issues, particularly in the eyes of the dominant power—burden
sharing and partnership commitment. The dominant power considers
the burden sharing legitimate because it provides all three allies with a
security guarantee regardless of their individual capabilities. It expects
that a capable ally should take part in burden sharing for both the ally's
own defense and that of a less capable ally; otherwise, the dominant
power might consider the capable ally a free rider.[17] That is, the dominant power believes that the burden sharing is closely related to security
commitment: no appropriate burden sharing, specifically in the form of
aid by the more capable ally to the less capable ally, means no shared
security commitment to each other, and vice versa.

As Snyder notes, a game is at work between allies or partners, just
as between enemies.[18] What I emphasize here is that partnership within
hierarchy, which has no rules between partners as seen in the security
triangle, makes the issues of burden sharing and commitment further
contentious on the ground that the extent of fear of both abandonment
and entrapment is not equal among the states with different capabilities.
The capable state worries about entrapment in a conflict in which the
less capable partner state is involved, but does not feel fear of abandonment by that partner. In contrast, the less capable state is always
afraid of the capable state's abandonment but does not really worry
about entrapment. This difference makes the states act differently. The
less capable one earnestly wants the capable state's expressed commitment and tries to secure economic and military assistance accordingly.
Exactly for this reason, the capable one tries to avoid such commitment.
The consequence is that the partnership commitment remains undefined and contentious until the dominant power intervenes between
these partners. The Japan-ROK disputes took place in this way; the
United States intervened in them because it believed that contention or dispute between the partners surrounding burden sharing and
commitment would damage its own interests and the security triangle
in its entirety.

As the dominant power in the two separate alliances, the United
States always avoided becoming formally mixed up in the disputes
between its allies. The United States approached each ally separately
and in different ways. Depending on each ally's position on the contentious issue, the dominant power used different methods of intervention.
Likewise, each ally solicited its support from the United States in different ways. Japan made attempts to trade its strategic significance for

U.S. support in the event of disagreements with South Korea. It tried to deal with most external issues in a broader context (e.g., providing economic aid to South Korea and South Vietnam while focusing on obtaining the reversion of Okinawa). In contrast, South Korea frequently resorted to moralistic appeals in its relations with Japan and demanded compensation for its "frontline costs" from Japan (e.g., requesting Japan to provide new economic aid in the early 1980s). Disputes often provoked serious antagonism between Japan and South Korea, particularly on the part of the latter toward the former. But the disputes neither broke up Japan-ROK relations nor seriously endangered the security triangle per se. For each state, the primary objective lay in maintaining or maximizing its interests, not in proving the legality or moral superiority of its own agenda.

U.S. Intervention

During the Cold War, the United States intervened in disputes between Japan and Korea, especially when it saw that they could possibly result in damage to its containment strategy. The U.S. intervention often involved superpower coercive pressure, apparently without concern for the legitimacy of its action. However, intervention did not always mean such coercive pressure; U.S. intervention in the Japan-South Korea disputes took diverse forms. A notable point is that the United States closely watched the domestic politics of its allies when deliberating the type of intervention and its possible impact on the two. In relation to U.S. intervention, two important points are observed: The more the United States considered the issue to be directly related to burden sharing and partnership commitment, the more likely it was to intervene earnestly (e.g., the United States' intervention in the Japan-ROK normalization talks, its drawing of the red line regarding Japan's approach to North Korea, its close cooperation with the Japanese government for protecting the ROK's legal standing in the UN, its promotion of Japan's economic aid to South Korea, and its mediation for the resolution of the comfort women issue). The more the United States perceived a situation to be distracting from its influence, the more likely it relied on superpower coercive pressure (e.g., the ROK's use of delaying tactics on the repatriation issue, Japan's and the ROK's foot dragging in normalization negotiations, and the ROK government's mismanagement of domestic scandal during the normalization negotiations).

Forms of Intervention

As Richard Solomon and Nigel Quinney note, in addition to the use of its superpower coercive pressure, the United States employs moralistic, businesslike, and legalistic approaches in negotiations.[19] Also, the United States often takes an ambivalent approach, which is a kind of nonintervention. In Japan-South Korea disputes, U.S. intervention took all forms, frequently combining diverse forms. First, the United States acted as a moralistic preacher in many instances. In the Wilsonian tradition of U.S. diplomacy,[20] presidents consistently drew attention to the U.S. mission to defend the world. During the Cold War, the mission was expressed in the strategy of containing communism. U.S. presidents used the catchphrase "defense of the Free World" whenever it pressed West European allies and Japan to share the financial burden. In the case of the U.S.-Japan-ROK security triangle, the United States used preaching based on moral superiority not only to exert its containment strategy but also to call for its allies' full commitment to that strategy.

Second, the United States took a businesslike approach in dealing with serious disagreements between its allies. The businesslike United States sometimes offered its good offices, but avoided becoming mixed up in the quarrels. In this case, the United States aimed to convince its allies "not of the logical rigor or philosophical integrity of the U.S. position but of its practical, concrete advantage."[21] Businesslike interventions took the form of leading concerted, collective efforts by the three governments in dealing with common problems and thus aimed to produce tangible outcomes. The U.S. position in the Six-Party Talks aimed at the denuclearization of North Korea best exemplified this approach. The United States tried to apply a staged engagement format, seeking the best possible common ground among the five states to induce North Korean cooperation.[22] The United States used businesslike interventions in the comfort women issue through the channels of U.S. embassies in Tokyo and Seoul. Realizing urgency in coping with the rise of China and the increasing North Korean nuclear threat, Washington persuaded its allies to reach the December 2015 agreement whereby Japan expressed an official apology and offered a fund for the victims, and in turn South Korea accepted the resolution as final and irreversible.[23]

Third, legalistic interventions by the United States involved calling for compliance by its two allies with regard to international laws, norms, and practices. More often than South Korea, Japan took advantage of these situations. When contentious issues arose, Japan was more inclined to rely on legal norms in responding, whereas South Korea would tend to resort to a historical or moral interpretation. An example of legalistic U.S. intervention was its suggestion during the Japan-South Korea normalization talks in the early 1960s that both governments bring the Dokdo/Takeshima case to the International Court of Justice (ICJ). Japan favored this suggestion, but South Korea persistently rejected it, declaring that no territorial dispute existed between the two states.[24] Another example of legalistic intervention occurred in 1959 at the culmination of the Japan-South Korea clash over the issue of repatriating Koreans to the North. The United States stressed freedom of movement and residence, a principle that Article 13 of the Universal Declaration of the Human Rights stipulates. While sacrificing South Korea's interests on the repatriation issue, the Eisenhower administration concentrated on the negotiations with Japan over the more important U.S.-Japan bilateral issue: revision of the security treaty.

Finally, the United States often applied superpower coercive pressure in its relations with the two allies. The United States used this form of intervention when moralistic, businesslike, or legalistic interventions appeared to fail and it assessed the damage caused by failure to be seriously undermining its influence. The dominant power normally exerted such coercive pressure over each ally separately, but it coordinated policy through its embassies in Tokyo and Seoul. Also, it is noteworthy that the United States exerted its superpower coercive pressure when intense domestic disturbances disrupted Japan-ROK negotiations.

Relevance of Domestic Politics

Domestic politics is not only a source of state behavior but also a factor in international politics.[25] Indeed, domestic politics in Japan and South Korea had a substantial impact on both governments' external behavior, and the United States paid attention to it particularly in times of tension between its allies. The forms of U.S. intervention had a certain relevance to the domestic issues involved.[26]

The United States was particularly attentive to the intensity of any disputes[27] and the distribution of power between the government and domestic forces.[28] First, the intensity of certain issues has differed between South Korea and Japan. In most cases during the Cold War and post–Cold War, the intensity of debates and protests in South Korea about Japan policy has been more severe than in Japan. For example, surrounding the comfort women issue, the civil society's protest in South Korea was so intense that even the intergovernmental agreement reached on December 28, 2015, was unable to diffuse civil criticism of the Korean government. On the other hand, the major Japanese domestic concern concentrated on how to eschew entanglement or entrapment in a U.S.-led conflict, and the Korea policy was a topic of relatively low-key discussion in the Japanese Diet. In a rare case, however, the Japanese domestic audience was inflamed by the abduction issue,[29] resulting in North Korea bashing in the mid-2000s, at a time when U.S. and South Korean efforts were focused on making progress in the multilateral nuclear talks with the North. The differences in the level of intensity between Japanese and South Korean politics not only produced differing governmental negotiation behavior but also called forth different types of U.S. attention and ensuing intervention. Intense domestic politics in South Korea over the Japan policy was likely to invite the United States' coercive pressure.

Second, distribution of power mattered in different contexts in Japan and South Korea. In South Korea, shifts in the distribution of power could be observed in the shifting state-society dynamics. For instance, when the Park-led military regime lifted the ban on political activity in 1963 and then top negotiator Kim Jong-pil's black money scandal was revealed, the domestic forces opposing the normalization talks were empowered (see chapter 4). Realizing the damaging impact of the scandal that was apparently narrowing the ROK government's flexibility, the United States exerted coercive pressure on the Park regime to send Kim abroad. The Japanese also experienced internal divisions and so invited pressure by the United States, which was concerned about the Japanese government's negotiating power. As the theories of "reactive state" and "gaiatsu" posit,[30] conservative politics in Japan was characterized by factional competition,[31] weak premiership at the top,[32] and infighting in the bureaucracy. The United States remained carefully attentive to Japan's domestic politics, and often intervened when it seemed necessary. For example, witnessing the protracted normalization negotiations, Secretary of State Dean Rusk, in an attempt to promote burden sharing, suggested that the designation of Japan's assistance to South Korea would not matter—whether "compensation" or "economic cooperation." In view of the Japanese opposition's reluctant but apparent acceptance of the term *economic cooperation*, Rusk's suggestion was a businesslike intervention that provided a kind of "alternative specification" to resolve the internal difference.[33] Indeed, the Japanese government did so, and all political groups in Japan accepted that alternative.

To sum up, U.S. intervention during the Cold War normally took a combination of diverse forms. Whatever the form of U.S. intervention, pressure in general was a built-in property because of the U.S.

status as the dominant power in the hierarchy. But the United States tried to avoid becoming mixed up in its allies' bilateral disputes because it harnessed the two alliances separately. In deliberating over intervention, the United States observed carefully the domestic politics of its allies. The United States was keenly attuned to both the nature of the dispute itself (its relevance to burden sharing and commitment) and the domestic politics involved (extent of intensity and power of opposition forces). It is noteworthy that Japan's preference for a legalistic approach in its Korea policy was largely aligned with that of the United States, thus receiving substantial U.S. support. In the post–Cold War era, U.S. intervention has taken a businesslike approach in coping with the North Korean nuclear issue and by and large a noninterventionist approach in dealing with the controversy over historical issues between Japan and South Korea.

Evolving Linkage between Burden Sharing and Commitment

The two U.S.-harnessed alliances had two different histories. With the end of the Pacific War, Japan, the defeated state, came under the control of U.S. forces. Japan's signing of the San Francisco Peace Treaty with the Allied Powers in September 1951 was immediately followed by the establishment of the U.S.-Japan alliance based on the bilateral security treaty. Having already sustained South Korea during the Korean War, the United States continued support to its war-torn ally militarily by establishing the Mutual Defense Treaty in October 1953. The American occupation and the Korean War were distinctive driving forces for the formation of the U.S.-led alliances with Japan and South Korea, respectively.

Japan and South Korea differed from each other in power and capability. Because of these differences, the United States provided each of its allies with separate, different roles in Cold War politics. Despite its surrendered-state status, Japan maintained intellectual and technological continuity. It retained its own prewar technology, including the means to produce all kinds of transport—ships, automobiles, and planes—and its well-trained administrative workforce. Furthermore, the manufacturing companies, despite the crackdown on conglomerates under the reform policy of the U.S. General Headquarters, retained great production capacity. They maintained prewar production techniques, product standardization, seniority-based wages, and technical training.[34] It was not a surprise, therefore, that as early as September 1948, George F. Kennan, then director of policy planning in the State Department and the architect of the containment strategy, considered Japan one of the five centers of industrial and military power in the world (the other four were Great Britain, Germany and Central Europe, the Soviet Union, and the United States).[35] Kennan's view was reflected in NSC 13/2, titled "Recommendations with Respect to U.S. Policy toward Japan," drafted in October 1948. Inasmuch as Kennan was keenly aware of Japan's importance for U.S. interests, NSC 13/2 detailed how to eliminate obstacles to Japanese trade with Asian countries and to draw an early conclusion of the Tokyo War Crimes Tribunal, both viewed as essential for building the new state.

Certainly, there was close connection between burden sharing and commitment. Following its achievement of de jure independence through the San Francisco Peace Treaty in 1951, Japan gradually assumed a central role in the Western Pacific, by shouldering partial economic responsibility for the success of the U.S. containment strategy. Interestingly Japan's middle power status in the U.S.-Japan-ROK security triangle and its increasingly important strategic value for the U.S. containment strategy were sources of differing expectations between Japan and South Korea due to the absence of rules governing their partnership. Recurrent disputes between the partners were centered on South Korea's higher expectations of Japan's intentions on the aid issue—indeed, U.S.-framed burden sharing in a broader sense—and partnership commitment to deterring communist threats. Just as burden sharing was evidence of alliance commitment in U.S.-Japan relations, so was Japan's aid expected by South Korea as evidence of partnership commitment in Japan-ROK relations. For discussion of this linkage, I divide the Cold War period into three phases, and then examine the post–Cold War period as the fourth phase.

The First Phase

With the establishment of the U.S.-Japan security treaty in 1952 (and its revision in 1960) and the U.S.-ROK defense treaty in 1953, the first phase, from 1952 to 1960, saw institutionalization of the hub-and-spoke alliances in East Asia. The U.S. policy focused on supporting Japan as the central security post in the Western Pacific. As evidenced in the NSC documents summarized in Tables 2.1 and 2.2, this policy was in line with Kennan's basic concept of embracing Japan as a center of industrial and military power, while South Korea was viewed as a useful trading partner for Japan. Indeed, Japan succeeded in restoring its industrial production: with the Korean War boom, Japan's economy started

Table 2.1. Selected NSC Documents Concerning Japan Policy of the United States

Number	Date	Objectives of Japan Policy	Korea-related Statements
NSC 61	Jan. 27, 1950	To promote Japanese economic recovery *through trade with Asian states*	South Korea noted as Japan's trade partner
NSC 73/1	July 29, 1950	To augment Japanese police force; to enhance Japan's *self-defense capability* and its assistance for U.S. defense strength	Start of the Korean War
NSC 48/5	May 17, 1951	To urgently conclude the peace treaty and negotiate bilateral security arrangements; to assist Japan in the *development of military forces*	
NSC 148	Apr. 6, 1953	To keep Japan as the *crucial security post in Western Pacific*	
NSC 5516/1	Apr. 9, 1955	To preserve Japan's security and independence; to seek Japan's *contribution to security of the Pacific*	
Report on NSC 5516/1	May 4, 1960	The security treaty revision, noted as *the single most important event in U.S.-Japan relations*	Rhee's resignation, viewed as opportunity for improving Japan-ROK relations
NSC 6008/1	June 11, 1960	To strengthen Japan's own defense; to keep Japan prepared to *complement U.S. Asia policy* and to economically support Free World	
NSAM 151	Apr. 24, 1962	To push prompt conclusion of Japan-ROK normalization talks	

continued on next page

Table 2.1. Continued.

Number	Date	Objectives of Japan Policy	Korea-related Statements
NSSM 9	Jan. 23, 1969	Japan's China policy, viewed as not in conflict with U.S. interests	Continuing Korean reluctance regarding defense cooperation with Japan observed
NSDM 13	May 28, 1969	To seek an *increasingly large Japanese role in Asia,* and U.S. maximum free use of Okinawa base	To use Okinawa base for defense of Korea, Taiwan, and Vietnam
NSSM 12	June unknown date, 1971	To channel Japan's desire for recognition as a great power into constructive areas	To seek *Japan's role for Korean stability* without significant U.S. presence
NSSM 172	July 27, 1973	Japan's *economic power and political and military potential* viewed as *global in scale*	To concert with Japan for Korea policy, in both two Koreas' UN membership and relations with North Korea
NSSM 210	Oct. 3, 1974	To promote economic powerhouse Japan's more important role in international relations	To seek Japan's maximum *support for South Korea and South Vietnam*
NSSD 6	July 20, 1982	To cultivate Japan's *partnership and interdependence*; to seek Japan's defense of its own territory; to maintain interoperability	To convince Japan of the *importance of Korean security for Japanese and regional security*

Source: Related files in *Japan and the U.S., 1960–1976, Japan and the U.S., 1977–1992, United States and the Two Koreas, Presidential Directives,* and *Presidential Directives, Part II,* in *Digital National Archive: The Documents that Made U.S. Policy* (ProQuest).

Table 2.2. Selected NSC Documents Concerning Korea Policy of the United States

Number	Date	Objectives of Korea Policy	Japan-related Statements
NSSM 27	Dec. 19, 1969	To seek increase in Korea's share of its defense cost	To achieve *greater Japanese contribution to Korean security*
NSDM 48	July 14, 1970	20,000 troop reduction by end of FY 1971	
NSC Memo. for President	Oct. 14, 1970	To deliberate another 14,000 troop reduction by end of FY 1973	To assure defense of Japan against nuclear aggression; to discourage Japan's nuclear ambition
NSSM 154	May 4, 1973	UN Command in Korea viewed not essential for U.S. military posture; change in UN policy deemed inevitable	Japan's Korea policy viewed with *no security commitment but with new aid programs*
NSSM 190	Dec. 31, 1973	To link military balance and UN Command issues to a broader balance on the Korean peninsula	To deliberate *4 + 2 scheme* on the Korea issue
NSDM 251	Mar. 29, 1974	To substitute U.S.-ROK command for the existent UN Command	To keep Japan informed of the two-track negotiation strategy (deleted in NSDM 262, July 29, 1974)
PD 12	May 5, 1977	To gradually withdraw the 2nd Division and supporting elements	

Source: Related files in *Japan and the U.S., 1960–1976, Japan and the U.S., 1977–1992, United States and the Two Koreas, Presidential Directives*, and *Presidential Directives Part II*, in *Digital National Security Archive: The Documents that Made U.S. Policy* (ProQuest).

recording remarkable growth beginning in the first half of the 1950s; the
GNP in 1950 totaled $11 billion, and it increased even further, reach-
ing $25 billion in 1955.[36] And Japanese politics settled down with the
establishment of the so-called Fifty-five System in 1955, in which the
conservative Liberal Democratic Party came to dominate politics, with
weak opposition from socialists and communists. Based on the increasing strength of its material base and political stability,[37] Japan geared
up the level of its security cooperation with the United States. With
the finalization of the security treaty revision in 1960, Japan came to
stand on an equal footing in its relations with the United States, even
if in a formal sense only. The United States also achieved an important result: "a voluntary reaffirmation by Japan of its close ties with the
U.S.," as noted in a report responding to NSC 5516/1.[38] The United
States obtained the right of virtually free use of bases and facilities in
Japan, even if formally constrained by a "prior consultation" proviso in
the revised treaty.

In the first phase, burden sharing was not a hot topic in the
U.S.-Japan-ROK relationship per se; however, at the end of the 1950s
it became a serious issue under the surface, as the United States experienced constraints on its budgetary allocations for overseas military aid.
On the other hand, commitment was a divisive issue between Japan and
South Korea. In the case of Japan's execution of repatriation of Korean
residents to North Korea, South Korea seriously questioned Japan's partnership commitment to anticommunism. This commitment issue, along
with the burden sharing issue, continued to strain Japan-ROK relations
in the coming years.

The Second Phase

The second phase—from the security treaty revision in 1960 to the
Okinawa reversion and the Sino-Japanese normalization in 1972—was
marked by strenuous U.S. efforts to press Japan to gradually shoulder
increased burden sharing, which was needed for security in the Western
Pacific and included aid for South Korea's development. In the pursuit
of Japan-ROK normalization in 1965, the United States put pressure on
both of its allies. NSAM 151, based on personal instructions by President
John F. Kennedy, reflected the U.S. position of intervening between
the allies to expedite the normalization negotiations. The NSC staff in
both the Kennedy and Johnson administrations advised their presidents
to exert extra pressure on the allies; they expected that the Japanese

aid money of between \$0.6 and \$1 billion would alleviate the U.S. burden.[39] While the United States employed coercive pressure to reduce its
own burden for supporting the South Korean economy and security, the
Sato cabinet in Japan, launched in November 1964, already considered
negotiations with the United States over the reversion of Okinawa a top
priority in its diplomacy. Japan finally obtained the U.S. pledge for the
reversion at the Nixon-Sato summit, held in Washington in November
1969. Inasmuch as the Okinawa reversion would have enormous political implications for territorial sovereignty, the Sato cabinet was ready to
make certain concessions to the United States, including both allowing
U.S. forces to continue using the bases in Okinawa and taking greater
financial responsibility for Asian countries at the culmination of the
Vietnam War.[40]

A notable point is that Japan's responsibility for burden sharing
was rationalized by its declared commitment, albeit not wholehearted,
to the Japan-ROK partnership. In the 1969 Nixon-Sato joint statement,
Japan's commitment to the partnership was expressed by the so-called
Korea clause, whereby Sato stated that the security of the ROK was
"essential to Japan's own security."[41] In view of the rising tensions in the
Korean peninsula owing to the North Korean navy's abduction of the
U.S. intelligence ship *Pueblo* in January of that year, Sato's statement was
a timely response to concerns of the United States and South Korea. To
be sure, the United States and South Korea considered the Korea clause
an evidence of Japan's commitment to both the U.S.-Japan alliance and
the Japan-ROK partnership.

Meanwhile, under the terms of the Japan-ROK normalization
agreement, Japan began to provide South Korea with grants and official and commercial loans: a total of \$800 million spread over ten years
from 1966 to 1975. One of the most remarkable South Korean economic accomplishments, the establishment of the Pohang Iron and Steel
Company (POSCO), was achieved with these funds.[42] POSCO became
the country's foundation for the heavy-chemical industrial drive of the
1970s. Later, it grew into an independent business group that diversified
its import lines of needed technology in the 1980s, thereby reducing
reliance on Japanese technology.[43] It is notable that there was an inverse
trend in economic aid from Japan and the United States to South Korea.
For example, the first five years of Japanese aid to South Korea were
followed by a reduction in U.S. aid payments to South Korea—from
\$131 million in 1965 to \$82 million in 1970 (see Tables 2.3 and 2.4).

Coinciding with this inverse trend in economic aid from Japan and
the United States to South Korea, the Nixon administration, through

Table 2.3 U.S. Aid to South Korea (Million USD)

	1965	1966	1967	1968	1969	1970	1971	1972	1973
Economic aid	131	103	97	105	107	82	51	5	2
Military aid	n.a.	n.a.	n.a.	665	450	384	598	536	n.a.

Source: Economic Planning Board, *Hanguk gyeongje gaegwan* [General Survey of Korean Economy] (Seoul: Economic Planning Board, 1974), 213; U.S. General Accounting Office, *U.S. Assistance for the Economic Development of the Republic of Korea: Report to the Congress* (Washington, DC: U.S. General Accounting Office, 1973), 57.

Table 2.4 Japanese Aid to South Korea (Million Japanese yen)

	1965 –1969	1970	1971	1972	1973	1974	1975	1976	1977	1978
Grant	396	0	130	394	563	500	500	1,000	717	415
Loan	67,728	7,200	38,040	21,600	21,600	31,320	23,420	23,500	24,000	21,000

Source: The Economic Cooperation Bureau of the Ministry of Foreign Affairs of Japan, ed. *Wagakuni no seifu kaihatsu enjo: kunibetsu jisseki* [Our Nation's Official Developmental Assistance: Country Report] (Tokyo: Ministry of Foreign Affairs, 1986), 117–19, and (1989), 45–51.

NSDM 48 issued on July 14, 1970, carried out a troop reduction of twenty thousand U.S. military personnel in Korea by the end of FY 1971.[44] This reduction was intended to meet the objective of the 1969 Nixon Doctrine, which aimed at both "Vietnamization of the Vietnam War" and "Asian defense by Asians." Again, the U.S. troop reduction was followed by Japan's additional loans to South Korea. An NSC report notes that Japan provided South Korea with new loans, although "Japan does not have and is not considering any direct security commitment to Korea."[45] Japan's reactive but corresponding responses to the U.S. strategic objective empowered Tokyo to exercise noticeably adventurous diplomacy. Witnessing the dramatic changes in Asia, such as the 1969 Nixon Doctrine and the 1972 Shanghai Communiqué, Japan immediately adapted to the changing circumstances and succeeded in achieving two important outcomes—the Okinawa reversion and the Sino-Japanese normalization in 1972.

In sum, from 1960 to 1972, Japan accepted the pressing U.S. requests for burden sharing in Asia, and in South Korea in particular. In legitimating Japan's aid to South Korea, the United States used, and South Korea supported, the Korea clause that stipulated the close relevance of security between the partners. In return, Japan gradually achieved its postwar national goals: restoring its own complete territorial sovereignty, and establishing normalized relations with mainland China.

The Third Phase

During the third phase of the Cold War period, from 1972 to 1990, the United States considered Japan an essential ally with which it consulted on important security issues in the Asia Pacific region. On the one hand, Japan, after normalizing relations with the People's Republic of China, became relatively independent in relation to Korean peninsula issues. On the other, Japan went along with the United States in dealing with the Korea question at the United Nations General Assembly (UNGA). After the PRC replaced the Taiwan as the representative of China at the UNGA in October 1971, the Korea question, especially North Korea's status and the UN Command in South Korea, became a contentious topic in the United Nations. The United States began to consult closely with Japan, while also requesting the latter's diplomatic support for U.S. efforts. As noted in NSSM 154 (May 4, 1973) and NSSM 190 (December 31, 1973), the United States seriously deliberated how to guarantee continued security in the Korean peninsula in

the event of the abolition of the UN Command, which had long func-
tioned to legitimate the U.S. military presence following the Korean
War. Eventually, the United States, with NSDM 251 (March 29, 1974),
decided to replace the existing UN Command with the ROK-U.S. Joint
Command, and adopted the balance of military power in the peninsula
as its basic policy objective (see Table 2.2). The allies established the
ROK-U.S. Combined Forces Command on November 7, 1978, while
the UN Command remained.

Japan's Korea policy in this period was characterized by the "two
Koreas policy," regarding which the ROK government seriously questioned Tokyo's commitment to its security partnership with Seoul.
Because of the U.S.-China rapprochement and the resultant détente
in East Asia, confrontational situations in the Korean peninsula were
difficult to justify. Both Koreas took an unprecedented step in 1972 to
reduce tension in the Korean peninsula: the July 4 Joint Statement
whereby the two Koreas pledged to unify Korea through three principles—no reliance on foreign forces, peace, and national unity. Given
this change, Japan expanded its approach to North Korea. Japan's two
Koreas policy became increasingly noticeable as North and South Korea
competed with each other through peace initiatives. Because of U.S.
warnings, Japan did not cross the red line of diplomatic recognition of
the Democratic People's Republic of Korea (DPRK) and abstained from
seeking a fishery agreement, which might have involved recognition of
territorial waters under North Korea's control. But Japan expanded cultural and economic exchanges with the North that, in turn, emboldened
the North in its dealings with the South. Despite South Korean protests,
the Japanese government allowed its business circles to export manufacturing plants to the North—until the latter's debt default problem
disappointed the Japanese exporters in the second half of the 1970s. In a
sense, Japan's two Koreas policy was an emulation of the U.S. approach
toward China and the Soviet Union. President Richard Nixon visited
Beijing in February 1972, and then he visited Moscow in May of the
same year. Nixon intended to drive a wedge between the communist
rivals and render them cooperative with Washington. Prime Minister
Tanaka Kakuei followed suit. He normalized relations with mainland
China in September 1972, and then visited Moscow in October 1973 to
discuss economic cooperation in Siberia. Then he extended this logic to
the two Koreas. Keeping normalized relations with South Korea, Japan
launched unprecedented exchanges with North Korea in the 1970s.

Corresponding to Japan's expanded influence on the Korean peninsula, the United States began to press Japan with the no free-rider prin-

ciple in security affairs. The United States considered the U.S. military forces in the Korean peninsula to be not simply a symbol of U.S. commitment to the security of the Korean peninsula but an actual "tripwire" in deterring any North Korean attack. In addition, the United States regarded the flexible use of U.S. forces in Japan as a necessary condition for deterring a North Korean attack, thus justifying its demand for free use of the Okinawa bases and the other bases on the main islands. This was the exact outcome that the ROK government desired. Also, the United States continued to press Japan not to remain a security free rider in the burden sharing. The United States pressed Japan to evidence its alliance commitment through taking part in burden sharing for peace on the Korean peninsula, particularly through aid to South Korea, as shown in a 1973 memorandum: "If Korea were essential to Japanese security, questions would be raised about its contribution to Korean security and Japan might consider more participation, such as non-lethal aid. If Japan considered U.S. presence in Korea important, the problem arose as to what it could do to facilitate the retention of that presence."[46]

The U.S. requests for Japan's increasing responsibility intensified as the Vietnam War drew to a close in April 1975. U.S. Secretary of Defense James Schlesinger, who visited Japan in August, defined Japan as a collective partner for the defense of the Western Pacific, using the concrete term *reciprocity*.[47] The U.S. positioning of Japan in its expanded role—with its corresponding responsibility—climaxed in President Gerald Ford's New Pacific Doctrine, declared in Honolulu on December 7. Ford stated that "partnership with Japan is a pillar of our strategy."[48] Continued requests by the United States for Japan's increased responsibility made the Japanese government sensitive to the point in the 1980s. Japan's 1980 Defense White Paper mentioned for the first time the "increasing Soviet forces and their activities in [the] Far East" as a "potential threat" to Japan. The 1981 version of the same document identified Japan as a member of the West sharing values and working together to prepare for any emergency in the Far East. From that year on, as an indication of sharing a concerted defense concept, the United States and Japan started holding regular meetings regarding equipment and technology. Japan's recognition of its increasing responsibility was reflected in the Nakasone cabinet's increased defense budget—reaching 1 percent of the GNP during the years 1982 to 1987.[49]

Japan's responsibility for South Korea's economy and security was further extended in 1983. With U.S. support, President Chun Doo-hwan, through his foreign minister, Lho Shin-yong, had requested in 1981 that Japan provide South Korea with $10 billion in aid. Prime Minister

Nakasone eventually offered $4 billion, which was noted to be unprecedentedly large. As a rationale, South Korea pressed the point that Tokyo should pay for South Korea's frontline cost for Japan's own security, calling the aid "security-based economic cooperation." But Japan maintained that the aid could not be linked to defense and made it clear that the money would be in the form of loans for economic cooperation.[50] Japan's economic aid, mainly in support of various infrastructure projects, continued until South Korea joined the OECD in 1996. No doubt the U.S.-framed burden sharing worked in this case, and South Korea made its utmost efforts to rationalize the Japanese aid to be linked to the ROK-Japan partnership commitment.

To sum up the Cold War period, the hierarchical relations in the U.S.-Japan-ROK security triangle essentially continued. The period was marked by increased Japanese responsibility in the U.S.-led Western Pacific security system. For the United States, Japan became increasingly vital for strategic and diplomatic reasons. Japan was also more robust economically than it had been before, and thus the United States relied more on Japan's burden sharing. In Japan-ROK relations, burden sharing consisted of Japan's aid to South Korea, but the absence of rules and the differing expectations between these partners made the aid issue contentious throughout the Cold War period. South Korea considered Japan's aid a compensation for colonial rule or frontline defense costs, whereas Japan tried to treat the aid issue as a matter of economic cooperation. What made the Japan-ROK relations further contentious were the two states' differing perception of and divergent approaches toward communism—South Korea's priority of deterring North Korean provocations versus Japan's normalization with China and its two Koreas policy while keeping an eye on Soviet naval expansion in the Western Pacific.

The Fourth Phase

By the time the Cold War began to thaw, a distinct change could be observed in the security triangle. In the relationship between Japan and South Korea, asymmetry substantially dissipated. The end of the Cold War opened opportunities for South Korea to expand its diplomatic and economic sphere outside the security triangle: it normalized relations with the Soviet Union and China in 1990 and 1992, respectively. Also, South Korea became a robust democracy with an expanding civil society, and it simultaneously graduated from Japanese aid and joined the OECD in 1996.[51] South Korea has clearly exhibited a kind of middle-power diplomacy, as shown in its hosting of the G20 Summit in 2010 and the Nuclear Security Summit in 2012. On the other hand, in the post-9/11 era, with its broadened security commitment and deepened military cooperation with the United States, Japan has further unfolded its already expanded scope of security, thus sacrificing its long tradition of pacifist principles. Also, through multinational collaboration, Japan has engaged in the issues of energy security, environment and climate change, human security, counterterrorism, sea lane security, and cyber security.[52] The difference between Japan and South Korea in reference to security has been further widened. South Korea has been preoccupied by all things having to do with deterrence against nuclear arming North Korea, whereas Japan regards the North Korea factor as just one of many significant security agenda items. In this context, new forms of tension intensified between Japan and South Korea, particularly between the Abe cabinet and the Park administration from 2013 to 2015—disputes over historical issues that had been submerged for decades during the Cold War.

The security triangle produces a feedback effect, but for different reasons for each member: for the United States, in countering the rise of China as well as new global threats; for Japan, in vigilantly coping with China's increasingly assertive behavior; and for South Korea, in coping with the increasing threat from North Korea. The deterrence against North Korea certainly has a cogent value for binding the three in the security triangle, but it is simply one part of a broader security agenda for the United States and Japan.

3

Repatriation of Korean Residents
from Japan to North Korea

The mass repatriation of Korean residents in Japan, first thought up as early as 1956 and launched in 1959, was a complicated international endeavor. On the surface, it was a project run by the Red Cross societies of Japan and North Korea and the International Committee of the Red Cross (ICRC). But the Japanese Red Cross (JRC) took the lead, rather than simply collaborating with the ICRC and the North Korean Red Cross (NKRC), in framing, preparing, and executing the project. The repatriation project actually involved intense political and diplomatic activity between five states: Japan, North Korea, South Korea, the United States, and the Soviet Union. The Kishi cabinet in Japan, backed by an unusual domestic consensus, decided on February 13, 1959, to officially sanction the mass repatriation of Koreans to North Korea. North Korea actively encouraged its affiliated organization in Japan, the General Association of Korean Residents in Japan (known in Korean as Chongryon), to mobilize the Korean community's support for the repatriation project. From the beginning, South Korea was vehemently opposed to the "deportation," since it was in severe competition with North Korea for legitimacy on the Korean peninsula. The United States recognized the complexity of the problem, but it supported the Japanese move while prioritizing political stability in Japan. The Soviet Union provided the transport vessels, thus alleviating Japanese worry about a South Korean naval blockade between Niigata in Japan and Wonsan in North Korea. After the signing of the Calcutta Agreement between the Japanese and North Korean Red Cross societies on August 13, 1959, the unprecedented mass repatriation project, involving 93,340 people, began in December of that year and continued until 1984.

How could such collaboration take place between countries in opposing camps at the height of the Cold War? And why did the United

States support the Japan-North Korea deal and ignore South Korean protests? These are legitimate questions to ask, particularly because South Korea, as well as Japan, was an ally of the United States and because Japan and South Korea, with U.S. help, were in the process of negotiating the normalization of their relations, although negotiations had stalled at that time. In addressing these questions, I concentrate on dynamics of the triangular relationship between Japan, South Korea, and the United States.

The logic of the hierarchy of U.S.-led alliances was at work here, with priority given to Japan above South Korea. While strongly resisting the repatriation project, South Koreans expected and requested the Japanese to keep a kind of commitment to an anticommunist partnership in dealing with North Korea. Because of differing interests and the absence of formal rules between Tokyo and Seoul, the Japanese did not feel obliged to acknowledge their partnership with the South Koreans. The South Korean government was in a weak bargaining position and had no diplomatic recourse, making it impossible for it to do anything other than solicit U.S. help. The United States supported the repatriation project, which was domestically popular in Japan; it needed to ensure the stability of the Kishi cabinet at a critical moment in negotiations on the revision of the U.S.-Japan security treaty. Far from being a "silent partner," in Tessa Morris-Suzuki's words,[1] the United States actually sustained the repatriation project and actively persuaded South Korea to find ways to minimize the project's negative impacts. The United States, in spite of its official noninterventionist position, intervened in the internationally controversial issue and sidelined South Korea's position.

Onset of the Problem

Emergence of the Idea of Mass Repatriation

Long before the mass repatriation started in 1959, some repatriations to the North had taken place in the late 1940s. In March 1947, based on an agreement of December 19, 1946, signed by the General Headquarters of the Supreme Commander of Allied Powers and the Soviet Union, 351 Koreans of North Korean origin were returned home. The agreement was intended to repatriate some tens of thousands of Koreans, but most of those who wanted to return were unable to do so because of delays and the outbreak of the Korean War. In its negotiations with its North

Korean partner in March 1959, the JRC treated the 1947 repatriation as a model for the mass repatriation that it was planning.[2]

On the other hand, South Korea's unilateral demarcation of the Peace Line in 1952 (the Japanese termed it the Rhee Line) and the ensuing dispute over detainees between South Korea and Japan contributed to the intensification of the contention over the mass repatriation issue. The Peace Line was drawn on January 18, 1952, by South Korean president Syngman Rhee's Presidential Declaration on Sovereignty over the Adjacent Seas. It marked a maritime boundary around the Korean peninsula, fifty to one hundred miles from the coast, including a group of rocky, uninhabited islands known as Dokdo/Takeshima. Whereas the ROK government argued that the Peace Line was intended to protect Korean fisheries, the Peace Line was designed to replace the MacArthur Line, which was due to be abolished once the San Francisco Peace Treaty came into force a few months later.[3] Within the Peace Line, the ROK authorities seized a number of Japanese fishing vessels and thousands of Japanese fishermen throughout the 1950s. The numbers of fishermen seized were 585 in 1953, 454 in 1954, and 498 in 1955; seizures dropped to 235 in 1956, but they continued throughout the second half of the 1950s.[4] These seizures, and the detention of the fishermen in Busan, obstructed Japan-ROK relations because they were intertwined with another complicated issue. The detention of Koreans in the Omura camp, for illegal entry into Japan or on criminal charges, was becoming a focus of attention for the ROK government. As of early 1956, the Busan camp held 681 Japanese fishermen, 267 of whom had already completed their sentences and were awaiting repatriation. The Omura camp contained 1,458 detainees, including 105 illegal migrants who the Japanese government believed should be deported. On the detention issue, the two governments seemed to be playing a game of chicken. The Japanese government criticized the Rhee administration's holding of Japanese fishermen as "hostage diplomacy" and insisted that the detainees on the two sides be exchanged. In response, Syngman Rhee accepted that the Omura camp detainees would be returned to the South because of their ROK citizenship, but at the same time he threatened to take retaliatory measures such as a trade embargo or a ban on visits to South Korea by Japanese. At this point, the United States exerted pressure on both governments, urging them to cooperate with each other. On his trip to Tokyo and Seoul in mid-March 1956, the U.S. secretary of state, John Foster Dulles, pressed the two governments to exchange detainees.[5]

Amid the dispute over the detention issue, there occurred an event in April 1956 that was to give birth to an idea of mass repatriation based on so-called free choice of residence. Forty-seven Koreans who wanted to go to the North staged a demonstration in front of the JRC office in Tokyo. Fearing deportation to South Korea against their will, the demonstrators demanded that the Japanese government send them to the North on the vessel that was being sent to repatriate Japanese nationals from North Korea.[6] This event marked a watershed in the development of the repatriation issue. At the end of April, the ICRC sent two officials to both North and South Korea, as well as to Japan, to investigate the humanitarian situation of the Busan and Omura detainees and the demands of the forty-seven demonstrators in Tokyo. Based on the analysis of that trip, the ICRC proposed in July 1956 a master plan for repatriation, or a "four-way movement" of Koreans: Japan to South Korea, Japan to North Korea, North Korea to South Korea, and South Korea to North Korea. In the meantime, the ROK government requested assistance from the United States in stopping Japan's plan to repatriate the forty-seven Koreans wishing to return to the North. The United States, however, took a noninterventionist position. With the assistance of the JRC and the ICRC, and with North Korea's cooperation, the forty-seven Korean demonstrators were eventually sent to the North in two waves: the first in December in 1956, and the second in March 1957.[7]

The ICRC's four-way movement proposal and Japan's return of the forty-seven Koreans to the North—combined with pressure from U.S. Secretary of State Dulles, in mid-March 1957—persuaded South Korea to enter negotiations with Japan over the exchange of the detained Japanese fishermen in Busan and the Korean parolees in the Omura camp. Indeed, the two governments reached an agreement in principle in April 1957 to cooperate on the exchange. But the Japanese government had to overcome some bureaucratic hurdles, particularly the justice department's viewpoint that agreeing to the return of only those fishermen who had completed their sentences might be seen as recognition of the legality of the Peace Line. In addition, the ROK government had to wait for stubborn President Rhee to make up his mind. Therefore, the final agreement on the exchange of detainees was not reached until December 1957 and was not acted upon until the spring of 1958.[8] Despite this development, South Korea's continued seizure and detention of fishermen fueled the Japanese public's frustration with and criticism against its own government. The families of the detainees and the fishing community in Japan put increasing pressure on the government.[9] This pressure contributed in part to the rising domestic support in Japan in 1958 for the repatriation of Koreans to North Korea, support that was associated with the Japanese discriminatory image of Koreans as a troubling minority, as shall be discussed later.

Convergence between North Korea and Japan

For repatriation or any other form of migration to take place, there needs to be a convergence of interests between the sending and receiving countries concerning the fate of those who wish to move. To be sure, there did exist a certain convergence of interests between Japan and North Korea. From early 1955, North Korea continued to repeat its willingness to accept the mass repatriation. On February 25, Nam Il, the foreign minister of the Democratic People's Republic of Korea (DPRK), proposed that North Korea open talks with Japan and expand trade and cultural exchanges, which was a positive response to Prime Minister Hatoyama Ichiro's indication that Japan was ready to enter into dialogue with the North.[10] Nam's proposal was an implicit invitation to Japan to engage in normalization talks, while at the same time it was intended to drive a wedge between Japan and South Korea, whose normalization talks had been suspended since a rupture in October 1953.[11] The Japanese government did not respond directly to Nam's proposal; instead, the JRC approached its North Korean counterpart with a view to discussing the repatriation of any Japanese remaining in the North.[12] Along with the return of Japanese from the mainland China, Japanese nationals in North Korea constituted one of the major concerns of the Hatoyama cabinet. The North's ensuing proposals and statements in the second half of 1955 directly touched on the issue of the detainees. North Korea expressed its concern that more Omura detainees might be returned to the South. On October 15, a DPRK Foreign Ministry spokesman denied the legitimacy of the Japan-ROK talks on the detainee issue and called for the Japanese government to uphold humanitarian principles and international conventions. In response, Foreign Minister Shigemitsu Mamoru announced in the House of Representatives on December 16 that he was willing to assist "foreigners" (i.e., Koreans) to return home freely.[13] In response, Nam Il, on December 29, repeated his normalization proposal and suggested that North Korea was willing to accept the returnees; Nam also insisted that the Japanese government ensure that the Koreans had the opportunity to "choose their residence." This proposal was immediately followed on December 31 by a letter from the chairman of the NKRC to the JRC president, Shimazu Tadatsugu, in which the NKRC suggested sending delegates to Japan in order to settle the question of the Korean residents.[14]

Observing international concern over the detention issue involving both Busan and Omura camps and the ICRC proposal for the four-way movement, North Korea became more assertive on the repatriation issue than before. In particular, as to the Japan-ROK agreement of December 31, 1957, on the exchange of detainees in Omura and Busan, North Korean foreign minister Nam Il declared that the repatriation of Koreans to South Korea was an illegal "forced deportation." Nam argued that the ROK was not entitled to represent the whole of Korea. Again, Nam highlighted the right of these individuals, particularly those released from the detention camps, to exercise their "free will" in choosing their place of residence.[15] It is interesting to note that North Korea used the term "free choice of residence," reflecting exactly the humanitarian principle at a time when the Japanese were deliberating mass repatriation. Apparently, North Korean insistence—on both repatriation of Koreans in Japan to North Korea and free choice of residence—encouraged the Japanese to seriously deliberate the mass repatriation issue. The North Korean insistence also enhanced the leverage of the Japanese government in dealing with South Korea on such issues as resumption of the stalled normalization talks and the talks on the repatriation of Koreans to the South.

Domestic Consensus in Japan

Had there not been a domestic consensus on the repatriation and mounting frustration about the detainee issue, the repatriation would not have been carried out. Also, the repatriation would have been impossible without organized support and enthusiasm within the Japanese society. North Korea–affiliated Chongryon in Japan became the prime mover of the organized support at the early stage of the rising enthusiasm, taking up the flurry of North Korean proposals and statements on the repatriation issue. The welcome messages in those proposals and statements gave added impetus to the desire of many Korean residents in Japan to move to North Korea, desire born out of a deep realization that in Japan they were the victims of discrimination.[16] In particular, Chongryon was encouraged to intensify its repatriation efforts by North Korean leader Kim Il Sung's speech on September 8, 1958, which commemorated the tenth anniversary of the DPRK. Kim stated that North Korea was ready to assist the prospective returnees to establish new lives in the North.[17] Representatives of Chongryon, Sohyo (the General Council of Trade Unions in Japan), and the Peace Committee met in

Tokyo on the same date that Kim delivered his speech and called for the immediate termination of the Japan-ROK normalization talks and the prompt repatriation of Korean detainees to the North. Chongryon organized an additional rally and demanded "mass repatriation" of Korean residents.[18] Applying the Korean term *gwigukundong* (*kikokuundo* in Japanese; meaning "returning-to-homeland movement" in both languages) to the repatriation, the headquarters of Chongryon launched an extensive drive to mobilize all its local branches, citing North Korean assurances and seeking assistance from sympathizers within the Communist Party, the Socialist Party, and Sohyo. By early October 1958, Chongryon's *gwigukundong* was already a nationwide movement. As of October 5, according to Chongryon data, 17,130 Koreans living in metropolitan areas had expressed a desire to return to North Korea: Tokyo (2,500), Osaka (5,300), Kobe (1,200), Aichi (4,150), Fukuoka (700), etc. Riding this wave of enthusiasm, Chongryon decided at a meeting of its extended central committee on October 10 that it would expand the movement and try to attract attention within Japanese political circles, collecting signatures among members of the Japanese Diet and calling for government support at municipal, prefectural, and central levels.[19] In support of Chongryon's efforts, Vice Premier Kim Il of North Korea promised in a statement issued on October 16, 1958, that North Korea would pay the travel expenses of the returnees and supply transportation for the returning-to-homeland project.[20]

With the formation on November 17, 1958, of the Council of Support for the Returning-to-Homeland Movement of Korean Residents (hereafter the Returning-to-Homeland Council), the repatriation became a national issue, rather than one that just concerned the Korean community, and this was seen as an irreversible trend by both politicians and the public. Indeed, many prominent Japanese politicians and opinion leaders joined the Returning-to-Homeland Council. Furuya Sadao, president of the Japan-Korea Association, was elected chairman, while Hatoyama Ichiro (former prime minister), Asanuma Inejiro (general secretary of the Socialist Party), and Miyamoto Kenji (general secretary of the Communist Party) joined the council as advisors. Hoashi Kei, a Socialist Party member of the House of Representatives (HR), was appointed chief secretary. Hoashi was regarded as having personal influence with Foreign Minister Fujiyama. Among the appointments to the council, probably the most interesting was that of LDP HR member Utsunomiya Tokuma as secretary. Utsunomiya was a conservative politician who was also sympathetic to communism. Already in the 1950s, he was advocating the normalization of Japan's relations with the two communist giants—

the Soviet Union and the People's Republic of China.[21] In other words, ideological differences between the Left and Right did not matter where support for the mass repatriation of Koreans was concerned.

What was it that united almost all Japanese—not to mention the North Korea–affiliated Korean community—on the repatriation issue? There were discrimination-related concerns about the high crime rate among Korean residents, as well as their dependence on welfare. For example, according to local government figures, 4,520 of the 40,915 Koreans living in Aichi prefecture were receiving government relief aid as of December 1958, nine times the rate for Japanese. According to the Aichi prefecture police, Koreans were involved in 2,219 of the 54,939 criminal cases in the prefecture that year, making the crime rate for local Koreans forty times that for Japanese.[22] It is widely recognized worldwide that poverty causes crime and that both poverty and crime are normally more prevalent in minority communities than in mainstream society. But those figures must have helped create the impression that Koreans were a troublesome minority that was causing social instability on the one hand and benefiting excessively from the burgeoning economy on the other.[23] In addition to this negative image, there were other reasons why the Japanese supported the mass repatriation of Koreans. These included a sense that Japan had a moral obligation toward the Korean community on account of its colonial history, humanitarian feelings for an oppressed minority, and a desire among leftists to counterbalance the influence of the United States in East Asia.[24] Whatever the reasons, it is clear that there was a convergence of interests among different groups in Japanese society on this issue. Most Japanese people wanted to see as many Koreans as possible repatriated to either the North or the South.

In this mood of rising enthusiasm, the only thing that remained was for the Japanese government to permit the Koreans to leave the country.[25] At some point around the beginning of 1959, the Japanese government seemed to reach the conclusion that it should sanction the domestically popular project. During talks with U.S. embassy officials on January 26, 1959, the Japanese Foreign Ministry revealed its position, saying that it was "ultimately impossible [to] deny [the] principle [of] voluntary repatriation."[26] On the flip side of this statement, the Japanese government had already discounted the utility of its talks with South Korea. At a press conference held on January 30, Foreign Minister Fujiyama expressed for the first time the government's official and determined position on the repatriation. Fujiyama stated that the government "would deal with the repatriation issue as soon as possible" and "would not pay attention to any possible negative impact on the long-awaited resumption of the Japan-Korea normalization talks."[27] Also, at the meeting with repatriation campaign leaders on that day, Fujiyama pledged to permit the voluntary departure of Korean residents on the basis of the internationally recognized principle of "freedom of residence."[28] The terms that he used to legitimize his policy were strikingly similar to those used by both the JRC officials and the North Koreans. Fujiyama's statement took place just two weeks before the February 13 cabinet decision that officially sanctioned the repatriation.

The February 13 cabinet decision was based on broad public support for repatriation in Japan. Other political issues at that time—the revision of the police law and the ongoing revision of the U.S.-Japan security treaty—were subjects of division between the ruling Liberal Democratic Party (LDP) and the opposition parties, including the socialists and the communists. The repatriation of Koreans, however, had the unanimous support of both the conservative ruling party and the opposition.

Triangular Dynamics: Two against One

Repatriation of individuals from one country to another requires both countries to work together at the governmental level. The legal procedures governing exit and entry for the returnees are matters of sovereignty. In this respect, the decision by the Japanese cabinet on February 13, 1959, which was initiated by Foreign Minister Fujiyama Aiichiro, was a decisive step toward the mass repatriation of Korean residents to the North. Riding the tide of the domestic consensus, the government officially endorsed the negotiations conducted by the JRC with its relevant partners, not only the ICRC but also the NKRC. The key points of the cabinet decision were: (1) that the Japanese government acknowledged the right of Koreans to return to their country, (2) that the government agreed that the repatriation would be carried out in accordance with the internationally accepted principle of freedom of movement and residence as set out in the Universal Declaration of Human Rights, (3) that the government would request the ICRC to confirm the wishes of the individuals concerned, and (4) that the repatriation would not imply recognition of the North Korean regime.[29] The February cabinet decision engaged both serious internal dynamics within the U.S.-Japan-ROK triangle and severe diplomatic competition among the three surrounding the ICRC's position.

The United States Siding with Japan

The above account—Japan-North Korea convergence and domestic consensus in Japan—is by no means the whole story of Japan's February 13
cabinet decision and the Kishi cabinet's determination to carry out the
repatriation project. There remains one pressing question: What made
the Japanese government decide to execute a risky, sensitive project at
a time of heightened Cold War confrontation? Japan was not an independent player in international politics, particularly with regard to U.S.
influence. It could not have implemented the controversial mass repatriation project without U.S. consent and support. This was especially
true at a time when the United States and Japan were preoccupied with
another sensitive and critical issue: revision of the asymmetrical security
treaty. In particular, the United States, from a strategic point of view,
considered the repatriation issue marginal in comparison to the revision
of the U.S.-Japan security treaty. Achieving success in the ongoing treaty
negotiations was the top priority. The United States had no incentive
to put Japanese interests at risk—even if it meant derailing Japan-ROK
normalization talks and having to deal with strong protests from South
Korea against the repatriation.

With regard to the security treaty revision, the United States
became concerned about Japan's domestic situation as early as in April
1958. The United States anxiously watched the domestic situation in
Japan, noting that neutralism and pacifism, the objectives of both the
socialists and the communists, were still influential, and that the Japanese people were unhappy about the "unequal" aspects of the security
treaty. For these reasons, the United States was eager to pursue early
treaty revision.[30] Furthermore, with the negotiation of the treaty revision,
the United States wanted to ensure that it retained the right to use its
military bases and facilities in Japan. No issues in U.S.-Japan relations
other than the treaty revision were given more serious consideration by
the White House or the State Department.

At their meeting in Washington on September 11, 1958, Secretary
of State Dulles and Foreign Minister Fujiyama agreed that the United
States and Japan would enter the long-awaited negotiations for the revision of the security treaty. For success of the negotiations, the U.S. officials were eager to trace the details of the political dynamic in Japan.[31]
Who was the preferred partner for the United States? From the U.S.
perspective, "nobody" but Kishi among Japanese politicians could be
trusted, and that included Ikeda Hayato who eventually became Kishi's
successor; for this reason, the stability of the Kishi cabinet was a primary

concern for Washington.[32] This was particularly true from October when the U.S.-Japan negotiations entered a crucial phase, with issues such as prior consultation, the domain of the Far East, and the introduction of nuclear warheads on the table.[33] There was little reason for the United States to jeopardize the Kishi cabinet's policy with regard to the repatriation issue, a policy that attracted popular support and that concerned a subject on which the government was facing mounting pressure. It is fair to say that maintaining the stability of the Kishi cabinet became a necessary condition for success in the treaty negotiations. Arguably, the Eisenhower administration wanted to avoid the Kishi cabinet's being damaged by the issue of Korean residents.

For its part, the Japanese government did its best to get the United States to understand Japan's position on the repatriation issue. Since Japanese foreign policy was constrained by the U.S.-Japan alliance, the Japanese government had to secure, or at least be able to infer, U.S. support for the mass repatriation prior to the February 13 cabinet decision. From time to time, Japanese Foreign Ministry officials delivered information concerning the repatriation to U.S. diplomats in Tokyo. Sometimes, the Japanese provided interpretations of politicians' statements. For example, in response to pressure from Socialist Diet member Okada Soji, Foreign Minister Fujiyama stated in October 1958 that he agreed with Chongryon's repatriation movement but needed to carry out "further study" before dealing with the issue.[34] The Foreign Ministry officials confirmed that Fujiyama was talking about the repatriation of "ordinary Koreans," in other words, not just those released from the Omura detention camp.[35] It is clear, therefore, that U.S. officials were aware of developments in Japan's plan for repatriation. But there is no evidence that the United States had expressed any particular disagreement or worry in relation to the way that the project was becoming redefined from the return of Korean detainees to North or South Korea into a mass repatriation to the North at the discretion of Japan.

In the run-up to February 13, the official position of the U.S. State Department was that the embassies in Seoul and Tokyo should "not intervene" and should "stay out of the dispute." But it later became clear that the U.S. position was one of tacit support for the Japanese decision, and this was the response that the Japanese government expected.[36] The United States tried to persuade South Korea not to use force—in the form, for example, of a naval blockade aimed at the transport vessels carrying the returnees to North Korea. The United States supported Japan's insistence on the humanitarian logic of the repatriation project and the ICRC's principle of freedom of choice of residence. The United

States dismissed the South Korean viewpoint that the repatriation of Korean residents in Japan to the North was not a genuinely humanitarian move but a political issue. Furthermore, the United States justified the Japanese plan by comparing it to other cases of voluntary mass repatriation that took place in the early 1950s, for example, that of Korean POWs at the end of the Korean War and that of Chinese to the communist-controlled mainland. The United States maintained that the repatriation of displaced people to their homelands did not imply recognition of the regimes in power in either North Korea or China.[37]

Sidelining South Korea

From the beginning, South Korea took a distinct stance that sharply differed from that of Japan and was incompatible with that of the United States. On numerous occasions, the Rhee administration registered protests with the Kishi cabinet and solicited U.S. understanding for the South Korean position. South Korea basically considered the mass repatriation of Koreans to be a political issue between South Korea and Japan. This position originated from the belief that, according to the UN General Assembly resolution of December 12, 1948, the government of North Korea had no legal authority. In Seoul's eyes, because the DPRK did not exist, there could be no diplomatic relations between Japan and North Korea and therefore Korean residents in Japan should be repatriated to the South. For South Koreans, the repatriation issue was a matter of legitimacy and sovereignty.

Realizing that its protests were no longer effective, however, South Korea tried two new approaches after the Japanese cabinet's decision on February 13: first, implying the use of force to block the repatriation vessels (an idea promoted by Yiu Tae-ha, the hardliner in the ROK mission in Tokyo); second, soliciting U.S. help in mediating the resumption of normalization talks and discussions on Japanese compensation for Korean returnees to the South (a proposal put forward by the moderate vice foreign minister, Kim Dong-jo). In response to U.S. support for Japan's position—support that contradicted Washington's expressed "no intervention" principle—the Rhee administration unveiled its two-pronged approach in February. On the one hand, in talks with the U.S. ambassador, Walter C. Dowling, in Seoul on February 21, Rhee suggested the possibility that South Korea might accept "all Korean residents in Japan if the Japanese government would meet ROK demands for due compensation" of the returnees.[38] Dowling's response was positive with regard to the U.S. role of offering its good offices for this purpose. On the other hand, the chairman of the Chiefs of Staff of the ROK navy, Yi Yong-un, warned on February 27 that South Korea might use force, saying that "the navy has the confidence and capability to block any ships carrying returnees."[39] The United States opposed this hardline approach. Because of the closeness of U.S.-ROK military relations, particularly the United States' operational control over the Korean armed forces, the United States feared that any mishap in the use of force by the ROK navy would threaten security relations in general. Thus, the United States put pressure on the Rhee administration, warning that the Japanese government was seriously considering bringing the issues of the Peace Line and the detention of fishermen to the UN. The logic of this warning was that if the case came to the UN, the Japanese would almost certainly prevail. Simultaneously, however, the United States obtained assurances from Kishi and Fujiyama that Japan would *not* refer the case to the UN.[40] The United States' duplicity in this matter was based on its judgment that any dispute in the UN between Japan and South Korea would be a tragedy from which only North Korea and, ultimately, the Soviet Union would benefit.

It is highly probable that South Korea's threat of force—regardless of whether it would be carried out—encouraged Japan to ask the Soviet Union to provide the ships for the repatriation rather than using either Japanese or North Korean vessels. The JRC submitted this request clandestinely through its Soviet counterpart. The JRC's Inoue Masutaro met the president of the Soviet Red Cross Society, G. A. Miterev, at a UNICEF meeting in Geneva in late March and asked for Soviet assistance with the "peaceful accomplishment" of the repatriation project.[41] Since the Soviet Red Cross Society had already indicated in early March its willingness to furnish vessels for the repatriation,[42] Inoue's meeting with Miterev was simply intended to confirm the Soviet assistance. The JRC's efforts paid off, as the use of Soviet vessels enabled the repatriation to follow a route that avoided the area under threat from South Korea—from Niigata in Japan to Wonsan in North Korea through the northern part of the East Sea/Sea of Japan. More important, the use of Soviet vessels proved to be a persuasive way of alleviating U.S. worries, in spite of complaints from Washington about the use of communist ships. One of Japan's concerns was resolved.

As direct negotiations started between the Japanese and North Korean Red Cross societies on April 13, 1959, the United States reiterated the principle of freedom of choice of residence and persuaded South Korea to accept the reality of the situation. The remaining question for the United States was how to "minimize the impact" of the mass repatriation. Here, the United States pledged to assist South Korea in reaching an agreement with Japan on the South Korea–bound repatriation, originally proposed by Syngman Rhee on condition that Japan paid compensation.[43] No doubt this scheme was intended to offset South Korea's dissatisfaction. It would seemingly enable South Korea to achieve two objectives at the same time: to weaken the impetus of the mass repatriation to the North, and to obtain a lump-sum payment from Japan for a possible Southbound repatriation, though not individual compensation for each returnee. In accordance with this reasoning, there was close collaboration between Undersecretary of State C. Douglas Dillon at the top, Ambassador Dowling in Seoul, and Ambassador MacArthur in Tokyo.

Japan's response to South Korea's more moderate approach and the U.S. proposal that the South be compensated for accepting returnees was lukewarm at best, and the Japanese even resorted to delaying tactics. Regarding the compensation, the Japanese Foreign Ministry seemed worried that if news of this leaked out it might encourage North Korea to demand the same. With the JRC and the NKRC on the point of reaching an agreement around mid-July 1959, Japan made an extremely modest offer to South Korea: it was willing to provide the Koreans with three five hundred–bed hospitals, although it believed that the repatriation should not be linked to compensation. The Japanese offer had been meticulously calculated: each hospital would cost Japan around 700 million yen, while Japan could save around 750 million yen per year in welfare payments by repatriating 200,000 Koreans (160,000 to the North, 40,000 to the South); the cost for providing three hospitals would be close to the savings from the welfare for three years. However, the Japanese government's expectation that 200,000 Koreans would volunteer for repatriation was unrealistic, despite the mushrooming of the returning-to-homeland movement within the Korean community.[44] On August 13, Foreign Minister Fujiyama, requesting the "strictest secrecy," promised Ambassador MacArthur that Japan would offer some kind of compensation for the repatriations to South Korea, though in the form of neither an individual nor a lump-sum payment.[45] Hours later, the JRC and the NKRC concluded the Calcutta Agreement. Japanese delaying tactics had worked.

Competition over the ICRC's Position

Even though the Japanese government had laid the groundwork for the repatriation, it still had some obstacles to overcome from the time of the February 13 cabinet decision, through the Calcutta Agreement between the JRC and the NKRC on August 13, to the departure of the first repatriation vessel on December 14. In addition to South Korean opposition, the most troubling concern for Japan was the ICRC's hesitation. The ICRC was reluctant to get involved in the repatriation for fear of possible political fallout in the event that it could not uphold humanitarian principles. ICRC involvement was crucial, however, so the JRC and the Kishi cabinet did their best to persuade the international organization to participate. Furthermore, believing that dropping the repatriation plans would be an act of political suicide, the Kishi cabinet offered the ICRC a political guarantee. In this process, the principles of free and voluntary repatriation, which the United States also insisted upon, went by the board.

There was a severe diplomatic competition centered on the role of the ICRC. On the ICRC's proposal of four-way movement of Koreans—presented in July 1956, repeated in August and December that year and again on February 1957—the JRC and the NKRC agreed, but the South Korean Red Cross rejected it on the grounds that the government of North Korea was illegitimate.[46] Since this proposal had been put forward, the JRC had lobbied the ICRC to permit the Red Cross, as a humanitarian organization, to conduct the mass repatriation. Given this background, it was not surprising that the Japanese government sought the ICRC's involvement in the project when the cabinet made its decision in February 1959. Indeed, from that date, the ICRC became the focus of intense diplomatic competition, with the United States requesting that it carry out extensive screening of the returnees, the Japanese and North Koreans favoring its limited, nominal involvement, and South Koreans wanting it to take no part in the repatriation. This struggle took place both at government level and at the Red Cross level.

At the outset, the United States expected the ICRC to be extensively involved in the project. For example, the Department of State and the U.S. embassy in Tokyo had expected the ICRC to be involved in polling Korean residents about voluntary repatriation. But doubt was cast on this plan when South Korea objected to the ICRC's engagement and even sent delegates to Geneva to persuade the ICRC to pull out. The United States immediately realized that the repatriation issue, if not handled carefully, would negatively affect its interests. Washington therefore became more involved, although it continued basically to support the Japanese position. As President Eisenhower stated later, the United States understood South Korea's concerns but could not work on behalf of Seoul at the expense of Tokyo.[47] The core element of the U.S. approach to the ICRC at this critical moment was to press it to take a bigger role in the process of repatriation.

Equally important to the United States were North Korea's attitude and the direct negotiations between North Korea and Japan. North
Korea was pleased with the Japanese cabinet decision but at the same
time feared that the ICRC's involvement would have a negative impact,
particularly on Chongryon's recruitment of returnees.[48] In this context,
the NKRC insisted on direct talks with its Japanese counterpart, bypassing the ICRC. In letters sent to the JRC and in statements issued by the
North Korean authorities, North Korea expressed its resolute opposition
to the Japanese government's call for "ICRC screening" of candidates for
repatriation to check that they were genuine volunteers. North Korea
called the screening an infringement of human rights and a barrier to
the voluntary return of Koreans.[49] Given this state of affairs, the ICRC
was faced with a dilemma. The situation pertaining to the repatriation
after February 1959 was different from that of 1956 and 1957 when the
ICRC had proposed a voluntary four-way movement of Koreans. The
ICRC, particularly President Leopold Boissier and Executive Director
Roger Gallopin, expressed their anguish at the political pressure that
the ICRC was receiving from all sides—South Korean opposition, the
U.S. insistence versus North Korean opposition to the full screening,
and the Japanese solicitation of the ICRC's help with the screening.
The ICRC was unsure about the scope of its involvement and worried
about the possibility of political fallout,[50] so it turned to the United
States, the country that it considered to be most influential with Japan
and South Korea, if not with North Korea. The United States, through
Henry Villard of the U.S. mission in Geneva, immediately confirmed the
necessity of ICRC involvement and urged it to ensure that all potential
returnees were allowed full freedom of choice. The ICRC "expressed
great appreciation for US government's views."[51]

The U.S. endorsement of the ICRC's involvement resulted in
an unexpected outcome—a diluted role for the ICRC in the screening process. In March, the ICRC decided that "the two Red Crosses
[Japanese and North Korean Red Cross societies] must tell what they
want . . . under the ICRC auspices."[52] The ICRC's approval of the
direct talks seems to have been the result of JRC's prior coordination,
as well as of the U.S. endorsement. Inoue Masutaro, the director of
international affairs of the JRC, left Tokyo for the ICRC headquarters
in Geneva a week after the February 13 cabinet decision. To the family members of the detained fishermen in South Korea who gathered at
the Haneda airport to see him off, Inoue expressed his determination to
resolve the detention issue in exchange of the repatriation of Koreans in
Japan to North Korea.[53] Inoue must have laid groundwork in advance

for the ICRC's decision about the JRC-NKRC direct talks. With the ICRC's approval of the JRC-NKRC talks, the repatriation issue entered a new phase and the chances of its success increased substantially. For the Japanese government and the JRC, the most important thing was that the ICRC would be involved in the repatriation—what form that involvement would take did not matter. In May, the JRC proposed to the ICRC that the JRC itself should play an extended role in organizing and implementing the overall plan. This would weaken the function of the ICRC, making it merely a "final court of appeal for complaints."[54] This proposal was also intended to appease North Korea and Chongryon over the screening issue.

In the end, the JRC proposal was accepted and the role of the ICRC was reduced from one of "supervising and controlling" the entire repatriation process to "advising" the JRC. The United States had not envisaged this reduction in the ICRC's role; however, it did enable the JRC to avoid a rupture with North Korea and it ensured the political safety of the Kishi cabinet. The United States, however, for the first time registered a protest concerning the possibility that the humanitarian principles behind the repatriation might be threatened by the JRC's excessive involvement and the Japanese government's support. At a meeting on June 11 with Vice Foreign Minister Yamada, Ambassador MacArthur argued that it would amount to a "fundamental departure" from the original plan if the ICRC were no longer to directly supervise the repatriation process. MacArthur said that the JRC, by entering into direct talks with the NKRC, was "play[ing] into communist hands." But Yamada defended the decision to reduce the ICRC's role, saying that the voluntary repatriation would be carried out "within the framework of the ICRC."[55] This was yet another watering down of the ICRC's role. In this changed situation, Undersecretary of State Dillon had no option but to step in again, instructing the Geneva mission and the embassies in Tokyo and Seoul to ensure that the ICRC "at minimum undertake screening itself."[56]

Faced with the anticipated dilution of the ICRC's role, North Korea relaxed its critical attitude in June, withdrawing its long-standing insistence on the use of Chongryon's list of applications.[57] As a consequence, on June 24, the two Red Cross societies reached a tentative agreement.[58] But this agreement did actually raise the ICRC's fears of political fallout and international criticism of its minimal involvement. In particular, the ICRC was concerned about the U.S. insistence that every potential returnee be screened to ensure that they had volunteered for repatriation.

At this critical juncture, the Japanese government made another important move. On July 17, Foreign Minister Fujiyama wrote to President Boissier stating that the Japanese government would assume "political responsibility" for the ICRC's role in the repatriation.[59] A week later, the ICRC expressed satisfaction with this and accepted in principle the JRC-NKRC agreement.[60] At the same time, the ICRC announced that all potential returnees would be subject to "individual screening" "before proceeding to the port of embarkation." It became clear that the ICRC would only have a technical role in the individual screening. Despite the ICRC's extremely limited role, the U.S. State Department stated that the international organization's pledge to carry out individual screening was a "most encouraging development."[61] Thus, the United States came to accept both the compromised JRC-NKRC agreement and the ICRC's limited technical role in the repatriation process.[62]

Once it had confirmed Japan's willingness to bear political responsibility and the United States' support for its minimal technical role, the ICRC finally made the decision to become involved on July 31. As Gallopin noted, the top officials of the ICRC were "not enthusiastic" about its involvement in the repatriation project, but they felt they had "more to lose than to gain by rejection" of the Japanese request.[63] The ICRC followed up its decision with a request to the Japanese and North Korean Red Cross societies to draw up their final agreement in a place other than Geneva. The ICRC suggested Calcutta, and this was where, on August 13, the JRC-NKRC talks were successfully concluded. According to the Calcutta Agreement, the JRC was to be in charge of the overall process of repatriation, including accepting applications and arranging domestic transportation, while the ICRC was to carry out formal but superficial screening of the returnees at the port of Niigata before embarkation. This outcome was a radical departure from the ICRC's humanitarian spirit.

Last-Ditch U.S. Intervention

With the repatriation almost in sight, the United States made a last-ditch effort to minimize its impact on U.S.-Japan-ROK relations. The U.S. effort became apparent in a conversation of July 17, 1959, between the vice foreign minister of the ROK, Kim Dong-jo, and Ambassador Dowling, and in the informal document that Dowling handed to Kim. The United States continued to preach that there were no logical or legal grounds for South Korea to oppose Japan's repatriation project, as long as the project abided by the principle of individual freedom; and it argued that where that principle was concerned the South had an advantage over the North. In addition, the United States urged South Korea to resume normalization talks with Japan, suggesting that normalization would contribute to the South Korean economy; in this connection, Dowling said that the United States was ready to extend its good offices to achieve the resumption of the talks.[64]

The U.S. offer of mediation was intended to convince the ROK to come to an agreement with Japan along the lines of the agreement between the Japanese and North Korean Red Cross societies. Also, the businesslike offer intended that the repatriation to the North should be limited to "the lowest possible" number of returnees. It was prompted by Washington's assessment of the implications of the repatriation for U.S. interests. The repatriation may have been an important political issue for the Japanese and the North and South Koreans, but the maintenance of political stability in Japan—which the repatriation would help—would serve U.S. interests. In connection with this assessment, Dowling noted in his conversation with Kim Dong-jo that the United States would not "countenance any action which might threaten peace or the security of the area."[65]

South Korea, clearly cornered in a losing game, requested U.S. mediation to facilitate the "unconditional" resumption of the normalization talks with Japan, but its strategy and objectives seemed unclear to American eyes. As usual, the United States pressed South Korea to clarify what it meant by "unconditional." During his conversation with Kim Dong-jo on July 29, 1959, Dowling suggested two conditions under which the United States would facilitate the unconditional resumption of the normalization talks. One was that South Korea must promise not to break up the talks, and the other was that it should accept a "financial settlement" instead of "compensation" for a possible Southbound repatriation of Koreans from Japan. South Korea refused to take responsibility in the event of a breakdown in the talks, and it also expressed skepticism about the Japanese method of settlement. No compensation for North Korea had been stipulated in the JRC-NKRC agreement of June 24, so it is clear that Japan had little reason to offer any to the South. In the eyes of the South Koreans, Japan apparently intended to include some additional aid in the claims settlement at the final stage of the normalization talks.[66] Despite the two sides' different understandings and objectives, Japan accepted the South Korean proposal for an unconditional resumption of talks on July 31.[67] It is noteworthy that Japan's acceptance coincided with the ICRC's final decision regarding its involvement in the repatriation project.[68]

The reaction of the Japanese public to the anticipated resumption of the Japan-ROK normalization talks was mixed. While cautiously
anticipating the return of the detained fishermen, the Japanese media
interpreted South Korea's move as either recognition of "the victory of
Foreign Minister Fujiyama's diplomacy" or an effort to obstruct the mass
repatriation project.[69] If South Korea's return to the negotiating table
represented a victory for Japan, the only remaining issue was the resolution of the Peace Line. In this regard, an *Asahi Shimbun* editorial of
July 31 stated that solving the Peace Line problem was a "prerequisite"
for settlement of the dispute between the two countries.[70] The editorial
reflected Japan's increasingly coercive strategy, which rendered the South
Koreans more and more isolated and helpless. Indeed, the resumption of
the normalization talks occurred one day before the August 13 Calcutta
Agreement; this made the talks meaningless as far as the repatriation
issue was concerned.

Conclusion

Along with the pull factor of North Korea's willingness to accept the
returnees, the push factor of public opinion in Japan ensured that the
repatriation project would be carried through. There were various reasons
why different segments of Japanese society were in favor of the repatriation of Korean residents; but in addition, the repatriation could be seen
as a way for the government to clear away the legacy of war, particularly as it existed in the presence of people from a former colony who
were now considered to be members of a troublesome minority. With
this domestic support behind it, the Kishi cabinet was determined to
assume political responsibility for this internationally controversial issue.
South Korea strongly protested the repatriation project, expecting Japan's
cooperation based on the anticommunist partnership, and the United
States insisted on the principle of the full screening of free will. But
Japan carried out the repatriation with only nominal screening of the
returnees by the ICRC. The ICRC's involvement was used to justify a
project that did indeed have inhumane consequences, as humanitarian
principles went by the board and were overshadowed by the political
interests of the states involved.

The United States was not simply the dominant power leading
the two alliances but also a prudent rational actor caught up in crucial
negotiations over the revision of the U.S.-Japan security treaty. Washington calculated that it had to put Japan's interests ahead of those of

South Korea. The Eisenhower administration wanted the most contro-versial issue—so-called prior consultation over the use of U.S. bases in Japan—to be settled in a way that favored U.S. strategic interests. For this to happen, the administration needed stability in Japanese politics centered on the Kishi cabinet. The United States was concerned that socialists and neutralists might be empowered. Aware of these concerns, the Japanese government, especially the Foreign Ministry officials, often let it be known that the Kishi cabinet would be in danger if the United States did not support the popular policy of repatriation. In this way, Japan justified the need for carrying out the repatriation, adroitly coun-tering protests from South Korea. It is notable that the United States, through its Geneva mission and the Tokyo embassy, was well aware of most of what was going on with the repatriation project. The only exception was the secret final stage of the talks between the JRC and its North Korean counterpart.

The United States varied the way in which it intervened between its two allies depending on the situation. First of all, when Japan made its audacious cabinet decision on repatriation in February 1959, the United States acted as a moralistic and legalistic mediator seeking to uphold the humanitarian principle of freedom of residence. Its preaching on this sub-ject reflected both its perception that the repatriation was inevitable and its genuine belief in humanitarianism. The preaching had certain ramifi-cations. It persuaded the ICRC to try to uphold humanitarian principles, although the ICRC failed to do so in reality. And it sidelined the South Koreans' protests that the repatriation was a political project disguised with humanitarian principles. Later, Prime Minister Huh Chung of the ROK took this up at a meeting with President Eisenhower on June 20, 1960: "They are pretending that the repatriation scheme is a humanitar-ian endeavor. . . . This is not exactly so . . . free choice is just a mask used by the Japanese." Huh's protest was in vain.[71] Second, at the final stage of the triangular dynamics, the United States became businesslike in dealing with its two allies. In view of its objective of establishing the U.S.-Japan-ROK security triangle, the United States sought to mini-mize the negative impacts of the repatriation. The Department of State worked hard to find common ground between Japan and South Korea by encouraging the repatriation of some Koreans to the South, although the effort had little consequence owing to Japan's delaying tactics.

The case of the repatriation demonstrates that Japan had the lever-age necessary to adroitly operate a risky Korea policy. Japan was able to deal with the two Koreas, although it did not formally recognize the legitimacy of the regime in the North. Japan could pursue its own interests in its relations with South Korea. Indeed, the repatriation sharply undercut the efficacy of South Korea's hardline approach toward Japan. When the protracted Japan-ROK normalization talks were resumed in the early 1960s, Park Chung-hee's military regime in South Korea, unlike the regime of Park's ousted predecessor Syngman Rhee, became business-like and pragmatic.

4

Japan-ROK Normalization Talks and Institutionalization of the Security Triangle

Because of the huge differences between the two sides, the Japan-ROK normalization talks were a painful, protracted process, lasting fourteen years from 1951 to 1965. The signing of the normalization treaty on June 22, 1965, not only marked the beginning of normal diplomatic relations between the former colony and its colonial master, but also institutionalized the security triangle consisting of the United States and its two allies, Japan and South Korea. It is significant that the normalization involved a money issue—U.S.-led burden sharing. From the end of the 1950s, the United States began to cut aid grants to developing countries, including South Korea. Washington saw Japan, by then an economic powerhouse, as a potential partner that could share the burden of financing development, in South Korea in particular. Indeed, the South Korean military regime, which seized power in May 1961, was in desperate need of money for the Five-Year Economic Plan, which was eventually launched in 1962. For a possible way of financing the economic plan, the Kennedy administration put pressure on Japan, and Japan reluctantly complied with the U.S. request for burden sharing, seeing it as inevitable. Because of the importance of burden sharing, the United States intervened in the talks in various ways and ensured that they were eventually successful.

The normalization talks, starting with the first preliminary meeting on October 20, 1951, were marked by antagonism between the two countries. As a starting point, South Korea, under Syngman Rhee, insisted that Japan acknowledge that its colonial rule from 1910 to 1945 had been illegitimate. The South Korean government's guiding principle for the normalization talks was "to keep historical insight and an independent attitude."[1] But Japan contended that the annexation of Korea in 1910 had been a legal act and that Japanese colonial rule had contributed to Korean modernization. There were emotionally charged exchanges between the two sides in relation to such contentious issues as the status of Korean residents in Japan, compensations, and fishing zones.[2] On January 18, 1952, the Rhee administration proclaimed the Peace Line, with the intention of taking the initiative in the coming negotiations. In response, Japan and the United States called it the "Rhee Line," signifying that it had no legitimacy in international law. Right after this, Japan prepared a guideline aimed at dragging out the negotiations. Among the arguments deployed by the guideline were the following: protracted negotiation is inevitable; the legitimacy of Japan's annexation of Korea should be maintained; Japanese claims to property remaining in Korea should be handled according to the principles of international law concerning a secessionist country; South Korean claims should be supported by evidence; many relevant South Korean documents had been lost during the Korean War; and South Korea did not effectively control the northern part of Korea.[3] In March, Japan registered a claim to property left behind in Korea by its citizens at the end of World War II. The Japanese claim intended to forestall any South Korean claims of compensation for Japan's colonial rule. On Japan's property claims, the United States remained ambivalent and avoided making an official interpretation of Article 4 of the San Francisco Peace Treaty, which pertained to property claims.[4] The United States wanted the two sides to resolve the claims issue themselves.[5] To make matters worse, the dispute over the detention issue and the repatriation project, as shown in chapter 3, obstructed the normalization talks until the early 1960s, when new governments came to power in all three countries—the Ikeda cabinet in Japan in July 1960, the Kennedy administration in the United States in January 1961, and the military regime of Park Chung-hee in South Korea in May 1961.

With the United States using its embassies in Seoul and Tokyo as go-betweens, Japan and South Korea reached a deal on the most contentious issue of compensations, which was recorded in the Kim-Ohira memo of November 1962. Japan would provide a US$300 million grant, a US$200 million governmental loan, and a commercial loan worth over US$100 million. This agreement became the basis of the normalization talks later; in turn, the normalization contributed to the formation of the security triangle, although its related documents did not contain any mention of security cooperation. Once relations between Japan and the ROK were normalized, the two sides entered an asymmetrical partnership—particularly in that South Korea became the recipient of Japanese aid. This chapter accounts for how the United States monitored and guided the Japan-ROK talks and the ways in which the dominant power intervened in the most contentious issues until normalization was complete. Also, the chapter pays special attention to the domestic dynamics of Japan and South Korea. Each government's stance was influenced by its own domestic politics in different ways, and thus the United States paid special attention to the dynamics of its allies' domestic situations and adjusted its intervention accordingly.

The Korean Junta as Japan's Negotiating Partner

The downfall of Syngman Rhee's autocratic regime as the result of a student uprising in April 1960 brought relief to Japan with regard to the Peace Line and the detention issue. Coincidentally, there was a change of government in Japan as well, when Prime Minister Kishi Nobusuke was succeeded by Ikeda Hayato in July that year. (The resignation of Kishi was attributed to the forced passage of the revision of U.S.-Japan security treaty in the Diet two months earlier.) In August, the new Chang Myon cabinet in South Korea was keen to resume the already-protracted normalization talks, but it was ill-equipped to deal with the erupting demands of the students or the labor movement, let alone the critical issues of poverty and corruption.[6] This situation provided the military with a chance to intervene in politics: a coup led by Major General Park Chung-hee on May 16, 1961. Only a week after the coup, South Korea's foreign minister, Kim Hong-il, who was controlled by the junta, announced that the government would resume the normalization talks with Japan.

Cuts in U.S. Aid

What made the resumption of normalization talks so urgent for the junta was its desperate need for external resources. Implementation of the Five-Year Economic Plan, which had been drafted by the Chang cabinet, was the junta's priority to accomplish its professed aim of eliminating corruption and poverty and to legitimize its rule. As levels of U.S. aid declined, the junta saw Japan as an alternative source of funding.

Both the South Korean military and the country's civilian economy had been sustained by U.S. aid up to the end of the 1950s. In those days, U.S. aid was directed at maintaining the security and stability of its ally, so there was no clear distinction between military aid and economic assistance.[7] Before the Korean War, the U.S. aid channeled through Government Aid and Relief in Occupied Areas (GARIOA) provided South Korea with food, clothing, agricultural products, and medical supplies. During the war, GARIOA was replaced by a massive program of emergency aid, which consisted mainly of food and military equipment. After the end of the war, aid based on the Mutual Security Act became the major means of meeting South Korea's need for raw materials, consumer goods, and services. In particular, the aid policy in the Eisenhower administration, inaugurated in 1953, enabled South Korea to maintain a large army of 650,000 troops, which would otherwise have been impossible for the poverty-stricken country.[8] U.S. aid diversified after 1954, when agriculture, mining, and technical assistance became crucial components. This aid made up a substantial part of the South Korean budget, and aid shipments accounted for a considerable portion of South Korea's imports throughout the 1950s (e.g., 86 percent of the total in 1957).[9]

However, the U.S. aid program in general and aid to South Korea in particular underwent a radical transformation in the late 1950s, with a change from grants to loans and a shift in focus toward economic development rather than the military.[10] Yielding to congressional pressure, the Eisenhower administration introduced the Development Loan Fund (DLF) in August 1957, which was intended to facilitate higher productivity and related institutional capacity for long-term economic development in the recipient countries.[11] Against this backdrop, the Eisenhower administration, which had deplored the waste and abuse of aid perpetrated under Syngman Rhee, pressed the Koreans to reduce their military expenditure. Two U.S. reports, NSC 5817 in 1958 and NSC 5907 in 1959, emphasized the need for the ROK to reduce its military forces. Even though the reports did not specify numbers, the force reduction issue became a bone of contention between the United States and South Korea. The Koreans argued that they needed to maintain existing numbers in order to deter North Korea, whereas the U.S. officials argued that there was no need for such a large military because of no sign of an imminent attack from the North. This fed South Korean suspicions that its ally was not fully committed to security, but the United States focused on linking the DLF to South Korea's infrastructure buildup.[12] The overall U.S. aid policy toward South Korea reached a turning point on October 25, 1960, with the "Dillon letter." In his letter to South Korea's finance minister, the U.S. undersecretary of state, C. Douglas Dillon, stated that in the future, aid would be tied to specific economic reforms in South Korea.[13] The Dillon letter became the foundation of the newly inaugurated Chang Myon cabinet's Five-Year Economic Plan, and

South Korea started to adjust itself to the U.S. demands for self-help in economic and military affairs. In the years ahead, it was the economic situation more than anything else that encouraged the military regime led by Park Chung-hee to be pragmatic in its negotiations on normalization with Japan.

The Junta Viewed through U.S. Eyes

The Japanese government regarded the South Korean junta's proposal to resume the normalization talks as an important sign of its willingness to develop bilateral relations. But Japan was still unsure whether the junta would become a viable negotiating partner in the failing talks. Given this situation, Japan relied on U.S. views of Park Chung-hee and the junta in the period up to the Ikeda-Kennedy summit, which took place in Washington on June 20, 1961.

The U.S. reaction to the coup was the result of careful observation. The commander in chief of the U.S. forces in Korea, General Carter Magruder, and the U.S. chargé d'affaires, Marshall Green, initially confirmed continued U.S. support for the Chang Myon cabinet, but Washington immediately discarded this position. President John F. Kennedy, who was on a visit to Canada, cautioned U.S. officials in Seoul not to make further comments on the Korean situation.[14] Kennedy's noninterventionist position was based on U.S. officials' background briefings as follows: first, authorities in the Chang cabinet were incapable of opposing the coup, and second, Park's coup did not appear to be communist-inspired, but anticommunist-motivated.[15]

As early as mid-June, the United States was treating Park's junta— the Supreme Council for National Reconstruction (SCNR)—as the de facto governing body of South Korea. One condition of de facto U.S. approval was early restoration of a representative civilian government. At the 485th meeting of the National Security Council on June 13, President Kennedy inaugurated a new Korea policy, based on Walt W. Rostow's idea of prioritizing economy over military to foster political stability and development in developing countries. NSC Action No. 2430 of June 13, which was adopted in response to the NSC meeting, stated that the new ambassador in Seoul, Samuel Berger, would act as a catalyst for South Korea-Japan relations and that he was authorized to invite the top leader of the South Korean junta to Washington. The document also suggested that if the ROK carried out economic reform, the United States would supply US$28 million in military aid and technical assistance for the Five-Year Economic Plan. Furthermore, it would give particular assistance to the country's vital power-generation industry, which was the weakest sector of South Korea's infrastructure. In consideration of Prime Minister Ikeda's imminent visit to Washington, the document suggested that Japan be urged to offer development assistance to South Korea in coordination with the U.S. aid program.[16] By means of this aid plan, the U.S. government virtually gave the South Korean junta the green light.

Originally, Prime Minister Ikeda was not interested in normalized relations with South Korea. Having witnessed that his predecessor, Kishi, had suffered political disgrace because of the unpopular revision of the U.S.-Japan Security Treaty, Ikeda did not want to provoke a possible political crisis in relation to the normalization talks. However, the Kennedy-Ikeda summit on June 20 provided Ikeda and his associates with both a view on the military regime in South Korea and a chance to consider resumption of the normalization talks.[17] At the summit, Kennedy, in line with his new Korea policy, put forth his views of supporting the military regime in South Korea and suggested that Ikeda develop Japan's relations with South Korea; then, in compensation, the United States would urge the junta to transfer power to a civilian government as soon as possible, something that was an important concern for Tokyo as well. In response, Ikeda stated that the coup was an "accomplished fact," and that the "situation must be dealt with as it now stands."[18] Now toeing the U.S. line on the junta, Ikeda must have been relieved; engagement with the junta seemed safer and more doable than before. This became clear when, upon his return to Tokyo, he suggested that the normalization talks be resumed.[19]

Japan's decision to do business with the junta was given powerful momentum after Park Chung-hee's August 12 statement announcing that he would establish a civilian government by the summer of 1963. This statement eased the Japanese government's concerns about possible criticism from the opposition over its dealings with the military regime in Seoul. Furthermore, Japan began to take into consideration the aid issue. In common with the United States, Japan was of the opinion that the aid would have a stabilizing effect on South Korean politics. It also took the view that, in comparison with such countries as Pakistan, Burma, and Turkey, where military rule had been prolonged, Park Chung-hee's plan to hand over power within two years was not too bad. In the light of this more positive assessment, Japan was prepared to resume normalization talks.[20]

The visit of the U.S. secretary of state, Dean Rusk, to Seoul on November 5 was an important event that marked recognition of the military regime by the United States. After attending the first meeting of the Joint U.S.-Japan Committee on Trade and Economic Affairs in Tokyo, Rusk flew to Seoul to meet the chairman of the SCNR Park Chung-hee. Rusk delivered a message that Washington was ready to help, if not mediate, the normalization talks, and stated that the U.S. government was "greatly impressed by the military government's efforts to deal with corruption."[21] The meeting certainly assured Park that his scheduled visit to Washington to meet President Kennedy would go well. It also reassured Japan that the junta in Seoul was a de facto partner for normalization talks.

Japan's Concerns

For Japan, the Kennedy-Ikeda summit and Rusk's visit to Seoul probably fulfilled a necessary condition for the resumption of normalization talks, but they were not sufficient to ensure the success of the talks. There were some points that worried the Japanese government. First, Japan did not know how, or to what degree, the United States would help improve Japan-South Korea relations. Japan was not interested in the United States' intermediary role on the grounds that the Koreans, as the weaker party, would be bound to seek U.S. support for their view. Given South Korea's desperate need for resources, direct U.S. mediation would mean earlier and faster settlement of differences between the two sides, which could be costly for Japan. Japan's worry disappeared in part as Rusk, while visiting Seoul, stated that Washington would not become a "mediator," although it was ready to do anything that would help the normalization talks.[22] This reflected the State Department's traditional caution where intervention was concerned, a stance that differed from that of the White House, which preferred direct intervention. Indeed, the State Department had already instructed the embassies in Tokyo and Seoul not to intervene in the talks. It did not want to take the blame in the event of failure.[23] But as I shall discuss below, the U.S. position changed from nonintervention to active, coercive intervention at a later stage.

Second, the Japanese were also worried that the United States would withdraw its commitment to South Korea, particularly its economic assistance, and that Japan would be expected to fill the gap. The issue of burden sharing was a difficult one for Japan at this particular juncture, when the protracted normalization talks were about to resume. This fear haunted Japan throughout the entire period of the negotiations. Indeed, the U.S. National Security Council (NSC) in particular adopted a strong position on burden sharing and the use of pressure. As one NSC memorandum to President Kennedy stated in April 1962, the U.S. interest lay in "early resolution" that would bring "Japan to assume a greater share of the burden of subsidizing South Korea."[24] (Later, another NSC memorandum to President Johnson stated that the Japan-ROK normalization, if concluded, would save the U.S. government a half-billion dollars.)[25] In this way, the NSC expected that burden sharing by Japan would be one of the most important aspects of the normalization.

Third, mainly on account of U.S. demands, Japan started deliberating its financial contribution to South Korea, but it wanted to exercise its discretion where the form of contribution and related agenda setting were concerned. The compensation, particularly settlement of claims, was certainly important for both countries, but it was far more serious for South Korea than it was for Japan. South Korea was in need of funds for economic development, so it was more concerned about the total amount of the compensation. Thus Japan was concentrating on promoting its preferred form of the compensation and the rationale for payment, and, more importantly, it was preparing the way for a proposal associated with South Korea's abolition of the Peace Line and the extension of the Japanese fishing zone. Also, Japan maintained the position that South Korea was not in control of the northern part of the Korean peninsula, even though the Republic of Korea was, according to the UN resolution of 1947, the only legitimate government of the country. The objective of this strategy was to reduce the ROK's demand for compensation and open the way to dealing with the two Koreas in the future.

U.S. Intervention and the
Dynamics of the Japan-ROK Talks

From September 1961 to November 1962, the relationship between the Kennedy administration, the Ikeda cabinet, and Park's military regime was a productive one. Japan and South Korea were both earnest about the negotiations. The involvement of the U.S. State Department consisted of its envoys in Tokyo and Seoul acting as businesslike go-betweens. Through a range of negotiations, the contentious compensation issue was settled in the form of so-called economic cooperation. The Kim-Ohira memo of November 1962 noted an agreement between the two about the amount of grants and governmental loans and the terms of disbursement and repayment, but avoided using terminology such as "compensation." This memo would become the basis of the normalization talks in the years following. But severe domestic criticism within South Korea aimed at the secret Kim-Ohira deal, the scandal involving Seoul's negotiator Kim Jong-pil, and the government's "submissive diplomacy" resulted in stalemate for an entire year in 1963. Domestic disturbances in South Korea caused the United States to apply direct coercive pressure on Seoul in 1964–65. South Korea, in a considerably weakened position, stuck to trying to secure additional loans and face-saving measures, mostly toeing the U.S. and Japanese lines on the interpretation of the important fishery-related issues.

Settling the Claims Issue, 1961–62: Businesslike U.S. Intervention

In essence, the property claims issue involved burden sharing, that is, Japan's taking part in the U.S.-framed burden sharing, and thus it was negotiated and settled in the context of the triangular relationship. At first, a series of bilateral negotiations began with the visit of Kim Yu Taek, director of the ROK's Economic Planning Agency, to Tokyo on September 1, 1961. During Kim's meeting with Japanese foreign minister Kosaka Zentaro, the amount of money became a central topic for the first time. The Rhee administration had unrealistically estimated the amount US$2 to 8 billion, but Kim reduced that figure to US$800 million: US$500 million for claims and US$300 million in grants.[26] It is interesting to note that when he suggested that amount, Kim also hinted at a possible concession on the troublesome Peace Line issue.[27] According to Lee Jong-won, an expert on the Japan-Korea relationship, Kim's suggestion was probably a bargaining ploy rather than the South Korean junta's Maginot Line. Kim indicated that the figure was based on political calculation, as he pointed out that Japan had paid out US$800 million in reparations to the Philippines.[28] However, Japan stressed that its decision on the payment would depend on the content of the Koreans' Five-Year Economic Development Plan.

Further bilateral negotiations regarding the amount were conducted by Park Chung-hee in November, during a stopover in Tokyo en route to Washington for his meeting with President Kennedy. The first Ikeda-Park meeting took place on November 12 without any aides present, and it was conducted in Japanese. This format obviously did not favor Park, although he was fluent in Japanese. Ikeda set the pace of the meeting. He was familiar with the details of the figures involved and the history of the normalization talks, whereas Park had a poor grasp of the details and lacked the skills to counter Ikeda's negotiating technique.[29] The meeting ended without any tangible agreement, and Park was dissatisfied not only with the result of the meeting but also with Japanese news coverage of it. Whereas Park stated at the subsequent news conference that the ROK would separate the settlement of claims from economic cooperation, the Japanese press reported that Japan would provide South Korea with a loan rather than a grant.[30]

The domestic viewpoint in Japan prior to the Ikeda-Park meeting contributed to its failure. Because of the huge difference between the two sides, Ikeda's associates and Japanese Foreign Ministry officials favored a cautious approach. These people believed that a hasty agreement might prove costly for Japan. Members of the ruling Liberal Democratic Party (LDP) and some government officials raised the possibility of settling the claims issue through "economic cooperation." In this atmosphere, a few days before the Ikeda-Park meeting the Japanese press reported that the *form* of the settlement would be the most salient issue discussed by the two leaders.[31] At the meeting itself, Ikeda did indeed roll out the term *economic cooperation*, and he was quoted as saying that Japan "would compensate those items for which there was clear evidence of claims, and for the rest of them, it would offer other forms of settlement, such as a low-interest loan, if the South Koreans were uneasy about receiving a non-repayable grant."[32]

While debate on the form of compensation was raging among the Japanese public and in government circles, Park flew to Washington for his November 14 meeting with President Kennedy. The Kennedy-Park meeting amounted to virtual recognition of the South Korean military regime and provided both of them with an opportunity for confirming alliance commitments between the two states. President Kennedy and Secretary of State Rusk emphasized that the ROK government should transfer available resources from the military to economic development; they reminded Park that the administration was under pressure from Congress to reduce long-term economic and military aid. In this context, they urged Park to speed up the development of Japan-South Korea relations. They reassured Park that the Japan-South Korea normalization would not result in the replacement of U.S. aid with Japanese aid. They promised that Japanese money would play a complementary role. On the other hand, the Kennedy administration promised a US$90 million aid package in return for Park's proposal to deploy South Korean troops in Vietnam. On this, Rusk complimented Park by saying that he thought one dollar in his hands was worth more than a dollar in the hands of previous Korean governments.[33]

With the opening of the "high-level political talks" in March 1962, the negotiations entered a new stage not only concerning the amount and form of money but also in the U.S. strategy of intervention. The Japanese side was represented by Prime Minister Ikeda and Foreign Minister Ohira, and the Korean side by the director of the Korean CIA (KCIA), Kim Jong-pil, a relative of Park's and a powerful supporter of the military regime. However, the Ikeda cabinet was not genuinely enthusiastic about the negotiations; it did not want to risk the unpredictable normalization talks becoming a campaign issue at the upper house election slated in July. The lack of Japan's enthusiasm presented the United States with a dilemma. Direct U.S. intervention in the negotiations—"in the middle," to use Kennedy's term, or "direct involvement," to use Rusk's—was not a desirable option, because fallout from failure would damage future U.S. management of its two alliances and complicate the normalization talks. The United States adopted a more subtle means to persuade the Japanese government: linking the triangular security commitment with burden sharing. Washington emphasized the geopolitical significance of Korea for Japan's security. Kennedy was quoted as telling the former Japanese prime minister, Yoshida Sigeru, during a meeting on May 3 that the United States "protected the security of Korea largely because of its importance to the security of Japan." In line with this, the United States pointed to the German government's extension of credit to South Korea as an example of an advanced country expanding its aid program and suggested that the economically burgeoning Japan provide South Korea with loans as part of the normalization package.[34]

The three states—South Korea, Japan, and the United States—showed divergent positions at this important moment. The South Korean junta was the most enthusiastic partner; the Japanese government was reluctant to deal with the situation due to its fear of being forced to carry a heavier financial burden; and the United States did not want to be mixed in between the two, although it wanted burden sharing by Japan. Given this situation, the State Department instructed the two U.S. ambassadors, Reischauer in Tokyo and Berger in Seoul, to work as go-betweens in the negotiations. Their job was to smooth the way to an agreement through a "confidential exchange of information" between the two ambassadors and the relevant governments.[35]

Owing to the two American ambassadors' groundwork, ideas about approximate amounts and the form of payment evolved from May to November. During a conversation with Nakayama, a Japanese Foreign Ministry official, in May, the U.S. ambassador in Seoul, Samuel Berger, suggested a figure of US$350–450 million in compensation and grants, exclusive of credit and loans.[36] This amount was less than the South Koreans were demanding, but it represented the middle ground between

Tokyo and Seoul. Despite the absence of additional documents, one may assume that there must have been a whole series of discussions or deliberations in the Japanese government, and that the U.S. embassy in Tokyo must have kept an eye on the Japanese response. In this context, the U.S. government made another suggestion. During the Ohira-Rusk meeting in New York on September 24, the U.S. secretary of state stated that South Korea would be satisfied with US$300 million in non-repayable money, obviously meaning a grant.[37] In view of this development between Japan and the United States, it was surely not a coincidence that the KCIA director, Kim Jong-pil, mentioned a similar amount at the subsequent high-level political talks: a grant of US$300 million, another US$300 million governmental loan, and an additional commercial loan.[38]

The high-level political talks reached their climax with Kim Jong-pil's two visits to Tokyo in October and November, which took place before and after a trip to Washington. At the Kim-Rusk meeting on October 29, Kim briefed Rusk on his talks with Prime Minister Ikeda and Foreign Minister Ohira, held on October 20–23.[39] Kim stated that the topics covered in the talks included not only the amount and form of the payment but also contentious issues such as fisheries, the Peace Line, and the disputed Dokdo/Takeshima. In other words, at the October talks the Japanese government was ready to make a final offer on the amount, and to do this in exchange for Japan's wish list. The Japanese side demanded that Kim drop the word *reparation* with regard to the claims payment, and Kim agreed in principle. In response to Japanese concern over the fishery and Peace Line issues, Kim said that South Korea would adopt a flexible stance for the benefit of both countries. As for Japan's insistence on a settlement of the Dokdo/Takeshima issue, Kim told Ohira that "a place for sea gull droppings" should be "blown up" so as to avoid the issue becoming a stumbling block in further negotiations.[40]

Given the developments above, the Kim-Ohira memo of November 12 did not come as a surprise. The memo stated that the two sides had agreed to a US$300 million non-repayable grant, a US$200 million governmental loan furnished through the Overseas Economic Cooperation Fund, and a commercial loan worth of US$100 million. There was no mention of reparation or compensation. The form of the Japanese settlement of the Korean claims was now economic cooperation. In Ohira's terms, it was deemed a gesture of "congratulations" for Korean independence."[41] The Kim-Ohira memo became the starting point for the subsequent stages of the normalization talks. The memo was important for both governments, but it attracted fierce criticism and resistance from opposition forces in South Korea.

Settling the Fisheries Issue, 1964–65: Coercive U.S. Pressure

The normalization talks were suspended throughout 1963, because of mounting criticism and opposition in South Korea and the scheduled political transition from military rule to civilian government. As Park Chung-hee, dressed in civilian clothes, was inaugurated president in December 1963, and negotiations on the fisheries issue proceeded in early 1964, opposition forces criticized the negotiations with Japan as anti-Korean and pro-Japanese. The domestic situation in South Korea caused anxiety for both Japan and the United States. Japan considered the Kim-Ohira memo to be a tentative agreement that would prepare the way for further talks on the remaining unresolved issues. Japan desperately needed early resolution of the Peace Line and fisheries issues.[42] The United States was now concerned about the continuing burden of aid to South Korea. This prompted a change in the U.S. stance beginning in 1964, to one of direct intervention and, specifically, coercive pressure. Consequently, "Washington, instead of Tokyo, became the center of the negotiations," as one Korean official noted.[43] The United States put pressure on both governments, but more pressure was put on South Korea. The U.S. government apparently believed that the main obstacle was on the South Korean side, particularly, the domestic disturbances surrounding the scandal of Kim Jong-pil's black money. The United States tried to correct the Park administration's possible miscalculation that time was on the South Korean side.[44] At the same time, the U.S. government, particularly the NSC, highlighted the need to put pressure on the Japanese government as well, on the grounds that the normalization would save the United States more than US$500 million, the amount Japan was supposed to be contributing to South Korea.[45] Inasmuch as the fisheries negotiations were the final hurdle in the Japan-South Korea talks, the United States decided to use coercive pressure on that issue.

One contentious point in the fisheries negotiations at the beginning of 1964 was that Japan laid claim to a twelve nautical miles exclusive fishing zone, while South Korea demanded a forty nautical miles zone.[46] Japan had long sought the abolition of the Peace Line in any form whatsoever, whereas South Korea aimed to secure the line as much as possible because it worried that technologically advanced Japanese fishermen would deplete fishing stocks in the East Sea, or the "Sea of Japan," as it was called by the Japanese. The Japanese proposal for a twelve-mile zone was based on a joint proposal for six miles of territorial waters and a six-mile adjacent fishery zone put forward by the United States and Canada at the Second UN Convention on the Law of the Sea, convened in Geneva in 1960. Although the U.S.-Canadian proposal failed to gain approval at that time, twelve-mile claims became legion in the late 1960s.[47] In view of the changing trend in territorial waters, the Japanese suggestion for a twelve-mile limit seemed internationally appealing and, more important, in accordance with the position of the United States. Another point of contention between Japan and South Korea was the issue of financial assistance for the modernization of the backward Korean fishing industry, particularly for the introduction of technology-based fishing boats. Japan wanted discussion of finance to take place at the commercial bank level, whereas South Korea wanted a "fishery cooperation fund" to be added to the Kim-Ohira memo.

Direct intervention by the United States—in the form of coercive pressure—was meant to provide the two countries with specific alternatives through the channels of the Tokyo and Seoul embassies. This kind of direct intervention differed from that in the first stage of the negotiations in 1961–62, when the ambassadors had worked merely as businesslike go-betweens. Now the State Department became the control tower, requesting information from the U.S. embassies and instructing them to find solutions in a straightforward way. For instance, the State Department's telegram to the Seoul embassy on February 12, 1964, which was based on information from the Tokyo embassy, instructed embassy staff to identify Korean intentions and actively look for a feasible solution: Korea would be prepared to accept Japan's proposal if Japan would be more forthcoming on the modernization of the Korean fishing industry and restrict its fishing in the area between the twelve-mile limit and the Peace Line.[48] Following suit, Ambassador Berger proposed to the State Department that Japan provide a US$70 million loan for fishery cooperation and temporarily restrict its fishing activities, while in return South Korea would accept Japan's twelve-mile limit. It is notable that there was a disagreement within the ROK government at that time. The Foreign Ministry came to realize that the twelve-mile limit was inevitable, whereas the Ministry of Agriculture, under pressure from opposition forces and the fishing community, pressed for forty miles.[49]

The U.S. government's direct intervention worked. The fisheries talks held in March and April between the Japanese minister of agriculture, Akagi Munenori, and his South Korean counterpart Won Yong-sok made progress, even if no conclusion was reached. The de facto abolition of the Peace Line was discussed: if a fisheries agreement was concluded, then the line would be dealt with in accordance with the agreement. Furthermore, the South Korean government tacitly approved the twelve-mile limit.[50] For the United States and Japan, this plan was a satisfactory solution that would allow a beleaguered South Korean government to save face.

As protests against the Park administration continued in South Korea through May and June 1964, the U.S. government gave Japan-ROK normalization "top priority" in Northeast Asian affairs. In a report in May to President Johnson, the NSC estimated that aid to the ROK had reached a total of US$6.6 billion—consisting of US$ 3.8 billion in economic and US$2.8 billion in military aid—and that another US$350–400 million was due to be spent in the fiscal year 1965. The average annual volume of aid to South Korea in recent years was estimated at US$300 million. Another NSC report in June suggested the need for extra pressure to be applied to bring about normalization, and it emphasized the impact of the Japanese funding that was expected to pour into South Korea: between six hundred million and a billion U.S. dollars. For the NSC, the long-term effect of burden sharing was the critical element; this would have a bigger impact than cutting the size of the South Korean military, which the U.S. government had long advocated as a way of reducing the need for U.S. aid.[51]

In line with the NSC's sense of urgency, in August the State Department tried to find effective means for adding new momentum to the negotiation process. One idea proposed by Ambassador Berger in Seoul, who always preferred coercive means, was the possibility of holding Japan-U.S.-ROK tripartite talks.[52] Berger's idea was opposed by the ambassador in Tokyo, Edwin O. Reischauer, and the State Department dropped it. Reischauer also believed that pressure was necessary, and he questioned whether the Park administration had the political skills necessary to handle domestic criticism. However, he feared that any formal mediation by means of tripartite talks would make the situation worse.[53] In the end, the State Department gave up the idea of tripartite talks or any other formal mediation, as it would require the United States to take political responsibility for any negative outcome. The State Department continued to apply direct pressure informally.

The United States put more pressure on South Korea than they did on Japan. In particular, Washington played the military aid card. Assistant Secretary of State William P. Bundy visited Seoul on October 1–3, after stopping off in Tokyo, in order to draw special attention to the Park administration's deployment of troops to Vietnam.[54] On this occasion, Bundy raised the possibility of cutting off military aid if the Park administration could not sort out the domestic situation and expedite the normalization talks. This threat was effective, and Prime Minister Chong Il-kwon expressed the government's determination to reach an agreement on the fisheries issue, stating that the Peace Line had "no standing as a boundary."[55] Chong's statement reflected South Korea's much softer position on the disputed border.

In November, U.S. pressure was extended to Japan also, although to a lesser degree. The newly inaugurated prime minister Sato Eisaku aired his views on how Japan should establish independent diplomacy at his first news conference held on November 10. He expressed an ambitious desire to open negotiations with the United States on the return of Okinawa, suggested an approach to Communist China, and said that he favored the rapid normalization of relations with South Korea.[56] Indeed Sato, as a prominent anticommunist politician before he became prime minister, had long supported Japan-ROK normalization, seeing it as important for the solidarity of the free world. For this reason, he was seen as the leader of an anti-Ikeda faction in the LDP.[57] In Washington's eyes, normalization was not simply one item on a list of diplomatic tasks;[58] normalization should *precede* all the other tasks.[59] Washington's prioritizing of normalization encouraged Japan to take a relatively flexible approach to the Peace Line issue, making nominal concessions in order to obtain substantial gains. At the Johnson-Sato summit held in Washington on January 12–13, 1965, the prime minister suggested that Japan might accept a de facto abolition of the Peace Line if the normalization treaty practically superseded it. What should be noted here is that, rather than anything else, Sato's interest at this summit was focused on *seikei bunri* (the separation of economics from politics), which would allow expansion of Japan's trade with Communist China. He was very sensitive to the rising interest in Beijing within the United Nations.[60]

The most protracted dispute between Japan and South Korea, the fisheries issue, was virtually resolved by means of a compromise reached in April 1965. The Sato cabinet made skillful use of U.S. pressure while accepting the Park administration's face-saving demands. At the ministerial meeting in February, the South Korean foreign minister Lee Dong-won asked his Japanese counterpart Shiina Etsusaburo to draft a new document to replace the Kim-Ohira memo, pointing out how much discontent the memo had aroused in South Korea.[61] Shiina refused to do this, but Lee did succeed in persuading the Japanese to raise the amount of the commercial loan, including the fishery cooperation fund, from "over US$100 million" to US$300 million. In this regard, as

Kimiya Tadashi aptly points out, the Kim-Ohira memo was not the end of the compensation negotiations but provided the context for further bargaining.[62] The South Korean government, faced with criticism at home, partially achieved its face-saving objective with the increase in the commercial loan. The Japanese, on the other hand, through a process of strenuous effort from March to the beginning of April, succeeded in obtaining their main objectives, including the abolition of the Peace Line, a twelve-mile exclusive fishing zone, and the establishment of a joint fishing control zone outside the exclusive zone. Equally important, Japan obtained South Korea's agreement that the right of trial for any fishing violations would belong to the flag state of the boat in question, a proviso that eliminated the possibility of South Korea seizing Japanese fishing vessels. For Japan, the increase in the amount of the loan had no real meaning. As the Japanese side reiterated in the talks, the commercial loan, unlike the grant, did not have a ceiling. For the South Korean government, the increase in the amount of the loan had *symbolic* meaning, rather than being an additional substantive benefit, at a time of deeply-felt and widespread domestic criticism of its diplomatic humiliation by Japan.

Dealing with History, 1965: U.S. Arrangement of Japan's Playing the Goodwill Card

The issue of Japanese colonial rule was submerged—at least at the governmental level—during the talks from 1961 to 1965. The negotiations during this period were based on interests. In view of the continuing domestic opposition in South Korea, however, placating Koreans' feelings concerning Japanese colonial rule certainly remained a critical issue in the final stages of the negotiations. Ambassador Reischauer, as an insightful historian, was keenly aware of this point. He believed that a goodwill visit by a Japanese official would alleviate the Korean people's anti-Japanese feelings to a certain degree. However, Reischauer realized that a genuine Japanese apology for its colonization of Korea was unlikely, partly because of the rise of nationalism in Japan and partly due to the absence of any regret among the public. In spite of South Korea's wishes, no one in the Japanese government was willing to apologize for what had happened in the past. For instance, in October 1953, the Japanese representative at the normalization talks, Kubota Kanichiro, had provoked Koreans by openly arguing that Imperial Japan had made an important contribution to Korean modernization. Foreign Minister Ohira expressed a similar view eleven years later. During a conversation

with William P. Bundy, the U.S. assistant secretary of state for Far Eastern affairs, in September 1964, Ohira said that South Korea was not
sufficiently grateful to Japan, despite copying all things Japanese, even
the names of its political parties. This exemplified the Japanese elite's
perceptions of both contemporary Korea and its former colony.[63] With
this in mind, Reischauer considered that a goodwill visit, even without
an apology, would be useful. But he believed that this card should not
be played until the final stage of the negotiations, that is, after tangible
outcomes had been achieved.[64] He seemed to believe that hasty use of
this card by Japan might cause misconceptions among the Koreans and
would adversely affect the negotiations.

It was South Korea that made the request for a goodwill visit.
Only a few days after his arrival in Tokyo in October 1964, the new
ROK ambassador, Kim Dong-jo, asked Reischauer to press the Japanese
to arrange a visit by a high-ranking official to Seoul as soon as possible.[65] Kim was a negotiator who certainly understood the meaning of
double-edged diplomacy—his request was aimed at a domestic audience
in South Korea as well as being framed in such a way as to avoid a negative response from the Japanese. At first, Reischauer was worried that
the Park administration might use the goodwill visit both to cover up
its own weakness and "to extract further concessions from Japan."[66] But
at a meeting in November, Reischauer did try to persuade the Japanese
foreign minister Shiina Etsusaburo that Japan should offer an apology
or a regret to demonstrate a forthcoming attitude.[67]

The Sato cabinet finally sent Shiina as a goodwill envoy to Seoul
on February 17–20, 1965. In a speech delivered on his arrival at Kimpo
airport, Shiina impressed the Koreans by saying that "it is really regrettable that there was an unhappy period in the long history of our relationship, and this should be a matter for reflection." This was the first
time that a high-ranking Japanese official had publicly uttered such terms
as *really regrettable, unhappy period,* and *reflection* in reference to Japan's
relations with Korea.[68] Yet the speech failed to make clear who was
responsible for the unhappy events in the past. As a result, South Korean
newspaper editorials and analyses pointed out that Shiina's speech did
nothing to change Korean perceptions of the Japanese. They urged that
Japanese goodwill, as displayed in the foreign minister's speech, should
not be limited to a diplomatic and ritual gesture, but should be followed up by concrete actions. Nonetheless, most South Koreans, with
the exception of student activists, received his speech favorably.[69] Those
who most welcomed Shiina's speech were ROK government officials.
During their first round of talks, Shiina's South Korean counterpart,

Lee Dong-won, praised Shiina, saying "the speech was based on a full understanding of the Korean people's remaining antipathy to Japanese" and "such a speech can only come from your broad vision and esteemed personal character."[70]

It is noteworthy that Shiina's visit and his speech were linked to his mission to finalize the already controversial draft of the Treaty on Basic Relations. The conclusion of the treaty involved two contentious issues: one was the rationale for the termination of the 1910 annexation, and the other was the extent of the Republic of Korea's jurisdiction, which determined the geographical scope of the treaty. First, concerning the rationale of Japanese colonial rule, the two sides came up with a middle-ground expression after two rounds of ministerial talks. Article 2 of the treaty stipulated that the annexation treaties "are already null and void," an ambiguous wording. South Koreans wanted it to be interpreted in such a way that the annexation treaties were null and void from the beginning, while the Japanese considered them null and void only after the establishment of the Republic of Korea in August 1948.[71] The South Koreans had wanted the treaty to denounce Japanese colonial rule as illegitimate and illegal. Japan's interpretation of the wording was connected with its interpretation of the payments made to South Korea at the time of normalization as a form of economic cooperation between the two countries, rather than as compensation for colonialism.

Second, in relation to the jurisdiction issue, there was another middle-ground solution. Article 3 of the Treaty on Basic Relations stipulated that "the Government of the Republic of Korea is the *only lawful government* in Korea *as specified* in the Resolution 195 (III) of the United Nations General Assembly" (author's italics). Resolution 195 (III), entitled "The Problem of the Independence of Korea" and adopted on December 12, 1948, noted the virtual division of Korea and the ROK's effective control over the southern part only. South Koreans had long insisted that the ROK's jurisdiction extended over the entire Korean peninsula, emphasizing that North Korea lacked both legal and diplomatic legitimacy. In contrast, the Japanese stressed that the ROK government had effective control only over the South and acknowledged its lawfulness based on the UN resolution. The expression in Article 3 was a compromise accommodating the stances of both countries: the inclusion of "only lawful government" reflected the South Korean point of view, and the addition of "as specified in the Resolution" was a concession to Japanese demands. Notably, these contrasting points of view reflected the stark difference in national interests between Japan and South Korea. For South Koreans, this jurisdiction issue was closely linked to the legitimacy of their state, particularly in view of the hostility of its sworn enemy in the North. For the Japanese, limiting the ROK's jurisdiction to the southern part of the peninsula was of significant strategic value. Although the U.S.-Japan Security Treaty and the imminent Japan-ROK normalization would constrain Japan's access to the Communist regime in North Korea in any legal or diplomatic sense, the Japanese government wanted to leave a possible opening for future relations with the North. As shall be discussed in the following chapter, Richard Nixon's visit to Beijing and the Sino-Japanese normalization in 1972 did indeed provide an opportunity for Japan to expand its economic and cultural exchanges with North Korea.

On June 22, 1965, the foreign ministers of the two governments finally signed the five normalization documents: the Treaty on Basic Relations, the Agreement on the Settlement of Problems Concerning Property Claims and on Economic Cooperation, the Agreement on the Legal Status and Treatment of Nationals of the ROK Residing in Japan, the Agreement on Fisheries, and the Agreement on the Art Objects and Cultural Cooperation. The South Korean legislature ratified the agreements on August 16, whereas the two houses of the Japanese Diet did the same on November 12 and December 11. With Japan-ROK normalization completed, the attention of the United States and its two allies quickly shifted to Vietnam. The United States continued to pursue its strategy of containing the Soviet Union there, and it extended the aerial bombing of North Vietnam, which had begun in February. The South Korean legislature approved another domestically contentious issue, the sending of troops to Vietnam, on the same day that they ratified the five normalization agreements. The Japanese government made great strides in its diplomacy in Southeast Asia in 1966 and 1967. More importantly, Japan put the reversion of Okinawa at the top of the agenda for the 1967 Johnson-Sato summit, quieting domestic criticism over the United States' use of its base on the island for the bombardment of North Vietnam.

How Did Domestic Politics Matter?

As for domestic politics in Japan and South Korea, it was the intensity of feeling about the issue and the distribution of power in each society that were the important variables that constrained the negotiators—that is, the governments.[72] Having carefully observed the combined effect of the two variables on the behavior of each of its allies, the United

States chose the form of its intervention. As shown below, the combined effect of this did not favor South Korea. The intensity of feeling on the normalization issue was distinctively different in the two societies. The high intensity of the issue in South Korea almost caused the talks to break down after the Kim-Ohira memo, as this document obstructed other elements of the negotiations. In Japan, normalization was a less intense issue, and the most important discussions about it took place in the Diet. The ruling party and the opposition shared common ground when it came to promoting or protecting the national interests. The Socialists had no intention of wrecking the negotiations.

The distribution of power between the government and society was also different in Japan and South Korea. In South Korea, during the initial stage of the negotiations, the Park junta was able to control the process without the distraction of domestic criticism or opposition. But at the time of the political transition in 1963, the leaking of the Kim-Ohira memo and the financial scandals surrounding the negotiator, Kim Jong-pil, resulted in a shift of balance. The activities of opposition forces in political circles and society considerably weakened the negotiating power of the new Park administration. In contrast, Japanese politics was by and large centered on the Diet, in which the LDP held a majority of seats, giving it control of the executive as well.

U.S. intervention obviously influenced Japan and South Korea in different ways. The pressure that the United States applied to South Korea was coercive, whereas much more gentle pressure was applied to Japan to persuade it to reach an early settlement. This difference may be attributed to South Korea's domestic unrest and the resultant protraction of the negotiations. The United States perceived this situation as prolonging the period in which Washington would have to bear the aid burden alone.

*The Impact of Domestic Disturbances on South Korea's
Negotiating Power*

When the military junta lifted the ban on political activities at the beginning of 1963, opposition forces in South Korea ignited criticism of the normalization talks. A primary target was Kim Jong-pil, who was accused by Kim Jun-yon and his fellow opposition party members in the National Assembly of accepting a US$130 million bribe.[73] Because Kim Jong-pil was both a relative of Park Chung-hee and the top negotiator at the high-level political talks, the allegation threatened the very existence of the Park regime, which had come to power pledging to

eradicate poverty and corruption. Students were also preparing to orga-
nize protests against the overall process of the normalization. They were
critical of the government's "submissive attitude" in the talks and feared
that normalization would result in the permanent division of Korea.[74]
In the eyes of Japan and the United States, both the allegation of corruption in high places and the students' criticism of normalization were
stumbling blocks in the talks.

The U.S. response to South Korea's domestic problems was swift.
Washington's reaction to the Kim Jong-pil scandal was particularly determined. As early as February 1963, the NSC suggested that pressure be
applied to the Park regime, and the State Department instructed the
embassy in Seoul to stop Kim Jong-pil using his intelligence machine,
the KCIA, to engineer the Democratic Republican Party (DRP) and
influence the result of the upcoming presidential election.[75] Whereas
the NSC was concerned about delays in Japanese money reaching South
Korea, the State Department worried about the fallout from Kim's political engineering and the ensuing instability.[76] An NSC memorandum for
President Kennedy warned that the performance of the military regime
was deteriorating, and pointed out Kim's involvement in corruption—
including an illicit stock exchange manipulation that brought him profits
of US$20–30 million.[77] (A CIA special report later stated that cash had
trickled into the hands of Korean rulers from Japanese businesspeople in
the first half of the 1960s: six companies paid US$66 million in total, and
individual contributions ranged from US$1 million to US$20 million.)[78]
Another NSC memorandum raised doubts about the effectiveness of
aid to South Korea, stating that U.S. aid "far exceed[ed] the strategic
interest" there.[79] The State Department, which had been reluctant to
apply pressure, eventually pressed the military regime to deal with the
scandals surrounding Kim and to persuade him to travel abroad, stating
that the "return of Kim Jong-pil to Korea would be most unfortunate."[80]
Shortly thereafter, Kim left the political scene for eight months, from
February to October 1963.

The inauguration of President Park in December 1963 did not
dispel U.S. concerns about the South Korean political situation and
the fate of the normalization talks, particularly on the fisheries issue.
The most troubling concern was that Park's negotiating power was seriously weakened, despite his continued enthusiasm for normalization. The
general-turned-president declared, in his first New Year's statement on
January 10, 1964, that his administration's priority was the expansion of
economic diplomacy in order to secure foreign funds, and he emphasized
the importance of settling all outstanding issues in the normalization

talks. However, throughout the first half of 1964, fierce demonstrations in favor of the Peace Line, which Japan desperately wanted to abolish, constrained the Park administration's flexibility on the fisheries issue.[81]

Indeed, as the fishery talks started discussions about the de facto abolition of the Peace Line, the protests intensified. On March 24, 1964, several thousand university students burned effigies of Ikeda and Kim Jong-pil, demanding the end of the talks, sinking of Japanese fishing boats caught violating the Peace Line, expelling Japanese monopoly capital, resistance against "comprador capital" in South Korea, ending U.S. involvement in the talks, and calling for a struggle against neo-imperialism and neocolonialism. In response, President Park met student leaders from eleven universities at the presidential office in an effort to convince them of the necessity of normalized relations with Japan.[82] Also, Park, seemingly in response to U.S. pressure, recalled Kim Jong-pil who returned to the negotiating table in Tokyo and replaced politically oriented representatives with civil servants. This measure was intended to avoid a repoliticization of the negotiation process.[83] But Park's efforts were in vain, as the domestic situation worsened.

In May and June 1964, the student protests spread throughout the country and developed into antigovernment demonstrations. The students denounced the existing regime for having its origins in a military coup, calling for an end to "nationalistic democracy," a unique form of polity based on nationalism and modernization that was advocated by the Park administration. To the students, the Park administration seemed both antinationalistic and pro-Japanese and pro-American.[84] A hunger strike by students further fueled the antigovernment demonstrations, and hundreds of university professors took to the streets. At this stage, the demonstrations were not simply against the normalization talks but had developed into a nationwide, popular protest against the government. On June 3, fifty thousand students and citizens took to the streets of Seoul alone, and violent clashes between police and demonstrators resulted in the burning of seven police stations. In the "June 3 incident," one student died and 630 others were arrested. On the evening of that day, Park declared a period of martial law which lasted until July 29.[85]

The disturbances and the government's repression of them reflected both the extremely high intensity of feeling on the issue and the shift in power to the opposition forces. This situation seriously constrained the government's ability to lead the normalization negotiations. Faced with criticism at home, the ROK government set its sights on nominal, and face-saving, gains rather than substantive ones. For example, on the one hand, the Park administration made concessions to Japan on the exclusive fishery zone and the joint control zone, and on the other, it pressed Japan to increase the amount of the commercial loans and to renegotiate the Kim-Ohira memo. Japan had no problem increasing the commercial loans, because private banks did not put a ceiling on such loans. Given this, the United States became anxious that South Korea's loss of flexibility might delay the normalization talks, something that would have been detrimental to its national interests.

Convergence of Interests between the Government and the Opposition Forces in Japan

Normalization was a relatively low-intensity issue in Japan, and its citizens were by and large indifferent to the matter.[86] Despite some criticism of the talks from the opposition, the government was not really constrained in its actions. The opposition's agenda on normalization largely overlapped with that of the government. The views of the Socialist Party and the SP-affiliated Sohyo (the General Council of Trade Unions in Japan) were similar to those of the government.[87] The Socialist Party in particular was an exemplary dual player: a leading vocal critic of the normalization talks and an advocate for Japan's interests. For example, they all agreed that the ROK could not represent the North,[88] and that the Peace Line was illegal and a legal resolution of the Dokdo/ Takeshima dispute was necessary.[89] The Socialists and the government only differed on the security implications of normalization. The opposition believed that Japan-ROK normalization would possibly contribute to the establishment of an Asian anticommunist military alliance, the so-called Northeast Asia Treaty Organization (NEATO), and Japan's entrapment into a regional conflict. Dismissing the possibility of such a scenario, the Japanese government maintained that normalization would simply enable it to develop friendly relations with South Korea. Consequently, the opposition's position solidified the government's negotiating position and persuaded the government to take a tougher stance toward South Korea.

The ruling LDP was relatively well prepared to cope with criticism from the opposition. This preparation came from experience gained during the political crisis of May–June 1960 over the revision of the U.S.-Japan Security Treaty. At that time, Prime Minister Kishi Nobusuke eventually had to resign, taking responsibility not only for the nondemocratic manner of ratification of the treaty but also for the content of the treaty itself. The LDP now made it a principle that the Japan-ROK normalization talks should be made known to the public, and it proactively promoted the legitimacy of the negotiations with the South Korean military regime. In December 1962, an article published in the party's monthly journal maintained that Japan had a responsibility to uphold the stability and prosperity of Asia by establishing normal relations with South Korea. The article endorsed the normalization process, arguing that a politically and economically stable South Korea would serve Japanese interests, that normalization would help consolidate Japan-South Korea economic cooperation, that the provision of grants to former colonies was a normal international practice, and that the junta would be succeeded by a civilian government of which Park Chung-hee would be the elected president.[90]

The Socialist Party's critical but supportive stance played an important role in the final stages of the negotiations, namely, the fisheries talks. In 1964, the Socialist Party analyzed the changes in the global situation in its own terms, concluding that normalization would strengthen the U.S.-led military alignment.[91] What the Socialists were most concerned about, however, was South Korea's possible misuse of Japanese funds, the dispute over the Peace Line, and the fisheries dispute. In particular, they pointed out that U.S. aid, which by early 1964 totaled US$3.6 billion, had not reduced poverty in South Korea in the previous decade. In these circumstances, they tried to ensure that the Japanese grant money would not fall into the hands of corrupt Korean rulers.[92] After the two foreign ministers had signed the five agreements in June 1965, the Socialists' concern was directed toward issues directly related to Japan's national interests. The Socialists were worried about missed opportunities for Japanese businesses in South Korea. In June, an article in the party journal bemoaned the slow pace of the normalization negotiations, contrasting the Japanese government's tardy actions with the rapid expansion of U.S. economic influence through the Agency for International Development in South Korea and growing investment there by German, British, French, and Swedish corporations.[93] The Socialists' main purpose was to ensure that the four agreements served Japan's national interests, rather than to oppose the normalization outright. This was especially true when ratification of the normalization by the Diet was only a matter of time.

Conclusion

With the Japan-ROK normalization, the U.S.-Japan-ROK security triangle of an asymmetrical hierarchy was solidified. The normalization was not intended to establish military cooperation between the two sides, but the influx of Japanese cash contributed to the development of the South Korean economy and consequently to the enhancement of its security as well. The institutionalization of the security triangle promised to have positive effects for all three states, albeit through painful processes of negotiation. The United States achieved its intended outcome: burden sharing with Japan for South Korean development and partnership between its allies. Japan was now able to bring its new objectives to the fore: negotiation with the United States for the reversion of Okinawa and the expansion of relations with China. South Korea obtained Japanese financial resources that were desperately needed if the country was to eradicate poverty and modernize its economy.

The consolidation of the security triangle would have been impossible without earnest, diligent work by the United States. As long as it aimed to achieve its burden-sharing objective and the establishment of a Japan-ROK partnership, the United States was willing to recognize the Korean junta as the legitimate government and to transmit this view to the Japanese. The United States exerted pressure on Japan and South Korea and intervened in a businesslike manner through its ambassadors in Tokyo and Seoul, particularly in negotiations on the compensation issue in 1961 and 1962. It also exerted coercive pressure on the Park regime when the Kim Jong-pil scandal in 1963 brought about domestic instability and when the antigovernment movement in 1964 obstructed the fishery negotiations. The United States viewed that further protraction of the negotiations or the crippling of the South Korean government would have been detrimental to its interests. However, the United States avoided an official mediation role—for instance, through holding tripartite talks. Pressure from and interventions by the dominant power on its two allies eventually brought about the conclusion of the treaty in June 1965.

Japan had the upper hand in its relations with South Korea. South Korea was ruled by a military regime that was urgently seeking external resources, and this was the weak point that Japan was able to penetrate. To settle the claims issue, Japan maneuvered the South Koreans into compromising over the amount and into accepting "economic cooperation" rather than reparation or compensation. It was also able to tie its grants and loans to the advancement of its business interests in South Korea. As for the fisheries issue, Japan achieved its main objectives: the abolition of the Peace Line, a twelve-mile exclusive zone, a joint control zone, and the right to try fishing crews who encroached into South Korean waters. Notably, Japan managed to enlist U.S. support in drawing up the fishing zones, sidelining the South Koreans.

Japan also made adroit use of U.S. intervention. The Japanese Foreign Ministry was in close contact, both formally and informally, with the U.S. embassy in Tokyo, and they assiduously analyzed the dynamics of the U.S.-Japan-ROK triangular relationship. The Japanese Foreign Ministry was familiar with the contents of communications between Seoul and Washington. During the final stage of the Kim-Ohira negotiations in November 1962 over the claims issue, Kim Jong-pil realized that Foreign Minister Ohira already knew about the exchanges between Washington and Seoul. At the fisheries talks, Japan suggested ideas that were more attuned to the U.S. position on emerging international norms concerning territorial waters. During the final stage of negotiation on the Treaty on Basic Relations, Japan ensured the maintenance of its stake in the Korean peninsula by virtually limiting the ROK's jurisdiction to the southern part only. Indeed, Japan followed this up with bold approaches to North Korea in the mid-1970s (see chapter 5). In contrast, South Korea, whose negotiating position was further weakened by mounting domestic criticism, was the unilateral target of U.S. pressure. In this way, U.S. intervention meant different things for each of the two allies.

5

Japan's Two Koreas Policy and
Its Commitment to
U.S.-Japan Alliance in the UN

During Richard Nixon's presidency, U.S. foreign policy, particularly its strategic contour of containing the Soviet Union, underwent a significant change. U.S. engagement with mainland China (PRC)—Kissinger's clandestine visit to Beijing in July 1971, the PRC's take-over of China's representation in the United Nations in October 1971, and Nixon's China visit in February 1972—aggravated the split in the communist block and opened the era of détente in international relations. This chain of events also had a direct impact on Japan's foreign policy. Japan became more independent than before, thus achieving its long-desired normalization with mainland China in September 1972.

For neighboring countries, the Sino-Japanese normalization in particular meant no less than the abandonment of Taiwan. Japan's severing diplomatic relations with the Republic of China (ROC) forced South Korea to nervously accept the reality of two Koreas, and at the same time encouraged North Korea to launch peace initiatives toward Japan and the United States as well as toward the South. Tension and confrontation on the Korean peninsula—which was exemplified in 1968 by North Korea's abduction of the U.S. intelligence ship *Pueblo* and the armed infiltration near the South Korean presidential residence—suddenly thawed, at least on the surface. And in turn, inter-Korean relations changed substantially, initiating a competition for peace initiatives. Japan's response was to deploy a two Koreas policy. It is fair to say that the development of Sino-Japanese relations had a more direct and penetrating impact on the Korean peninsula than the U.S.-China rapprochement. Despite the continued Japan-ROK partnership anchored by the United States, Japan was not concerned about the ROK government's demands, protests, or wishes,[1] while it tried to expand its relations with the North. Thus, Japan's position was seriously questioned by South Korea as to whether Tokyo was sincerely committed to the anticommunist cause. In this way, the asymmetrical relationship between Japan and South Korea and disputes over their commitment became more apparent in the first half of the 1970s.

This chapter addresses the following questions: What were main differences between Japan and South Korea in interpreting the partnership commitment? What maintained the security triangle intact—or specifically, what was the role of the United States in the security triangle? This chapter covers the period from 1972 to 1975, the years from the Sino-Japanese normalization to the unification of Vietnam under socialist rule.

Japan's Way of Independent Diplomacy

Following the end of World War II, the United States turned its wartime enemy Japan into an ally and incorporated it into the strategy of containing the Soviet Union. Japan faithfully played the role of sustaining the U.S. strategy, for instance, by providing supplies and logistical support to the U.S. forces during the Korean War. In response, Japan took advantage of the wartime procurement, amounting to close to a half-billion dollars, for its own economic growth.[2] As time passed, the United States expected Japan to gradually shoulder some share of the burden for the security of Asia in general and for South Korea in particular. As shown in the previous chapter, during the Japan-ROK normalization talks the United States pressed Japan to share responsibility for the development of the South Korean economy.

With the announcement of the Nixon Doctrine in 1969, which was succinctly dubbed the "Vietnamization of the Vietnam War" and "Asian defense by Asians," the United States gradually disengaged from Asia, particularly by reducing deployed American forces. In line with this policy, the Nixon administration withdrew the U.S. Seventh Division, amounting to around twenty thousand soldiers, from South Korea between 1970 and 1972. With the force reduction, South Korean leaders' fear of abandonment heightened. But there is a more telling story. During his Beijing visit in July 1971, Kissinger discussed the reduction issue with Zhou Enlai, and Zhou relayed it to North Koreans at his visit to Pyongyang in the same month. If the ROK leaders had been aware of the Kissinger-Zhou-North Korean conduit of the information, they would have been horrified by the U.S. move.[3]

Japan was not insensitive to the U.S. force reduction issue, but was more concerned about the possibility of being entrapped militarily than anything else. The Japanese government's first reaction was to question why the reduction started in Asia rather than somewhere else.[4] In the eyes of the United States, the Japanese government, particularly Prime Minister Sato Eisaku, was "far from ready" for the U.S. force reduction on the peninsula. Indeed, the Japanese government avoided the security issue at the Japan-ROK ministerial conference in 1970, a regular meeting that had been established after normalization in 1965.[5] Nevertheless, Japan provided new loans to South Korea in the early 1970s: $160 million in 1971, $100 million in 1972, and $100 million in 1973. Japan made it clear that the loans were not directly related to the force reduction on the peninsula, denying the linkage between aid and defense.[6]

The main concern of the Japanese government was that South Korea would try to persuade Japan—or the United States would press Japan—to provide the U.S. government with a kind of "automatic approval" for redeployment of U.S. forces stationed in Japan. To Tokyo officials, the automatic approval meant Japan's *embroilment*, or entrapment in a conflict on the Korean peninsula. They feared that circumstances might arise in which Japan would have to take over the U.S. military role in the peninsula. In this vein, Defense Agency director Nakasone stated that the Japanese government would not play such a role.[7] The Japanese fear of embroilment was no doubt associated with domestic politics. The opposition parties, including the Socialist Party and the Communist Party, sought evidence of any possibility that Japan would be entrapped into supporting U.S. military actions. It is notable, however, that the tension in domestic politics, ironically, contributed to Japan's unanimous resistance to its entrapment. In sum, there was a gap between the U.S. expectations and Japan's response, but Japan's alignment in economic terms with the U.S. strategic moves encouraged Tokyo to develop a pathway of its own with regard to China policy and Korea policy.

Sino-Japanese Normalization and the Abandonment of Taiwan

U.S. President Nixon's July 1971 announcement of his plan to visit Beijing stunned the Japanese people. In particular, the manner in which the information was delivered to its Tokyo ally was a shock—*shokku*, in Japanese. Japanese prime minster Sato Eisaku was informed of the policy change only a few minutes in advance of the announcement through a telephone call from the Japanese ambassador in Washington, Ushiba Nobuhiko. Perhaps the event might have reminded Sato and Japanese officials of the famous nightmare reported by Asakai Koichiro, Japanese ambassador in Washington from 1957 to 1963: in his dream the United States shook hands with China without giving notice to Japan.[8]

Taking into account the cautious, but distinct, American approaches to the PRC even before Kissinger's secret visit to Beijing, it is fair to say that Nixon's July announcement was not a shock but a diplomatic opportunity for Tokyo.[9] As to the issue of representation of China in the UN, the United States and Japan had witnessed in 1969 that the "Albanian Resolution" supporting PRC's representation was gradually gaining support in the General Assembly (forty-eight for and fifty-six against) despite U.S. support for the ROC's continued representation. The United States, in response, prepared a countermeasure in 1970: to refer the ROC's case as an "Important Question" under Article 18 of the UN Charter, which required two-thirds approval for any country's expulsion from the UN. No doubt this was a last-ditch effort by the United States to prevent the ROC from being expelled. But the Albanian Resolution received even more support in 1970 than the previous year; it secured for the first time a simple majority at the UNGA (fifty-one for and forty-nine against). Should this trend continue, it seemed obvious that even the Important Question would not be able to defend Taiwan in 1971.[10]

It is noteworthy that Japan continued to maintain a certain degree of flexibility in dealing with the China representation issue, even while it aligned with the United States in terms of UN diplomacy in general. To the U.S. request for Japan's cooperation with its dual representation proposal (representations by both the PRC and ROC in the UN) in 1971, Japan's reaction was negative initially. Japan believed that the dual representation proposal would not gain approval. Although Japan went along with the United States at the UNGA voting held on October 25, the result proved Japan's judgment to be correct. The voting on the Important Question for maintaining the ROC's membership status succeeded in getting a majority (sixty-one for and fifty-three against), but the Albanian resolution to seat the PRC received surprisingly strong support (seventy-six for and thirty-five against), greater than two-thirds even though only a simple majority was required. This result showed that many countries that had supported the Important Question on the ROC defected to support the Albanian Resolution for PRC representation— a situation that reflected a bandwagon effect prompted by the PRC's rising international status.[11] Also, the result demonstrated that Taiwan was theoretically in a position to maintain its UN membership, even though the PRC took over China's representation in the UN. However, the ROC's UN ambassador walked out just before the vote on the Albanian resolution and abandoned such a scenario of maintaining its membership.

In view of the developments described above, it is highly likely that the Japanese government realized by 1970, at the latest, that the China representation issue was turning in favor of the PRC. And thus Nixon's announcement in July 1971 of his plan to visit Beijing must have been viewed as an opportunity for Japan's normalization with the PRC government. Indeed, Japan waited for the opportune time to take advantage of the already rising "China fever" in Japanese society in order to achieve its goal of deepening economic relations based on normalization. In 1970 the volume of trade between Japan and China had already reached US $826 million, which was around 30 percent of Japan's total trade volume and brought Japan a surplus of US $318 million.[12] With the absence of diplomatic normalization, however, most Japanese firms, except Nippon Steel, had to accept the PRC's unilaterally imposed conditions that prohibited Japanese firms from engaging in trade with the PRC and trading with Taiwan simultaneously. Given this situation, the political circle prepared for the development of Japan-PRC relations by establishing, in December 1970, the League of Diet Members for the Restoration of Japan-China Normalization; as early as 1971, the Japanese business community separately raised its voice demanding normalized relations with the PRC.[13]

From early 1972, Japan's official position regarding China, particularly Prime Minister Sato's viewpoint regarding the Taiwan Strait, changed drastically. Originally, Sato had been negative with regard to scrapping the Japan-ROC Peace Treaty, even though he had endorsed the principle that Taiwan was a part of China. Sato's commitment to the peace treaty and diplomatic relations with Taiwan had been officially expressed as the "Taiwan clause" in the Joint Statement of the Nixon-Sato summit issued on November 21, 1969, which read: "The Prime Minister said that the maintenance of peace and security in the Taiwan area was also a most important factor for the security of Japan."[14] However, a month before Nixon's visit to Beijing, Sato reversed his previous position on the Taiwan clause. At a news conference held right after the second Nixon-Sato summit, on January 7, 1972, the prime minister stated: "I do not believe that the expression [Taiwan clause] used at that time is still applicable today. . . . The Taiwan clause disappeared."[15]

Even though his foreign minister, Fukuda, tried to extinguish the fire ignited by the prime minister's abrupt statement and the ensuing fall-out, the logic behind Sato's statement was that the United States was obliged militarily to defend Taiwan but Japan had no such obligation. Also, Sato's statement meant that the 1969 Joint Communiqué, even if not scrapped, was now applicable only to U.S.-Taiwan relations. Sato's statement exactly indicated Japan's changed position on the China issue. Sato confirmed this point again in his speech in the Diet on April 27, 1972, stating that the political situation in the Far East differed greatly from that of 1969, thus rejecting the validity of the Taiwan clause.[16]

As the Taiwan issue became a focal point of Sino-Japanese relations from late 1970 to early 1972, South Korea came to fear Japan's apparent change in its Korea policy. In the 1969 Nixon-Sato Joint Communiqué, the "Korea clause," along with the Taiwan clause, had been a critical component, reflecting the escalated tension centering around the *Pueblo* incident and North Korea's armed infiltration into the South in 1968. The Korea clause read: "The President and the Prime Minister specifically noted the continuing tension over the Korean Peninsula. The Prime Minister . . . stated that the security of the Republic of Korea was essential to Japan's own security."[17] As early as late 1971 and early 1972, however, an important question for South Korea was: If the Japanese government no longer respected the Taiwan clause, then what would be the fate of the Korea clause? For South Koreans, scrapping the Korea clause would mean Japan's withdrawal of its commitment to the ROK, including economic aid. South Korea's anxiety snowballed as North Korea accepted a flurry of visits by Japanese politicians, both ruling Liberal Democratic Party (LDP) members and opposition party members. The Japanese visits to Pyongyang coincided with, or preceded, their visits to Beijing.

At first appearance, Nixon's visit to China, in February 1972, appeared to generate Japanese concern: "We have been left behind."[18] But the change of prime minister in July, from Sato Eisaku to Tanaka Kakuei, turned the sense of being left behind into one of high expectations regarding the development of Japan-China diplomatic relations. Indeed, at his first press conference Prime Minister Tanaka expressed his strong desire for normalized relations with the PRC. The press conference, attended by an unusually large number of foreign correspondents, lasted one hour and fifty minutes. Tanaka was eager to explain his ambitious foreign policy, particularly regarding normalization with China, rather than avoiding direct answers to questions.[19] The manner of Tanaka's press conference was new and uncommon compared to those of previous prime ministers.[20] Along this line, Tanaka, right after his cabinet's inauguration, made an "unusual political determination" whereby he ordered his close associates to prepare for Sino-Japanese normalization, while bypassing the Foreign Ministry's high-ranking officials who had stuck by the traditional two-China formula.[21]

In relation to Korea in particular, Tanaka stated in July that the Korea clause was nothing more than an expression of the view that the security of South Korea was linked to Japan's security. Also he stated that the Taiwan clause reflected the U.S. and Japanese perception at that moment regarding the confrontational situation in the Taiwan Strait. Tanaka added that the situation had undergone considerable change and that the "possibility of an armed conflict [had] virtually disappeared."[22] Tanaka reiterated his view on the changed situation on the occasion of Kissinger's Tokyo visit on August 19. Tanaka and his foreign minister Ohira articulated the following points: due to the changes in the regional situation there would be little possibility of military conflict; the U.S.-Japan security alliance would be compatible with Japan-PRC normalization; and Japan was ready to sever diplomatic relations with the ROC if Japan's trade with and investment in Taiwan could be ensured.[23]

In a series of rapid changes occurring from early 1971 to mid-1972 (reduction of U.S. forces in South Korea, PRC's obtaining representation in the UN, Nixon's China visit, Japan's imminent abandonment of Taiwan, and Japan's virtual abandonment of the Korea clause), North Korea became more daring, and South Korea moved quickly. A result was the historic agreement between South and North Korea, the so-called July 4 Joint Statement. It is noteworthy that South Korea accepted the three concepts for national unification—independence, peaceful unification, and national unity—concepts which North Korea had long insisted on as the basis for withdrawal of U.S. forces from the peninsula.

The subsequent Nixon-Tanaka summit, held in Hawaii on August 31 and September 1, 1972, focused on two issues: trade-imbalance adjustment and Tanaka's planned Beijing visit. As to his scheduled Beijing visit, Tanaka tried to persuade Nixon regarding Japan's changed policy toward the PRC and Taiwan. In response, Nixon cautioned that Tanaka's adventurous diplomacy was tilted too much toward the PRC, and he tried to avoid creating a "Tanaka shock" comparable to the shock Japan had suffered at Nixon's July 1971 announcement. The summit ended with carefully expressed negotiated differences between the two states. For instance, the U.S. was unable to realize its wish to mention the U.S.-Japan security treaty's relevance to the defense of the ROK and Taiwan. Also, the allies differed from each other in wording the draft

of the joint statement, particularly in interpreting the potential implications of Tanaka's scheduled China visit for Asian security. The joint
statement read that "the Prime Minister and the President welcomed the
recent opening of dialogue in the Korean Peninsula" and that "they [the
Prime Minister and the President] shared the hope that [the] forthcoming visit of the Prime Minister to the People's Republic of China would
also serve to further the trend for the relaxation of tension in Asia."[24]
It is noteworthy that the Japanese original draft was worded "shared the
view," but at U.S. insistence, the joint statement finally adopted the
wording "shared the hope."[25]

Despite the above-mentioned difference, the Nixon-Tanaka summit was considered a success for the Japanese. For example, Komeito
chairman Takeiri Yoshikatsu stated that for the first time the Japanese
prime minister had met the U.S. president "on equal and independent
footing" and achieved "U.S. recognition of its [Japan's] means of normalizing relations with the PRC." Media also mentioned that it was the first
major test of Japan's ability to carry out an independent foreign policy.
In line with such a cheerful atmosphere in Japan, Tanaka declared in his
return statement on September 5 that Japan would enter a "new stage"
in international relations.[26] Indeed, the Japanese government made it
explicit that the relations with Taiwan would have to be sacrificed in
order to normalize with the PRC. Again, Japan's rationale of the Taiwan
abandonment was that, unlike Washington with its defense treaty with
Taipei, Tokyo had no such defense commitment and for this reason had
a free hand with regard to the Taiwan issue.[27]

During Tanaka's China visit, from September 25 to 30, 1972,
Japan and the PRC achieved their intended objectives. Among the
many points adopted in the Zhou-Tanaka Joint Communiqué on September 29, the following were of special importance: the Japanese government recognizes the PRC government as the "sole" legal government
of China, and it "fully understands and respects" that Taiwan is an
inalienable part of the territory of the PRC; the PRC renounces its
demand for war reparations from Japan; and the two governments have
decided to establish diplomatic relations immediately, putting an end
to the abnormal relations.[28] As for the Taiwan issue, the two governments did not formally nullify the Japan-ROC peace treaty, as China
had wanted.[29]

On the Japanese domestic front, the Zhou-Tanaka Joint Communiqué was a result of convergence of interests among ruling and
opposition parties and business circles. Accordingly the communiqué
was the first major diplomatic achievement that the opposition parties,

spearheaded by the Japan Socialist Party, unanimously supported. Also it was welcomed by business groups that had long wanted the expansion of their trade relations. Furthermore, on the diplomatic front, the United States recognized that Japan retained "freedom of action" in the operation of the U.S.-Japan Security Treaty. Undersecretary of State for Political Affairs Alexis Johnson underscored that the Zhou-Tanaka Joint Communiqué provided Japan with discretion of action in the event of hostilities, however unlikely, in the Taiwan Strait. The PRC exactly expected this point.[30]

For the ROK government, the Zhou-Tanaka Joint Communiqué meant Japan's abandonment of Taiwan. And this viewpoint must have prompted, and rationalized, South Korean president Park Chung-hee's extension of power in domestic politics. On October 17, only two weeks after Tanaka's China visit and the Joint Communiqué, Park declared the launching of the Yushin regime in Korea, allegedly naming it after the Japanese Meiji Ishin in 1867 (Yushin and Ishin both mean "restoration"). The Yushin regime was a clear departure from the existing procedural democracy. With a presidential special decree, the regime suspended the constitution, dissolved the National Assembly, banned all party and political activities, and declared nationwide emergency martial law. There are different answers to the question of why Park chose that new, authoritarian model at that particular juncture,[31] but a notable point is that he viewed the U.S.-China rapprochement, the Sino-Japanese normalization, and the Taiwan abandonment as a break from the status quo on the peninsula and as a change favoring North Korea.

Deployment of Japan's Two Koreas Policy

Japan's extended diplomatic advance was distinctive in its policy toward the Korean peninsula as well. While virtually abandoning its commitment to its partnership with South Korea between 1972 and 1975, expressed in the Korea clause, Japan audaciously approached North Korea, in particular with politicians' visits and the expansion of economic relations. South Korea strongly opposed Japan's North Korea policy, and expressed worries and warnings that Tokyo's move would undercut Seoul's security. Washington drew the red line that Tokyo should not cross at political recognition, which would allow the North to seriously damage to the U.S.-Japan-ROK security triangle.[32] For Japan, however, drawing the red line meant recognition of a certain boundary within which Japan was able to enjoy freedom in pursuit of its external policy.

Peace Initiative Competition between the Two Koreas

In the aftermath of the development of Sino-Japanese relations, the improvement of Japan-DPRK relations seemed only a matter of time. In Japan, a kind of "North Korea fever"—which followed China fever—suddenly emerged. For North Korea, the painful memory of the 1965 ROK-Japan normalization still lingered, but the new change in the Japanese attitude was encouraging news. Indeed, convergence was emerging between Japan's China fever and its expanded interest in North Korea, on the one hand, and North Korea's aim to develop a new relationship with Japan, on the other.

At the dawn of 1972 there was a stream of visits to North Korea by Japanese politicians. One of the most important visits to Pyongyang was that made by members of the Diet, from January 16 to 29. The group was led by Kuno Chuji, an LDP member, and included members of the Japan-North Korea Friendship Promotion League. At the planning stage, there was controversy in the LDP over the visit. Top LDP leaders were concerned about Japan-ROK relations and thus registered strong opposition to the plan. As Kuno did not give up the visit, the party leaders warned him that he would be turned over to a disciplinary session upon returning to Tokyo. Their warning was for the benefit of South Korean audiences also.[33]

The Japan-North Korea Friendship Promotion League's visit to Pyongyang led by Kuno was not simply a courtesy visit but resulted in tangible outcomes. At the meeting with North Korean leader Kim Il Sung, Kuno's group expressed remorse about Japan's colonialism and made a formal apology; and Kuno expressed a desire for establishing Japan-DPRK normalization.[34] This was the first time that Japanese politicians in office, even if not members of the administration, openly uttered apologies to Kim Il Sung. It is noteworthy that Kuno and North Korea, on January 23, signed the Agreement on Japan-North Korea Trade Promotion, which would remain in effect until December 31, 1976. This agreement called for expansion of two-way trade from $58 million in 1972 up to $380–510 million annually by 1976.[35] According to this agreement, Japan was expected to export manufacturing plants related to weeding machines, automobiles, and oil refining, whereas Japan was supposed to import tools, pig iron, compound metals, and nonferrous metals. Opposition parties and business groups in Japan welcomed the agreement; in particular, business groups rushed to request that the government allow North Korean technicians to enter Japan, which was considered a necessary condition for exporting manufacturing plants.[36]

Also, major Japanese newspaper editorials unanimously demanded that the Japanese government should change the existing discriminatory policy toward North Korea, and should not back off despite South Korean protest.[37]

Kuno's Pyongyang visit and the ensuing trade agreement were immediately followed by another group's visit led by Kawasaki Kanji, the director of the International Affairs Bureau of the Japan Socialist Party. Whereas Kuno's visit underscored the expansion of trade relations, Kawasaki's visit contributed to highlighting North Korean leader Kim Il Sung's posture of "reasonableness" and "flexibility" with regard to security issues. Using the opportunity of a visit by such a high-ranking official of Japan's progressive party, Kim Il Sung announced his new peace initiatives to Japan and the world. He stated that the existing unfriendly relations would end if relations between the two countries were normalized; that the U.S. forces should be withdrawn from the South, and the UN Commission for the Unification and Rehabilitation of Korea (UNCURK) should be dissolved; that the North and the South should establish a peace treaty; and that following the U.S. troop withdrawal, the two Koreas should implement arms reduction. Interestingly, Kim did not insist on the removal of U.S. forces as a condition of signing a North-South peace treaty, and he stressed the significance of Japan-DPRK normalization as a means to ending the hostility between North Korea and the United States.[38] Kim's new peace initiatives contained seemingly flexible elements as well as old doctrines.

In mid-1972 Japanese politicians were engaged in a kind of race to visit Pyongyang. The Komeito representatives, led by Takeiri Yoshikatsu, visited North Korea from May 30 to June 7 and concluded a joint statement. The statement called for withdrawal of foreign forces from the peninsula, establishment of a trade representative office, and normalization based on mutual interests and equality.[39] The Pyongyang trip, July 18 to 28, by the Socialist Party's Special Committee for the Korean Problem marked the first visit after the July 4 North-South Joint Statement and right after the inauguration of the Tanaka cabinet on July 7. It is noteworthy that at the meeting with the visitors Kim Il Sung evaluated the Tanaka cabinet positively for the latter's forthcoming attitude toward the North, compared with previous cabinets; furthermore, Kim expressed North Korea's changed attitude toward the United Nations, stating his willingness to send a representative if invited to the discussion about Korean affairs at the UN General Assembly in the coming fall.[40]

Notably, the Japanese government's position was in accordance with the viewpoints of the visitors to Pyongyang, such as the unusually progressive LDP member Kuno, the Komeito representatives, and the Socialist Party representatives. For example, in response to the protest by an ROK embassy official, in January 1972, against the Japanese government's permission particularly for Kuno's visit, Sunobe Ryozo, the director of the Bureau of Asian Affairs in the Foreign Ministry, made it clear that the Japanese government would "diversify" its diplomatic efforts, attempting to persuade the Korean government that it should also be "flexible."[41]

Furthermore, although the Japanese officials denied the legal standing of the Agreement on Japan-North Korea Trade Promotion, they contacted the leader of the North Korea–controlled Chongryon (the General Association of Korean Residents in Japan). In February 1972, a high-level official in the Ministry of International Trade and Industry (MITI), on behalf of the minister, participated in the ceremony marking the establishment of the Japan-North Korea Export and Import Corporation and had a meeting with the Chongryon president, Han Dok-su. This meeting signified a green light from the Japanese government in relation to direct economic exchanges between the two countries in spite of the absence of diplomatic relations. Foreign Minister Fukuda Takeo, in a response to the ROK ambassador's complaint about the meeting, steadfastly defended the establishment of the Japan-North Korea Export and Import Corporation. Fukuda said that this corporation followed Japanese domestic law and was similar to Mitsui & Co., which had been a window for Japan-South Korea trade.[42]

The government's approval of extended business relations with North Korea became more apparent in subsequent months. In March, it approved the opening of de facto regular shipping lines between Japan and North Korea. The three shipping companies in Tokyo—Tokai, Seiwa, and Eiwa—originally intended to submit their registrations as regular lines, but the government advised them to register as irregular lines in order to avoid the ROK government's objections. Although the companies had to submit a shipping report for each transaction, the reporting was a formality only. In regard to this development, the ROK ambassador in Tokyo sent a telegram to Seoul stating that "the development of Japan-North Korea relations would be inevitable," owing to Japan's improved relations with communist China.[43] In the face of the apparently rapid expansion of Japan-North Korea economic exchanges, South Korea became defensive and nervous.

It is noteworthy that as early as mid-1973 the Japanese government put forward the concept of a two Koreas policy and expressed its intention to further develop Japan-North Korea relations, if not to the point of normalization itself. Believing that Korean unification was not feasible, the Japanese government, at the U.S.-Japan talks held in Washington, held in May 1973, expounded that there was "no alternative to a two-Korea solution" and expressed the need for an international framework for this arrangement.[44] Such a Japanese position exactly reflected the two Koreas' competitive peace initiatives, which essentially represented competition for legitimacy in the Korean peninsula. Also, the position was associated with its stance at the United Nations, a place where North Korea was riding an increasingly favorable tide following the PRC's obtaining of China representation.

The two Koreas' competitive peace initiatives pertained particularly to the unification issue. One tussle between the two Koreas was ignited on June 23, 1973. South Korean president Park Chung-hee announced the Special Declaration for Peaceful Unification, whereby the ROK government would admit the existence of two Koreas in the international community. In this declaration, Park stated that his government would not oppose the simultaneous entry of South and North Korea to the United Nations.[45] Before issuing the declaration, Korean legal experts carefully scrutinized it to ensure that there was no logical contradiction between the internationally recognized two Koreas and the domestically legitimized one Korea.[46] The declaration was intended to allow international organizations and foreign countries to recognize the two Koreas, while avoiding open recognition of the North by the ROK government and people.

Park's adventurous peace initiative was immediately countered by North Korean leader Kim Il Sung's declaration on the same day of the Five Points for Peaceful Unification. In this declaration Kim called for establishment of a Korean Confederation and opposed Park's proposal for two Koreas' entry into the United Nations. For him, the building of a Korean Confederation was the precondition for one UN membership of the entire nation.[47] Also, Kim reiterated the DPRK's determination to achieve national unification without foreign influence, depicting Park's idea as prolonging the division of Korea. Kim's peace initiative was followed by a number of concrete actions: North Korea entered the WHO and made efforts to open UN observer offices, both in New York and Geneva, and also actively cultivated good relations with the states that had already opened diplomatic relations with the ROK.

The Japanese government welcomed the two declarations presented by Park Chung-hee and Kim Il Sung. At a news conference on June 23, Foreign Minister Ohira Masayoshi appraised Park's declaration as "practical, constructive foreign policy." Also, on June 28, Ohira stated at the

Committee for Foreign Affairs of the Upper House that the Japanese government would carefully pursue development of Japan-DPRK relations within a range that would not be damaging to existing Japan-ROK relations. In a similar vein, major Japanese newspapers welcomed Park's practical approach to the international recognition of two Koreas. *Asahi Shimbun* published, on June 24, an editorial entitled "Two Koreas and Japan's Diplomacy," which interpreted the South Korean declaration as de facto recognition of two Koreas and the pursuit of peaceful coexistence. A *Yomiuri Shimbun* editorial, entitled "South Korea's Policy Shift Reflecting the Reality," characterized the North's and South's declarations in a unique way: "South Korea's internationalization of the Korean issue, and North Korea's intra-nationalization of the Korean issue."[48]

The two Koreas' peace initiatives solidified the Japanese government's two Koreas policy. On the one hand, the South's proposal opening the possibility of two UN memberships would mean legitimizing Japan's even freer access to the North. On the other, North Korea's welcoming of Japanese visitors, from both political and business circles, and its proactive international involvement justified Japan's trade relations with the North.

Impact of the Kim Dae-jung Incident on Japan's Tilt to North Korea

Meanwhile, on August 8, 1973, there occurred an incident that seriously damaged the image of South Korea under Park Chung-hee while strengthening the pro–North Korean atmosphere in Japanese society. The incident was the abduction of opposition leader Kim Dae-jung. Kim, who had been Park's opponent in the 1971 presidential race, was kidnapped from the Grand Palace Hotel in Tokyo by members of the Korean Central Intelligence Agency (KCIA). He was found alive near his home in Seoul around a week after his disappearance. The incident constituted open and unprecedented infringement by South Korean agents upon Japanese sovereign territory.

In both domestic Japanese politics and Japan-ROK bilateral relations, the Kim Dae-jung incident became the most controversial and sensitive issue that had occurred following the 1965 normalization. The Japanese media took the lead in expressing critical views on the abduction incident, raising the possibility of the South Korean government's involvement. On August 23, the *Yomiuri Shimbun* attributed to an unnamed ROK official the admission that KCIA officials had been involved. In reacting to the Yomiuri's report, the U.S. Embassy in Seoul expressed the view in its communications with Washington that the source of that report might have been one of Prime Minister Kim Jong-pil's personal associates; the reasoning was that the Yomiuri correspondent had long enjoyed friendly relations with high-ranking officials, including the prime minister.[49] The ROK government swiftly responded to the report on the following day by ordering the closure of the Yomiuri bureau in Seoul. But there were signs of discord within the ROK government. As a U.S. Embassy report to the State Department noted, some high ranking officials, including possibly the prime minister, advocated dismissal of "responsible" KCIA officials, probably KCIA Director Yi Hu-rak or Deputy Director Yi Chol-hi.[50] In the end, the U.S. Embassy in Seoul reported that "in actual fact" KCIA director Yi led the abduction and President Park might have either ordered or at least implicitly approved the operation.[51] The truth-finding report, which was finally published in Korea in 2007, reached a conclusion similar to that of the U.S. Embassy report.[52]

The Kim Dae-jung abduction pushed Japanese politics into a frenzy in the following months. Prime Minister Tanaka and Foreign Minister Ohira were inclined to take a relatively cautious approach to the incident, being concerned about the effect of any negative fallout on bilateral relations. However, the progressive LDP politician Utsunomiya Tokuma viewed Kim Dae-jung as a political refugee and asked the Japanese government to make efforts to have him released by the ROK government. Opposition forces attempted to use this opportunity to corner the ruling party. Diet members Narazaki Yanosuke and Den Hideo of the JSP used the incident as a chance to press their own government, by providing evidence that included photos of a Mercedes with diplomatic plate number 48-52 being driven away from the hotel at the time of incident. Another JSP member, Kato Kiyomasa, pressed the Tanaka cabinet in a session of the Diet, calling for punitive measures in relation to economic aid to South Korea. As politicians in the ruling LDP also began to denounce the alleged South Korean involvement, MITI minister Nakasone Yasuhiro answered in the Diet that he was mulling over harsh measures, including termination of economic aid.[53] It is noteworthy that the rationale for addressing questions regarding the Kim Dae-jung incident differed between the ruling party and the opposition forces, but their interests converged—pressing the ROK government by cornering their own government.

The U.S.-led alliance's politics became involved in relation to the South Korean agents' infringement on Japanese jurisdiction. At first, the Japanese government attempted to use the United States' influence to resolve the incident, urging Washington to pressure Seoul at least to secure the latter's public apology. But there was a subtle difference between the positions of Japan and the United States. The U.S. government considered it a "clear threat" to leave the strain between its two allies unsettled, but it intended to seek a quiet solution of the incident. Despite Japan's wishes, the U.S. government did not apply harsh measures against the South Korean government. Instead, the United States delivered Japanese messages to the ROK government, but without using the exact Japanese terms. The United States wanted not only to avoid getting caught between its allies but also to settle the issue in an expedited manner. It chose the moralistic approach of "preach[ing] reason and compromise" to both Japan and South Korea. Also, the United States considered Kim Dae-jung's safety one of the most important issues.[54] Thus, top Japanese authorities, particularly Prime Minister Tanaka, came to mull over a kind of negotiated settlement, despite strong resistance from the home affairs and justice ministries.[55]

In response, the ROK government established a special police command and began an investigation, but this action was a gesture to shield itself from the growing criticism in Japan and the Japanese government's request for an investigation. Indeed, the ROK government strenuously sought a political resolution through negotiations. Apparently as the United States intended, Prime Minister Kim Jong-pil visited Japan and issued an apology, but at the personal level rather than publicly, to Japanese prime minister Tanaka on November 2, 1973. With the apology, the ROK government considered that it had washed its hands clean in relation to the abduction incident. The solution was reached through negotiation. The means of resolving the incident was the apology the Japanese wanted, whereas the manner was personal, as the South Korean side wished.[56]

Why did the United States not exert direct coercive pressure on or take harsh measures toward the ROK government? The U.S. approach concerning the Kim Dae-jung incident proved that its priority was the maintenance of the security triangle, particularly the partnership between Japan and South Korea. Japan was diplomatically empowered by both the Sino-Japanese normalization and improved Japan-North Korea relations, whereas South Korea was further weakened on the diplomatic front and its image was tarnished in Japanese society, as shown below. Given these circumstances, the United States sought a compromise political solution, resisting Japan's request for U.S. coercion against the ROK.[57] For the United States, such a solution was essential, especially at a time when trilateral cooperation was indispensable in relation to the Korea question at the UN General Assembly.[58] At that time, not only South

Korea but also the United States was focused on the Korea question as North Korea geared up its peace initiatives.

The Kim Dae-jung incident's impact on both Japan-ROK relations and Japanese society was enormous, not only because of the nature of the incident—South Korean agents' infringement upon Japanese sovereign territory—but also because of the Park regime's human rights violation against its political opponent. As a result, the incident strengthened pro-North Korea sympathies in Japan. The opposition parties quickly started a campaign for gearing up Japan-DPRK relations. The JSP took the lead. It initiated the establishment of the National People's Assembly for Japan-DPRK Normalization and convened its first meeting in Tokyo on September 8, 1973. At this meeting, the party chairman, Narita Tomomi, underscored in his speech that the Japanese government had aligned itself more closely to Park Chung-hee than before by trying to resolve the abduction incident politically and forgoing pressure for an investigation. Narita added that Japan's approach would obstruct the wishes of the Korean people, that is, for the unification of the Korean peninsula.[59] The Kim Dae-jung incident now became a political issue whereby the Socialists pressed for a new debate on the government's policy toward the Korean peninsula. In this way, the situation differed from that of the period before the incident.

Japan's increasing pro–North Korean tilt coincided with Japan-North Vietnam normalization on September 21. Japan became the sixty-second country to normalize relations with socialist Vietnam. Major Japanese newspapers carried articles the next morning proposing that the last remaining step be Japan-DPRK normalization. And the newspapers reported that the Japanese government was deliberating the possibility of providing an Export-Import Bank loan to North Korea for exporting manufacturing plants. Because the Export-Import Bank was completely government subsidized, in the view of the ROK government the bank loan to the exporters signified the Japanese government's involvement in economic exchange with the DPRK. The more sensitive issue for the ROK government was that there were officials in the Japanese foreign ministry who openly argued that the effect of the 1965 Japan-ROK Treaty (Treaty on Basic Relations between Japan and the Republic of Korea) was nil, legally speaking, in the northern part of the peninsula where the ROK's jurisdiction was unable to reach. To this, the South Korean ambassador in Tokyo hurriedly sent a telegram to Seoul about the changed atmosphere in the Japanese government as well as the cooling public attitude toward Park's authoritarian practices, aggravated by the Kim Dae-jung abduction.[60]

Encouraged by the Japanese government's two Koreas policy and the growing pro–North Korea public attitude in Japanese society, Pyongyang was further emboldened to propose negotiation of a U.S.-DPRK peace treaty. In this proposal, Pyongyang tried to project its reasonableness and flexibility on the diplomatic front. The Supreme People's Assembly in North Korea adopted, on March 25, 1974, a "Letter to the Congress of the United States." The letter stated two points: first, Korean unification should be independently achieved by the Korean people themselves; second, the DPRK must have direct negotiations with the United States, because the latter maintained its forces in the peninsula and exercised command over all military forces, including those of South Korea.[61] This letter was the first North Korean initiative that officially proposed direct negotiations with the United States for a peace treaty, while excluding South Korea. Kim Il Sung repeated the peace treaty proposal at the thirtieth anniversary of the Workers' Party of Korea on October 9, 1975.[62] Since then, a U.S.-DPRK peace treaty has become one of the most frequently cited demands in North Korean peace initiatives.

The aggressive North Korean peace initiatives in turn encouraged the Japanese politicians' further tilt toward Pyongyang. Diet member Utsunomiya Tokuma's Pyongyang visit, August 5–15, 1974, was probably the most troubling case for South Korea and one of the most encouraging developments for North Korea. Utsunomiya was a member of the progressive faction, led by Miki Takeo, in the LDP; he was a career Diet member who had been elected seven times since 1942; his progressive tendencies had first appeared in his visit to the mainland in 1959 as an envoy for Sino-Japanese normalization. At the time of his Pyongyang visit in 1974, he was leading the Asia-Africa Alliance, a leftist organization composed of Diet members from both the ruling LDP and the opposition parties. At a press conference in Beijing on the way home, Utsunomiya delivered Kim Il Sung's idea of the Korean unification model, particularly a Korea Confederation under which the two different systems would coexist. He went on to note that Kim had told him that "the Japan-ROK Treaty's Article 3 that defines the ROK as the sole legal government in the Korean peninsula is unreasonable, but if DPRK-Japan relations normalized, the DPRK would not object to that article."[63] Utsunomiya's Pyongyang visit and remarks afterward rendered Kim Il Sung more emboldened than before and made Article 3 of the 1965 treaty a controversial one in the political discourse of Japan. In this regard, Utsunomiya's visit had larger ramifications than Kuno's 1972 visit.

Owing to both the changed Japanese attitude and Japan's two Koreas policy, Japan-ROK relations suffered their worst period, which lasted until the Miki-Ford summit on August 6, 1975. Partly relieving South Korean security concerns, the Miki-Ford Joint Announcement to the Press included the so-called new Korea clause: "They [the prime minister and the president] agreed that the security of the Republic of Korea is essential to the maintenance of peace on the Korean peninsula, which in turn is necessary for peace and security in East Asia, including Japan."[64] Nevertheless, this new Korea clause could not completely soothe South Korean worries. This was because the clause was not adopted at Miki's initiative but because of the U.S. request for repeating the clause, which had already appeared in the 1969 Sato-Nixon Joint Statement.[65]

North Korea Fever: Expansion of Economic Relations

The changed Japanese attitude toward North Korea and the ensuing two Koreas policy coincided with the expansion of economic relations, a situation that might be called "North Korea fever." LDP Diet member Kuno's visit to Pyongyang in early 1972 paved the way for expanded trade between the two countries. The Agreement on Japan-North Korea Trade Promotion, adopted at the time of Kuno's visit, was not a government-level agreement, and for this reason, no legal protection in trade with and investment in the risky country was guaranteed. But the agreement was a kind of political substitute for a governmental guarantee, in view of its tacit approval by the Japanese government at that time.

The July 4 North-South Joint Statement, which was considered a landmark agreement between the two Koreas, was an encouraging sign for Japanese business circles interested in North Korea. As seen in Table 5.1, trade volume in 1972 doubled compared to that of the previous year; in particular, a sudden jump in exports—which more than tripled—produced a surplus in Japan's trade with North Korea during the same period. However, there were two contentious issues in Japan and in Japan-ROK relations: one was the export of manufacturing plants, and the other was the use of the government-owned Export-Import Bank's loans.

This rapid increase in trade largely reflected the export of manufacturing plants, and for this reason South Korea registered protests with the Japanese government. For South Koreans, the export of manufacturing plants and factories would strengthen the war potential of North Korea, whether or not the facilities were directly related to military industry in

Table 5.1. Japan's Trade with North Korea (Thousand USD)

	Export	Import	Total	Balance
1970	23,344	34,414	57,758	−11,070
1971	28,907	30,059	58,966	−1,152
1972	93,443	38,311	131,754	55,132
1973	100,160	72,318	172,478	27,842
1974	251,914	108,824	360,738	143,090
1975	180,630	64,839	245,469	115,791
1976	96,056	71,627	167,683	24,429
1977	125,097	66,618	191,715	58,479
1978	183,347	106,862	290,209	76,485
1979	283,848	152,027	435,875	131,821

Source: Iljo muyeokhoe [Japan-Korea Trade Association], Niccho boeki [Japan-Korea Trade], No. 305 (March 1985), 16–17.

the North. South Koreans believed that introduction of new facilities, accompanied by advanced technology that the North did not already possess, would facilitate economic growth and technological improvement, and in turn, would contribute to modernization of the existing military industry in North Korea. This might have been theoretically true, but South Korea could not deflect Japanese firms' rising interest in doing business with North Korea. Fourteen manufacturing plants were exported to the North in Japan's fiscal year 1972 (from April to March of the following year); the total value reached US $45 million. In fiscal year 1973, fewer plants were exported to the North (eleven altogether), but the total value quadrupled in comparison to the previous year, reaching $188 million. It is notable that this total amount in 1973 was almost three times that of Japan's export of manufacturing plants to South Korea in the same period; also, North Korea ranked third in importing Japanese manufacturing plants, after the PRC and Brazil. The plants and facilities that Japan exported, or attempted to export, included a cement factory ($120 million) and a towel-making factory ($2 million) in 1973, a bolt-nut factory ($2.4 million) in 1974, and a vinylon weaving plant ($6.4 million), a newspaper intaglio rotation machine ($5 million), and a standard weighing system related to physics and chemistry ($2.6 million) in 1975.[66]

In response to this expansion of industrial exports, the ROK Foreign Ministry repeatedly instructed its embassy in Tokyo to make utmost efforts to block them. In the first half of the 1970s, Korean embassy officials spent a lot of time meeting with both foreign ministry officials and business leaders sympathetic to the South to try to convince them that the manufacturing plant exports would improve North Korean military capability, particularly during the North's accelerated Six-Year Economic Plan from 1971 to 1976.

The more troubling issue was the use of Export-Import Bank loans. For exporters, the export of plants and facilities involved capital mobility problems. The exporting of manufacturing plants was not followed by immediate payment from the importers; long-term deferred payment was a usual practice. For this reason, Japanese exporters attempted to avail themselves of low-interest loans, at lower than commercial bank rates, from the Export-Import Bank, a procedure administered by the Ministry of International Trade and Industry.

The Export-Import Bank loans had discriminated against communist countries for almost a decade before the Japanese government developed relations with the PRC in the early 1970s. In particular, the Japanese government had suspended Export-Import Bank loans to mainland China following the so-called Yoshida letter, dated May 7, 1964, in which the former prime minister pledged to Taiwan that Japan would not approve the export of Nichibo's chemical fiber plant to mainland China through the Export-Import Bank.[67] No doubt the letter had long been considered equally applicable to North Korea. The Japanese government, however, suggested an end to the validity of the Yoshida letter in the fall of 1971, when U.S.-China rapprochement unfolded and the development of Japan-PRC relations deemed imminent. Finally, Foreign Minister Ohira confirmed the change at a press conference in July 1972 by stating that there was no reason to discriminate against China. At the Diet session on October 28, Minister of Finance Matsuda stated that the considerations pertaining to the Yoshida letter no longer applied, suggesting approval of Export-Import Bank loans for exports of manufacturing plants to China.[68]

As Japan's policy to support China-bound exports with Export-Import Bank loans seemed imminent, the ROK government began to panic. An internal government document, dated October 11, 1972, analyzed the trend of Japan's trade with the North, including plant and factory exports, and expressed concern about the practical difficulties in differentiating exported Japanese materials, whether or not they were CoCom-listed strategic materials that might support the North's military capability. The document suggested that stopping Export-Import Bank loans might be the best strategy for undercutting the increasing trend of Japan-North Korea trade and preventing Japanese firms from exporting large plants to North Korea.[69] From then on, the South Korean strategy of protest against the Japanese government focused on obstructing Export-Import Bank loans, not simply opposing the export of manufacturing plants.

Japanese enthusiasm for economic relations with the North began to deflate in the mid-1970s. As an indicator, the volume of trade between Japan and North Korea, which reached a peak in 1974, began to drop off; a sharp decline in exports was visible, from $251 million in 1974 to $96 million in 1976, and the trade surplus also showed a sharp decrease, from $143 million to $24 million in the same period (see Table 5.1). There were two reasons for the decline in Japanese enthusiasm. One was the impact of the unification of Vietnam in 1975 and the Japanese government's heightened security concerns, which eventually brought about loss of Japanese business interest in North Korea. The other was the debt problem, which began in 1974. North Korea's debt reached $1,999 million in total (as of December 31, 1976), with its debt of $300 million to Japan the largest owed to an individual country, exceeded only by its debt of $900 million to the entire socialist bloc. Also, North Korea had debts to Western states: $162 million to France, $130 million to Sweden, $125 million to West Germany, $90 million to Austria, $70 million to the Netherlands, $60 million to the UK, and a few others.[70] It is noteworthy that beginning in 1974 one-third of North Korea's debt to Japan suffered delayed payment and that the North was unable to pay the principal and interest after December 1975. Japanese business groups, represented by the Japan-North Korea Trade Association, frequently visited Pyongyang in 1976, not to expand their business but to negotiate the debt issue. The result of the negotiations was their approval of postponement and lowered interest rates, but in fact North Korea has made no payment on its debts even up to the present.

The Korea Question in the UN: Japan as an Assertive U.S. Ally

In the first half of the 1970s, Japan's commitment to the U.S.-Japan alliance, and its middle-power status in the security triangle, was distinguished by its close coordination with the United States in the UN in dealing with the Korea question. Although its two Koreas policy worried South Korea, Japan's diplomacy in the UN with regard to the Korea question was evidence of its commitment to the U.S.-Japan alliance, through which Japan believed that its commitment to the partnership with South Korea was demonstrated.

The Korea question in the UN was about the Korean unification issue in general, which had not been seriously discussed since 1948 UN General Assembly Resolution 195 (III) but nevertheless was raised as an annual ritual. The Japanese government had normally followed the U.S. position in the United Nations. However, taking advantage of diverging interests within the triangle, North Korea tried to make the Korea question a real agenda item in the UN. As an initial step, North Korea interpreted the July 4 Joint Statement in 1972, particularly the clause stating that "unification should be achieved independently without reliance upon outside force or its interference," as a pretext for removing foreign influence from South Korea. Specifically, North Korea aimed at suspension of the activities of the UN Commission for the Unification and Reconstruction of Korea (UNCURK), abolition of the UN Command (UNC), and withdrawal of foreign forces following a North-South peace treaty. And North Korea expressed its wish to send representatives to the UN General Assembly for debates on the Korea question, which the United States had so far prevented from being considered as an agenda item.

In support of the North Korean position, the PRC advocated dissolution of UNCURK and the UNC at the meeting between PRC UN Representative Huang Hua and U.S. National Security Advisor Henry Kissinger held on July 26, only three weeks after the July 4 Joint Statement.[71] To this, the United States, in an attempt to resolve the issue quietly, replied that it would dissolve UNCURK in 1973 should China cooperate with the United States for the postponement of the discussion about the Korea question at the fall UNGA session. In accordance with this, the United States acted jointly with Japan to postpone discussion of the Korea question in the UN fall 1972 session.[72] This implies that the United States must have informed Japan of the result of the Huang-Kissinger meeting.

In 1973, the Japanese government became proactive in dealing with the Korea question. Japan expressed its preference for maintaining the UNC and the U.S. forces—precisely speaking, the U.S. forces under the UN flag. At the U.S.-Japan talks held in May 1973 for discussing the Korea question, Japanese officials stated that the UNC in South Korea was useful although not essential. The logic of this statement was that in the event of South Korea coming under direct attack, the UN-flagged U.S. forces would legitimize their use of bases in the Japanese territory for the sake of Japan's security as well as for the defense of South Korea. In other words, the Japanese government would not have to face any domestic criticism on "embroilment," which had long been raised by the opposition parties. Of course, Japan did not want anything close to such a situation to develop. On the other hand, Japan presented the idea of dissolving UNCURK, which remained a nominal UN organization more than two decades after its establishment in 1951.[73]

Amid shifts in the positions of Japan and the United States, South Korean president Park Chung-hee declared, in a Special Declaration issued on June 23, 1973, that he would not object to North and South Koreas' simultaneous entry into the United Nations. It was a preventive measure designed to cope with expected pro–North Korean initiatives at the UN session in the fall. In retrospect, the issue of simultaneous entry into the UN by divided states was not unique to the Korean peninsula during this period of détente in the early 1970s. For instance, on December 21, 1972, East and West Germany had signed the Basic Treaty (*Grundlagenvertrag*) that paved a way for both to be recognized by international organizations. As a result, both Germanys were admitted to membership in the UN on September 18, 1973.[74]

Meanwhile, Algeria became the spearhead of the supporters of North Korea's position and proposed the so-called Algerian Resolution. This resolution called for the dissolution of UNCURK and the UNC and withdrawal of foreign forces from South Korea. As the time approached for the UN meeting in the fall of 1973, when both South and North Korea would participate as observers for the first time, there emerged a compromise between the U.S.-ROK position and the Algerian Resolution: to dissolve only UNCURK. For this compromise, the United States worked with its allies, not only with the ROK but also with Japan, the UK, and Australia.[75] And the compromise was possible owing to the U.S.-PRC agreement. At the Kissinger-Zhou Enlai meeting in Beijing on November 11, right before the Korea question was moved to the UN General Assembly, they agreed that UNCURK would be dissolved at the 1973 session and the UNC at the 1974 session.[76]

Against this background, the Japanese government stated at the United Nations First Committee (political and security), on November 14–21, 1973, that it would "not support dissolution of the UN Command . . . until the moment that the existing armistice agreement would be replaced by any other mechanism of ensuring effectively sustaining the armistice." Also, the Japanese government supported the ROK's June 23 Special Declaration that proposed the two Koreas' simultaneous entry to the UN.[77] To be sure, Japan was an important partner, rather than a follower, of the United States in relation to the Korea question.

As the Korea question focused on the UNC issue in 1975, Japan became a more assertive ally of the United States in proposing its own

ideas. The Japanese government proposed that Washington hold informal, preliminary talks with North Korea. Japan wished them to reach
an agreement on the dissolution of the UNC and the maintenance of
the Armistice Agreement. But the United States was reluctant to do so,
because it believed that such an agreement would be self-contradictory.
For the United States, the UNC existed in order to supervise the Armistice Agreement. In addition, the United States was concerned about the
possible political fallout that would result from bypassing South Korea at
its first talks with North Korea. That is, sidelining South Korea might
mislead North Korea into supposing that the United States considered
the DPRK, instead of the ROK, to be the only legitimate government
in the Korean peninsula.[78]

What made the U.S. approach toward North Korea eventually
unnecessary was the UN General Assembly's adoption of two different
and contradictory resolutions proposed by the two Koreas. The ROK
proposal, put forward at the thirtieth General Assembly on November
18, 1975, focused on dialogue for peaceful unification, indispensability of
the Armistice Agreement, and negotiations for dissolution of the UNC.
The North Korean proposal concentrated on replacement of the Armistice Agreement with a peace agreement, dissolution of the UNC, and
the withdrawal of all foreign troops.[79] The General Assembly's adoption
of the two resolutions at the same time put an end to the competition
between the two Koreas in the United Nations. This move made use-
less future debates about the Korea question in general and the UNC
issue in particular.

The fact that Japan put forth a proposal for U.S.-North Korea talks
six months after the fall of South Vietnam indicated that the Japanese
perception of the Indochina situation substantially differed from that of
South Korea. South Korea feared that North Korea would be emboldened to prepare another war on the peninsula. Perceiving the situation
differently, Japan continued its two Koreas policy and placed top priority
on peaceful coexistence between South and North.

Conclusion

In the 1970s, the security triangle survived South Korea's protests against
Japan's approach to the North. The United States controlled the red line
or boundary with regard to the security of the three states—especially,
that there be no diplomatic ties between Japan and North Korea. The first
half of the 1970s exposed four key characteristics in the U.S.-Japan-ROK

security triangle. First, there were sharp differences in interests, scope, and policy preferences between Japan and South Korea. Japan, a burden-sharing partner of the United States, launched in the early 1970s its assertive policy toward mainland China and deployed its two Koreas policy. In particular, through its two Koreas policy Japan intended to seek a balance in its exchanges with both Koreas and encourage them to compete and coexist with each other, while not trespassing the red line. Considering Taiwan's abandonment the core of the Sino-Japanese normalization, South Korea feared that the Japanese approach to the North would not only embolden the latter's diplomatic ventures but also strengthen its war-making capacity. Since there was no shared rule or agreement about security, South Korea persistently questioned Japan's partnership commitment to anticommunism. It registered protests against Japan's economic cooperation with the North and made efforts to block Japanese Export-Import Bank loans to the exporting companies. But the most effective constraint on Japan's approach to the North was the U.S. initiative of reviving the Korea clause in the 1975 U.S.-Japan Joint Announcement, which stipulated the significance of the ROK's security for the security of East Asia as a whole, including Japan.

Second, Japan's middle-power status in the security triangle was distinctive in its close collaboration with the United States in the UN in dealing with such important security issues as China representation and the Korea question. While maintaining its two Koreas policy, Japan remained a strong supporter of the ROK position. Why did Japan do so? Not only did Japan recognize the utility of the UNC and the Korean Armistice Agreement for its own security, but Japan also considered the UN an important international arena where it could expand its own diplomatic power. Certainly, Japan was an assertive player that projected its own formulas and ideas when necessary. When the pro–North Korean resolution was riding a rising tide in 1975, Japan put forward to the United States (even though it later proved unnecessary) the idea of dissolving the UNC while protecting the Armistice Agreement. Also, even before the ramifications of the unification of Vietnam had dissipated, Japan suggested that the United States approach North Korea to negotiate a compromise on the Korea question.

Third, Japan's foreign policy in general, and its Korea policy in particular, not only depended on political leaders—for example, the current prime minister—but also reflected Japan's national interests. No doubt, Sato Eisaku was a pro-American conservative politician, but he swiftly adapted in early 1972 to the changed international environment at that particular juncture of the U.S.-China rapprochement. Sato virtually discarded the Taiwan clause unilaterally, a move that smoothly paved the way for Japan's proactive approach to mainland China and the ensuing Sino-Japanese normalization. Conversely, Tanaka Kakuei was certainly an audacious pro-China politician, but he could not have achieved Sino-Japanese normalization without already rising Japanese political and economic interests in China. In line with Japan's China policy, Tanaka was able to expand Japan-North Korea economic relations.

Finally, and most importantly, the United States actively managed the security triangle to yield a feedback effect to the three. In the Kim Dae-jung incident, the United States avoided becoming mixed up between the other two, but intervened to orchestrate a negotiated, low-key solution: the ROK prime minister's apology. The United States aimed to save face for Japan, but it did not corner the ROK government, which was already nervous about North Korea's emboldened diplomacy. The forms of U.S. intervention were moralistic and businesslike, and their intent was for the Japan-ROK partnership to be maintained even if it was asymmetrical and contentious. Also, the United States, along with Japan, managed to keep the Korea question in the UN under control, thus sustaining the ROK's position and its legitimacy in the international institution. The United States made a concession in the dissolution of UNCURK, but collaborated with Japan to maintain the UNC and the Armistice Agreement. On the other hand, with its continued aid to South Korea and its commitment to the U.S.-Japan alliance in the UN diplomatic maneuvers, Japan evidenced a certain degree of security partnership with South Korea, although not altogether allaying Seoul's suspicion of Tokyo's intention to expand its access to Pyongyang.

6

Japan-ROK Security-Based Economic Cooperation

U.S.-Framed Burden Sharing

Sino-Japanese normalization in 1972 not only facilitated economic cooperation between the two countries, but also elevated Japan's standing in East Asia, particularly in the affairs of the Korean peninsula (see previous chapter). After the Vietnam War ended, the United States began to press Japan to play a bigger role in defending the so-called free world. In what is known as the Ford Doctrine or New Pacific Doctrine—unveiled in Hawaii on December 7, 1975—President Gerald Ford identified specific ways of containing the Soviet Union in the Western Pacific: raising U.S. strength, solidifying partnership with Japan, establishing normalization with China, and assuring security in Southeast Asia.[1] In response to this move, Japan increasingly identified itself as a partner of the United States and as a member of the Western bloc for both security and economic purposes in the second half of the 1970s.[2] Japan came to redefine its Self-Defense Forces (SDF) as a part of the Western collective defense system aimed at containing the Soviet Union.[3]

The new international conflicts and political changes at the end of the 1970s—such as the Vietnamese offensive against Cambodia in December 1978, the Soviet invasion of Afghanistan and the Islamic Revolution in Iran in December 1979, and the Iran-Iraq War starting in September 1980—made the United States more vigilant than ever about the Soviet Union's military buildup and its presence around the world. Indeed, as Zbigniew Brzezinski has noted, "the Soviet offensive thrust reached its apogee in the 1970s."[4] Soviet presence reached into Indochina, the Middle East, Africa, the Caribbean, the Indian Ocean, and the Persian Gulf. State-of-the-art Soviet weaponry, such as SS-20 missiles and Backfire bombers, targeted the NATO allies in Western

Europe and South Korea and Japan in the Far East. The Soviet Union threatened the West's sphere of influence at sea with its naval capability. What the United States was most concerned about was the Soviet threat to sea lanes at a time when oil imports were particularly unstable.[5] In this context, for the United States, the establishment of a partnership with an economically thriving Japan was essential.[6]

The U.S.-Japan alliance would have been of no consequence without burden sharing. The United States encouraged and pressed Japan to expand its share of the burden of defending the Western Pacific in particular and strategic areas around the world in general. Every U.S. administration from Ford to Carter to Reagan, as soon as it embarked, put pressure on Japan to increase its economic aid, arguing that Japan had had a free ride as far as defense was concerned. The pressure started after the unification of Vietnam, and it continued throughout the rest of the Cold War period. In response, Japan substantially increased the amount of its foreign aid, doubling it in 1978–80 and doubling it again in 1980–85. Also, the scope of Japan's aid expanded from East Asia to diverse regions around the world, and it was aimed at economic development and humanitarian relief. But U.S.-framed burden sharing meant more than just financial aid; it also meant incorporation into the linkage between aid and defense, linkage that was intended to strengthen strategically significant and sensitive but materially weak countries.

In this chapter, I show that Japan's aid of US$4 billion to South Korea in 1983, the largest package since the economic aid that was offered at the time of normalization in 1965, took place within the scheme of the U.S.-framed burden sharing. First, I illustrate how the United States pressured Japan to increase its share of the burden for the security of the free world. Then, I identify the rationales of the three states—the United States, Japan, and South Korea—in requesting and providing this aid. Notably, the three states were motivated by different interests, as is apparent from the different terminology used to describe the aid. The United States obviously saw the aid in the context of security burden sharing; South Korea called it *anbo gyeonghyeop*, or "security-based economic cooperation"; and Japan simply termed it "economic cooperation," recognizing no linkage between aid and defense.

U.S. Pressure on Japan for Burden Sharing

With regard to burden sharing, the United States exerted pressure on the Japanese government to do four things: (1) increase the quantity and quality of its official development assistance (ODA) to strategically important countries; (2) strengthen its SDF so that it could effectively defend the Northwest Pacific sea lanes that were vital for Japan's economic security; (3) define cooperative military roles and missions and to improve U.S.-Japan defense cooperation, including joint planning and technological cooperation; and (4) give more diplomatic support to the United States on issues of common interest.[7] Of the four, Japan was most forthcoming on (1), that is, increasing its ODA to strategically important areas. The logic behind Washington's request for this type of burden sharing was that the two states shared common strategic interests around the world. In response, Japan apparently believed that the expansion of its ODA could complement its reluctance in defense cooperation with the United States. Japan also acquiesced on (4), and Japanese and U.S. officials were frequently involved in exchanges of views on the international situation from the mid-1970s. For Japan, however, the defense cooperation noted in (2) and (3) was extremely sensitive due to domestic constraints in particular, so the Japanese were cautious in responding to the U.S. requests. As shown below, Japan at first resisted any admission that its ODA to strategic areas, including South Korea, was related to defense. As time passed, however, Japan's ODA gradually came into line with U.S.-framed burden sharing.

It is noteworthy that while Japan's ODA began to increase at the end of the 1970s, U.S.-Japanese differences also increased. In response to pressure from the United States, Japan at first pledged to considerably increase its ODA to strategically important countries. At the G7 summit held in Bonn on July 16–17, 1978, Prime Minister Fukuda Takeo stated that he would "strive to double Japan's official development assistance in three years."[8] The United States urged Japan to step up the expansion of its aid program, requesting that it be done "as rapidly as possible," for instance, a 50 percent increase in dollar terms in 1978 alone. This pressure was based on recognition of the unprecedented foreign exchange reserve in Japan and the appreciation of the Japanese yen at that time. The U.S. pressure was not limited to the amount of aid, but extended to urging Japan to adopt Western standards of disbursement. The United States considered that Japan's aid program was implemented unfairly, and thus Washington requested that Tokyo relax the terms of its ODA—that is, to cease the practice of tied loans (tying them to the advancement of Japanese businesses).[9] However, as the U.S. pressure became increasingly specific, Japan expressed its own preferences. As to how the increase should be measured, the United States expected it to be in constant dollars, but the Japanese government defined the doubling in terms of current dollars. Also, the Japanese government said that it was willing to discuss the ODA issue with the United States, but it was "not prepared to negotiate." In other words, the Japanese made it clear that the decision to expand ODA was its own and that the issue was *not* an item for negotiation.[10]

Japan is frequently described as a "reactive state" in terms of its external policy. According to reactive state theory, the development of which owes much to Kent E. Calder's innovative studies of Japanese politics, external pressure may become a catalyst for a change in attitude on the part of the divided actors toward reaching a consensus.[11] Indeed, there are many instances of the timely and wise application of U.S. pressure helping to build a consensus in Japan on economic and trade issues. However, external pressure was not always helpful, particularly where security burden sharing was concerned. Japanese politicians and officials did not want straightforward pressure from the United States, and they pointed out that such pressure might be counterproductive. The former U.S. ambassador to Japan Michael Armacost has aptly noted that "Japanese passivity invited American pressure. Pressure in turn provoked Japanese defensiveness."[12] Japanese politicians and officials themselves worried that U.S. pressure might incite protectiveness and watchfulness in various sectors of society rather than aid the emergence of domes-tic consensus. In particular, the Japanese resisted Washington's requests concerning the defense budget on the grounds that this was interference in their domestic affairs. Another reason for this resistance was that in contrast to economic and trade issues, security burden sharing had no support base in Japan.[13] As time passed, the United States recognized this point.

Between 1978 and 1980, Japan's ODA expanded geographically as well. The program started with aid to Asian countries, such as Korea, the Philippines, Thailand, Bangladesh, Pakistan, and Indonesia, and then extended to other areas, such as mainland China, the Middle East, and Central America.[14] The substantial amount of ODA supplied to coun-tries in the Middle East is noteworthy. In 1978, Japan made a US$15 million loan to Egypt and started to explore the possibility of a joint power generation project with Saudi Arabia worth US$300 million.[15] The Japan-Saudi project was intended to involve Sudan and Yemen as well as Egypt. This kind of aid was in line with U.S. strategic aid policy. Also, this aid was quite timely. Egypt, in particular, had come in for severe criticism from neighboring Arab states for President Anwar Sadat's conciliatory posture toward Israel.[16] Against this backdrop, Japan, along with the United States and the countries of Western Europe, intended to use ODA projects to enhance Egypt's political and eco-nomic stability and to involve Saudi Arabia and Egypt—two moderate states—with other Arab countries.[17] Of course, Japan was also motivated by the need to stabilize its oil imports from the Middle East, but there is no doubt that the Japanese were encouraged and even pressured to provide aid to the region by the United States. Japan's aid to Pakistan was also remarkable in that it was intended to strengthen the country's economy and to assist refugees who had fled Afghanistan after the Soviet invasion. The Japanese aid was accompanied by a medium-term military modernization program provided by the United States. Likewise, the Khmer relief aid was aimed at alleviating the humanitarian crisis caused by refugees fleeing to Thailand from the Khmer Rouge's reign of terror and the ensuing Vietnamese invasion of Kampuchea. This relief aid was provided alongside a U.S.-funded UNHCR program and bilateral food aid to Thailand where the Khmer refugees were accommodated in camps.[18]

To be sure, the geographic expansion of Japan's foreign aid fell in line with U.S. strategic considerations. In this regard, the Japanese aid should be described as strategic aid in terms of its content, whether Japan was willing to acknowledge it as such or not.[19] And Japan's aid was obviously a part of the burden sharing that was initiated and framed by the United States.[20] But the efficacy of such strategic aid was ques-tionable. The strategically framed aid was most focused on relief aid or items convertible to military use, and thus was not intended to enforce the conditionality required for economic reforms.[21]

Despite the strategic characteristics of its aid, Japan was opposed to its being used to fund military buildups in the recipient countries. The Japanese government tried to avoid the linkage between aid and defense, and Japanese officials publicly argued that the aid was limited to economic and humanitarian projects. They maintained that there were two obstacles preventing Japan from providing military aid: one was its pacifist constitution, and the other was domestic resistance that reflected the spirit of that constitution. This argument was well understood by the United States. For example, the U.S. national security adviser Zbigniew Brzezinski admitted in a January 1980 memorandum to the secretaries of state and defense that Japan "could not send military aid but . . . was prepared to step up economic and humanitarian aid." This memoran-dum referred to Japanese aid to Pakistan, which had particular strategic importance at the time of the Soviet invasion of Afghanistan. It was obvious that President Carter was informed of Japan's stance and that he directed the administration's officials to push for this nonmilitary aid.[22]

Since that time, there has indeed been little disagreement between the United States and Japan about the characteristics of Japanese aid to developing countries. Japan was willing to contribute to Western security within the framework of its constitution but it was not willing to see a massive increase in defense spending.

U.S. pressure increased with the advent of the Reagan administration. At the end of 1980, Stephen Solarz visited Japan as a congressional delegate and met with politicians and top officials in the Foreign Ministry and Defense Agency. Solarz's mission was to ask Japan to increase its ODA. His argument was that Japan should rid itself of the stigma of being a free rider, thus enabling the United States to spend more on military aid to strategic areas and strengthening the third world allies of the United States. Indeed, the Japanese side understood that every new administration in the United States would make new demands on Japan and accuse it of being a free rider where defense was concerned.[23]

There was a remarkable increase in Japan's ODA in the early 1980s. Between 1980 and 1985, Japan once again doubled its amount of aid, totaling US$21.4 billion. Aid in 1983 reached US$3.76 billion (see Table 6.1). Japan already ranked third after the United States and France among the OECD countries with respect to ODA. Also, there

Table 6.1. Net Flow of Japan's ODA, 1980–83 (Bilateral and Multilateral) (Million USD)

		1980	1981	1982	1983
ODA total		3,303.7	3,170.9	3,023.3	3,761.0
	Increase over previous year	25.3%	–4.1%	–4.7%	24.6%
	Percentage of GNP	0.32%	0.28%	0.2%	0.33%
Bilateral assistance		1,960.8	2,260.4	2,367.3	2425.0
	Grants, including technical assistance	652.6	810.4	805.2	993.0
	Development lending and capital	1,308.2	1,450.0	1,562.1	1,432.0
Multilateral agencies	Grants, capital, loans	1,342.9	910.5	656.0	1,336.0

Source: Japan's Foreign Aid Policy, Briefing Paper, Department of State, June 18, 1984, Digital National Security Archive: Japan and the U.S., 1977–1992, No. JA01222.

was a sign that the previous practice of tying loans to contracts for Japanese firms was giving way to untied loans. Japan disbursed a significant portion of ODA in 1981 without tying, although its practice of tied loans was not eliminated. What the United States was concerned about was that Japan would not be able to achieve its goal of doubling its aid again in 1980–85 because of budget constraints and the depreciation of the yen. Despite U.S. concerns, Japan was able to address the need to provide aid to strategically important areas as well as help resolving the economic problems of the poor majority among developing countries.[24]

The U.S. stepped up pressure on Japan to increase its own defense budget as well. While welcoming Japan's efforts to build up its defense, U.S. Secretary of State Alexander Haig Jr. stressed in a letter to the Japanese foreign minister in February 1982 that the upcoming Japanese medium-term defense plan for 1983–87 should include an increase in force level and accelerate procurement of U.S. weapons systems, such as antisubmarine helicopters and air defense equipment, for their joint defense cooperation.[25] The United States cautiously suggested the idea of role sharing, recalling the agreement made at the Reagan-Suzuki summit in 1981. Also, Haig urged Japan "to take up an even larger burden of its own defense and at an even faster pace in order to contribute significantly to our joint efforts to deter aggression." Haig stressed that the United States spent a much larger share of its national economy on defense in general and deterring Soviet aggression in particular. Indeed, the United States increased its defense budget by more than 10 percent in fiscal year 1982, which constituted more than 5.5 percent of GNP.[26] Japanese defense spending constituted only 5.2 percent of the budget and 0.9 percent of GNP in 1980.[27]

Japanese aid was distributed in line with U.S.-framed comprehensive security burden sharing in the 1980s. Japan extended its aid to countries of "sensitive strategic concern" to the United States. Included in the Japanese list were Pakistan, Indonesia, South Korea, China, and Thailand in Asia; Egypt, Turkey, Oman, and North Yemen in the Middle East; Jamaica and Honduras in Central America; and Kenya and Sudan in Africa.[28]

Japan's Aid to South Korea

Although U.S.-framed burden sharing dominated Japan's ODA policy, Japan's aid to South Korea, which is the subject of this chapter, was raised by South Korea itself in 1981. At that time, South Korea was in desperate need of foreign aid. The United States had substantially reduced military aid to its allies, including South Korea, since 1974, and by 1977 military aid to South Korea was terminated completely. Also, by 1975 the US$200 million worth of Japanese governmental loans to South Korea, arranged at the time of normalization in 1965, had already been disbursed. In 1981, the general-turned-president of South Korea, Chun Doo-hwan, made appropriate use of the U.S.-framed burden sharing idea in his request for U.S. mediation to obtain new aid from Japan. Chun's idea was that Japan should share the ROK's defense burden because the ROK armed forces were playing a role in keeping Soviet forces in the Far East dispersed and deterring Soviet expansionism, not to mention preventing North Korean aggression.

In a similar vein, South Korea made tactful use of the new Korea clause that appeared in the joint statements issued after U.S.-Japan summits. The Korea clause, which had first been mentioned in the joint statement issued after the 1969 Nixon-Sato summit, rationalized the relevance of the security of the ROK to Japan's security. The inclusion of the clause in the joint statements meant a kind of declaration on Japan's part, not to mention that of the United States, of its commitment to security partnership with South Korea. But the Korea clause was virtually disregarded in Japan at the height of "China fever" and the ensuing "North Korea fever" in the first half of the 1970s. It was after the fall of South Vietnam that the Korea clause was resurrected in the joint statement of the Ford-Miki summit of August 6, 1975, which contained the phrase: "[T]he security of the Republic of Korea is essential to the maintenance of peace of the Korean peninsula, which in turn is necessary for peace and security in East Asia, including Japan." This resurrection had a special meaning for South Korea, which termed it the "new Korea clause," because South Korea considered it Japan's declared partnership commitment to their common security. The new Korea clause was repeated in the Carter-Ohira joint statement of May 2, 1979, and the Reagan-Suzuki joint communique of May 8, 1981.[29] There is no doubt that the ROK government worked hard to get the Korea issue included as an agenda item in U.S.-Japan summits.

President Chun's aid request, and the rationalization of partnership commitment to security, in 1981 was well positioned and timely. The request was in accordance with the U.S. containment strategy and followed the trend toward increasing burden sharing by Japan in strategic areas around the world. Also, the South Korean call for the United States to act as mediator—specifically, delivering the message to the Japanese and encouraging consensus building in Japan—eventually worked. The result was Japan's provision in 1983 of a US$4 billion aid package to South Korea. On the Japanese side, the Nakasone cabinet was the prime mover for the aid decision. But Nakasone's personal leadership or his perception of communism was not the only reason for the aid decision. Japan had been substantially increasing its ODA since the end of the 1970s. Japan's aid to South Korea was part of this expansion, which was in turn an evidence of Japan's alignment with U.S. strategic assistance policy.

South Korea's Need for Aid

South Korea's request for Japanese aid was motivated by its concern over the change in U.S. policy on military aid to Asia in the 1970s. U.S. military assistance reached its peak in 1973, when it was worth about US$4.3 billion. However, it declined sharply to US$1.5 billion in 1974 and to US$0.5 billion in 1976 (constant value in 1972).[30] This dramatic cut was related to the "Vietnamization" of the Vietnam War in line with the 1969 Nixon Doctrine, but it also affected military aid to South Korea. In the South Korean case, the United States had replaced its remaining grant aid with the Foreign Military Sales (FMS) program—credits or loans for weapons purchases. In an Action Memorandum prepared in 1974 for Secretary of State Henry Kissinger, the NSC under the Ford presidency noted that the time had come to tell the ROK that the U.S. government would "phase out grant aid with the exception of training and some minor programs by the end of FY 1976."[31] In reality, the grant aid was substantially decreased between 1974 and 1977, and terminated completely in 1977.[32] The cuts in U.S. military grant aid were accompanied by scheduling the withdrawal of all U.S. combat troops by the Carter administration. This made the South Koreans feel both nervous and abandoned by the United States.[33] Until the withdrawal plan was cancelled in June 1979, U.S.-ROK relations were unprecedentedly tense.

To make matters worse, Japan's aid to South Korea declined substantially in the second half of the 1970s. The flow of US$200 million in Japanese governmental loans, agreed upon in 1965 at the time of normalization, was terminated in 1975 (see Table 6.2). The level of Japanese ODA fluctuated. It reached US$198,000 in 1978 and then declined, finally reaching zero in 1979 (see Table 6.3). If South Korea's Fifth Five-Year Economic Development Plan for 1982–86 was to be implemented, South Korea had to obtain more assistance from Japan.

Meanwhile, South Korea underwent a period of political turmoil in 1979 and 1980. In October 1979, President Park Chung-hee was

Table 6.2. Japan's Disbursement of Governmental Loans to South Korea (Million Japanese yen)

1966	1967	1968	1969	1970	1971	1972	1973	1974	1975	Total
16,084	9,860	6,412	3,985	3,202	2,880	10,749	14,330	—	225	67,727

Note: The total 67,727 million yen (= US$200 million) is the amount that was agreed at the time of normalization in 1965.

Source: "Gukgyojeongsanghwa ihu Ilboneui daehan gyeongjehyeomnyok hyeonhwang, 1966–1981 [The Trend of Korea-Japan Economic Cooperation after the Normalization, 1966–1981]," in Nakasone Yasuhiro Ilbon susang banghan [Japanese Prime Minister Nakasone Yasuhiro's Visit to Korea], January 11–12, Vol. 1 of three volumes, Roll 2013-0030.

Table 6.3. Japanese ODA to South Korea (Thousand USD)

1970	1971	1972	1973	1974	1975	1976	1977	1978	1979	1980	1981	Total
—	115,651	21,930	123,104	123,104	—	75,503	62,250	198,440	—	83,790	88,350	769,018

Note: This ODA differs from the governmental loans in Table 6.2, which were agreed upon at the time of normalization. In addition to this ODA, Japan provided rice aid worth US$479 million and Export-Import Bank (EXIM) loans worth US$131 million from 1965 to 1981.

Source: "Gukgyojeongsanghwa ihu Ilboneui daehan gyeongjehyeomnyok hyeonhwang, 1966–1981 [The Trend of Korea-Japan Economic Cooperation after the Normalization, 1966–1981]," in Nakasone Yasuhiro Ilbon susang banghan [Japanese Prime Minister Nakasone Yasuhiro's Visit to Korea], January 11–12, Vol. 1 of three volumes, Roll 2013-0030.

assassinated by his close associate, the KCIA director Kim Jae-gyu. This was followed in December by a mutiny led by Major General Chun Doo-hwan, which in turn sparked the Kwangju uprising of May 1980 against the military's intervention in politics. In August, three months after the bloody suppression of the uprising, Chun retired from the army, and in September he was inaugurated as president, having forced President Choi Kyu-ha to resign. In view of the decline in foreign aid in the second half of the 1970s, the Chun administration saw no prospect of an influx of aid from the United States or Japan in the 1980s.

South Korea's Request for U.S. Mediation

Against this backdrop, the general-turned-president, Chun Doo-hwan, made an official visit to Washington in February 1981. For Chun, his summit meeting with President Reagan was most successful. First of all, that the meeting took place at all was evidence that the U.S. government recognized the legitimacy of Chun's rule. Indeed, this meeting with Chun was the newly inaugurated U.S. president's first summit. Furthermore, Reagan stated that the United States would never put overt pressure on South Korea on human rights, assuring Chun that the issue would be dealt with in a "proper manner." Reagan's assurance was notable in view of the fact that the United States had pressed Chun's predecessor, President Park Chung-hee, on his human rights violations, and it had subsequently criticized Chun's violent suppression of the Kwangju uprising. This indicated that Reagan took into consideration the fact that right before his Washington visit, Chun had commuted the death sentence passed on the prominent dissident Kim Dae-jung to life imprisonment. In another concession, Reagan pledged to suspend discussion of U.S. troop withdrawal. Although Carter had announced the cancellation of the withdrawal at the Seoul summit in 1979, Reagan's pledge reconfirmed the United States' commitment to the defense of South Korea, which came as a relief to Chun and all South Koreans. It was obvious that the Reagan administration prioritized stability and order in South Korea and on the Korean peninsula as a whole. In response, Chun stated that political and social stability must precede economic development and defense buildup. Chun also announced his political schedule for the coming months: a presidential election in February under the new constitution was to be followed by elections to the National Assembly in late March or April and the inauguration of the ROK's Fifth Republic.[34]

Chun Doo-hwan's essential mission at the summit was to solicit U.S. mediation in the matter of Japanese aid. The logic behind the request was that South Korea's defense efforts contributed to the security of Japan. At a meeting with Secretary of State Haig on February 2, 1981, just before the Reagan-Chun summit, Chun stated that:

> Korean and U.S. forces have contributed to the defense of not only the Korean peninsula but also Northeast Asia and the Pacific Ocean. Japan has received the benefit of their [Korean and U.S.] efforts. Therefore, Japan must take a part of the defense burden of the ROK and the United States. . . . Korea and the United States have been a bulwark or a frontline to Japan, and thus Japan has been able to rise to a robust economic power. . . . Not only does Japan need to invest more in its defense, but it must share the burden of the defense of the ROK from both moral and realistic viewpoints. . . . Japan needs to provide Korea with economic aid equivalent to the amount needed to maintain *two infantry divisions*.[35] (Author's italics)

In calling attention to South Korea's need for Japanese aid, Chun made skillful use of the notion of burden sharing. Chun's statement, prepared on the advice of his associates and officials, demonstrated an improvement in South Korea's presentation of its expectations and preferences. In principle, the statement was in line with U.S. strategic aid policy around the world and the long-term expectations of the United States concerning Japan's expanded burden-sharing role. Also, the use of a specific term such as "two infantry divisions" was intended to deliver a message concerning the implications for Asian security. South Korea had sent two infantry divisions, as well as medical and engineering units, to South Vietnam during the war there, and the number of U.S. troops stationed in South Korea in 1981 approximated two full infantry divisions. Chun was indicating that Japan's contribution to keeping the communists at bay was inferior to that of either South Korea or the United States. Chun's carefully worded statement of aid-defense linkage received a positive response; Haig stated that the United States was willing to discuss the issue of aid to South Korea with the Japanese government.

At the subsequent summit, Chun made adroit use of other rhetoric, which Reagan and other top U.S. officials were familiar with: Soviet aggressive military buildup around the world. And Chun focused on the ROK's pivotal role in containing the Soviets. Indeed, the deployment

of Soviet forces in the Far East had expanded to the extent that the
United States and its allies were threatened. The Soviet Union's forty-six
divisions, with about a half-million troops, and its strengthened air and
naval forces in the Far East were apparently penetrating into the regional
power vacuum in the military sense. This vacuum had ostensibly been
created by the Carter administration's Europe-first orientation and the
relatively low priority it gave to Asia.[36] For instance, the dispatching
of part of the Seventh Fleet to the Persian Gulf and the Indian Ocean
weakened the new administration's naval force deployment in the Far
East.[37] Chun tried to link this military imbalance in the Far East to a
possible miscalculation of the situation by North Korea.

Chun submitted an official request to Reagan that the United
States use its influence to persuade Japan to take on a burden equal to
that of two infantry divisions. Chun used the term *economic cooperation*,
although he really meant security-based burden sharing. He recognized
that Japan had insisted on the use of "economic cooperation" during the
normalization negotiations in the first half of the 1960s, and he would
have been aware of Japan's aversion to the concept of an aid-defense
linkage from the late 1970s when Japan was expanding its burden sharing. Reagan offered "no disagreement." Surprisingly, Reagan also gave
Chun a number of gifts that South Korea had long desired: defense
technology transfers, the expansion of FMS loans, and the reporting of
F-16 sales to Congress.[38]

U.S. Mediation and Japan-ROK Compromise: Delinking Aid and Defense

After Chun's visit to Washington, the United States embarked upon its
mediating role. In March 1981, a Department of State briefing paper
mentioned the request for aid "equivalent to the cost of maintaining
two divisions." On the other hand, it noted Japanese arguments that
the South Koreans were pressing too hard without proper regard for
Japan's internal political dynamics and the Japanese government's need
to carefully handle the Korean issue in the Diet.[39]

From April, the South Korean request for Japanese aid became
an agenda item in discussions between the United States and Japan. In
particular, Chun's soliciting of U.S. mediation became a pressing issue
for the U.S. government with the approach of the Reagan-Suzuki summit in Washington, scheduled for May. The United States wanted to
see the development of Japan-ROK economic relations—specifically for
Japan to undertake burden sharing with regard to the ROK regardless

of the formula. The U.S. embassy in Tokyo became the prime mover in delivering South Korea's aid request and in discovering Japan's stance on the matter. According to embassy officials, Japan was insisting that South Korea's improved economic standing made it difficult to maintain the existing level of economic aid. By 1980, South Korea's per capita GDP had risen to US$1,500; as far as Japan was concerned, it was no longer a less-developed country. Japan would have preferred money to flow into South Korea from the commercial sector. The U.S. embassy officials thought that there was a need for "groundwork" to be done in the Japanese government, which apparently meant there was a need for more discussion to take place and a consensus to be formed.[40] Meanwhile, the ROK foreign minister Lho officially requested the Japanese government, through Ambassador Sunobe Ryozo in Seoul on April 23, for a US$10 billion aid package.[41] It seems that South Korea timed the request to coincide with the upcoming Reagan-Suzuki summit, when the United States was expected to raise the aid issue. However, the Japanese were shocked by the amount requested, and wondered whether the Koreans had mistakenly added a zero to the figure. More importantly, the Japanese did not accept the South Korean logic of aid-defense linkage.[42]

Observing the above-mentioned development, U.S. diplomats in Tokyo concluded that putting pressure on Japan at the upcoming summit would be counterproductive. One basis for this conclusion was that the issue of Japanese aid to South Korea, and particularly South Korea's wish for aid levels to return to their 1978 peak or even to pre-1978 levels, had not been discussed at any level beyond aid-related agencies in Japan. Japan had already shifted its priorities with regard to ODA in line with U.S. strategic considerations, with priority being given to such countries and areas as Jamaica, Turkey, Pakistan, and Africa, as well as refugee relief. The U.S. embassy also took into consideration the fact that the Japanese did not accept South Korea's complaints about Japan's large trade surplus and thus could "not justify the aid to the ROK as compensation" for it. Finally, U.S. diplomats had been informed by their Japanese counterparts that Japan considered the figure put forward by the South Koreans in April to be "incredible" and "unrealistic."[43]

It is believed that the subject of Japan's aid to South Korea did not come up at the Reagan-Suzuki summit in Washington, on May 8. The joint communique of the summit, however, included the "new Korea clause," and thus South Korea's hopes were kept alive with regard to the aid issue. The communique reaffirmed that the two leaders shared the common goal of maintaining world peace and that they were willing to share the burden of achieving this goal. It stated that they agreed "to continue respectively to expand cooperative relations with the People's Republic of China, . . . [and] to promote the maintenance of peace on the Korean Peninsula as important for peace and security in East Asia, including Japan." The communique also stated that "the Government of Japan will strive to expand and improve its official development assistance under the New Medium Term Target and that the Government [of Japan] will strengthen its aid to those areas which are important to the maintenance of peace and stability of the world."[44] For South Korea, the summit and the communique opened the possibility that they would be included on Japan's list of ODA recipients.

On the negative side, the aftermath of the Reagan-Suzuki summit demonstrated that the defense issue remained a sensitive one in Japanese domestic politics. As soon as he returned to Japan, Suzuki was bombarded with questions and requests for explanation concerning the statement in the communique that "in insuring peace and stability in the region and the defense of Japan, they [Reagan and Suzuki] acknowledged the desirability of an appropriate division of roles between Japan and the United States." Fearing domestic opposition, Suzuki virtually reversed the meaning of this sentence, claiming that "division of roles" did not imply a dramatic shift in Japan's military responsibilities.[45] As Mike Mansfield, the U.S. ambassador in Tokyo at that time, has pointed out, Japan's domestic politics meant that even a prime minister could not act independently but had to take into consideration "how the public at home views the summit."[46] Prime Minister Suzuki must have followed this logic. The prime minister and top government officials were neither prepared to accept the U.S. request that Japan take on a military role nor ready to face up to domestic resistance to such a role. For the South Koreans, this implied that any aid-defense linkage was not acceptable to the Japanese.

Meanwhile, news of the ROK request for US$6 billion in aid began to appear in the Japanese press at the end of July 1981.[47] What the top officials in Japan were most concerned about was the potential political fallout from the South Korean idea of linking the aid to defense and security. In the end, Japanese dissatisfaction with the South Korean attitude erupted on the eve of a meeting between the Japanese and South Korean foreign ministers, Sonoda Sunao and Lho Shin-yong, which was held on August 20, 1981, in Tokyo. Sonoda was quoted as saying that "if they want aid they must say that. But why do they try to link the issue to defense and security?" Because of this difference, the meeting failed to produce a tangible result.[48]

The first earnest bilateral talks on the aid issue took place at the Japan-ROK ministerial conference held in Seoul on September 10–11, 1981, but the two sides could not narrow their differences. The main differences lay in the nature and the amount of the aid. South Korean delegates insisted that Japan's aid was necessary for the defense of the Korean peninsula. Their reference point was the new Korea clause that stated that security and peace on the Korean peninsula were essential for the peace and stability of the Northeast Asian region, including Japan. South Koreans saw this as the most important element keeping the U.S.-Japan-ROK triangle together, and thus Japan had to take into account the benefit it gained from South Korean efforts to deter North Korean aggression. The South Koreans noted that 36.8 percent of their budget or 6.6 percent of their GNP was devoted to defense in 1980, compared to 5.2 percent of the budget and 0.9 percent of GNP in Japan in that year. This was money that could have been diverted to economic development.[49] South Korean officials stated that if Japan provided US$6 billion in ODA and US$4 billion in private loans, the ROK would be able to use this money for infrastructure development and use its own resources for defense buildup. But this scheme was unacceptable to Japan. Japan's position, expressed by Foreign Minister Sonoda Sunao, was to stick to four principles with regard to aid: (1) no defense aid, (2) priority allocation for poorer countries, (3) mainly private sector flows to South Korea, and (4) an annual consultation to decide on specific projects.[50]

As early as December 1981, Japan began sending constructive but mixed messages. Right after his appointment, the new foreign minister Sakurauchi Yoshio suggested that the two sides could negotiate the total amount of the aid. Sakurauchi said that Japan was willing to provide aid to South Korea, but the amount they had requested was excessive and that any link to defense was unacceptable. The South Koreans recognized that Sakurauchi's negotiation idea might help them to reach a deal on the amount. Thus, there was some optimism in South Korea in early 1982, despite the lack of concrete progress. In his address on national politics delivered at the National Assembly in January, President Chun praised "the Japanese government's proactive stance for early resolution" of the aid issue.[51] Lho Shin-yong, the foreign minister, was also optimistic, and he said that it was President Chun who had conceived the idea of requesting US$10 billion in governmental loans and JEXIM bank loans over five years. Most notably, South Korea changed its justification for the Japanese aid package—from aid-defense linkage to "economic cooperation," a term that Japan preferred. Also, South Korea excluded from the list of targeted projects various defense-related items that had been considered "unacceptable to the Japanese in earlier talks."[52]

Recognizing that the United States was mediating on its behalf, South Korea continued to press its case with Japan in 1982. The Koreans focused their argument on the need to correct the economic imbalance between the two sides, rather than stressing any links to defense. They pointed out that postnormalization economic cooperation had resulted in a huge trade deficit for South Korea. Between 1965 and 1982, Japanese aid to South Korea totaled US$1.3 billion—about US$80 million per year on average—and this included ODA, rice aid, and JEXIM loans. Over the same period, South Korea's trade deficit with Japan increased to US$23 billion, 70 percent of the country's total trade deficit.[53] This imbalance was the result of Japanese aid being tied to Japanese business advancement. Normally, 70–80 percent of the Japanese loans was used for the procurement of Japanese products (see also Table 6.4).

To be sure, in 1982 the main difference between Japan and South Korea in the aid negotiations was not so much the aid-defense linkage

Table 6.4. South Korea's Trade Deficit with Japan (Million USD)

	Export	Import	Balance
1966	66	294	−228
1967	85	443	−358
1968	100	624	−524
1969	133	754	−621
1970	234	809	−575
1971	262	954	−692
1972	408	1,031	−623
1973	1,242	1,727	−485
1974	1,380	2,621	−1,241
1975	1,293	2,434	−1,141
1976	1,802	3,099	−1,297
1977	2,148	3,926	−1,778
1978	2,627	5,981	−3,354
1979	3,353	6,657	−3,304
1980	3,039	5,858	−2,819
Total	18,172	37,212	−19,040

Source: "Ilboneui daehanguk gyeongjehyeomnyeok hwakdae [Expansion of Korea-Japan Economic Cooperation]," Economic Planning Board, 1981, in Hanil gyeongje heomnyok silmuja hoedam, je8cha [The 8th Korea-Japan Economic Cooperation Working-Level Meeting], Tokyo, January 28–29, 1983, Roll 2013-0092.

issue but the total amount and the way the aid was to be divided between ODA and JEXIM loans. In April, the deputy director general of the Japanese Foreign Ministry Yanagiya Kensuke visited Seoul as a special envoy for the aid negotiations. He offered a so-called final proposal for a total of US$4 billion, consisting of US$1.5 billion in ODA and US$2.5 billion in JEXIM loans. But the ROK foreign minister Lho Shin-yong countered this by proposing ODA of US$3 billion and JEXIM loans of US$1 billion. In the absence of a response from Japan, the newly appointed foreign minister Lee Bum-suk went to Tokyo in early July to submit a new proposal for US$2.3 billion of ODA and the remaining US$1.7 billion in JEXIM loans. Lee's proposal represented a break with normal diplomatic practice in that it nullified the counterproposal that his predecessor had made a few months previously.

At a time when the main difference between the two sides was how the aid should be split between ODA and JEXIM loans, the controversy over the Japanese school textbooks, which whitewashed Japan's behavior during the colonial and wartime period, caused the entire aid negotiations to collapse. The controversy erupted when the main Japanese newspapers, including *Asahi Shimbun* and *Mainichi Shimbun*, reported that the textbooks had described Imperial Japan's aggression as "advancement." The use of such a term to describe Japan's wrongdoings was not new, however. As the South Korean sociologist Shin Yong-ha has noted, the most problematic points were the use of the term *accommodation* to describe the Japanese way of depriving Korea of diplomatic power and Japan's intervention in Korea's domestic affairs in 1905. Another problematic point in the textbooks was in regard to Japan's language policy; they falsely described that "the Korean language, along with Japanese, was used as a common language," when the truth was that Koreans were actually forbidden from using their native tongue.[54] Shin warned that these misrepresentations were a prelude to "neo-militarism" in Japan, and he saw the textbook issue in the context of Japan's five-year defense development plan from 1983 to 1987.[55]

The textbook controversy was the main reason for the cancellation of Sakurauchi's scheduled visit to Seoul in August, which had been seen as an ideal opportunity to conclude the aid issue. There was a consensus among the public, politicians, and officials in South Korea that resolution of the textbook issue was more important than the continuation of the aid negotiations. In the midst of this crisis in bilateral relations, Japan's chief secretary of the cabinet Miyazawa Kiichi made a conciliatory public statement on August 26, 1982. And then the Japanese government adopted a *kinrinkokujoko* (neighborhood clause) that was designed to reassure Japan's neighbors that their views would be taken into account when compiling history textbooks. These concessions enabled aid negotiations between Japan and South Korea to survive the textbook controversy.

After Nakasone Yasuhiro became prime minister in November 1982, the two-year-long aid negotiations entered their final stage. On December 28–29, a special envoy of the prime minister paid a secret visit to Seoul and delivered a personal letter from Nakasone to President Chun. The specific contents of the letter have yet to be made public, but it seems that a final agreement on the amount of aid was made during the envoy's visit. And then Nakasone chose South Korea for his first official visit.[56] At their summit meeting on January 11–12, 1983, Nakasone and Chun officially concluded an agreement on the economic aid issue, which was dubbed "economic cooperation" by the Japanese and "security-based economic cooperation" by the Koreans. Japan pledged to provide its largest package of economic aid to South Korea since normalization. The US$4 billion aid package, which would be disbursed over seven years, was to be composed of US$1.85 billion of ODA and US$2.15 of JEXIM loans. This aid to South Korea was an exception to Japan's overall ODA policy, which at that time was focused on less-developed countries.

Not surprisingly, the joint statement issued by the two leaders after the summit included expressions similar to the "new Korea clause," which had appeared repeatedly in U.S.-Japan joint statements, such as those issued after the Ford-Miki summit in 1975, the Carter-Ohira summit in 1979, and the Reagan-Suzuki summit in 1981. According to the Nakasone-Chun joint statement, "the president and the prime minister . . . shared the perception that peace and stability on the Korean peninsula is essential to peace and stability in East Asia including Japan."[57] The inclusion of this Japan-ROK version of the new Korea clause in the joint statement meant that Japan implicitly, even if cautiously, recognized South Korean security interests and rationales, that is, that Japanese aid would be provided in the context of the two countries' common understanding of the international situation surrounding the Korean peninsula. Also, the inclusion meant that not only the ROK government but also the U.S. government were seriously concerned about the Japan-South Korea aid negotiations.

Responses to the summit in South Korea, Japan, and the United States were generally positive.[58] The South Korean media depicted it as a new step toward improved bilateral relations. Also they expressed the hope that, along with the aid, Japan would make an effort in other areas, such as increasing technology transfers, correcting the trade imbalance, improving the status of Korean residents in Japan, etc.[59] The six major Japanese newspapers were of the opinion that the summit had recognized South Korea's contribution as expressed in the Japan-ROK version of the new Korea clause. In particular, a *Sankei Shimbun* editorial suggested that the Japanese government should confidently explain to the public the legitimacy of that clause. The newspaper specifically noted that Japan had to make its "due contribution" to the South Korean efforts and that economic cooperation should not be regarded as compensation for past misdeeds but should be conducted in an atmosphere of equality and mutual respect.[60] More importantly, the U.S. reaction to the Japan-ROK summit was fairly positive, highlighting the aspect of triangular cooperation. David F. Lambertson, the director of the Office of Korean Affairs in the State Department, praised Nakasone's visit to Seoul, calling it a "historic and dramatic event." Lambertson said that coming as it did just a week before Nakasone's summit with Ronald Reagan, it reflected increased U.S.-Japan-ROK triangular cooperation.[61] It is noteworthy that two weeks after the summit, the U.S. government listed South Korea as a country of vital, core strategic importance, along with Egypt, Sudan, Pakistan, Thailand, Turkey, and Chad.[62] These countries were also recipients of Japanese aid, which was in accordance with U.S.-framed burden sharing.

Conclusion

Japan's 1983 aid package for South Korea represented a microcosm of Japan's role in U.S.-framed security burden sharing. At the request of South Korea, the United States intervened in aid negotiations between its allies; however, Washington did not apply coercive pressure, but adopted a form based on moralistic preaching (emphasizing the two states' common values and shared strategic interests) and businesslike requests (Japan's engaging in further burden sharing and removing the stigma of a free rider). The United States transmitted the South Korean message to Japan and waited until a consensus had been formed in Japanese political circles. The remaining differences were resolved through direct negotiation between the two parties concerned, Japan and South Korea. Also, the United States recognized domestic constraints on the Japanese government, as well as the country's constitutional constraints where defense was concerned and resistance to any aid-defense linkage. The United States did not force Japan to officially accept the aid-defense linkage, but in reality it guided the Japanese aid program toward U.S.-framed burden sharing.

During the initial stage of the aid negotiations, the main difference between Japan and South Korea concerned the nature of the relationship between aid and defense. Japan strongly resisted any linkage between the two. Once the United States took on the mediation, the focus of the negotiations swiftly shifted to the question of how much aid would be provided and how it would be split between ODA and JEXIM loans. The negotiations resulted in a US$4 billion package and a split that was a compromise between the Japanese and South Korean proposals. The aid was called "economic cooperation," as the Japanese wanted, although it was dubbed "security-based economic cooperation" by the South Koreans. It is certain, however, that in nature the US$4 billion package represented strategic aid that compensated for the reduction of U.S. aid to South Korea. Japanese aid in the 1980s enabled South Korea to concentrate on its economic development, as it no longer had to divert its own limited resources of the civilian economy to the military. The strategic nature of the aid was indicated by the inclusion of the new Korea clause, which repeatedly appeared in the joint statements of the U.S.-Japan summits from 1975 onward. This clause was a formal acknowledgment of the connection between stability on the Korean peninsula and peace and security throughout East Asia, including Japan. The reiteration of that clause in the joint statement of the 1983 Nakasone-Chun summit demonstrates that Japan was providing South Korea with strategic aid, whether or not Japan admitted the aid-defense linkage.

The aid issue was actually less contentious than the issues dealt with in previous chapters—that is, the repatriation of Korean residents in Japan to North Korea, the Japan-ROK normalization talks, and Japan's two Koreas policy. The United States, Japan, and South Korea were well practiced in presenting their own preferences and thus maintaining their respective national interests in the security triangle. Consequently, despite the ups and downs in the negotiations, caused by disagreements over the aid-defense linkage and the Japanese textbook controversy, the aid issue eventually had a reinforcing feedback effect on the security triangle in general and on each state in particular. First, while requesting the United States to apply pressure to Japan, South Korea took into account U.S. worries about continued Soviet expansionism as well as North Korea's military adventurism. President Chun made an effort to demonstrate that South Korea's armed forces could play a complementary role in deterring the Soviet Union in the Far East. Also, in its negotiations with Japan, South Korea avoided stubborn insistence on formalities, such as the title of the aid package, but sought instead to maximize its national interests. Second, the United States, as the dominant power, adroitly mediated between Japan and South Korea. Instead of using coercive pressure, it took into account Japan's aversion to any linkage between aid and defense. Japan's decision on aid to South Korea was taken in the context of its rapidly expanding security burden sharing. On this point, the United States was in agreement with South Korea. Thus, the United States tried, particularly in its joint statements with the Japanese, to link the security of the Korean peninsula to that of Japan, as shown in the new Korea clause. Finally, having agreed to an aid package for South Korea, Japan entered a reciprocal relationship with the United States. Thus Japan's standing in the security triangle became firmer than ever before.

7

Controversy over Historical Issues

In the post–Cold War era, the most contentious issues between Japan and South Korea have been those concerning the Korean "comfort women," or military sex slaves, and the islets of Dokdo/Takeshima. With the passage of time, these issues have become more troubling both on the diplomatic front and within the two societies. Diplomatic tension between Japan and its neighbors has not been limited to the comfort women issue; the Nanjing massacre is another case that has caused Japan diplomatic tension, in this instance with China. Likewise, Japan has other territorial disputes with its neighbors apart from the one with South Korea concerning Dokdo/Takeshima, including the disputes over the Northern territories/Southern Kuril and the Senkaku/Diaoyu islands.[1] Not surprisingly, disputes over historical events have gone hand in hand with competing territorial claims. With U.S. intervention, the ROK and Japan reached an agreement on December 28, 2015, whereby Tokyo admitted the Imperial Army's involvement in sex slavery, expressed apology, and offered financial support (one billion Japanese yen, equivalent to $8.3 million) for the establishment of a foundation for the victims; in return, Seoul accepted the resolution as final and irreversible.[2] Strictly speaking, the agreement was not a resolution but a product of negotiation. Long enmity entrenched in each society is not likely disappear anytime soon.

In explaining Japan's disputes with its neighbors, most accounts have adopted one of two approaches. Those favoring the nationalism approach attribute these problems to the rise of Japanese nationalism, or more broadly a "clash of nationalisms," in East Asia,[3] whereas proponents of the collective memory approach have identified channels of memory, using terms and concepts developed in interdisciplinary contexts—such as psychological defense mechanism[4] and cultural identity.[5] Although both of these approaches have their merits, neither of them accounts for why contentions over historical issues emerged at this particular time, that is, in the mid-1990s. This chapter shows the ways in which the contentions, which had been suppressed during the Cold War, came to the surface and continued to trouble the Japan-ROK relations.

I argue that internal dynamics in the security triangle—incremental changes in South Korea and Japan during the Cold War and a substantial balancing between the two as the Cold War thawed—allowed these historical issues to reemerge. For South Korea, the internal dynamics meant a record-breaking rate of economic development and an impressive process of democratization before the end of the Cold War, and a rise in its middle-power standing in the post–Cold War era. South Korea normalized its relations with the Soviet Union in 1990 and with China in 1992, and in 1996 it ceased to be a recipient of Japanese aid and joined the OECD, becoming a donor of official development assistance (ODA) and humanitarian aid around the world. Advocacy groups within South Korea's increasingly empowered civil society have taken up such long-suppressed issues as the rights of the victims of state-sponsored violence, human rights violations, and gender discrimination. The advocacy groups have also unearthed the painful stories told by former comfort women.

In Japan, the internal dynamics meant particularly the rise of right-wing views and a crisis mentality after the bursting of the bubble economy and the rise of China.[6] In these circumstances, historical revisionism provided a way of erasing the perceived dishonor of the postwar regime. Therefore, the rise of historical issues in the 1990s should be attributed to the changes taking place within the security triangle, rather than simply to anti-Japanese nationalism in South Korea or to psychological defense mechanisms against the apology politics adopted by the Japanese government.

While taking into account the internal dynamics of the security triangle, this chapter focuses on how revisionism reemerged in Japan to raise contention and dispute over these issues in the post–Cold War era. It shows that the U.S. strategy of containing the Soviet Union sowed the seeds of contention over historical issues and territorial disputes between Japan and its neighbors. As part of this containment strategy, Japan was transformed "from an enemy to an ally" of the United States.[7] In this regard, the United States "is complicit in, and has been a primary architect of, Japan's historical amnesia."[8] The premature closure of the Tokyo War Crimes Tribunal resulted in some perpetrators of atrocious war crimes escaping justice, while some politicians who should have borne responsibility for the war were allowed to become leading figures in mainstream conservative politics in the postwar period. Likewise, the ambiguous treatment of territorial issues in the San Francisco Peace Treaty sowed the source of the contention between Japan and its neighbors. During the Cold War, the revisionist views of the rehabilitated politicians favoring constitutional revision and rearmament were suppressed by the Yoshida doctrine, which focused on economic development and placed Japan's security in the hands of the United States. However, in the post–Cold War era, these revisionist views have found new adherents among younger politicians. What the old and new revisionists have in common is a desire to maintain Japan's own grand strategy and uphold its honor and status. In this context, contention over the comfort women and Dokdo/Takeshima has reemerged.

Setting One: Tokyo War Crimes Tribunal and the Comfort Women Issue

The issue of the Korean comfort women exemplifies how the way that Japan's responsibility for the war was dealt with in postwar international politics has affected its view of history. At the Tokyo War Crimes Tribunal, which took place from January 1946 to November 1948, the United States, as the leader of the Allied Powers, prioritized the prosecution of Japanese who were guilty of crimes against peace, that is, Class A criminals. The U.S. prosecutors, led by Joseph Keenan, focused on punishing those engaged in the surprise attack on Pearl Harbor, rather than seriously dealing with conventional war crimes and crimes against humanity (Classes B and C).

The issue of wartime sex slavery in Japan was investigated by the prosecutors, but nobody was brought to trial for that crime. Prosecutors collected evidence on the operation of brothels in areas occupied by the Imperial Army, particularly military facilities housing Dutch women in Borneo. Yuma Totani argues that the "synopsis method" used in the prosecution procedure prevented the inclusion of detailed evidence concerning the crime of sexual slavery.[9] Totani thus refutes the "victor's justice" perspective, which implies that the Allied Powers unilaterally treated Japan as a defeated aggressor state while ignoring the sufferings of Japanese colonies, such as Korea and Taiwan.[10] The victor states did indeed regard the colonial subject populations, most of whom had been mobilized by the Imperial Army, as collaborators with the aggressor rather than as victims. However, careful scrutiny reveals that far from refuting the victor's justice perspective, Totani's view that the synopsis method was responsible for the tribunal's failure to deal with the sexual slavery issue actually supports it. Indeed, the Allies were themselves colonial powers, and thus their status prevented them from addressing humanitarian issues concerning Japan's colonies. The victor's prime concerns were not with the crimes the aggressor had committed against the people of its colonies, such as sexual slavery and forced labor. Therefore, it was not simply due to the procedural methods of the Tokyo Tribunal that the use of sex slaves by the Imperial Army was overlooked; it is also attributable to the Allied Powers' status as colonialists.

More importantly, discussion of the failure to recognize colonial people's concerns, including sexual slavery, must go beyond the points mentioned above. From a broader perspective, U.S. policy regarding Japan's future strategic role caused war crimes in general and sexual slavery in particular to be overlooked. At the time of the Tokyo Tribunal, the United States was intensifying its strategy of containment against the Soviet Union. By the first half of 1948 at the latest, the United States had begun to transform Japan into an ally to serve its containment strategy, which is why the Tokyo Tribunal was hurriedly terminated. The central figure in this strategy was George Kennan, who became director of the policy planning staff at the Department of State in May 1947. In a document dated March 25, 1948, Kennan detailed the U.S. policy toward postwar Japan. He stressed that "economic recovery should be made the prime objective of United States policy in Japan for the coming period," and recommended removing all obstacles to Japan's trade with other Asian countries. As for the ways to build a new elite structure in Japan, Kennan recommended easing off on the purge and hastening the termination of the Tokyo Tribunal. In particular, he advocated "early deadlines for the termination of the War Crimes Trials of 'A' suspects."[11] He clearly prioritized the early restoration of Japanese power, rather than the pursuit of retributive justice.

Given this situation, many Class A suspects were released early, and the Tokyo Tribunal was speeded up, so that it ended eight months after Kennan submitted his recommendations. Moreover, the GHQ introduced a series of measures to rehabilitate more than twenty-five thousand politicians and bureaucrats in October 1950, and again in June and August 1951. The expedited tribunal and the rehabilitation of former leaders contributed to the restoration of a revisionist stream, which in turn joined the broader mainstream of conservative politics in Japan led by Yoshida Shigeru.

Japan's formal acceptance of the judgments of the Tokyo Tribunal was contained in Article 11 of the Treaty of San Francisco. According to that article, Japan had to carry out the sentences handed down at the tribunal and could not reduce them, or grant clemency or parole, without the approval of the governments that had handed them down. Not surprisingly, feelings ran high within Japanese society in favor of the early release of the war criminals. The movement for early release was led by the families of the prisoners, and the Justice Ministry took note of their demands. In response, both conservative and progressive politicians supported a resolution for the release of the war criminals in the House of Representatives on June 12, 1952. The conservatives supported the resolution because, in their heart of hearts, they did not recognize the legitimacy of the Tokyo Tribunal, whereas the socialists did so out of sympathy for the prisoners.[12] More importantly, on September 4, 1952, the Truman administration set the ball rolling when it issued an executive order establishing a Clemency and Parole Board for War Criminals to look into arranging the release of Class B and C criminals. Interestingly, Joseph Keenan, the chief prosecutor of the Tokyo Tribunal, also supported the idea of early release. He believed that the objective of the tribunal—to make the Japanese understand the consequences of the war—had already been achieved. Other states followed suit and released Class B and C criminals over the years 1952–54. On the initiative of the United States, on September 7, 1955, the eight states that had participated in the Tokyo Tribunal finally decided to grant parole to all Class A criminals who had served at least ten years in prison. This decision resulted in the release of all thirteen criminals by the end of 1956. One important reason for the U.S. leniency lay in its strategy of trying to win the hearts of the Japanese, "so as not to make Japanese anti-American," to use the words of the then U.S. ambassador in Tokyo, John Allison.[13]

U.S. policy toward postwar Japan, which was in line with the containment strategy, had an enormous impact on Japanese politics. The rehabilitation of politicians who had served the wartime government and of war crime suspects ("reverse course," or *gyaku kosu* in Japanese) allowed them to rejoin political life. Hatoyama Ichiro and Ishibashi Tanzan were two such examples. Both served as prime minister, Hatoyama from 1954 to 1956 and Ishibashi in 1956–57. Others who benefited from the rehabilitation included Ando Masazumi, Okubo Tomejiro, Miki Bukichi, and Kono Ichiro, who were all close associates of Hatoyama.[14] All of them were banned from politics while Yoshida Shigeru was prime minister, and when they eventually joined mainstream conservative politics, they became his opponents. Whereas Yoshida had focused on economic development and let the United States take care of Japan's security, the rehabilitated politicians were revisionists who supported revision of the constitution and rearmament. The core shared element

between the revisionists and Yoshida was their common policy preference of "hug[ging] the United States," as Richard Samuels puts it.[15]

Kishi Nobusuke is a prime example among the released Class A
suspects.[16] Kishi, a former minister in the Tojo cabinet, was arrested in
1945 but released without trial three years later. He served as a Liberal Party member of the Diet when Yoshida was the party leader, but
later joined the newly formed Democratic Party led by Hatoyama, and
subsequently became general secretary of the party. Kishi was one of
the architects of the merger of the two parties that formed the Liberal
Democratic Party (LDP) in 1955, which marked the beginning of that
long period of conservative rule that is known as the "1955 system."
After he became prime minister in February 1957, his cabinet entered
into negotiations with the Eisenhower administration and in 1960 completed the revision of the U.S.-Japan Security Treaty in the face of
strong domestic opposition.[17] Kishi's grandson, Abe Shinzo, also served
two terms as prime minister, in 2006–07 and 2012–16 (he is still prime
minister at the time of writing). Adopting the slogan "overcoming the
sengo rejimu (postwar regime)," Abe has staunchly advocated not only
amendment of the constitution but also patriotic education;[18] he has
vehemently denied that the comfort women were subject to coercion,
and he has tried to play down the importance of the issue.

Setting Two: The San Francisco Peace Treaty and the Dokdo/Takeshima Dispute

That Dokdo/Takeshima was not on the list of territories Japan had to
surrender under the San Francisco Peace Treaty was the result of deliberate ambivalence on the part of the United States. In dealing with this
potentially contentious issue, the United States took into consideration
its own national interests and the desperate need to contain communism.
As Kimie Hara notes, this was not limited to Dokdo/Takeshima but also
applied to the Northern territories/Southern Kuril. This ambivalence was
the cause of Japan's disputes with South Korea and Russia.[19]

Close analysis of the process leading up to the San Francisco Treaty
reveals that Japan made strenuous efforts to promote its position on
Dokdo/Takeshima and that the United States accepted Japan's position.
Inasmuch as Japan was crucially important for Washington's containment strategy, there seems to have been a certain convergence of interests between the two states, although they had different objectives. At
first, both the supreme commander of the Allied Powers in Japan and

the U.S. ambassador in Seoul, John Muccio, supported South Korea's claim to the islets. But the Japanese government gradually succeeded in undermining the South Korean position and persuading Washington to support its claim. In 1947, Japanese officials prepared a pamphlet on the territorial issue and lobbied General MacArthur's political advisor William Sebald. In turn, Sebald became the author of a report entitled "Comment on Draft Treaty of Peace with Japan," dated November 19, 1949, which noted the need to take into account "strategic considerations" in dealing with the Dokdo/Takeshima issue. As a result, the sixth draft of the San Francisco Peace Treaty of December 8, 1949, recognized Dokdo/Takeshima as Japanese territory, reversing the description of it in the previous versions.[20]

   After John Foster Dulles took charge of the treaty negotiations in April 1950, and with the outbreak of the Korean War two months later, the situation began to favor Japan. As Dulles, an advocate of the containment strategy, seemed ready to accept Japan's argument, Prime Minister Yoshida Shigeru gave the impression that Japan's strategic interests were incompatible with those of South Korea. In a document entitled "Korea and the Peace Treaty," dated April 23, 1951, and delivered to Dulles during his visit to Tokyo, Yoshida maintained that the ROK should not be a signatory of the San Francisco Peace Treaty. He argued that if the ROK was allowed to participate in the treaty, it would join with Korean communists living in Japan in making excessive demands for compensation, which would eventually damage the Japanese economy.[21] The image that Yoshida portrayed of a zero-sum game in Japan-South Korea relations succeeded in winning over Dulles and, in particular, led to South Korea's position on Dokdo/Takeshima being ignored.

   Of particular interest is an exchange of arguments between the United States and South Korea over the issue of the islets. On July 19 and August 2, 1951, the ROK ambassador to the United States, You Chan Yang, sent letters to Secretary of State Dean Acheson in which he put forward the South Korean position with regard to some sensitive outstanding issues in Japan-South Korea relations, namely, recognition of Dokdo and Parangdo as South Korean territories, the legal transfer of Japanese property to South Korea, and the continued existence of the MacArthur Line. By means of these letters, Yang intended to secure the islets and the vast fishing grounds surrounding them for South Korea and to obtain a certain degree of leverage with Japan concerning the property claims. However, the ROK embassy was unable to locate Parangdo on the map, so it later dropped its claim to the island. This blunder undermined Korean efforts to convince the U.S. government, so Yang was only partially successful. In a letter to Yang on August 10, the assistant secretary of state for Far Eastern affairs, Dean Rusk, stated that the MacArthur Line would continue only until the treaty came into force and that he recognized South Korea's claim to Japanese colonial property in South Korea. He also stated that, according to U.S. information, Dokdo/Takeshima had been under the jurisdiction of Japan's Shimane prefecture since 1905.[22] Against this backdrop, it is not surprising that from the tenth draft of August 7, 1950, onward, the islets were not identified as belonging to any country.[23]

Observing how unfavorable this situation was for South Korea, on January 18, 1952, just three months before the San Francisco Treaty was due to come into force, President Syngman Rhee declared the Peace Line (known as the Rhee Line to the Japanese, most likely in an effort to demonstrate that it had no legal force). This boundary was basically the same as the MacArthur Line and it included Dokdo/Takeshima within Korean territory. After the San Francisco Peace Treaty came into effect, U.S. strategic ambivalence developed into a policy of nonintervention in the Japan-ROK territorial issue. For instance, in his 1954 report of his mission to the Far East, James Van Fleet, the former commander of U.S. forces during the Korean War, said that the United States had "declined to interfere in the dispute." He also stated that the United States recommended that Japan and the ROK take their dispute to the International Court of Justice (ICJ).[24] The Japanese concurred on this, and from September 25, 1954, onward and throughout the protracted normalization talks, they demanded that the ROK government bring the case to the ICJ.[25]

It is important to note, however, that the situation at the time the treaty was drafted did not always favor the Japanese. The British in particular took a hardline position on the issues of territory and war reparations. The British draft of the San Francisco Peace Treaty was the first, and the last, in which Japanese territory was defined by drawing a line on the map. This map, titled "The Territory under Japanese Sovereignty as Defined in Art. 1 of the Peace Treaty," drawn up in April 1951, was attached to the draft treaty. The map included, as Japanese territory, the four main islands and Shikotan and Habomai, but not Kunashiri and Etorofu. It did not include the Ryukyu Islands, Senkaku/Diaoyu, some other islands south of Kyushu, or Dokdo/Takeshima. This delineation of Japanese territory demonstrated British efforts at retribution for Japan's aggression. Apparently, the British position had not been influenced by Japanese lobbying.[26] What should be noted is that the British map did not form part of the final draft of the treaty, which was a compromise between the U.S. and British drafts. The U.S. desire to protect Japan by means of its ambiguity over the territorial issue prevailed over the British notion of peace and justice based on retribution.

The ramifications of the failure to include the map in the final draft of the treaty were enormous in terms of current territorial disputes involving Japan. As Jung Byung Jun notes, "If the San Francisco Peace Treaty had adopted such a map clarifying Japan's territory and the islands Japan had renounced, it could have prevented Japan's territorial disputes with its neighbors."[27] But all the draft versions of the treaty, with the exception of the British draft of April 1951, and the final version simply listed the islands that Japan was obliged to surrender. In the end, Article 2 (a) of the San Francisco Peace Treaty read as follows: "Japan recognizing the independence of Korea, renounces all right, title and claim to Korea, including the islands of Quelpart, Port Hamilton and Dagelet."[28]

The lack of clarity in the treaty concerning Dokdo/Takeshima and the Northern territories/Southern Kuril enabled the United States to enhance its strategic advantage. This ambiguity was meant to complicate the relations between Japan and its neighbors.[29] The treaty's lack of clarity would have enabled the United States to keep the East Sea/Sea of Japan within its sphere of influence even if the South had lost the Korean War. Indeed, the lack of clarity gave the United States more influence over Japan's relations with the Soviet Union. When the Soviet Union approached the Hatoyama cabinet in January 1955 seeking to restore bilateral relations, the United States asked the Japanese government to raise the issue of the return of Japanese territories. The U.S. request was based on the calculation that the territorial issue might hamper the negotiations and limit the development of Soviet-Japanese relations to a certain degree. Indeed, this calculation appeared in part in "NSC 5516/1: Progress Report on Policy toward Japan," which was adopted on April 9, 1955.[30] This report stated that the United States did not oppose normalization between Japan and the Soviet Union, but it supported Japan's territorial claims over the islands of Habomai and Shikotan. It is interesting to note that the United States did not mention the other two islands, Kunashiri and Etorofu, which Japan must have borne in mind.[31] As the United States had anticipated, Japan normalized its relations with the Soviet Union in October 1956, but the two sides failed to conclude a peace treaty on account of the thorny territorial issue. The United States' half-hearted support for Japan's rapprochement with the Soviet Union did drive a wedge between the two states, although it did not derail the normalization completely.

The dispute over Dokdo/Takeshima was put on the back burner in the second half of the 1950s, owing to the prominence of another contentious issue, the repatriation of Korean residents in Japan to North Korea. But the territorial dispute took on a new shape as the Japan-ROK normalization negotiations entered a critical phase in the first half of the 1960s. For the most part, South Korea wanted to avoid contention over the issue, whereas Japan continued to insist that the dispute be referred to the ICJ until the final stage of the normalization talks. Compared to its stance during the San Francisco Peace Treaty negotiations, the United States took a low-key approach on the territorial issue during the Japan-South Korea normalization talks, while having sided with Japan in legalistic interpretation of the issue. Because the United States considered the normalization the top of its list of priorities in Northeast Asia at that time, particularly regarding the need for burden sharing with Japan for South Korea's development, it pressed South Korea to give up the Peace Line within which the Dokdo/Takeshima was included, but avoided allowing the dispute over the islets to become a stumbling block in the normalization talks. In contrast to the case of the Northern territories/Southern Kuril, U.S. ambivalence on this issue was used passively, not negatively, during the Japan-South Korea normalization talks. As a consequence, Japan failed to include it in any form in the Japan-ROK treaty or to bring it to the ICJ.

Post–Cold War Trajectories

Strictly speaking, the comfort women issue is different in nature from the Dokdo/Takeshima dispute. The former pertains to the violation of human rights and crimes against humanity in which there are perpetrators and victims, whereas the latter is a territorial dispute between two sovereign states. The Japanese government has claimed that the contention over Dokdo/Takeshima, unlike the comfort women case, is purely a sovereignty issue that should be resolved through legal procedures. In contrast, the ROK government has maintained that both issues are closely related to the history of Japan, even though they arose in different contexts. For South Korea, it was as a result of Japanese imperial expansionism both that Japan occupied the islets during the Russo-Japanese War and that it forced Korean women into sexual slavery during the Pacific War.

It is noteworthy that in Japanese society today, these two areas of contention are intermingled. This is because right-wing politicians and scholars view Japan's wartime history from a revisionist perspective. Their most important goal is to rewrite history; as a result, references to the comfort women have gradually disappeared from students' textbooks, and the islets are increasingly described as being illegally occupied by the South Koreans.

The Unfolding of the Comfort Women Issue

The issue had remained silent during the Cold War. Articles appeared in various publications suggesting that the Imperial Army had organized sexual slavery. For instance, Nakasone Yasuhiro mentioned in his memoir that he was involved in the establishment of military brothels when he was an Imperial Army officer in the Philippines and Borneo.[32] However, for decades, none of the former comfort women testified about their painful experiences. There were three reasons for the delay of the revelation of the issue. First, none of the perpetrators of the sexual slavery were prosecuted by the Tokyo War Crimes Tribunal. Second, the absence of any provision for war reparations in the San Francisco Peace Treaty discouraged the victims from testifying to their painful experiences. Third, the Japan-South Korea normalization treaty of 1965, which settled the issue of South Korea's claims against Japan in terms of economic assistance, deprived the Korean victims of the right to raise individual claims against Japan for the atrocious crimes. But democratization in South Korea stimulated the revelation of the issue of the comfort women. After the June 29 declaration in 1987, which was a pact between the ruling authoritarian regime and opposition forces concerning a transition to democracy, gradual democratization empowered trade unions and civic groups, particularly women's organizations. The long silence on the comfort women issue was broken when Professor Yun Chung-ok publicized her research on the subject in 1988 and a former Korean "comfort woman," Kim Hak-soon, testified publicly on August 14, 1991, at a meeting organized by a Korean women's organization: the Korean Council for the Women Drafted for Military Sexual Slavery by Japan.

Yun's research and Kim's public testimony changed the situation. In 1992, soon after they broke the silence on the issue, Yoshimi Yoshiaki discovered documents related to comfort women in the library of the Japanese Defense Agency. According to these documents, the Ministry of the Army, the Ministry of Internal Affairs, and the offices of the governors-general of Korea and Taiwan were all involved in the recruitment and transportation of the women from as early as 1938. The documents revealed that the military had managed and controlled the comfort women stations, which were located all over Southeast Asia after the outbreak of the Pacific War in 1941. With the collaboration of human traffickers, the mobilization of women for sexual slavery reached its peak between 1943 and 1945. The largest group of victims was Korean, numbering between 170 and 200 thousand. Obviously, sexual slavery was a violation of various international laws, most of which Japan had agreed to observe. In particular, it violated laws against child prostitution and the trafficking of women.[33] One of the stated objectives of operating military brothels in conflict zones was to prevent Japanese soldiers from raping local women, but despite the existence of the brothels, rape was widespread throughout the Pacific War.[34]

As details of these atrocities began to be revealed, the new reformist cabinet led by Hosokawa Morihiro, the first non-LDP prime minister since the advent of the conservative "1955 system," inaugurated the diplomacy of apology. Chief Secretary of the Cabinet Kono Yohei issued a statement on August 4, 1993, admitting that the Japanese military had been involved in the operation of brothels. Kono admitted that "honied words and coercion were used in the recruitment, transportation, and management, and all in all, these acts took place against the will of those women."[35] This was the first time that a top Japanese official had publicly admitted the existence of organized sexual slavery during the war, although even now there was no mention of legal responsibility or compensation. Prime Minister Hosokawa himself delivered an apology during his visit to Kyongju, South Korea, on November 7; he mentioned specific issues, including the comfort women, Koreans being forced to use Japanese names, and forced labor during the colonial period. Furthermore, on August 15, 1995, Japan's first Socialist prime minister, Murayama Tomiichi, issued a special statement titled "On the Occasion of the 50th Anniversary of the War's End," which included the finest expressions of contrition the Japanese have ever made before or since, including "deep remorse" and "heartfelt apology" for the sufferings inflicted as the result of "a mistaken national policy."[36] The Murayama statement, along with the Kono statement on the comfort women, included more specific information on Japan's wartime actions and more sincere expressions of remorse and apologies than any other such statements had done.[37] There is no doubt that the Murayama statement was welcomed by most Asian people. The Japanese government also supported the creation of a private organization, the Asia Women's Fund, which was established to provide the former comfort women with compensation. Following suit, the compilers of history textbooks started including information about the comfort women issue. Most middle school textbooks for 1995–96 mentioned it in one way or another.[38] As a consequence, middle school textbooks in the second half of the 1990s contained more accurate information on Japan's wartime aggression, including the comfort women and the Nanjing massacre, than any others before or since.

However, those conciliatory moves by the Japanese government had political repercussions at home.[39] In an interview printed in *Mainichi Shimbun* on May 5, 1994, the newly appointed justice minister, Nagano Shigeto, fired the first salvo, describing the Nanjing massacre as a "fabrication." Watanabe Michio, a long-serving Diet member who had served as foreign minister from November 1991 to April 1993, upset the South Koreans when he said on June 3, 1995, that "the 1910 annexation was an international treaty and was achieved smoothly." The contention spread to the Diet that year when it deliberated a resolution endorsing the Murayama statement under preparation. Not only the opposition parties but also Murayama's coalition partner, the LDP, opposed the initial draft of the resolution. The resolution's opponents emphasized differences in historical understanding and war responsibility among different countries. As a consequence, the Diet resolution, which provoked much opposition but was eventually adopted on August 9, was not so forthright about Japan's wartime actions as Prime Minister Murayama's August 15 statement. For instance, the Diet resolution used the somewhat unspecific, watered-down term *those acts* instead of Murayama's term, *aggression*.[40]

Meanwhile, the controversy over the comfort women was having significant ramifications internationally. Advocacy groups were set up in South Korea, Japan, Canada, and the United States in the 1990s. The activities of these groups succeeded in bringing the issue to the United Nations: in 1998, Gay McDougall, the UN special rapporteur on systematic rape and sexual slavery practices in armed conflict, submitted her report to a subcommittee of the Commission on Human Rights.[41] The advocacy groups, on the initiative of the Violence Against Women in War Network Japan (VAWW-NET Japan), succeeded in organizing an international people's tribunal in December 2000—the Women's International War Crimes Tribunal on Japan's Military Sexual Slavery. The tribunal raised the issue of the legal responsibility of the Japanese emperor and the military for the treatment of these women. It pointed out that the Tokyo War Crimes Tribunal was "incomplete" in that it had failed to bring charges against those individuals involved in sexual slavery.[42] Furthermore, the tribunal contributed to the empowerment of former comfort women by stating that the victims should be able to claim against the Japanese state, that the perpetrators should not be allowed to use a statute of limitations defense, and perpetrators should admit their guilt in order to restore the dignity of their victims.[43]

The comfort women issue resonated with concern over other examples of organized sexual violence at the time, including those in conflict zones such as Rwanda and the former Yugoslavia, for example. The issue became a focal point around which people concerned about such gender-related crimes were able to share their views internationally. In this respect, as Carol Gluck notes, the comfort women issue was "becoming part of a transnational memory with social, legal, and moral consequences that transcended national or cultural borders."[44]

Reemergence of the Dokdo/Takeshima Dispute

This territorial dispute did not reemerge until two decades after Japan-South Korea normalization. When it did come to the fore again, it was centered on Shimane prefecture. As early as 1987, the prefectural government had attempted to link Dokdo/Takeshima to the Northern territories case. These efforts were supported by a series of public conferences and the publication of materials advocating Japan's claim to the islets. This activity eventually attracted the attention of politicians in Tokyo, and by 2003 the Japanese foreign minister was sending congratulatory messages to some of these conferences in the prefecture.[45] Another important move was made on March 16, 2005, the one hundredth anniversary of the islets' annexation, when the prefectural assembly designated February 22 "Takeshima Day." The South Koreans registered a strong protest against this move, and North Kyongsang province ended its sister relations with Shimane prefecture. The protests were followed by a South Korean maritime exploration mission into waters near the islets in April 2006, when there was nearly a military confrontation between the two democracies. As Paul Midford notes, this incident exemplified South Koreans' historically rooted mistrust of Japan and rendered "democratic reassurance" almost impossible in such a territorial standoff. Democratic reassurance refers to the positive signals that one democratic state may transmit to another to reassure the latter that the former's disposition or intentions are constructive.[46]

The Japanese government bases its claim to the islets on two points, which it considers to be decisive. One is the official incorporation of the islets into Shimane prefecture in 1905; the other is Article 2 (a) of the San Francisco Peace Treaty, which does not include Dokdo/

Takeshima among the islands Japan renounced. Japan interprets the fail-ure to specify Dokdo/Takeshima in this article as evidence supporting its claim. In contrast, the ROK government maintains that there is no ter-ritorial dispute over the islets. The evidence it uses to support that view is as follows: Korea recognized the islets as early as the fifteenth century and officially integrated them in 1900; SCAP Instruction (SCAPIN) 677 of January 29, 1946, noted that the islets, along with Jeju Island, were part of a special area from which Japanese administrative con-trol was removed; SCAPIN 1033 of June 22, 1946, which established the MacArthur Line, excluded the islets from Japanese administrative control and the Japanese fishing zone; and the ROK has had effective control of them since 1952 when President Syngman Rhee declared the Peace Line (see Table 7.1).

Table 7.1. Japanese and South Korean Positions on Dokdo/Takeshima

	Japan	*South Korea*
Geographical recognition	• Kaisei Nippon yochi rotei zenzu in 1779	• Sejong sillok jiriji in 1454 • Dongguk munheon bigo in 1770
Official incorporation	• Incorporation into Shimane prefecture in 1905	• Empire of Korea's Imperial Decree No. 41 in 1900
Presented evidence	• Article 2 (a) of San Francisco Peace Treaty of 1951	• SCAPIN 677 & 1033 in 1946 • Effective control since 1952
Counterargument	• ROK's 1952 Rhee Line had no legal authority	• Japan's incorporation in 1905 was expansionist and illegal
Suggested solution	• Referral to International Court of Justice	• No territorial dispute

Source: Web sites of the Japanese and South Korean ministries of foreign affairs. The ROK's basic position appears in the site entitled "Dokdo, Beautiful Island of Korea," whereas the Japanese site is entitled "Japanese Territory: Takeshima." (accessed March 4, 2015); Jon M. Van Dyke, "Legal Issues Related to Sovereignty over Dokdo and Its Maritime Boundary," *Ocean Development & International Law* 38, nos. 1–2 (2007): 183.

The Politics of Historical Revisionism in Japan

The Japanese government's apologies regarding the comfort women were met with domestic resistance. The more the government, particularly the reformist Hosokawa cabinet and the Socialist Murayama cabinet in the period 1993–96, tried to be conciliatory on historical issues and drew the attention of neighboring countries, the more domestic resistance was strengthened. Why? Behind the resistance against any admission of guilt there has been historical revisionism as a driving force. There has been a "political struggle," to use the strongest term, or "interest politics" and "negotiation between social actors," to use more moderate terms, over what counts as legitimate knowledge and values.[47] The comfort women issue, along with the Nanjing massacre, forms the political agenda of the revisionists, and the Dokdo/Takeshima issue, along with other territorial disputes, has been drawn into it. My analysis of this revisionism concentrates on: main arguments that gained new momentum in the post–Cold War era; attractors that have united these revisionists (such as the publication of revisionist middle school textbooks and the movements to adopt them); and political objectives that revisionists have advocated (such as national honor, revision of the constitution, and military buildup), just as their predecessors did in the 1950s.

The post–Cold War revisionism has been centered on descriptions of the main wartime atrocities in middle school history textbooks. Tsukurukai (Atarashii rekishi kyokasho o tsukurukai, or the Japanese Society for History Textbook Reform) became the locus of the revisionism. The central figures in this society, which was founded in December 1996, were Nishio Kanji, Fujioka Nobukatsu, Takahashi Shiro, and Kobayashi Yorinori. Tsukurukai worked to refute the new discoveries that had been made concerning Japanese war crimes, particularly those pertaining to the comfort women and the Nanjing massacre; to spread its revisionist interpretation of history, especially among the youth; and to discourage authors and publishers of history textbooks from dealing with these issues. Its founding members shared a crisis perception with regard to the events occurred in Japan in the mid-1990s, and used it as a means to justify their revisionist ideas. For instance, when the Japanese government announced on August 14, 1996, that it was paying compensation to Filipino comfort women, Fujioka criticized his own government by calling the government's action "a huge crime that followed the mismanagement of the disastrous Hanshin earthquake [in January 1995] and Aum Shinrikyo's gas attack on the Tokyo subway [in March 1995]."[48] To Fujioka, in the midst of such domestic crises, the government's handling of the historical issue only contributed to portraying Japan's vulnerable status and the nation's uncertain future. In the same vein, in a book published by Fusosha, Tsukurukai interpreted Japan's situation in the first half of the 2000s as a "watershed of crisis versus vision," with crisis indicating threats to Japan's future. Tsukurukai and other revisionists believed that the development of weapons of mass destruction by North Korea and the Iraq War were examples of this crisis, whereas they considered Kim Jong Il's admission that North Korea had abducted Japanese nationals, Japan's alignment with the United States in the Iraq War, and the defeats suffered by Socialists and Communists in local elections as positive signs of the development of the future vision, if not solutions to the crisis.[49]

Tsukurukai's revisionism called for the restoration of Japan's honor and status.[50] These values originated with the founders of the Empire of Japan and had been taken up by the rehabilitated revisionist politicians gathered around Hatoyama and Kishi. The statement announcing the establishment of the society in December 1996 accused contemporary middle school history textbooks of "making verdicts on modern Japanese history as a history of crimes. . . . The description of the comfort women was kind of the final destination of a devil that had been wandering for a long period of time."[51] The statement basically rejected the objectivity of these historical facts, warning that there would be "no easygoing sharing of historical understanding with other countries."[52] The society obviously stood for particularism and subjectivism in both the understanding of history and the writing of it.

Nishio Kanji and Fujioka Nobukatsu were the prime proponents of these revisionist views. Nishio stated in 1996 that "in the study of history, there is good and evil that is peculiar to each particular time." In his view, the basic purpose of studying history is not to judge history with the eyes of people living now. Historical revisionism denied that history is a discipline based on evidence.[53] It was Fujioka who first used the term *masochism* to describe history education in contemporary Japan. He maintained that the critical view of Japan as the perpetrator represented a masochistic understanding of history. Masochism became a popular term among the revisionists, both academics and politicians, from the end of the 1990s.[54] On the comfort women issue, Fujioka argued that publicly investigating it would be equivalent to labeling Japan a state that was guilty of sexual slavery. To include it in middle school history textbooks, he argued, would be masochistic behavior.[55] Fujioka's logic was that if young students, who are learning about sexual relationships for the first time, are taught about the comfort women issue, they may acquire distorted views of sex. He worried that if the comfort women issue was the students' first experience of hearing about sex, they might see sex as extreme and unnatural.[56]

Inspired by these revisionist views, from the end of the 1990s Tsukurukai did all it could to influence the comfort women issue. In January 1997, representatives of Tsukurukai met Minister of Education Machimura Nobutaka to request deletion of the comfort women issue from the middle school history textbooks. Furthermore, Tsukurukai lobbied several prefectural education committees to encourage schools to adopt Tsukurukai's own textbook, *Atarashii Rekishi* (New History). Meanwhile, another nationalistic organization, Nippon Kaigi, wrote to Prime Minister Hashimoto asking him to remove descriptions of the comfort women issue from textbooks.[57] The membership of Tsukurukai and Nippon Kaigi overlapped to a great extent and the two organizations were closely linked.[58]

Tsukurukai's efforts were partly successful. The movement for the adoption of its own history textbook by schools became the focus around which like-minded revisionist people united. Also, the movement forced other textbook publishers to gradually water down, or avoid altogether, descriptions of the comfort women, which had already become a very sensitive topic in the textbook publication sector.[59] However, this change did not automatically raise the rate of the adoption of Tsukurukai's textbook by schools. On the failure of Tsukurukai's textbook adoption movement in 2000 and 2001, an internal division began to open up in September 2005.[60] The division was initiated by Nippon Kaigi, the Fuji-Sankei media conglomerate, and a leading politician of the postwar generation, Abe Shinzo. Many founding members of Tsukurukai left the organization and joined the new revisionist coalition, leaving only Fujioka and a small number of his associates. This division resulted in attracting stronger, more organized political support for a new revisionist coalition. The new coalition was also interested in publishing revisionist history textbooks, and in July 2007 it called itself Kyokasho Kaisen no kai (Association for Textbook Improvement). Tsukurukai and Kyokasho Kaisen no kai shared same revisionist views of past atrocities, maintaining that there was no coercion involved in the recruitment of comfort women, that the massacre in Nanjing was no different from killings that had taken place in other wars, and Okinawans had not been forced to commit suicide.[61]

Kyokasho Kaisen no kai's main supporter was the Nippon Kaigi Giren (League of Diet Members of the Nippon Kaigi), to which half of all LDP Diet members and many members of the Democratic Party of Japan (DPJ) belonged.[62] Other revisionist political groups that had close connections with Kyokasho Kaisen no kai were Rekishi Kyokasho Giren

(League of Diet Members Concerning History Textbooks), Ianfu Mondai to Nankin Jiken no Shinjitsu o Kenshosuru Kai (the Association for Truth-Finding about the Comfort Women Issue and the Nanjing Incident Issue), and Chugoku no Konichi Kinenkan kara Futona Shashin no Tekkyo o Motomeru Kai (the Association for the Elimination of Unfair Pictures from the Memorial Museum of Chinese People's Anti-Japanese War). All these organizations were established in the first half of 2007 when Abe Shinzo was prime minister.[63]

It is noteworthy that these organizations were filled with politicians from the young, postwar generation. The number of young politicians, particularly from the LDP, increased substantially after the elections to the Upper House in July 1989 and the Lower House in February 1990. This new breed of politicians benefited from the atmosphere of public distrust and discontent with the old politics of corruption, which centered on the Recruit scandal. They took note of the rapid changes that were occurring both internationally and domestically: the collapse of communism, the development of a North Korean nuclear capability, the rise of China, and the bursting of the bubble economy at home. They maintained a strong preference for strengthened alliances, collective self-defense, the expansion of Japan's own defense capability, and amendment of the constitution. Their views were different from those of the mainstream conservative politicians.[64]

Among this postwar generation of politicians, Abe Shinzo, who served as prime minister from 2006 to 2007 and again from 2012 (he is still in office at the time of writing), has been the most prominent. He was involved in the dissemination of revisionist historical views. It is known that on January 29, 2001, when he was deputy secretary to the cabinet, Abe put pressure on an NHK producer, in the name of "fair broadcasting," to change the content of a TV program on the comfort women issue. After his meeting with Abe, the producer returned to his studio and instructed his production team to delete three scenes, including interviews with former comfort women, just before the program was due to be aired.[65] When a group of U.S. congressmen led by Michael Honda proposed a congressional resolution calling for the Japanese government to issue an apology for the treatment of comfort women in 2007, Prime Minister Abe maintained that the military brothels were not problematic. Abe's main point, in common with Tsukurukai and Kyokasho Kaisen no kai, was that the women were not subject to coercion. Since then, he has continued to call public attention to his narrow definition of coercion, thus trying to deny the existence of the sexual slavery altogether.[66]

When the *Washington Post* became involved in the debate, the revisionist groups unfolded a new concerted media strategy. Forty-four Diet members, eight professors, four political commentators, and two journalists sponsored an advertisement in that newspaper on June 14, 2007. They refuted the arguments of a similar advert sponsored by an advocacy group for comfort women that had appeared in the *Washington Post* two months earlier. The revisionists argued that the young girls involved were not forcibly rounded up, but were lured to Manchuria for prostitution by brokers. However, this argument avoided the critical point that the use of comfort women was an organized crime committed by the state and the military. The revisionists maintained that the comfort women were not sex slaves but licensed prostitutes whose incomes exceeded those of field officers.

The revisionists' efforts to publicize their view in the U.S. media actually backfired. Michael Honda, backed by 167 cosponsors at the House of Representatives, led the adoption of HR Resolution 121 on July 30, 2007, which stated that the Japanese government "should formally acknowledge, apologize, and accept historical responsibility" for the Imperial Army's coercive sexual slavery system. The resolution was neither legally binding nor did it demand that the Japanese accept legal responsibility, but the perceived pressure on the Abe cabinet and the revisionist groups must have been enormous. However, Prime Minister Abe, along with younger LDP and DPJ politicians, still argued that there was no evidence of coercion.[67]

Not surprisingly, the revisionist turn regarding the comfort women went hand in hand with the reemergence of the territorial issues. The Japanese government had always maintained that the Dokdo/Takeshima issue was a territorial dispute that had to be resolved through legal procedures, particularly at the ICJ. But from around 2005, the issue of the islets became involved in the increasingly prominent textbook issue. Of the middle school textbooks used between 2001 and 2005, only one, written by Tsukurukai and published by Fusosha, described the islets as Japan's territory. Between 2006 and 2009, however, as many as four textbooks described Dokdo/Takeshima as Japanese territory both "historically and legally."[68] In April 2011, all fourteen middle school textbooks approved by the Japanese Ministry of Education claimed that the islets belonged to Japan, with some describing South Korean control of them as an "illegal occupation."[69] These textbooks described Japan's territorial claim even more forcefully than previous ones had. The trajectory of Japan's handling of this issue in school textbooks reflected the standing of the political groups advocating historical revisionism.[70]

The textbook approval decision of 2011 occurred just as South Koreans were enthusiastically donating to the relief fund for victims of the Tohoku earthquake in March, and thus it aroused even more frustration and anger there and made Koreans suspicious of Japan's intentions. For South Koreans, the Dokdo/Takeshima issue is not simply about territory; it is one of the most sensitive historical issues affecting the country, and it has attracted an extraordinary amount of national attention. It was in this context that on August 10, 2012, President Lee Myung-bak, whose term of office had only six months to run and whose popularity was waning, visited Dokdo for the first time as the incumbent president. And Lee's visit was for the most part supported by South Koreans despite the opposition party's skepticism about his political motives.[71]

Since Abe became prime minister again in December 2012, revisionism has been further intensified at the official level. It was probably the Abe cabinet's reexamination of the 1993 Kono statement admitting the Japanese military's involvement in the operation of brothels that had the most detrimental effect on understanding of the comfort women issue. On June 20, 2014, the cabinet released a report on its reexamination that claimed that the Japanese and South Korean governments had consulted several times on the wording of the Kono statement.[72] The report also implied that the content of the statement had been influenced by the sixteen former comfort women's testimonies that the Japanese government had never verified. The release of this report was apparently intended to undermine the Kono statement's admission of coercion with respect to comfort women.[73] Although the Japanese government dismissed the possibility of withdrawing the Kono statement, the reexamination had the effect of watering down Japan's admission of responsibility for its wartime wrongdoings.

The release of the report had enormous ramifications in Japanese society. Evidently, Japanese social memory of the comfort women was questioned and even overturned. The immediate target was *Asahi Shimbun*, which during the 1990s had carried reports about the wartime comfort women based on interviews with the Japanese novelist Yoshida Seiji. Yoshida had stated that women were rounded up on the Korean Jeju island during the Pacific War. But his statements were later found to be fabrications, which in turn caused a crisis of credibility at the newspaper in August 2014. CEO Kimura Tadakazu and top managers apologized for printing the fabricated reports and retracted them. The government's reexamination of the Kono statement had an impact on the history textbook issue too. Many textbook publishers expressed willingness to reexamine the descriptions of the comfort women issue.[74] Furthermore, it was obvious that the revisionist groups would likely increase their scrutiny of how the issue was handled in history textbooks, and thus publishers tended to be more cautious and discourage the inclusion of sensitive content.

Ten years after the government of Shimane prefecture declared February 22 Takeshima Day, Japan introduced a dramatic change of policy on Dokdo/Takeshima. On April 6, 2015, the Ministry of Education approved a number of middle school textbooks in social studies and history that described the islets as Japanese territory; more importantly still, textbooks are increasingly depicting them as illegally occupied by South Korea. Also, Japan's Diplomatic Bluebook, published on April 7, 2015, stated that "Takeshima is traditionally a part of Japanese territory in terms of both history and international law," as well as noting that "the comfort women issue was legally and completely solved."[75]

In sum, the textbook issue has become part of the revisionists' political agenda at a time of increasing vulnerability. This political agenda has been incompatible with South Koreans' increasing awareness of the rights of the victims of Japan's colonial rule and wartime atrocities, particularly those of comfort women. For the revisionists, there is no difference between historical issues and territorial issues. They have used the historical and territorial issues to attract political support. Thus, revisionism in Japan has involved the expansion of likeminded logrolling coalitions.[76] The logrolling began with a few right-wing academics and politicians, and gradually extended to include most LDP politicians and even many opposition party members. The logrolling has continued to gain momentum through the textbook adoption movement and thus intended to change young people's views of history and their understanding of wartime history in particular. The logrolling has certainly tainted the descriptions of the wartime period. In the second half of the 1990s, school textbooks contained relatively fair descriptions of such issues as the comfort women and the Nanjing massacre. However, over the following two decades these descriptions have gradually disappeared. This change has had a far-reaching impact on young people's understanding of Japanese history in general and of the comfort women issue in particular, and it also has had an enormous negative impact on Japan's external relations. Criticism from South Korea and China over the Japanese government's approval of textbooks that glossed over Japanese war crimes—criticism that intensified particularly in 2001, 2005, 2011, 2013, and 2015—has complicated diplomatic relations between Japan and its neighbors.[77] Despite some enthusiastic collaboration in historical research at the nongovernmental level, the Japanese government has continued to approve textbooks that contain denials of the country's past crimes.

U.S. Intervention on the Comfort Women Issue

Both Dokdo/Takeshima and the comfort women issue have been sources of diplomatic tension between Japan and South Korea, but the comfort women issue has had a far more detrimental impact on bilateral relations in particular and on Japan's relations with its neighbors in general than the territorial dispute.[78]

As important indicators of progress with regard to the comfort women issue, there were two court rulings, one in Japan and the other in South Korea. On April 27, 2007, the Japanese Supreme Court made an important ruling in the case of the kidnapping, detention, and repeated rape of two Chinese girls by the Japanese military in Shanxi province in 1942. Acknowledging the extreme suffering that was inflicted on the victims, the ruling confirmed that coercion had been used in the recruitment of comfort women, a point that Japanese revisionists have consistently denied. On the other hand, the court ruled against the victims' rights to demand compensation on the grounds that the 1972 Japan-China Joint Communique had renounced war reparations.[79]

On August 30, 2011, the Constitutional Court in South Korea ruled that the ROK government's nonfeasance with regard to the comfort women constituted a breach of the constitution. This ruling stated that despite different interpretations of Article 2, Section 1, of the "Agreement on the Settlement of Problems Concerning Property Claims and on Economic Cooperation between the Republic of Korea and Japan," the ROK government must refer to Article 3 of the agreement in protecting the rights of plaintiffs guaranteed in the constitution.[80] Article 3 stipulates that any dispute concerning the interpretation of the agreement shall be settled primarily through diplomatic channels. In this context, the court mandated the government to resolve the plaintiffs' requests for compensation through those channels.

Despite those court rulings of the two countries, the two governments did not make sincere efforts to work toward a diplomatic solution until the 2015 negotiations. The Japanese government, particularly the Abe cabinet that launched in December 2012, has not actively explored this possibility, and has instead argued that the issue of claims against Japan was settled by the agreement of normalization in 1965. In response, the ROK government, particularly the Park Geun-hye administration that inaugurated in February 2013, has dismissed the possibility of holding a summit meeting, the highest level of diplomacy, to reduce the friction incurred by the historical issue. This stalemate delayed the first summit between Park and Abe until November 2015, when it took place on the sideline of the ROK-China-Japan trilateral summit held in Seoul.

Until early 2014, when it started its earnest intervention, the U.S. government had not expressed any strong opinion on the disagreement over the comfort women issue. To be sure, Prime Minister Abe's revisionist views have damaged U.S. national interests by causing a deterioration in Japan-ROK relations and undercutting Japan's ability to deal with sensitive issues related to China.[81] But the U.S. government has not singled out the Japanese as being responsible for the ongoing tensions surrounding the historical issues. This was so because for Washington, Abe was not only a revisionist but also a realist, as Gilbert Rozman aptly notes. Abe as a revisionist wanted to revise the description of the wartime history, to refute the verdict of the Tokyo War Crimes Tribunal, and to restore Japan's honor and status, whereas the prime minister as a realist intended to build a stronger U.S.-Japan alliance to cope with China and to expand its security role in the world.[82] With the motto of "positive pacifism," the realist Abe established the National Security Council and prepared to reinterpret the constitution to legitimize the right of collective self-defense. Such realist measures were in accordance with U.S. global strategy, even if they have been viewed by South Koreans as a move toward a militarist path. Thus, the United States was not in support of South Korea's position, particularly President Park's continued refusal or indifference to the improvement of bilateral relations.[83]

The United States intervened seriously in 2014 and 2015. First of all, depending on party affiliation, members of the Congress often took different positions over the comfort women issue; however, their demands and pressure eventually worked, in effect, to induce Japan's forthcoming move and South Korea's accommodating stance in December 2015. On June 27, 2014, eighteen members of the House of Representatives sent an official letter to the Japanese government through Japan's ambassador in Washington, Sasae Kenichiro, in which they criticized Japan's reexamination of the 1993 Kono statement and demanded that the Japanese accept responsibility for the comfort women issue. The letter stressed that the issue was a matter of both victims' rights and human dignity. The main signatories were Michael Honda, Loretta Sanches, Garry Cornelly, Peter Roskam, and Mike Kelly—a group that was bipartisan in its composition.[84] These efforts seemed in vain, as Abe failed to express repentance or make an apology in his April 2015 address at the joint meeting of Congress.[85] But key Republicans such as senators John McCain and Cory Gardner and Representative Matt Salmon made additional efforts on the comfort women issue. They took a low-key approach that suggested that Japan and South Korea earnestly negotiate with each other.[86]

The congressional move mentioned above was not sufficient to influence the allies. If there had been no action on the part of the administration, U.S. efforts would have been without consequence. In order to cope with China's increasing influence in the Asia Pacific and North Korea's increasing threat, the Obama administration considered restoration of the partnership between its allies a desperately needed and indeed inevitable strategic requirement, not a choice. Deputy Secretary of State Anthony J. Blinken aptly described this point by saying that "this [repair of Japan-ROK relations] wasn't a question of wanting our two friends to get along; it mattered strategically."[87] The Obama administration's intervention took place in two ways. First, Obama himself arranged a trilateral summit on March 25, 2014, at the U.S. ambassador's residence during the Hague nuclear security summit. Although all talking points were about the North Korean nuclear threat, the arranged summit provided Prime Minister Abe and President Park with momentum to begin negotiations on the comfort women issue. Second, the Obama administration followed the traditional approach in intervening in this issue: not to be mixed in between its allies, but to access them individually through embassies. With the State Department as the control tower, Ambassador Mark Lippert in Seoul and Ambassador Caroline Kennedy in Tokyo accessed the individual foreign ministries and tried to make use of the opportunity presented by the arrival of the year 2015—the seventieth anniversary of the end of World War II and the fiftieth anniversary of the Japan-ROK normalization.[88]

Meanwhile, several incidents threatened the negotiations. For instance, U.S. Undersecretary of State for Political Affairs Wendy Sherman, at a conference in Washington on February 27, 2015, criticized all political leaders who tried to earn "cheap applause by vilifying a former enemy."[89] Although she did not indicate any specific leader and the State Department made efforts to calm the uproar, her remarks aroused hostility in South Korea in particular. But the aftermath did not sink the government-level negotiations over the comfort women issue between Japan and South Korea. Separating the historical issue from economic and security issues, the South Korean government continued the negotiations with the Japanese government in a veil of secrecy. Both governments, as in the case of the normalization talks in the early 1960s, feared potential political fallout in the event that the contents of the negotiations were revealed while they were ongoing. Indeed, the comfort women issue was highly sensitive, and public attention in each society was intense.

The agreement on the comfort women issue between South Korea and Japan, reached on December 28, 2015, was a result of U.S. diplomatic intervention. For the United States, intervention was certainly a better policy than ambivalence between its allies, as many had suggested.[90] At the agreement, the Japanese government admitted the Imperial Army's involvement and offered Prime Minister Abe's apology to the victims. In addition, Japan pledged a financial contribution worth of one billion Japanese yen to establish a foundation for the restoration of the honor of the victims. In response, South Korea promised its consultation with civic organizations in seeking to relocate the statue of a girl that had been erected in front of the Japanese embassy in Seoul. The statue has symbolized the victims and supported the movement advocating for their rights, but Japan has considered it defamatory in its position relative to the embassy building. Also, Seoul and Tokyo confirmed that the comfort women issue had been "resolved finally and irreversibly."

Conclusion

In this chapter, I have shown that contentions over the comfort women issue and Dokdo/Takeshima were situated in the U.S.-led alliance's politics. Following Cold War logic, the United States subordinated these important legacies of the war to the necessity of containing the Soviet Union. In this context, revisionists rose to power in Japan and put forward an agenda that included amendment of the constitution and assertive security. In post–Cold War Japanese society, revisionism has reared its head again and tried to convince the general public that Japan should extricate itself from the postwar regime and restore its national honor and status, overcoming its feelings of crisis and vulnerability. Revisionism has inherited the agenda of the predecessors, including the assertive security policy. What lies behind today's revisionism in Japan may be found in the way that the United States embraced Japan after its defeat, particularly its cursory treatment of the issue of responsibility for the war in the early years of the Cold War. In this regard, the United States cannot be excused of the responsibility for the disputes over historical issues between Japan on the one hand and South Korea and China on the other.

Just as in many other cases during the Cold War, the United States earnestly intervened in the comfort women issue because it believed that delaying a resolution would be detrimental to the interests of the United States and the security triangle as a whole. But the consequence of the Japan-ROK negotiations has not been a complete, clean resolution of the comfort women issue or the historical issues as a whole. Arguably, the negotiated settlement will not be able to eliminate the deep-seated animosity in each society and thus may not end persistent resistance or backlash in each country anytime soon. The Abe cabinet's decision in December 2015 was an uneasy compromise—coaxing revisionists to restrain, on the one hand, and restoring partnership with Seoul for a realist, activistic security agenda, on the other. The Park administration, focusing on the North Korean threat, did not consult with the victims in the process of negotiation. As a result, revisionists in Japan criticize that Tokyo made too many concessions, whereas advocates for victims' rights in South Korea argue that the agreement without consultation with the victims is null. Compared to previous disputes between the troubling partners, the comfort women case is likely to reverberate in each society for a long period of time.

On the other hand, the 2015 agreement provided new momentum for the dominant power—the United States—to exert pressure on its allies and thus institutionalize a further strengthened security triangle. For Washington, the intervention was a success in binding the three, in view of another provocative action by North Korea, the fourth nuclear test on January 6, 2016, which took place only a week after the agreement on the comfort women issue had been reached.

8

North Korea Factor and the
Persistence of the Security Triangle

In the post–Cold War era, South Korea's enhanced economic and dip-lomatic standing, as well as its democratization, has helped to make the Japan-ROK relationship more symmetrical than before and altered the hierarchy within the security triangle as well. Despite this change, the security triangle continues to operate today. Not only do the two U.S.-led alliances persist, but also Japan and South Korea have to collaborate with each other, however differently they interpret the benefits of that collaboration. This chapter addresses the following questions: Does the post–Cold War security triangle differ from the Cold War one? In particular, how differently is each state acting now? Why does the Japan-ROK partnership persist today even without burden sharing, especially in the absence of aid from Japan to South Korea?

To stipulate, the security triangle cannot persist without a certain amount of feedback effect. In the post–Cold War era, the increasing threat posed by a nuclearizing North Korea has helped to bond the three states together and maintain the security triangle. North Korea's repeated nuclear tests (in 2006, 2009, 2013, and 2016) and numerous missile tests have aroused international concerns over nuclear proliferation and have increasingly destabilized regional security. Neither does this mean that all three states perceive the North Korean threat to be equally serious, nor that the feedback effect is equal for all three. For the United States and Japan and for the U.S.-Japan alliance, a rising China is the most important reference point for establishing and revising their security policies; North Korea is not a priority, even though it is by no means marginal. In contrast, South Korea does perceive a nuclear threat from North Korea seriously and thus gives serious consideration to deterrence against the threat in framing its security policy.

Just as in other cases discussed in previous chapters, Washington's intervention and mediation continue to tie the three together on the security front. The U.S.-led military information sharing, set up in December 2014, is a good example. The U.S. intervention and the Japan-ROK agreement in December 2015 on the long, contentious comfort women issue—which was immediately followed by a coincidental event, North Korea's fourth nuclear test, in January 2016—is another example. North Korea's continued nuclear advancement has facilitated an unprecedented, strengthened military cooperation both between the troubled partners and in the security triangle as an entirety.

U.S. Access to North Korea and Trilateral Coordination in the 1990s

As soon as the Cold War thawed, the ideological tension that had prevailed during its years was substantially relaxed. South Korea swiftly moved to normalize its relations with the Soviet Union in September 1990 and with China in August 1992. Meanwhile, having witnessed how the ROK had gained access to the Soviet Union, North Korea started political talks with Japan in September 1990 and began normalization talks in January 1991.[1] North Korea also opened political talks with the United States in an attempt to end its long-standing international isolation.

The attempts by both North and South Korea to throw off the Cold War legacy were followed by high level talks between the two, starting in September 1990; at this time, these talks were conducted more earnestly than ever before. After several rounds of talks in both Seoul and Pyongyang, the two Koreas signed the South-North Basic Agreement in December 1991. This agreement was the first of its kind to include a nonaggression clause, under which the two Koreas pledged to coexist peacefully. The two Koreas also issued the Joint Declaration on the Denuclearization of the Korean Peninsula in December 1991, agreeing to use nuclear technology for peaceful purposes only. As the backdrop to this joint declaration, the United States and South Korea agreed in October 1991 to withdraw all tactical nuclear weapons from the Korean peninsula (the U.S. Department of Defense declared the withdrawal completed on July 2, 1992). In this initial stage of the post–Cold War period, both sides made enormous efforts; however, on balance, the North's diplomatic overture was defensive in comparison to that of the South.

The unprecedented direct contact between the United States and North Korea originated from Pyongyang's strenuous efforts to approach

Washington. From the end of the 1980s, North Korea had intention-
ally allowed U.S. intelligence satellites to observe its nuclear facilities.
In one sense, North Korea succeeded in its intent. It was because of its
concerns about nuclear proliferation that the United States agreed to
establish direct contact with the North. In January 1992, the secretary of
international affairs of the Korean Workers' Party, Kim Yong-sun, trav-
eled to the United States to meet Arnold Kanter, the undersecretary of
state for political affairs. They conducted a high-level talk for the first
time in the history of the relationship between the two states. Kanter
urged Kim Yong-sun to permit inspections of the North's nuclear facilities by the International Atomic Energy Agency (IAEA) and to give
up the nuclear weapons option.[2] In exchange, he proposed that a U.S.
air base in South Korea undergo simultaneous inspection.[3] Eventually,
on January 30, North Korea signed the IAEA safeguards. Pyongyang's
compliance was mainly attributable to its enthusiasm for relations with
the United States and its wish to avoid international isolation. The
Kim-Kanter meeting had important implications for the relationship
between the former adversaries. For the first time, the United States
and North Korea were treating each other as counterparts in negotiations regarding such significant issues as nuclear proliferation and the
development of bilateral relations.

One of the most important achievements of the direct bilateral
contact between the United States and North Korea was the Geneva
Agreed Framework of October 1994. The background to the framework
was as follows. As the IAEA began engaging with North Korea in May
1992, it discovered that there was a serious discrepancy between Pyongyang's report concerning its nuclear facilities and what the IAEA inspec-
tors found. The IAEA asked North Korea to allow a special inspection
of its two undeclared facilities. However, Pyongyang rejected the request
and in March 1993 announced its exit from the Nonproliferation Treaty
(NPT), an event that marked the "first nuclear crisis" on the Korean
peninsula. As this crisis developed, the United States prepared various
options to cope with North Korea's possible military provocation; they
included imposing sanctions on North Korea, evacuating U.S. citizens
from South Korea, and adding twenty thousand U.S. troops in South
Korea. Also, the U.S. forces, under Secretary of Defense William Perry's
instructions, prepared a surgical strike as a contingency plan, although
it was not planned to execute it. At this critical moment, former president Jimmy Carter visited Pyongyang and met North Korean leader
Kim Il Sung to defuse the crisis.[4] With the opportunity presented by the
Carter-Kim meeting, in June 1994, North Korea's vice foreign minister

Kang Sok-ju and the U.S. assistant secretary of state Robert Gallucci could enter into high-level talks in Geneva in an effort to bring an end to the nuclear deadlock. The result of these talks was the Agreed Framework, under which North Korea agreed to freeze its graphite-moderated nuclear reactors in Yongbyon in return for receiving two light water reactors for electricity generation.

South Korea had virtually no role at all in the 1994 Geneva talks, although it had a vital stake in the North's willingness—or otherwise—to agree to nuclear nonproliferation. Despite no participation in the talks, South Korea, rather than the United States, became the main financial contributor to the Korean Peninsula Energy Development Organization (KEDO), a consortium that was established in March 1995 to provide the light water reactors. South Korea was supposed to assume 70 percent of the total financial burden of the KEDO project, although by the time it was wound up in 2005 it had only assumed 53 percent (see Table 8.1). In compensation, the Korea Electric Power Corporation (KEPCO), South Korea's state-sponsored electricity company, became the primary supplier of the reactors. South Korea's proactive participation in KEDO tells us two things. One is that South Korea was able to afford such a large share of the financial burden. In 1996, South Korea became a member of the OECD, thus graduating from being an aid recipient and expanding its aid to other developing or less-developed countries. Thus, South Korea's willingness to assume a large share of the KEDO burden was not simply a reflection of its feelings of brotherhood toward the North. The other thing its participation in KEDO tells us is that South Korea was already capable of designing its own nuclear power plant, the Korean standard model, the OPR 1000. This plant was a significantly

Table 8.1. Financial Contributors to KEDO, 1995–2005 (Million USD)

	Total	South Korea	Japan	U.S.	EU	Others
Construction	1,562	1,137	407	—	18	—
Management	118	37	39	32	10	—
Heavy oil aid	501	—	—	373	95	33
Total	2,181	1,174	446	405	122	33

Source: Ministry of Unification, "Gukgam jaryo, gyeongsuro saeop [Materials Prepared for the National Assembly's Inspection of Administration Affairs, Light-water Reactors Project]," October 10, 2006.

modified version of one originally designed by the U.S. firms Westing-house and Combustion Engineering.[5]

South Korea's largest contribution and the U.S.' and Japan's shar-ing at the KEDO were a new mode of burden sharing, unseen in the Cold War period. The negotiations were led by the United States, and the ensuing financial division was by and large framed by the United States; that is, the Agreed Framework and the KEDO project were a product of the dominant power's initiative. However, South Korea was economically empowered and thus able to take on the largest share of the KEDO project. Equally importantly, Japan demonstrated its security commitment regarding the North Korea issue by declaring its contribu-tion to the KEDO in November 1998.[6] To be sure, this was a significant change in the burden-sharing scheme: from the Japan-to-South Korea distribution of aid during the Cold War to the South Korea-led project in the post–Cold War in which Japan and the United States participated.

In the second half of the 1990s, the United States conducted another series of direct talks with North Korea concerning the latter's development of ballistic missiles. The talks started in April 1996 and continued until the publication of the Perry report in September 1999. The Perry report was written in response to North Korea's firing of a long-range missile, called Taepodong-1, on August 31, 1998.[7] The missile flew more than 1,600 km, passing over Japanese territory and finally falling into the Pacific Ocean. North Korea tried to avoid inter-national condemnation by claiming that the rocket was designed for launching a satellite. As to this incident, Japan expressed its unusu-ally serious concern about the security threat posed by North Korea. For example, the spokesman for Japanese Foreign Ministry stated that "[w]e are seriously concerned about this because the deployment of mis-siles by North Korea does affect Japanese security and it also affects peace and stability in Northeast Asia. It also is of serious global concern, in terms of the proliferation of weapons of mass destruction."[8] In this regard, the Perry report advocated a "comprehensive and integrated approach" toward North Korea and suggested short-, medium-, and long-term poli-cies—that the North should agree to a moratorium on missile tests and suspend its development of nuclear program and missile technology, with the long-term aim of ensuring stability on the Korean peninsula.[9]

It is noteworthy that the Perry report was prepared with unprec-edented trilateral coordination between the United States, South Korea, and Japan. In order to complete his report, William Perry consulted U.S. government departments, the Congress, and various experts. As a con-crete move to institutionalize the coordination between the three states,

Perry as the U.S. North Korea Policy Coordinator, South Korea's Senior Presidential Secretary Lim Dong-won, and Japan's Ministry of Foreign Affairs Director-General Kato Ryozo created the Trilateral Coordination and Oversight Group (TCOG), which met six times in Washington, Seoul, Tokyo, and Honolulu during 1999 and 2000.[10] In line with the Perry report, several rounds of U.S.-North Korea talks were held, and the North Korean attitude impressed the United States. As to this positive development, Perry stated that "North Korea was ready to accept the cooperative strategy we had presented."[11] This increasingly cooperative mood culminated in high-level political exchanges between the two sides in October 2000, including the visit by Cho Myong-rok, the political commissar of the North Korean army, to Washington and the resultant U.S.-DPRK joint communique, and the return visit of U.S. Secretary of State Madeleine Albright to Pyongyang.[12] This was an exemplary development that was based on equal-footing cooperation in the security triangle on the particular issue of the increasing North Korean threat.

The development of U.S.-North Korea relations, sustained by South Korea's and Japan's engagement, failed to result in any tangible outcome such as normalization. Progress did not occur until the final year of the Clinton administration, and thus the time to achieve such an outcome ran out. Of the two remaining significant foreign policy issues to be dealt with before his term ended, that is, the Israel-Palestine peace treaty and U.S.-North Korea normalization, Clinton chose the peace treaty in the Middle East as the priority.[13]

Despite cooperation on the North Korea issue, there were differences between South Korea and Japan with regard to security. South Korea accorded the North Korea issue the highest priority and thus welcomed the development of more conciliatory relations between Washington and Pyongyang. In contrast, Japan's main concern was the growth of Chinese power and thus its security policy was far broader in scope than South Korea's. One of the most notable developments was the revision of the Defense Cooperation Guidelines in September 1997, whereby the United States and Japan identified the scope of their alliance as "situations in the areas surrounding Japan." This was far wider than just the defense of Japan. The "situations" apparently meant any potential incidents in the Taiwan Strait or on the Korean peninsula.[14] The revision of the guidelines "diluted Japan's traditional postwar policy against the use of force in the absence of a direct attack."[15] More importantly, from September 1998 U.S.-Japan security cooperation extended to joint research on missile defense (MD) technology. Japan's decision regarding MD was prompted by North Korea's test firing of a Taepodong-1 missile in August, which passed over Japanese territory.[16] For China, however, the U.S.-Japan cooperation on MD was one of the most sensitive issues. China regarded it as an attempt to nullify the offensive capabilities of its own missile system and to counter any means China might have of coercing Taiwan.[17] From the Chinese point of view, the MD cooperation must have seemed more serious than the revision of the U.S.-Japan Defense Cooperation Guidelines in 1997.

In sum, the United States had direct access to North Korea in the 1990s and pursued major deals between the two sides. In the first half of the 1990s, South Korea and Japan were by and large excluded from the U.S. approach toward North Korea. In the late 1990s, the trilateral security cooperation achieved through the TCOG and the preparation of the Perry report reached an unprecedented level. But it is notable that South Korea and Japan differed in the breadth of security that each professed. South Korea continued to focus exclusively on the North Korean nuclear and missile programs, whereas Japan tried to proactively broaden its security policy, taking into account the China factor as well as the North Korean issue.

Divergence and Cooperation in a Multilateral Context in the Post-9/11 Era

After his inauguration in 1998, President Kim Dae-jung achieved a certain degree of success in inducing North Korea to open up to the South. The opening up of Mount Geumgang to South Korean tourists in 1998 was the result of Kim's efforts to develop inter-Korean relations; the inter-Korean summit of June 2000 was followed by the launch of the Gaesong Industrial Complex project two months later. However, the terrorist attacks of September 11, 2001, had an enormous impact throughout the world, including on the Korean peninsula. The United States concentrated its security strategy on terrorists and so-called rogue states, among which it included North Korea. The Nuclear Posture Review (NPR), which was submitted to the U.S. Congress on December 31, 2001, stated that North Korea was posing threats to the United States and its allies and that the U.S. government needed contingency plans for the use of nuclear weapons.[18] In his State of the Union address in January 2002, President George W. Bush branded Iraq, Iran, and North Korea the "axis of evil." In a speech delivered at the West Point in June that year, Bush strongly suggested the possibility of a preemptive attack against terrorists and dictators. Indeed, the National Security Strategy

(NSS), published by the White House in September, declared that the United States would seek out terrorist threats in advance and use all possible means to destroy them.[19] It became obvious that North Korea was one of the potential targets of this security strategy.

More than any other state, North Korea took the new U.S. security strategy seriously. Apparently recognizing the significance of the NPR and the NSS, the North Korean party organ *Nodong Sinmun*, on September 22, 2002, denounced the United States and analyzed the direction of the U.S. security strategy. According to the newspaper's analysis, the United States had adopted a new strategy that differed from its old deterrence strategy in order to cope with the new threats posed by terrorists and rogue states. The North Korean analysis was quite accurate, and it was accompanied by Pyongyang's growing perception of threat. Notably, in the wake of the U.S. invasion of Iraq in 2003, North Korea declared a policy of "nuclear deterrence" for the first time in June that year.[20] This was a bold declaration for a state that had yet to conduct a nuclear test. At that time, the U.S.-China-DPRK tripartite talks concerning the North Korean nuclear issue were in progress and the Six-Party Talks were under preparation; thus, many observers overlooked the significance of North Korea's declaration, regarding it as a negotiating tactic. But the declaration was the result of a careful assessment of its security environment. Afterward, North Korea consistently argued that it could not accept U.S. denuclearization demands, saying that Iraq was invaded due to its absence of deterrent power.

The so-called second nuclear crisis, from 2002 to 2004, occurred in this context—the conflict between the new U.S. security strategy, including the use of preemptive attacks, and North Korea's perception of a U.S. threat and its determination to continue its nuclear program. The trigger for this nuclear crisis was North Korea's admission that it had a uranium enrichment program. In response to pressing inquiries from U.S. Assistant Secretary of State James Kelly during his visit to Pyongyang in October 2002, North Korea's first vice foreign minister, Kang Sok-ju, admitted that the country had a uranium enrichment program. Kang was quoted as saying that "the United States designated the DPRK as part of the axis of evil and is now planning a preemptive attack. We are prepared to produce further advanced weapons. The United States, which threatens to use nuclear weapons, has no right to demand that we stop our uranium enrichment program."[21] The enrichment program violated many agreements that were still theoretically valid but in fact were on the verge of collapse at that time. They included North Korea's obligations under the NPT, which it had signed in 1985, the Joint Declaration on the Denuclearization of the Korean Peninsula of 1991, its safeguards agreement with the IAEA of 1992, and the Geneva Agreed Framework of 1994.

Unlike the direct, bilateral approach it had used to deal with the first nuclear crisis, the United States chose a multilateral approach this time. This resulted in a sharp turn from the Clinton administration's direct access to North Korea, which was based on trilateral coordination in the security triangle, particularly through the TCOG. Washington refused North Korea's request for bilateral talks, although the second crisis erupted in a bilateral context. The reason for this refusal was that the Bush administration did not want to exhaust itself while it was waging war in Iraq. It apparently tried to lock North Korea in with the consultation with its allies South Korea and Japan and with the help of China and Russia, rather than once again struggling alone with the rogue state's destabilizing behavior. In particular, it took into account China's potential to negotiate a resolution of the crisis. Knowing that China would want to avoid a military conflict breaking out on the Korean peninsula, the Bush administration expected China to play an active role in persuading its old ally North Korea to cooperate.[22] The result was the Six-Party Talks of 2003–08, between China, the United States, Russia, Japan, and the two Koreas, with China in the chair.[23]

After two years of negotiations, the Six-Party Talks issued the Joint Statement on September 19, 2005. This contained some significant points, including the verifiable denuclearization of the Korean peninsula, abiding by the principles of the UN Charter, the promotion of economic assistance to North Korea, the establishment of peace and stability in Northeast Asia, and application of the principle of action for action. But the Bush administration's North Korea policy during the Six-Party Talks remained coercive, and the North still did not trust the United States. This resulted in a vicious circle of U.S. sanctions and North Korean defiance. After the U.S. authorities froze North Korean funds held by the Banco Delta Asia in Macau, Pyongyang carried out its first nuclear test in 2006. Deadlock over the question of the authenticity and completeness of North Korea's declaration of its nuclear activities was accompanied by a second test in 2009.[24] It is interesting to note that the vicious circle regarding the nuclear issue at the Six-Party Talks coincided with the alternation of sanctions and defiance with regard to Iran's uranium enrichment program at the P5+1 negotiations.[25]

In the multilateral negotiations, the positions of the United States and North Korea remained extremely divisive. China's most notable contribution was its effort to bring the United States and North Korea together, particularly after the eruption of the second nuclear crisis in 2002. South Korea was a nodal point where information on each state's views was collected. Russia played an important role in drawing up the 2005 Joint Statement. When the United States and North Korea were sharply divided over the definition of denuclearization, Russia suggested that the participants refer to the 1991 Joint Declaration on the Denucle-arization of the Korean Peninsula, which had been signed by the two Koreas. Despite Chinese, South Korean, and Russian mediation efforts, the negotiations were eventually wrecked by key divisions between the United States and North Korea.

What did these multilateral negotiations mean for the security tri-angle? From their outset in 2003, the negotiations obviously changed the relationship between the United States, Japan, and South Korea. Where the issue of North Korea was concerned, it put the three states on an equal footing in more than a simply formal sense. But the three states revealed differences: South Korea's active engagement, Japan's adherence to the abduction issue, and the United States' mixed approach of engagement and coercion. The differences revolved not merely around the question of how to deal with North Korea but also on the ways in which the North Korean nuclear issue was factored into each state's broader security and military strategy.

In the Six-Party Talks in the 2000s the South was an indepen-dent, constructive player, which tried to mediate between the other participants. During the drafting process of the 2005 Joint Statement, the South Korean representative acted as the nodal point where information concerning the other five states' preferences and interests was gathered and disseminated.[26] It was in South Korea's interest to play this role because it had such a high stake in the denuclearization of the peninsula. Also, the policy consistency between the two progressive administrations of Kim Dae-jung and Roh Moo-hyun made this engagement possible.

Japan also substantially changed its approach in the multilateral context. At the Six-Party Talks, Japan frequently insisted on discuss-ing the issue of the abduction of Japanese nationals by North Korean agents during the Cold War. This issue had already emerged in the early 1990s and served to complicate the Japan-North Korea normaliza-tion talks. The Japanese had long hoped to achieve a breakthrough on this issue, and thus Prime Minister Koizumi Junichiro visited Pyongyang in September 2002.[27] But his visit actually had the opposite outcome. Although Kim Jong Il admitted that the abductions had taken place and expressed his apologies during his meeting with Koizumi, and in their joint statement, the Pyongyang Declaration, the two leaders pledged to cooperate in diplomatic, economic, and security affairs, the Koizumi visit caused Japan to reverse its policy on North Korea.[28] When North Korea returned five abductees to Japan in October that year, it had the effect of intensifying public fury about the absence of information concerning the many other alleged abductees. Given this situation, the Koizumi cabinet made it clear that it would not be able to provide economic aid to North Korea.[29] Koizumi's unexpected second visit to Pyongyang in May 2004 did nothing to alleviate the public's fury. Although the prime minister returned home with several agreements under his belt, including a promise that the children of abductees would be returned, public anger was not only targeted at North Korea but extended to the Japanese government.[30] In one example, the father of the youngest abductee, Yokota Megumi, said that he felt betrayed by his own government.[31]

The abduction issue tarnished Japanese relations with North Korea, and for that reason, the sanctions subsequently imposed by Japan were indiscriminate.[32] In May 2003, the Japanese Diet passed the War-Contingency Laws that were intended to facilitate cooperation between U.S. and Japanese armed forces and to permit certain domestic measures in the event of an emergency. These laws were prepared long before the abduction issue emerged; however, in view of the timing, the deterioration in relations caused by the abduction issue must have had an impact on the legislation. In February 2004, the Diet passed a revised version of the Foreign Exchange and Foreign Trade Law that imposed trade sanctions on Pyongyang and banned remittances to North Korea by Chongryon, the pro-North Korea organization in Japan.[33] When North Korea conducted a ballistic missile test and a nuclear test in 2006, Japan, along with the United States, played a key role in the imposition of sanctions on Pyongyang by the UN Security Council (for the UN resolutions, see Table 8.2, page 178). On top of the international sanctions, in January 2007 the Japanese government proposed a revision of the Customs Law that was designed to curb illegal trade with North Korea and cut off the flow of funds from Chongryon.[34] More importantly, even when the Six-Party Talks began to make some progress in February, the Japanese government refused to join the other four participants in providing heavy fuel oil to North Korea.[35] In other words, the spirit of engagement at the Six-Party Talks was incompatible with Japan's punitive approach toward North Korea.

Whereas Japan's sanctions-oriented approach toward North Korea was not followed by other participants in the Six-Party Talks, Japan was free to proactively strengthen its military cooperation with the United States. In response to North Korea's nuclear tests and missile

Table 8.2. UN Security Council Resolutions on North Korea

July 15, 2006, UNSC resolution 1695
—responds to ballistic missile test (July 4, 2006)
—does not invoke Chapter VII of the UN Charter, in line with request of China and Russia
—bans sale of material or technology that would serve North Korea's weapons program
—calls on North Korea to suspend ballistic missile program and commits to moratorium on missile launching
—calls upon North Korea to rejoin the Six-Party Talks

October 14, 2006, UNSC resolution 1718
—under Chapter VII, Article 41 of the UN Charter
—responds to North Korea's first nuclear test (October 9, 2006)
—prohibits North Korea from conducting future nuclear tests or launching a ballistic missile
—urges immediate return to the negotiating table
—bans imports and exports to North Korea, and imposes assets freeze and travel ban
—prohibits imports of luxury goods
—monitoring mechanism: committee

June 12, 2009, UNSC resolution 1874
—under Chapter VII, Article 41 of the UN Charter
—responds to the second nuclear test (May 25, 2009) "in violation and flagrant disregard" of the previous resolution
—strengthens 1718, and imposes sanctions on additional goods, persons, and entities
—calls on states to inspect and destroy any cargo in violation of sanctions and to limit financial transfers
—expands arms embargo
—urges immediate return to the negotiating table
—monitoring mechanism: committee assisted by seven-member expert panel

January 22, 2013, UNSC resolution 2087
—under Chapter VII, Article 41 of the UN Charter
—responds to rocket launch (Eunha 3) (December 12, 2012) violating the two previous resolutions
—calls on North Korea to completely abandon nuclear programs in verifiable and irreversible way and to join Six-Party Talks
—notes states' rights to seize and destroy materials suspected of violating sanctions
—reiterates travel bans on suspected persons
—monitoring mechanism: no new one

March 7, 2013, UNSC resolution 2094
—responds to the third nuclear test (February 12, 2012)
—calls on North Korea to completely abandon its nuclear programs in a verifiable and irreversible way
—calls for a resumption of the Six-Party Talks
—makes it harder for North Korea to access hard cash and technical equipment (strengthens existing sanctions)
—calls for states to inspect and detain any suspect cargo and shipments
—expands list of names and luxury goods
—monitoring mechanism: calls to update the list of sanctions

March 2, 2016, UNSC resolution 2270
—responds to the fourth nuclear test (January 6, 2016) and a ballistic missile launch (February 7, 2016)
—calls on North Korea to abandon all nuclear weapons and suspend activities related to ballistic missile program
—targets proliferation networks to limit the ability to smuggle and evade sanctions
—imposes new cargo inspection and maritime procedures
—imposes sectoral sanctions targeting North Korea's exports of mineral resources
—imposes new financial sanctions targeting North Korea's banks and assets
—includes a new list of names of people, agencies, and vessels

Source: "UN Documents for DPRK," in Security Council Report. http://www.securitycouncilreport.org/un-documents/dprk-north-korea/; accessed May 9, 2016.

firings, Japan consistently adhered to MD cooperation. This cooperation bore fruit in December 2007 when Japan's Maritime Self-Defense Force (MSDF) destroyer *Kongo* shot down a ballistic missile by using the Aegis detecting and tracking tool.[36]

MD cooperation was accompanied by, and associated with, military information sharing between the allies. At the 2+2 security conference in May 2007 (talks held between the U.S. secretaries of state and defense and their Japanese counterparts), the two sides agreed to establish a General Security of Military Information Agreement (GSOMIA), which would allow the exchange of top military information. The GSOMIA that was signed on August 10 covered operational intelligence, training information, and technical data. In line with this agreement, the Air Self-Defense Force began linking its early warning radar networks to the U.S. 5th Air Force at Yokota Air Base. In return, Japan was able to get access to information on both North Korean ballistic missiles and Chinese aerial military activities collected by U.S. reconnaissance satellites and air patrols.[37] Such systematic information sharing was a requirement of effective cooperation in the MD system. In a similar vein, Japan authorized the use of its space program for military purposes. The Diet passed the revised version of the Basic Law on Space in May 2008.[38] It should be noted here that Japan had already launched three military satellites starting in 2003, five years before this law was passed. The purpose of these satellites must have been to counter not only North Korea's ballistic missiles but also China's assertive military use of its own space program.[39]

To sum up, the security triangle in the post-9/11 era, specifically during the Six-Party Talks from 2003 to 2008, revealed a subtle disharmony in relation to the North Korea issue. South Korea was the most willing to engage with the North, the approach of the Bush administration was one of engagement in negotiations within the framework of its coercive security strategy, and Japan adopted consistently punitive measures. The lack of coordination within the security triangle, along with China's and Russia's lenient attitudes toward North Korea, hindered the effectiveness of the talks, while at the same time it opened up a new chapter in Japan's military cooperation with the United States.

Institutionalization of Military Cooperation

After the Six-Party Talks reached deadlock in 2008, North Korea's behavior became more provocative, and this contributed to solidifying the U.S.-Japan-ROK triangle again. Pyongyang's continued nuclear tests in May 2009, February 2013, and January 2016, and the test firings of ballistic missiles, alerted all three states to the threat posed by North Korean weapons of mass destruction (WMDs). When North Korea sank a South Korean naval corvette, the *Cheonan*, in March 2010 and shelled the island of Yeonpyeong in November that year, military cooperation in the security triangle reached an unparalleled level. With North Korea's fourth nuclear test in 2016, South Korea and Japan, after a standoff over the comfort women issue from 2013 to 2015, geared up the level of bilateral cooperation.

Limited, cautious military cooperation between Japan and South Korea can be traced back to the 1990s. In the years after the two states held their first defense ministerial meeting in 1994, the ROK navy and the Japanese MSDF conducted a number of exchange visits. In August 1999, the two sides conducted their first joint search and rescue exercise near Jeju Island.[40] However, more than any other North Korean provocation, the sinking of the *Cheonan* and the artillery attack on Yeonpyeong in 2010 caused closer military cooperation between South Korea, the United States, and Japan than ever before. At the Security Consultative Meeting (SCM) held in October 2010, South Korea and the United States agreed to establish the Extended Deterrence Policy Committee (EDPC).[41] At the trilateral foreign ministerial meeting in Washington on December 6, 2010, Hillary Rodham Clinton of the United States, Seiji Maehara of Japan, and Kim Sung-hwan of South Korea issued a trilateral statement in which they stressed not only the two alliances but also a "partnership" between Japan and South Korea with the purpose of maintaining peace and stability in Asia.[42] To be sure, North Korea was the factor that made the three states commit to common security.

The United States immediately tried to turn the emerging momentum of trilateral military cooperation into an institutional arrangement. This was hinted at a speech to a Senate hearing on March 1, 2011, given by Kurt Campbell, assistant secretary of state for Asia Pacific affairs. He was quoted as saying that "institutionalization of trilateral cooperation will be an important focus of U.S. diplomatic efforts in the coming year." Recalling the trilateral statement of December 2010, Campbell stressed the necessity of doing this not only to cope with North Korea's destabilizing behavior but also to shape a new regional strategic environment.[43] No doubt the United States viewed the trilateral cooperation in a much broader context than did South Korea. On June 21–22, 2012, the United States led the first joint ROK-U.S.-Japan naval exercise in international waters south of Jeju Island. The exercise was, according to the U.S. command, intended to deter the threat posed by North Korea's long-range missiles and its submarine operations. The Chinese expressed their disapproval of the exercise in a carefully worded statement by a Foreign Ministry spokesman who said that "the Asia-Pacific states should do something that may enhance peace and security in the Korean peninsula and in Northeast Asia, but should not do the opposite things."[44]

The most distinctive development in Japan-South Korea security affairs was an admittedly failed attempt to reach two military agreements on June 29, 2012: a GSOMIA and an Acquisition and Cross-Servicing Agreement (ACSA). Owing to domestic opposition in South Korea amid the dispute over the historical issues, the two sides called off the agreements, which had been in preparation since January 2011, just an hour before they were due to be signed. The GSOMIA would have boosted the sharing of information about North Korea, whereas the ACSA was designed to enhance mutual cooperation in services and supplies in the event of overseas peacekeeping operations. If the two agreements had been concluded, South Korea, in particular, would have had another source of much-needed information about North Korea's missiles, antisubmarine warfare, and minesweeping operations, collected by Japanese satellites, Aegis ships, and early warning and antisubmarine aircraft.[45] Japan would have secured an extra channel for human intelligence and timely information on North Korean missile trajectories. Indeed, when North Korea launched the Eunha-3 long-range rocket in April 2012, Japan desperately needed real-time radar data from the Korean Aegis ship *Sejongdaewang*.[46] In this respect, the Japanese were extremely enthusiastic about the GSOMIA, and thus Foreign Minister Genba Koichiro called it the "first full-fledged attempt at defense cooperation between the two neighbors" and a "historic event" if signed.[47]

South Korea had already concluded GSOMIA-type agreements with twenty-two other states, and the Government Legislative Agency in Seoul did not envisage any security problems or financial issues that would prevent such an agreement with Japan. But public opinion in South Korea was resolutely opposed to any attempt at military cooperation with Japan. Civic groups and politicians fiercely criticized the agreement as a secret deal with a former colonial power. Many newspapers, regardless of their ideological orientation, denounced the GSOMIA on the grounds that it would pave the way for an expansion of Japan's military ambitions. In the face of this domestic criticism, President Lee made a surprise visit to the Dokdo islets in August 2012. This visit was apparently intended to boost the president's declining popularity given Dokdo's symbolic significance as a focus of Korean nationalism.

As the North Korean threat escalated, South Koreans felt the need for trilateral security cooperation. North Korea's third nuclear test in February 2013 shocked the entire international community, South Korea in particular. After this, few South Koreans believed that the North Korean nuclear issue could be solved diplomatically, especially through the Six-Party Talks.[48] In the midst of this gloomy atmosphere, North Korea started insisting on negotiations over nuclear arms control.[49] Pyongyang's subsequent provocative statements, including the ending of the sixty-year long Armistice Agreement, led the newly inaugurated Park administration to take a principled approach toward North Korea. The new administration's "trust-building process" was based on a spirit of strict reciprocity. At the same time, South Korea accelerated the establishment of its own defense system for deterring North Korean WMDs—the Kill Chain and the Korea Air and Missile Defense System—while continuing to expand its military cooperation with the United States and Japan. In August 2013, South Korea, along with Japan, participated in a U.S.-led multinational training exercise off Hawaii. The exercise tested various forms of communication and interoperability between the United States, South Korea, and Japan, in a way that had not been seen for decades.[50]

North Korea's third nuclear test in 2013, and its increasing threats, had a certain degree of impact on South Korean public opinion regarding the sharing of military information with Japan. By September 2013, one poll indicated that 60.4 percent of the public considered a GSOMIA to be necessary, compared with 44.3 percent in July 2012. However, after Prime Minister Abe Shinzo paid a controversial visit to the Yasukuni shrine, the support for information sharing dropped to 50.7 percent in January 2014.[51]

Certainly, Japan's provocations over the historical issues limited the ROK government's forthcoming attitude to the institutionalization of military cooperation with Japan. As symbolic for the historical animosity, the Park administration that took office in February 2013 refused to hold summit with the Abe cabinet that had been inaugurated in December 2012. It was not until November 2015 that the first Park-Abe summit occurred, on the occasion of the ROK-China-Japan trilateral summit held in Seoul (see chapter 7). Amid the standoff on the comfort women issue particularly, China apparently employed a wedging strategy regarding ROK's relations with Japan and more broadly in the security triangle. Chinese president Xi Jinping's speech at Seoul National University on July 4, 2014, held on the occasion of his visit to Seoul, stressed the sweat-and-blood collaboration between Chinese and Korean people against the Japanese militarist aggression.[52] South Korea's hedging toward China, partly affected by Beijing's wedging strategy and partly motivated by Seoul's need to denuclearize North Korea, culminated with President Park's appearance at the Chinese military parade commemorating the Seventieth V-Day in Beijing in September 2015.

Amid the deteriorating partnership between its allies because of the historical issues, the United States made efforts to institutionalize information sharing between them. Since the United States had already signed a GSOMIA with South Korea in September 1987 and one with Japan in August 2007, any form of information sharing between Japan and South Korea, even if it fell short of a GSOMIA, would inevitably enable trilateral information sharing. One possible solution would be information sharing via the United States, an idea that would not incite so much domestic criticism in South Korea over military cooperation with Japan. As part of the groundwork for this, the two sides issued a joint fact sheet after the ROK-U.S. summit on April 25, 2014, in Seoul. The fact sheet insisted that trilateral information cooperation would contribute to a "comprehensive and cooperative response against North Korean threats."[53] With the ROK president's backing, some form of trilateral information sharing became an important item on the agenda of the security triangle. At the U.S.-Japan-ROK defense ministers' meeting held in Singapore in May, they agreed to set up a working group on a trilateral arrangement. Finally, on December 29, the three states signed the Trilateral Information Sharing Arrangement (TISA).[54]

The 2014 TISA differed in terms of its legal standing from the proposed GSOMIA of 2012. Whereas the latter was supposed to be a kind of treaty that needed ratification by the legislature in both sides, the TISA was an arrangement between the military authorities of the two governments and thus was not legally binding. The TISA did not allow direct exchanges of military information between South Korea and Japan. In order to placate the domestic audience, the ROK government stressed that information would not be handed over directly to the Japanese military authorities. Furthermore, the TISA stated that only information related to North Korea's nuclear and missile threat should be shared. This was intended to forestall criticism in South Korea that information sharing would heighten tension with neighbors such as China.[55] It should be noted that information sharing through the United States would not allow the flow of real-time data, thus preventing MD cooperation between the three states. This may have alleviated, to some extent, South Korean worries that they were being entrapped into joining the U.S.-led MD system.

The content of the TISA was not so different from the aborted GSOMIA. The information sharing was the same, covering as it did "oral, visual, electronic, magnetic, or documentary form, within the definitions of information covered by existing bilateral information sharing agreements."[56] Moreover, many observers in South Korea expressed their continued concern that the TISA would be the first step toward a GSOMIA, which would eventually allow exchanges of all the real-time data necessary for an MD system. There was a reason for this concern, as the U.S.-led MD system was designed not only to deter the immediate threat from North Korea but also to carry out surveillance of Chinese and Russian missile systems.[57] In this sensitive strategic environment, South Korea is faced with a dilemma that is reflected in various alliance theories. South Korea needs accurate, timely information to cope with the North Korean threat, but it may find itself obliged to commit more than it originally intended. The cost of this overcommitment would be the possibility of unintentionally antagonizing neighbors such as China and Russia.[58] Conversely, if it does not cooperate fully, South Korea will not be able to take full advantage of its membership in the security triangle, and may have to face the increasing threat from North Korea alone—whether it is a direct nuclear threat or a nuclear-backed conventional provocation. Recognizing this dilemma, South Korea has tried to limit the TISA to military information concerning North Korea only.

Japan's attitude to this trilateral information sharing arrangement was most accommodating and welcoming. Right after the signing, defense minister Nakatani Gen stated, "The pact is meaningful to heighten the security of our country, the United States and South Korea."[59] Japan had long been working with the United States on the development of an MD system, so the two countries were willing to accommodate South Korea's wishes, apparently expecting the TISA to develop into a comprehensive agreement for the exchange of military information. Not surprisingly, North Korea registered a strong protest against the TISA. *Nodong Sinmun* called it "an attempt to be the hegemon in the Asia-Pacific region."[60]

The trilateral military cooperation, despite its newness, was not yet full-fledged. This was particularly because South Korea remained suspicious of Japan's intentions. South Korean concerns focused on Japan's initiatives to revise its traditional defense-centered policy. On July 1, 2014, the Abe cabinet reached a "Cabinet Decision on the Development of Seamless Security Legislation to Ensure Japan's Survival and Protect Its People." This reinterpreted the Japanese constitution in a way that would permit collective self-defense.[61] It would allow the SDF to use force not only in the event of an armed attack against Japan itself but also in the event of an armed attack against an ally.[62] On the basis of this decision, the Abe cabinet worked with the Obama administration on the revision of the U.S.-Japan Guidelines for Defense Cooperation, which had last been revised in 1997. The guidelines, which were finalized at the 2+2 meeting held in Washington on April 30, 2015, highlight the *global* nature of the present U.S.-Japan alliance. Whereas in the 1997 version, the scope of the defense cooperation was limited to areas surrounding Japan, the new guidelines expand the scope of cooperation and remove the geographical limits on SDF operations. Furthermore, the new guidelines stipulate that in the event of armed attacks on foreign countries that have close ties with Japan, SDF operations would involve the use of force.[63] In response to these moves by Japan, the South Korean government made it clear that no Japanese collective self-defense operations would be allowed in the Korean Theater of Operations (KTO). In the event of a contingency equivalent to war, the commander of the ROK-U.S. Combined Forces will conduct operations to repel North Korean armed forces in the air, on land, and at sea in the KTO. This mention of the KTO was intended to prevent Japan's collective self-defense and U.S.-Japan joint cooperation from overruling the ROK-U.S. Combined Forces Command.[64] In this context, when Japan enacted a set of security laws in September 2015, South Korean President Park Geun-hye urged the Japanese government to be transparent in their implementation.[65] In this vein, the ROK foreign ministry stressed that South Korea "will not tolerate" Japan's practice of collective self-defense on the Korean peninsula without its prior consent of the territorial state.[66]

South Korea's cautious stance on military collaboration has not been limited to its military cooperation with Japan but has been extended to its position on the possibility of the U.S. deployment of the Terminal High Altitude Area Defense (THAAD) system on Korean territory. Despite U.S. denial, the THAAD has been viewed as a means to not only counter North Korean missiles but also to deter Chinese and Russian missile capability. Thus, all three states—North Korea, China, and Russia—have expressed their opposition to the deployment on the ground that THAAD poses a new type of threat to their security. In particular, China has pressed South Korea to refuse the United States permission to deploy the system on the Korean peninsula. Concerned about the damaging effect on its relations with an important trading partner, South Korea has been reluctant to express an opinion on this issue.[67] South Korea's attitude has contrasted with Japan's continued efforts to deepen all forms of cooperation with the United States, including MD cooperation.

However, North Korea's fourth nuclear test on January 6, 2016, made South Korea's view proactive on military cooperation with the United States and Japan. North Korea's provocative test removed Seoul's aforementioned concern and enhanced the possibility of the THAAD deployment on Korean territory. A few days after the North's nuclear test, President Park stated that the government would decide the deployment purely on the basis of military perspective. This was the first time that the highest authority in South Korea mentioned the possibility of the deployment. After North Korea's fifth nuclear test on September 9, South Korea finally decided to allow the deployment of THAAD on the Korean soil. In the same vein, the South Korean defense ministry declared that it would set up a new military information network between the ROK, the United States, and Japan by the end of 2016. With the establishment of the network, South Korea would exchange real-time data with the two, and thus the ROK military would be incorporated into the U.S.-led MD system eventually.[68]

To be sure, North Korea's nuclear ambitions have resulted in a vicious circle of military confrontation on the Korean peninsula over the past decade. North Korea's destabilizing behavior backed up by its development of nuclear weapons has led to the increasing U.S.-ROK cooperation in the realm of extended deterrence,[69] enhancement of the global role of the U.S.-Japan alliance, and the development of U.S.-Japan-ROK military cooperation.

Conclusion

The security triangle persists in the post–Cold War era because of the increasing threat posed by North Korea's nuclear advancement. But persistence does not mean consistency. The security triangle has experienced ups and downs, and these fluctuations have been largely due to global changes. The U.S. war on terror since 9/11 has had an enormous impact on the security triangle in East Asia as well. The U.S. security strategy has focused on deterring terrorists and "rogue states," including North Korea. With the passage of time, U.S. security strategy in the Obama administration has gradually rebalanced, shifting its focus from Europe to the Asia Pacific region, where China is the prime reference of security and insecurity. In line with this change, the United States has recently made efforts to gear up its military cooperation with its allies in Asia Pacific—for example, the 2014 TISA, the 2015 revision of the U.S.-Japan Guidelines for Defense Cooperation, and U.S.-Japan-

Australia trilateral joint statement and their joint military exercises in 2015. Apparently, Pyongyang, in view of China's unwillingness to abandon it amid increasing U.S.-Chinese rivalry, has continued to ignore the two powers' firm opposition to its nuclear defiance. In response, Washington is making more efforts to institutionalize the trilateral military cooperation.

Within the security triangle, South Korea's status has changed over the last few decades. The enhancement of South Korea's economic and diplomatic power has brought about a change in its standing. In particular, South Korea's relationship with Japan is less asymmetrical: no longer a recipient-donor relationship. On the security front, South Korea plays a role that is commensurate with its economic power and diplomatic standing. Specifically, South Korea's new standing in burden sharing has made itself an independent and active player in dealing with North Korea. As shown in the KEDO case, South Korea was the largest contributor, followed by Japan and the United States. In preparing the Perry report and implementing it, trilateral coordination was the working principle, as seen in the TCOG, although the United States was the prime mover. At the Six-Party Talks, South Korea was an active partner and mediator of facilitating a consensus. In response to North Korea's increasing nuclear threat, South Korea has independently developed its missile defense system, such as the Kill Chain and the Korea Air and Missile Defense.

Meanwhile, one important development has occurred in the role of Japan. In the Cold War era, Japan was a core ally of the United States, especially where the defense of the Western Pacific was concerned. While it expanded its strategic aid around the world and enhanced its own defense, Japan went along with the U.S. containment strategy. In the post–Cold War era, the U.S.-Japan alliance is not only the foundation of both states' security and prosperity but also a global partnership. The change in Japan's role is exemplified by the widening scope of its security concerns. As set out in the 2015 Guidelines for Defense Cooperation, Tokyo's concerns have changed from ensuring the stability of the area surrounding Japan to being involved in international security affairs in such increasingly contentious areas as the East China Sea, the South China Sea, Iraq, and Syria. For example, in coping with the gradually assertive China in the South China Sea, Japan contributes to solidifying a "minilateral" architecture led by the United States and joined by Australia.[70] In this regard, Japan is a nodal point of weaving and connecting the two different and overlapping security triangles in the Asia Pacific: the U.S.-Japan-ROK triangle and the U.S.-Japan-Australia triangle.

9

Conclusions

The security triangle in East Asia demonstrates that a partnership within a hierarchy inevitably entails as a built-in property the likelihood of disputes between the allies of the dominant power (who are called "partners"). This study has analyzed why these disputes arise and how the states in the triangle manage to live together despite them. Although the study has focused on one particular case in one region, the findings may have implications for intra-alliance politics in general and other cases of U.S.-led alliances in the Asia Pacific in particular. In the partnership within a hierarchy, disputes arise surrounding two issues, burden sharing and partnership commitment. The partnership engaged in the dispute is stabilized when the dominant power effectively intervenes between its allies to resolve it. The intervention may take the form of superpower coercion, or preaching, or businesslike mediation, or legalistic approach, or nonintervention. The method of intervention depends on how relevant the dispute is to the interests of the dominant power and to the maintenance of the security triangle.

Partnership within Hierarchy: Underexplored Intra-Alliance Politics

One might assume that the dominant power in a hub-and-spoke alliance structure, in this case the United States, would be able to define the role and status of each of its allies and would not need to intervene in any business between its partners, in this case Japan and South Korea. But this is not true. There are at least two rank systems in the security triangle under investigation: one between the dominant power and its two allies, and the other between these allies. This hybrid form of hierarchy breeds a discrepancy between official relations between individual sovereign states, on the one hand, and unofficial rank based on different

189

capabilities, on the other. This situation creates a host of differing, conflicting expectations and preferences, which eventually develop into disputes, particularly between the partners anchored by the dominant power. The disputes between partners invite intervention by the dominant power. Whether this intervention takes place depends on whether it is in line with the dominant power's own strategic objective, whether it is likely to yield the desired benefits, and whether it can ensure the security of the allies.

Just as in other forms of alliance politics, the two elements that sustain the partnership within the hierarchy examined in this study are burden sharing (i.e., a capable partner's assuming a share of the dominant power's burden of supporting a less capable partner) and commitment (i.e., the dominant power's assurances vis-à-vis its allies' contribution to mutual defense and maintenance of a red line, and diplomatic and military cooperation between partners). With regard to these elements, there is usually a consensus between the dominant power and its allies through close communication. But the partners, particularly the capable partner, do not feel the need for, and are not obliged to enter into, any kind of agreement on burden sharing or an alliance-type commitment with each other. Given this problem of informality, the dominant power is likely to worry that disputes between the partners over the burden sharing and commitment issues may damage its core interests and give an advantage to the enemy.

All of the serious disputes between Japan and South Korea in which the United States has intervened have pertained to burden sharing and commitment. During the Cold War, U.S. intervention worked to balance the benefits among the three parties, particularly through Japan's aid to South Korea within U.S.-framed strategic aid. The burden sharing went hand in hand with the security commitment, and the Korea clause included in U.S.-Japan joint statements repeatedly rationalized the burden sharing. In the post–Cold War era, the donor-recipient relations or the so-called security-based economic cooperation between Japan and South Korea ended, and thus asymmetry between them was substantially balanced. This change has caused the resurgence of the controversial historical issues. In the dispute over the comfort women issue in particular, the United States tried to avoid being mixed in until the Japan-ROK partnership was exhausted, as seen from 2013 to 2015. Even after the December 2015 agreement on the comfort women issue between the U.S. allies was reached, a few potentially damaging historical issues lie ahead and are likely to trouble the partnership in the future. North Korea's increasing nuclear threat continues to produce alliance commitment and consequently contributes to the persistence of the security triangle; however, it is the United States, and the two U.S.-led alliances, that links Japan and South Korea on the military front.

Shifting Reference of Security:
From the Soviet Union to China?

There is an internal logic of persistence in the security triangle that may be called the feedback effect. The feedback effect means that cooperative relations within the mechanism yield specific benefits for each member state, although in varying degrees and in asymmetrical ways, and in turn makes exit highly costly. What binds the partners together is a certain common reference of security, or insecurity, and related red lines: for example, containing the Soviet Union and deterring its protégé North Korea during the Cold War, and checking China and deterring North Korea in the post–Cold War era. Notably, the rise of China and the resulting shift in reference regarding security has accentuated the subtle differences in the security triangle. This situation differs from that which characterized the Cold War, when the security triangle stood uniformly against the Soviet Union.

The significance of China to the security triangle meant different things to each of the three member-states during the Cold War era. For the United States, China was useful for driving a wedge into the communist bloc and isolating the Soviet Union after the U.S.-China rapprochement of 1972. During the initial stage of cooperation, the United States gave China detailed military intelligence about the Soviet Union, including reconnaissance images of force deployments and related facilities, in order to establish an anti-Soviet bond.[1] Despite the utility of this bond, the United States did not develop it into a full-fledged partnership nor did it abandon its means of checking China over the issue of Taiwan. The United States gave up diplomatic relations with the Republic of China while maintaining its security alignment with Taipei. For this reason, it took seven years for Washington to establish normalized relations with Beijing after President Richard Nixon's historic visit to China. Washington managed to continue its arms sales and military assistance to Taiwan under the terms of the 1979 Taiwan Relations Act, which was passed by Congress right after the U.S.-PRC normalization.

Japan had long recognized the economic opportunities offered by China. As U.S. diplomats, particularly those in Tokyo, described it, the Japanese could not live without China. "China fever" was on the rise in Japan even before the U.S.-China rapprochement; for this reason, Nixon's sudden announcement in 1971 of his planned visit to Beijing, coming right after his national security adviser Henry Kissinger had made a clandestine visit there, was seen as a shock by the Japanese; however, the announcement was an opportunity for Japan to gain access to China. Therefore, Japan abandoned Taiwan and normalized relations with the PRC without reservation. After the brutal crackdown on the Tiananmen demonstrators in 1989, Japan walked a tightrope between condemnation of Beijing and recognition of its own interests in economic relations with China. Indeed, Japan was the first country to lift the ban on China after Tiananmen.[2]

For South Korea, China was a sworn enemy throughout the Cold War on account of the Chinese People's Liberation Army's involvement in the Korean War. The two developments that the South Koreans found most alarming were the PRC's entry into the United Nations in 1971, replacing the Republic of China on Taiwan, and the U.S.-PRC rapprochement and subsequent Sino-Japanese normalization in 1972. The abandonment of Taiwan made the South Koreans nervous, and at the same time emboldened North Korea. The North Koreans became proactive in their peace initiatives directed at Japan and the United States as well as South Korea. Paradoxically, these developments made South Korea anxious to gain access to China. In 1983, taking advantage of the resolution of a hijacking incident when a Chinese civilian aircraft made an emergency landing on South Korean territory, Seoul granted China permission for its civilian flights to fly through the South Korean flight information region and started nonpolitical exchanges with China.[3]

The end of the Cold War brought about a sea change. China now is neither a Soviet Union nor a China under Mao. China has changed and grown up, particularly in terms of its material power. In 2009, China became the largest trading state in the world, surpassing Germany; in 2010, the Chinese economy overtook that of Japan, and it is said that in 2020, China's economy will exceed that of the United States in terms of purchasing power parity.[4] China is now adopting an assertive security strategy that is commensurate with its material power. In this respect, there are differing views on China. Based on Mearsheimer's theory that China cannot rise peacefully,[5] some observers warn of the possibility, or even the inevitability, of war between China and the United States, and they highlight the need for Washington to exercise deterrence by denial.[6] Others focus on the limited scope of China's security strategy or the fact that it is motivated by uncertainty, insecurity, and opportunism. They emphasize that the United States should create an environment in which China is able to make rational decisions.[7] One thing that they all agree on, however, is that the United States, and its ally Japan, should be aware of the danger of conflict in the Asia Pacific and be ready to employ preventive diplomacy in order to avoid a worst case scenario.

In response to China's rise, the United States has strengthened its military cooperation with Japan. According to the 2015 revision of the Defense Cooperation Guidelines, Japan's SDF may respond to attacks on U.S. forces even if Japan is not directly attacked. Furthermore, the revised guidelines extend the geographical scope of Japan's military role, from areas surrounding Japan to anywhere in the world.[8] More importantly, it is not only the United States that has changed its view of China; the perception of Japanese conservative politicians has changed dramatically in the past two decades. As an example, one leading politician, Aso Taro, remarked that China and Japan have not enjoyed good relations for the last 1,500 years.[9]

In contrast, the end of the Cold War opened new opportunities for South Korea in its diplomatic, economic, and strategic relations with China. The thaw allowed South Korea to normalize its relations with China in 1992. South Korea has invested its diplomatic energy into persuading China to cooperate in dealing with the North Korean nuclear issue, although China has adopted a dual policy—taking a lenient attitude toward North Korea's provocations while cooperating with the international community in working toward the goal of nonproliferation.[10] Since 2004, China has been South Korea's top trading partner, and the Free Trade Agreement of June 2015 should intensify their economic interdependence. It is noteworthy that the South Korean approach toward China is neither jumping on the bandwagon nor assuming a posture of primary deference to China, but rather a kind of renegotiation in the era of newly emerging order.[11] Thus, the approach, of hedging toward China, has not directly damaged Seoul's alliance with Washington.[12]

Just as important as the rise of China in the world, so has China facing the Pacific become a significant factor in the operation of the security triangle. China today differs from the Soviet Union, which vetoed all American proposals. The United States regards China both as a collaborator and a competitor, as seen in their cooperation and disagreement over the content of the UN Security Council resolutions to punish North Korea's four nuclear tests. Japan has strengthened its alliance with the United States and extended the scope of its security in order to cope with China's rise and to engage in global affairs more broadly. South Korea has employed a hedging strategy toward China in an attempt to attract Beijing's support for its North Korea policy, and China has tried to apply a wedging strategy aiming to force a division between South Korea and Japan and create a schism in the security triangle. In relation to the security triangle, the rising China today is more complex than the Soviet Union.

The Two Faces of Burden Sharing

Burden sharing is one of the most contentious issues in any example of intra-alliance politics. For example, "Burden sharing debates have always been part of NATO."[13] Likewise, burden sharing was a thorny issue in the security triangle in East Asia, particularly during the Cold War. On the one hand, the U.S.-framed burden sharing revolved around the question of how and to what extent the more capable Japan should help the weaker South Korea. There was a certain degree of convergence of interests between the United States and South Korea—that is, Japan should not remain a free rider in defense of the Far East and the Western Pacific. On the other hand, burden sharing, which is closely interconnected with commitment, has two seemingly conflicting faces— a binding effect and asymmetrical interdependence. For this reason, with the absence of a contentious burden-sharing issue between the partners in the post–Cold War era—specifically, with no aid passing between Japan and South Korea—the relationship between them has become more equal.

Both directly and indirectly, the United States requested that Japan provide South Korea with aid packages so that Washington could reduce its share of the burden of supporting South Korean economic development and military buildup. In the first half of the 1960s, burden sharing was the main motivation behind U.S. efforts to facilitate Japan-ROK normalization. In the second half of the 1960s and throughout the 1970s, the United States persuaded Japan to take on a part of burden of supporting the Southeast Asian states as well. After the fall of South Vietnam in 1975, the United States saw Japan as a crucial ally, although the Japanese did not openly use that term. Prime Minister Fukuda Takeo's initiative of 1977, known as the Fukuda Doctrine, enabled Japan to engage more deeply in Southeast Asian affairs.[14] Japan also sustained U.S. strategy in the Western Pacific through its enhanced commitment to contain the Soviet naval presence. Under the U.S.-framed burden sharing, Japan agreed to provide a new aid package to South Korea in 1983. South Korea skillfully solicited U.S. support in obtaining this aid, and the United States was only too eager to do the necessary groundwork. Certainly, South Korea's negotiating skills evolved as it, more than Japan, learned from past experience and became skillful in dealing with outstanding issues. In comparison to the normalization talks in the first half of the 1960s, the negotiations regarding Japanese aid in the early 1980s were carried out much more efficiently and adroitly by the Koreans who were adept at articulating their interests, creating an agenda, and responding to the other side's preferences and demands. South Korea made full use of the fact that the United States wanted Japan to take on a bigger share of the burden.

The burden sharing, which stemmed from differing capabilities to assume the cost of containing the Soviet Union and its protégé North Korea, made the three states asymmetrically interdependent. Because of differing capabilities and contributions, the United States expected Japan and South Korea to play different roles, and actually laid out different assignments for them. South Korea was the front line in deterring North Korea, which was backed by the Soviet Union, whereas Japan was the key ally of the United States in containing the increasingly threatening Soviet naval presence in the Western Pacific. In this situation, historical issues between Japan and South Korea, even though they caused resentment in South Korea, were suppressed and submerged. Burden sharing made the relationship between the United States, Japan, and South Korea more than just a set of two alliances; it was a trilateral bond under hierarchy.

For the dominant power, burden sharing and partnership commitment to security are interconnected. Indeed, what legitimized the burden sharing—specifically the U.S. request that Japan provide aid to South Korea, and South Korea's soliciting U.S. support to obtain the Japanese aid—was the "Korea clause" and the "new Korea clause" in the joint statements issued after the U.S.-Japan summits. The clause recognized that the security of the Republic of Korea was essential to the security of Japan. But because of different views between the three about its relevance, there was intense diplomatic activity among them concerning whether to include the clause in the joint statements and the wording of the clause.

What did the end of burden sharing, particularly the end of Japanese aid to South Korea in 1996, mean for the security triangle? It contributed to the change in the relationship between the partners. The end of South Korea's reliance on Japanese aid followed three dramatic changes on both domestic and external fronts from the end of the 1980s to mid-1990s: democratic transition, economic empowerment, and the normalization of relations with the Soviet Union and China. South Korea's graduation from aid recipient status and its entry into the OECD dissipated the previously asymmetrical relationship between South Korea and Japan. It also ended disputes between the two over such issues as the trade imbalance, the amount of aid, and the aid-defense linkage. Given this, the dispute over historical issues emerged in the early 1990s and has continued to trouble the relationship between the partners. The end of the donor-recipient relationship has certainly relaxed asymmetry between the partners, and their cooperative commitment to security, deriving from newly increasing external threat, have been based on an equal footing in dealing with North Korea at least.

The empowered South Korea tried to play a constructive role in dealing with the issue of denuclearization of North Korea, an important nonproliferation subject. South Korea became the major contributor to the construction of the light-water reactors that were provided in exchange for Pyongyang's freezing its nuclear facilities under the 1994 Geneva Agreed Framework. South Korea also became an active promoter of the Six-Party Talks from 2003 to 2008, dealing with important security issues on an equal footing with the other parties. However, amid the increasing North Korean nuclear threat, the territorial dispute and contentions over the comfort women issue have paralyzed the Japan-ROK partnership. Symbolizing the paralysis of the partnership, South Korean president Park Geun-hye and Japanese prime minister Abe Shinzo held no summits from 2013 to 2015. With the damaged partnership, South Korea refused the full-scale military information sharing in the security triangle in 2012, but accepted a minimum level of information exchange cooperation in 2014. The intervention of the United States, which felt the seriousness of the fallout, eventually helped the allies to mend their damaged partnership through the December 2015 agreement, as discussed in chapter 7.

Why Do the Historical Issues Matter Now?

The historical issues between Japan and South Korea are retroactive and retrospective, and disputes over them tend to obstruct and exhaust cooperation between the partners. The issues not only provoke emotionally charged protests but also breed distrust of each other's security posture. In one example, just one hour before the 2012 GSOMIA—the agreement on the sharing of military information—was due to be signed,

Seoul pulled out because of strong opposition from the South Korean public. South Koreans were concerned about the possible reemergence of Japanese militarism, amid the situation in which the controversy over the comfort women had yet to be resolved.

An important question is why the historical issues became so salient at this particular moment. Disputes over historical issues have different origins and backgrounds, and they follow different internal dynamics—i.e., political and social changes—in each state. The emergence of the disputes also coincided with two significant changes in the U.S.-Japan-ROK triangle: the dissipation of asymmetry based on the donor-recipient relationship between Japan and South Korea, and the divergence between the U.S.-Japan alliance and South Korea on the issue of China. These changes have created a context in which the historical issues have prevailed in the Japan-ROK relationship. Indeed, the disputes over the historical issues cannot be attributed to historical animosity alone. The ways in which the issues are raised between the two states differ from those in the Cold War period—emotionally charged protests have been replaced by demands for appropriate descriptions of Japan's actions in the past and legally based compensation.

Some scholars, including Glosserman and Snyder, identify issues of national identity and historical factors as the main obstacles to productive relations between Japan and South Korea.[15] However, disputes over historical issues not only revolve around, and reinforce different views on, past history per se but are also closely related to the above-mentioned dynamics of the security triangle. The impact of the much relaxed asymmetry between them has made the historical issues prohibitively difficult to resolve.

Diplomacy would be helpful in resolving these disputes, or compromising differences at least, if both sides were prepared to make earnest efforts, despite the emotional nature of the problem. The United States intervenes in the historical issues as it comes to feel that acrimony between allies would be detrimental to its interest and the bond of the triangle. When the comfort women issue was viewed as damaging the Japan-ROK cooperation over the North Korean nuclear threat, President Obama and the U.S. ambassadors in Tokyo and Seoul carefully but diligently engaged with the allies. The consequence was a negotiated deal between foreign ministers on December 28, 2015, in Seoul. The U.S. reluctance or delay in intervening lay in its fear of being mixed up in this highly sensitive, complex issue. What should be noted is that even after the December 2015 agreement, troubling issues lie ahead in the

Japan-South Korea relationship—such as the territorial dispute, compensation for forced labor, description of wartime history in Japanese textbooks, as well as ramifications of the comfort women issue.

The Implications for the Newly Emerging
U.S.-led Partnership in the Asia Pacific

The U.S.-Japan-ROK security triangle is a prime example of intra-alliance politics in which the dominant power leads at least two different alliances and its allies both have a stake in regional security. In the Asia Pacific, the United States has maintained alliances or cooperative relations with various states, including Australia, Thailand, the Philippines, and Pakistan, not to mention Japan and South Korea, during and since the Cold War. It has recently extended its security cooperation to Vietnam, Malaysia, Indonesia, and India in order to cope with China's assertive maritime activities in the South China Sea and to ensure the security of the Indian Ocean. But apart from Japan and South Korea, no allies of the United States in the Asia Pacific have such a history of intense cooperation and recurrent contentions. In the triangular category, the U.S.-Japan-Australia triangle is similar to the U.S.-Japan-ROK triangle; however, the former is only a decade old and now undergoing a test.

When relations between the allies of the dominant power become intense, divergent interests and expectations often give rise to contention and dispute. Unlike collective security organizations such as NATO, there are no rules governing the relationship between allies of the United States. For example, there is no institutionalized control of boundaries that each partner is forbidden to cross and no system for settling disputes. Given this situation, U.S. intervention has been crucial in resolving contention and dispute, as shown in the U.S.-Japan-ROK security triangle. Today, the U.S.-Japan-Australia security triangle, which emerged with the Trilateral Security Dialogue in 2006 and the Japan-Australia Joint Declaration of Security Cooperation in March 2007, is undergoing a test based on how differing interests and expectations may arise and develop into contentions, and how adjustments and compromises can produce a settlement. Despite pledges between Japan and Australia with regard to security cooperation, there is a significant difference between the two states. Japan has been enthusiastic about security cooperation with Australia, whereas Australia has been cautious—or at least not as enthusiastic as Japan expected it to be—in developing security relations with Japan. Their difference stems from divergent views of the Beijing regime and different economic relations with China.[16] For geopolitical reasons, Australia is not as sensitive about China's assertive behavior as Japan is; furthermore, China is now Australia's largest trading partner, having overtaken the United States.

The United States has been seriously concerned about China's land reclamation activities in the South China Sea since 2015, and for that reason has encouraged Japan and Australia to join in the U.S.-led security cooperation. For example, on May 30, 2015, the U.S. defense secretary and the Australian and Japanese defense ministers issued the Joint Statement in which they stressed the importance of maintaining the status quo in the South China Sea and said that they expected early agreement on an ASEAN-China code of conduct on the territorial disputes there. They also stated that the three states would extend security cooperation with ASEAN, through the ASEAN Defense Ministers' Meeting-Plus (ADMM-Plus) framework, and provide maritime security assistance to ASEAN. In July, the United States led joint military exercises in the Northern Territory and Queensland, Australia, in which Australian forces and officers from the Japanese GSDF participated.[17]

However, the U.S.-Japan-Australia triangle reveals that the three states have different priorities and policy preferences. The United States is interested in building a regional architecture, Japan is trying to prioritize China and regards trilateral cooperation as an instrument of deterrence, while Australia is not so concerned about countering China.[18] More importantly, as the trilateral cooperation develops into providing military assistance to the ASEAN states, differences over such issues as burden sharing and partnership commitment—not to mention differing perceptions of and approaches to China—are likely to emerge.

The U.S.-Japan-ROK security triangle also has implications for recent U.S.-led cooperation in Southeast Asia. Surrounding the South China Sea, the United States has enhanced its bilateral cooperation with ASEAN states such as the Philippines, Vietnam, Indonesia, Singapore, and Malaysia. These states are in geopolitically significant locations and have the kind of sophisticated infrastructure that may help U.S. maritime operations.[19] The Philippines and Vietnam, the states most affected by China's recent territorial claims, have conducted joint training with the United States and have lobbied ASEAN for a common position. Indeed, ASEAN has called for a common code of conduct in disputed waters in order to deescalate disputes and to prevent miscalculations by claimants of disputed territory on both sides—that is, China and ASEAN member-states. However, ASEAN has revealed its own disunity through the lack of a consensus on how to manage disputes among its members. For example, there are overlapping claims to islands, rocks, and low tide elevations in the Spratlys involving Malaysia and Vietnam, the Philippines and Malaysia, and the Philippines and Vietnam.[20] ASEAN is also divided on how to cope with China's assertive behavior. The Philippines and Vietnam have been the most proactive in raising their voices internationally, whereas Cambodia and Laos, as non-claimant states, remain ambivalent and Malaysia and Brunei are reluctant to take an active approach.[21] In this regard, as Ross correctly notes, ASEAN is "more divided today than at any time since its formation."[22]

While enhancing its security cooperation with the ASEAN states, the United States has also tried to expand the U.S.-Japan-Australia trilateral cooperation to include ASEAN in its entirety. Notably the involvement of Japan, which has a high stake in the security of sea lanes in the South China Sea, makes the security cooperation under the U.S. leadership in Southeast Asia more complex than that within the U.S.-Japan-ROK security triangle. The Japanese coast guard, as a de facto fourth branch of the Japanese military, has participated in U.S.-led multilateral antipiracy exercises in the South China Sea for the last decade. In connection with this, in 2006 Japan provided the Indonesian and Philippine coast guards with fast patrol craft.[23] In October 2014, Japanese Self-Defense Force officers observed the first U.S.-Philippine amphibious exercise since the military agreement between Washington and Manila allowing U.S. troops to be based in the Philippines was signed in April that year.[24] In May and June 2015, Japan conducted its first joint military exercise with the United States and the Philippines in the South China Sea.[25] Having engaged in this area, Japan will likely find itself involved not only in disputes with China but also in discord with other partners. Japan's cooperation with the ASEAN states, under the U.S. leadership, will be likely to complicate—and be complicated by—the overlapping claims between some ASEAN states in the Spratlys in particular.

The burden sharing issue goes along with security cooperation. The United States has provided the Philippines with US$300 million in military aid since 2001 and provided another US$40 million in 2015; this aid was intended to help modernize the Philippine military.[26] As tension rises in the South China Sea, the U.S. burden may be expected to increase, and the United States is likely to request that Japan share this burden. This prompts us to ask how far Japan is prepared to go in financing the Philippine military. Both the nature and the amount of this aid has already become a hot topic in trilateral relations between the

United States, Japan, and the Philippines. The issue of burden sharing is not limited to the Philippines but also extends to other ASEAN states.

The emerging U.S.-led partnership in the Asia Pacific differs from the U.S.-Japan-ROK triangle in terms of goals, composition, background, and geopolitics. But the lesson of the East Asian security triangle is that security cooperation within hierarchy tends to have built-in contentions and disputes. If the U.S.-Japan alliance or the U.S.-Japan-Australia triangle contemplates further military cooperation with ASEAN states such as the Philippines and Vietnam, then two problems—burden sharing and partnership commitment—should be resolved in the newly emerging partnership. Just as the question of who pays how much is an emerging burden-sharing issue, so will the question of who commits to what kind of security become a commitment issue. The turn of the Philippines to China observed in late 2016, whether temporary or long-term, signifies a challenge that arises from the game surrounding burden sharing and commitment.

Notes

Chapter 1. Introduction

1. It is noteworthy that, traditionally, Japan has been keenly aware of its status in international relations, as Kenneth B. Pyle lucidly observes: "As Japan entered the international system . . . the awareness of hierarchy as an ordering principle was bound to be unusually strong in the Japanese consciousness." See *Japan Rising: The Resurgence of Japanese Power and Purpose* (New York: Public Affairs, 2007), 107.

2. See Michael Schaller, *Altered States: The United States and Japan since the Occupation* (Oxford: Oxford University Press, 1997), 7–30.

3. Thomas J. Christensen, *Worse Than a Monolith: Alliance Politics and Problems of Coercive Diplomacy in Asia* (Princeton: Princeton University Press, 2011), 262.

4. See James Mahoney and Kathleen Thelen, eds., *Explaining Institutional Change: Ambiguity, Agency, and Power* (Cambridge: Cambridge University Press, 2010), 1–37; Orfeo Fioretos, "Historical Institutionalism in International Relations," *International Organization* 65 (Spring 2011): 367–99; and James G. Miller, *Living Systems* (New York: McGraw-Hill, 1978), 36.

5. While defining Japan-ROK relations as a "quasi-alliance," Victor Cha addresses the question of when the quasi-alliance act cooperatively or competitively. Cha's view is that this variation comes from symmetry or asymmetry between the two U.S.-led alliances in relation to fear of abandonment/entrapment. See Victor D. Cha, *Alignment Despite Antagonism: The US-Korea-Japan Security Triangle* (Stanford: Stanford University Press, 1999).

6. Glenn H. Snyder, "The Security Dilemma in Alliance Politics," *World Politics* 36, no. 4 (July 1984): 461–95, and *Alliance Politics* (Ithaca and London: Cornell University Press, 1997).

7. Cf. Brad Glosserman and Scott A. Snyder, *The Japan-South Korea Identity Clash: East Asian Security and the United States* (New York: Columbia University Press, 2015). They focus on the notion of national identity as the main obstacle to productive relations between Japan and Korea. Their book attributes the bilateral clash mostly to historical factors.

8. For the notion of persistence despite institutional changes, see John Ikenberry, *After Victory: Institutions, Strategic Restraint, and the Rebuilding of Order after Major Wars* (Princeton: Princeton University Press, 2001); James Mahoney and Kathleen Thelen, eds., *Explaining Institutional Change: Ambiguity, Agency, and Power* (Cambridge: Cambridge University Press, 2010).

9. See also Scott Snyder, "The China-Japan Rivalry: Korea's Pivotal Position." in *Cross Currents: Regionalism and Nationalism in Northeast Asia*, ed. Gi-Wook Shin and Daniel C. Sneider (Stanford: The Walter H. Shorenstein Asia-Pacific Research Center at Stanford University, 2007), 241.

10. See Shin Bongkil, *Hanjungil hyeomnyeogeu jinhwa: 3guk hyeomnyeogsamu-guk seolipgwa hyeomnyeogeu jedohwa* [Evolution of the ROK-China-Japan Cooperation: The Establishment of the Trilateral Cooperation Secretariat and the Institutionalization of Cooperation] (Seoul: Korea University Asiatic Research Institute, 2015).

Chapter 2. Partnership within Hierarchy

1. Helen Milner, "The Assumption of Anarchy in International Relations Theory: A Critique," in *Neorealism and Neoliberalism: The Contemporary Debate*, ed. David A. Baldwin (New York: Columbia University Press, 1993), 153–62.

2. Kenneth D. Bailey, *Sociology and the New Systems Theory: Toward a Theoretical Synthesis* (Albany: State University of New York Press, 1994), 51.

3. Niklas Luhmann, *Social Systems* (Stanford: Stanford University Press, 1996), 191, 395.

4. David Lake, *Hierarchy in International Relations* (Ithaca and London: Cornell University Press, 2009), 9.

5. David Kang, *East Asia before the West: Five Centuries of Trade and Tribute* (New York: Columbia University Press, 2010), 17.

6. Robert O. Keohane, *After Hegemony: Cooperation and Discord in the World Political Economy* (Princeton: Princeton University Press, 1984), 32.

7. As a classic model of hegemony, Albert Hirschman analyzes Germany's use of trade relations as a means to render target countries constrained during the period between the two world wars. The German policy was intended to increase the dependency of the target countries on Germany. See Albert O. Hirschman, *National Power and the Structure of Foreign Trade* (Berkeley: University of California Press, 1980), 34–35.

8. Glenn H. Snyder, *Alliance Politics* (Ithaca and London: Cornell University Press, 1997), 359.

9. David Kang, "Getting Asia Wrong: The Need for New Analytic Frameworks," *International Security* 27, no. 4 (2003): 57–85.

10. Evelyn Goh characterizes the post–Cold War order in East Asia as a multilayered hierarchy: the United States at the top, China and Japan in the

middle, and South Korea and ASEAN at the bottom. See *The Struggle for Order: Hegemony, Hierarchy, and Transition in Post–Cold War East Asia* (Oxford: Oxford University Press, 2013), 208–22.

11. Stephen M. Walt, *The Origins of Alliances* (Ithaca and London: Cornell University Press, 1990), 5–6.

12. Lake, *Hierarchy in International Relations*, 68–71.

13. For the analysis of asymmetrical interdependence, see Miyashita, "Gaiatsu and Japan's Foreign Aid," 695–732.

14. Sang-young Rhyu and Seungjoo Lee, "Changing Dynamics in Korea-Japan Economic Relations: Policy Ideas and Development Strategy," *Asian Survey* 46, no. 2 (2006), 195.

15. James Mahoney and Kathleen Thelen, "A Theory of Gradual Institutional Change," in *Explaining Institutional Change: Ambiguity, Agency, and Power*, ed. James Mahoney and Kathleen Thelen (Cambridge: Cambridge University Press, 2010), 11.

16. Victor D. Cha, *Alignment Despite Antagonism: The US-Korea-Japan security Triangle* (Stanford: Stanford University Press, 1999).

17. John R. Oneal, "The Theory of Collective Action and Burden Sharing in NATO," *International Organization* 44, no. 3 (Summer 1990): 379–402; Malcolm Chalmers, "The Atlantic Burden-sharing Debate: Widening or Fragmenting?" *International Affairs* 77, no. 3 (2001): 569–85; Astri Suhrke, "Burden-sharing during Refugee Emergencies: The Logic of Collective versus National Action," *Journal of Refugee Studies* 11, no. 4 (1998): 396–415.

18. See Snyder, *Alliance Politics*, 34.

19. Richard Solomon and Nigel Quinney, *American Negotiating Behavior: Wheeler-Dealers, Legal Eagles, Bullies, and Preachers* (Washington, DC: United States Institute of Peace Press, 2010), 19–45.

20. Wilsonianism has been the foundation of U.S. moralistic intervention and institution building in world affairs. Indeed President Woodrow Wilson justified not only diplomatic engagement but also military intervention. For example, President Wilson described the American decision to enter World War I as following "the principles of mankind." Cited from Kenneth W. Thompson, "Ethics and National Purpose," in *Moral Dimensions in American Foreign Policy*, ed. Kenneth W. Thompson (New Brunswick, NJ: Transaction Books, 1994), 3.

21. United States Institute of Peace, "U.S. Negotiating Behavior," Special Report 94 (October 2002), 8.

22. See Sung Chull Kim and David Kang, eds., *Engagement with North Korea: A Viable Alternative* (Albany: State University of New York Press, 2009).

23. See Juliet Eilperin, "Agreement on 'Comfort Women' Offers Strategic Benefit to U.S. in Asia-Pacific," *Washington Post*, January 9, 2015.

24. For details on the territorial dispute, see Seokwoo Lee, "Dokdo: The San Francisco Peace Treaty, International Law on Territorial Disputes, and Historical Criticism," *Asian Perspective* 35, no. 3 (July-September 2011): 361–80; Seokwoo Lee and Jon M. Van Dyke, "The 1951 San Francisco Peace Treaty

and Its Relevance to the Sovereignty over Dokdo," *Chinese Journal of International Law* 9, no. 4 (December 2010): 741–62; Kimie Hara, "50 Years from San Francisco: Re-Examination of the Peace Treaty and Japan's Territorial Problems," *Pacific Affairs* 74, no. 3 (Fall 2001): 361–82.

25. See Lisa L. Martin and Beth A. Simmons, "Theories and Empirical Studies of International Institutions," *International Organization* 52, no. 4 (Autumn 1988), 749. For general discussion on coalition building or logrolling of domestic groups and the impact on external behavior, see Jack Snyder, *Myths of Empire: Domestic Politics and International Ambition* (Ithaca and London: Cornell University Press, 1991) and Etel Solingen, *Regional Orders at Century's Dawn: Global and Domestic Influences on Grand Strategy* (Princeton: Princeton University Press, 1998).

26. Many works on the impact of domestic politics have been developed under the theoretical umbrella of the two-level game, which shows that the negotiator, that is to say, the government, sometimes tries to use domestic constraints as a tool to press the counterpart for enlarging gains. For the seminar work on this topic, see Robert Putnam, "Diplomacy and Domestic Politics: The Logic of Two-Level Games," *International Organization* 42, no. 3 (Summer 1988): 427–60.

27. See Peter F. Trumbore, "Public Opinion as a Domestic Constraint in International Negotiations: Two-Level Games in the Anglo-Irish Peace Process," *International Studies Quarterly* 42, no. 3 (September 1998): 545–65.

28. For the distribution of power in the domestic aspect of the two-level game, see Frederick W. Mayer, "Managing Domestic Differences in International Negotiations: The Strategic Use of Internal Side-Payments," *International Organization* 46, no. 4 (September 1992): 793–818; Jongryn Mo, "The Logic of Two-Level Games with Endogenous Domestic Coalitions," *Journal of Conflict Resolution* 38, no. 3 (September 1994): 402–22; Jongryn Mo, "Domestic Institutions and International Bargaining: The Role of Agent Veto in Two-Level Games," *American Political Science Review* 89, no. 4 (December 1995): 914–24; Robert J. Schmidt Jr., "International Negotiations Paralyzed by Domestic Politics: Two-Level Game Theory and the Problem of the Pacific Salmon Commission," *Environmental Law* 26, no. 1 (Spring 1996): 95–140.

29. In the 1970s and 1980s North Korean agents abducted an unknown number of Japanese nationals from Japanese territory. In response to Japanese Prime Minister Koizumi Junichiro's visits in 2002 and 2004, the North Korean leader Kim Jong Il expressed apology for the incident and sent five victims and their five children to Japan. There has been no more progress since then.

30. See Kent E. Calder, "Japanese Foreign Economic Policy Formation: Explaining the Reactive State," *World Politics* 40 (July 1988): 517–40; Akitoshi Miyashita, "Gaiatsu and Japan's Foreign Aid: Rethinking the Reactive-Proactive Debate," *International Studies Quarterly* 43, no. 4 (December 1999): 695–731; T. J. Pempel, "Structural Gaiatsu: International Finance and Political Change in

Japan," *Comparative Political Studies* 32, no. 8 (December 1999): 907–32; Michael Blaker, Paul Giarra, and Ezra Vogel, *Case Studies in Japanese Negotiating Behavior* (Washington, DC: United States Institute of Peace Press, 2002); Yang Ki-woong, *Ilbonui oegyo hyopsang* [Japanese Diplomatic Negotiation] (Seoul: Sohwa, 1998).

31. See Haruhiro Fukui, *Party in Power: The Japanese Liberal-Democrats and Policy-making* (Berkeley: University of California Press, 1970), 107; Quansheng Zhao, *Japanese Policymaking: The Politics behind Politics* (Westport, CT: Praeger/Oxford: Oxford University Press, 1993).

32. For example, in order to rise to power prime minister hopefuls depended on factional support. With the support of the Tanaka faction and its successor Keiseikai, Ohira Masayoshi, Suzuki Zenko, Nakasone Yasuhiro, Takeshita Noboru, Hashimoto Ryutaro, and Obuchi Keizo became prime minister. Also, the two factions backed Uno Sosuke, Kaifu Toshiki, and Miyazawa Kiichi to become prime minister. See Oshita Eiji, *Keiseikai Takeshita gakko* [The Keiseikai Takeshita School] (Tokyo: Kodansha, 1999).

33. For the notion of alternative specification, Leonard J. Schoppa, "Two-Level Games and Bargaining Outcomes: Why Gaiatsu Succeeds in Japan in Some Cases but not Others," *International Organization* 47, no. 3 (Summer 1993): 353–86.

34. Laura E. Hein, "Growth versus Success: Japan's Economic Policy in Historical Perspective," in *Postwar Japan as History*, ed. Andrew Gordon (Berkeley: University of California Press, 1993), 103–105.

35. John Lewis Gaddis, *Strategies of Containment: A Critical Appraisal of American National Security Policy during the Cold War*, revised edition (Oxford: Oxford University Press, 2005), 29.

36. Andrew Gordon, *A Modern History of Japan: From Tokugawa Times to the Present* (Oxford: Oxford University Press, 2003), 246.

37. It should be noted that beginning in the 1950s, Japan made an attempt to develop *kokusanka*, meaning national technology-based production, of defense production as well. Japanese techno-nationalism contributed to the country's postwar industrial power in general. Michael J. Green, *Arming Japan: Defense Production, Alliance Politics, and the Postwar Search for Autonomy* (New York: Columbia University Press, 1995).

38. Operations Coordinating Board, Washington, DC, Report on Japan (NSC 5516/1), May 4, 1960, *Digital National Security Archive: Japan and the U.S., 1960–1976*, JU00038.

39. Memorandum from Robert W. Komer of the National Security Council Staff to President Johnson, Washington, July 31, 1964, *FRUS 1964–1968, Korea*.

40. Muroyama Yoshimasa, *Nichibei anpo taisei* [Japan-U.S. Security System] (Tokyo: Yuhikaku, 1998), 291.

41. See the document at http://www.ioc.u-tokyo.ac.jp/~worldjpn/documents/texts/docs/19691121.D1E.html; accessed January 12, 2012.

42. For the construction of the plant, which continued from 1968 to 1976, the South Korean government invested some 10 percent of the $300 million grant and about 45 percent of the $200 million governmental loan. See Nagano Shinichiro, *Sogoizon no Nikkan keizai kankei* [Japan-Korea Economic Relations of Interdependence] (Tokyo: Keisoshobo, 2008), 308; Horikane Yumi, "1970 nendai kankoku no jukagaku kogyoka to Nikkan keizai kyoryoku: Pohang Sogo Seitetsu to yondai kakukojou purojekuto o chushin to shite [South Korea's Heavy and Chemical Industrialization Push and Japan-Korea Economic Cooperation in the 1970s: The Cases of POSCO and the Four Core Projects]," *Meji daigaku shakai kagaku kenkyujo kiyo* 45, no. 1 (October 2006): 75–99.

43. Rhyu and Lee, "Changing Dynamics in Korea-Japan Economic Relations," 214.

44. For the United States' troop reduction plans in the late 1950s and the early 1960s and withdrawals of them, see Park Tae-gyun, "1950–60 nyondae Migukui Hangukgun kamchungnongwa Hanguk chongbuui Taeung [The U.S. Policy of Korean Troop Reduction and the Korean Government's Response in the 1950s and the 1960s]," *Kukje jiyok yongu* 9, no. 3 (Fall 2000): 31–53.

45. US Policy Concerning the Korean Peninsula (Reference NSSM 154), May 4, 1973, Appendix F, 5–6, *Digital National Security Archive: United States and the Two Koreas*, KO00143.

46. U.S.-Japan Talks—May 9, Memorandum of Conversation, Department of State, May 9, 1973 Microfiche No. 01731, *Japan and the United States: Diplomatic, Security and Economic Relations, 1960–1976*.

47. Muroyama, *Nichibei anpo taisei* [Japan-U.S. Security System], 342–44.

48. See Address of President Gerald R. Ford at the University of Hawaii, December 7, 1975, at http://www.fordlibrarymuseum.gov/library/speeches/750716.asp; accessed March 17, 2015.

49. Muroyama, *Nichibei anpo taisei* [Japan-U.S. Security System], 456–57, 495.

50. Kim Yong-ho, *Nikkan kankei to Kankoku no tainichi kodo* [Japan-South Korea Relations and South Korea's Response to Japan] (Tokyo: Sairyusha, 2008), 137–59; Son Kisup, "Hanil anbogyeonghyeop oegyo jengchaek [Policymaking of the Korea-Japan Security-Economic Cooperation: Japanese Governmental Loan to Korea, 1981–1983]," *Gukjejeongchi nonchong* 49, no. 1 (2009): 305–28; Son Kisup, "Ilbonui daechungguk wonjojeongchaekui pyonhwawa teukjing [The Change and Characteristics of Japan's Aid Policy to China: Compared with the Aid to Southeast Asia and Korea]," *Ilbonyeongu nonchong* 21 (2005): 63–103.

51. B. C. Koh, "South Korea in 1996: Internal Strains and External Challenges," *Asian Survey* 37, no. 1 (January 1997): 1–9.

52. See Purnendra Jain and Lam Peng Er, "Japan's 21st Century Strategic Challenges: Introduction," *Japan's Strategic Challenges in a Changing Regional Environment*, ed. Purnendra Jain and Lam Peng Er (London and Singapore: World Scientific, 2013), xi–xxvii.

Chapter 3. Repatriation of Korean Residents from Japan to North Korea

1. Tessa Morris-Suzuki, *Exodus to North Korea: Shadows from Japan's Cold War* (Lanham, MD: Rowman and Littlefield, 2007), 198–207.

2. Outgoing Telegram from Department of State to Embassy in Seoul (Seoul's 430), March 5, 1959, 294.9522 in RG59, Central Decimal File 1955–1959.

3. On September 23, 1952, the commander of the United Nations forces, General Mark W. Clark, established the Clark Line, which was almost identical to the Peace Line. The purpose of the Clark Line was to enhance security in the East Sea/Sea of Japan, and it continued to exist until the end of the Korean War in July 1953. Kim Dong-jo, *Kan-nichi no wakai* [Korea-Japan Reconciliation] (Tokyo: Saimaru Shuppansha, 1993), 8–9, 97.

4. See Lee Won-deog, *Hanil gwageosa cheorieui wonjeom: Ilboneui jeonhu-cheori oegyowa Hanil hoedam* [Original Point of the Settlement of the Korea-Japan Past History: Japan's Diplomacy for Postwar Settlement and Korea-Japan Normalization Talks], (Seoul: Seoul National University Press, 1996), 85.

5. Kim Dong-jo, *Kan-nichi no wakai* [Korea-Japan Reconciliation], 111–13.

6. Park Jung Jin, "Dare ga kikoku undo o suishin shitanoka [Who Led the Returning-to-Homeland Movement?]," in *Kikokuundo towa nandattanoka* [What Was the Returning-to-Homeland Movement?], ed. Takasaki Sozi and Park Jung Jin (Tokyo: Heibonsha, 2005), 185–86.

7. See "Jaeil hanineui Bukhan songhwan kyeonggwa, 1955–1957 [The Process of the Repatriation of Korean Residents in Japan to North Korea, 1955–1957]," in Jaeil hanin Bukhan songhwan mit Han-Il yangguk eokryuja sangho seokbang gwangyecheol, 1955–1960 [Compiled Documents Related to the Repatriation of Korean Residents in Japan to North Korea and the Mutual Release of Detainees in ROK and Japan, 1955–1960], Vol. 7, Ministry of Foreign Affairs, ROK, C1-0011, 11; Morris-Suzuki, *Exodus to North Korea*, 118–19, 126–31.

8. Kim Dong-jo, *Kan-nichi no wakai* [Korea-Japan Reconciliation], 112–13.

9. Telegram from Embassy in Tokyo to Secretary of State (No. 1803), March 6, 1959, 294.9522.

10. "Hokusen, tainichikosho yobikake: boeki, bunkakoryumondai nado [North Korea Proposes Exchanges with Japan: Trade, Cultural Exchanges, etc.]," *Asahi Shimbun*, February 25, 1955, evening.

11. The rupture was caused by Japan's insistence on upholding its nationals' property rights in Korea during the colonial period, and by the "Kubota statement" that justified colonial rule and argued that it had played a constructive role in Korean modernization. For the details, see Lee Won-doeg, *Hanil gwageosa cheorieui wonjeom* [Original Point of the Settlement of the Korea-Japan Past History], 63–77.

12. "Kikokumondai no kaito motomu: Nisseki kara Hokusen ni daden [Asking Response about the Repatriation Issue: Telegram from JRC to North Korea]," *Asahi Shimbun*, April 13, 1955, evening.

13. Record of 23rd House of Representatives, Foreign Affairs Committee, Japan, No. 12, December 16, 1955.

14. See "Statement of the Spokesman of the Foreign Ministry of the DPRK," October 15, 1955; "Statement of the Foreign Minister of the DPRK," December 29, 1955; "Chairman of the CC of the Korean Red Cross Society Sends Telegram to the President of the Japanese Red Cross Society," December 31, 1955, in *On the Question of 600,000 Koreans in Japan* (Pyongyang: Foreign Languages Publishing House, 1959) in Jaeil hanin Bukhan songhwan mit Han-Il yangguk eokryuja sangho seokbang gwangyecheol, 1955–1960, Vol. 7, C1-0011, MOFA, ROK.

15. "Statement of the Foreign Minister of the DPRK," January 4, 1959, in *On the Question of 600,000 Koreans in Japan.*

16. For example, "Statement of Vice Minister of Education of the DPRK," June 10, 1956; "DPRK Cabinet Order No. 53 on Stabilizing the Living of the Korean Citizens Returning from Japan," June 20, 1956, in *On the Question of 600,000 Koreans in Japan.*

17. "An Excerpt from Premier Kim Il Sung's Speech Made on the 10th Anniversary of the Founding of the Democratic People's Republic of Korea," September 8, 1958, in *On the Question of 600,000 Koreans in Japan.*

18. Telegram from Embassy in Tokyo to Secretary of State, September 9, 1958, 320 JAPAN-ROK, in *Hanil hoedam gwangye migukmubu munseo* [The Department of State of the United States Documents Related to Korea-Japan Talks], ed. National Institute of Korean History, Vol. 4 (1956–1958) (Seoul: NIKH, 2008), 414–15.

19. "Kikokukibo wa ichimansanzennin: Chosensoreni owaru [Thirteen Thousand Koreans Want to Return: The Central Committee of the Chongryon Ends]," *Asahi Shimbun*, October 11, 1958.

20. "Answers of Vice Premier Kim Il to the Questions Put by the Correspondent of the Korean Central News Agency in Connection with Earliest Realization of the Urgent Desire of the Korean Nationals to Return Home from Japan," October 16, 1958, in *On the Question of 600,000 Koreans in Japan.*

21. Park Jung Jin, "Dare ga kikoku undo o suishin shitanoka [Who Led the Returning-to-Homeland Movement?]," 190.

22. Korean Problem in Nagoya Consular District, Foreign Service Dispatch from Consulate in Nagoya to Department of State (No. 59), March 10, 1959, 294.9522.

23. For the discussion of such negative image making about ethnic Koreans in postwar Japanese society, see Taku Tamaki, *Deconstructing Japan's Image of South Korea: Identity in Foreign Policy* (New York: Palgrave Macmillan, 2010), 99.

24. For the various reasons for this extensive public support, see Sato Katsumi, *Waga taikenteki chosen mondai* [Korean Problem as We Experienced] (Tokyo: Toyo Keizai Shimposha, 1978), 14–15.

25. Park Jung Jin, "Dare ga kikoku undo o suishin shitanoka [Who Led the Returning-to-Homeland Movement?]," 197.

26. Telegram from Embassy in Tokyo to Secretary of State (No. G439), January 26, 1959, 294.9522.

27. "Hokusen kikoku chikaku kettei: gaishodan, Nikkankaidan to kirihanashi [Repatriation to North Korea Will be Decided Soon: Minister of Foreign Affairs, Repatriation Issue Separated from Japan-ROK Talks]," *Asahi Shimbun*, January 30, 1959, evening.

28. Telegram from Embassy in Tokyo to Secretary of State (No. 1534), January 31, 1959, 294.9522.

29. For the Japanese government press release, see Telegram from Embassy in Tokyo to Secretary of State (No. G484), February 18, 1959, 294.9522.

30. Letter from the Ambassador to Japan (MacArthur) to the Assistant Secretary of State for Far Eastern Affairs (Robertson), April 18, 1958, in Madeline Chi and Louis J. Smith eds., *Foreign Relations of the United States* (*FRUS*) 1958–1960, Japan, Korea (Washington, DC: United States Government Printing Office, 1994), 24–25.

31. "Nihon seifu wa kangei: kosho wa Fujiyama-Ma taishi de [The Japanese Government Welcomes: Negotiations Will Be Held between FM Fujiyama and Ambassador MacArthur]," *Asahi Shimbun*, September 12, 1958, evening.

32. Telegram from the Embassy in Japan to the Department of State, August 1, 1958, *FRUS* 1958–1960, Japan, Korea, 46–49; "Security Arrangements with Japan," Memorandum of Conversation (Secretary of State, Ambassador MacArthur, and eight other participants), September 8, 1958, *FRUS* 1958–1960, Japan, Korea, 58–63; Telegram from the Embassy in Japan to the Department of State, December 7, 1958, *FRUS* 1958–1960, Japan, Korea, 108–10.

33. Telegram from the Embassy in Japan to the Department of State, October 5, 1958, *FRUS* 1958–1960, Japan, Korea, 92–95.

34. Record of 30th House of Councilors, Foreign Affairs Committee, Japan, No. 4, October 21, 1958.

35. Telegram from Embassy in Tokyo to Secretary of State, October 24, 1958, 320 JAPAN-ROK, in National Institute of Korean History, ed., *Hanil hoedam gwangye migukmubu munseo* [The Department of State of the United States Documents Related to Korea-Japan Talks), Vol. 4 (1956–1958), 426.

36. Outgoing Telegram from Department of State to Embassy in Tokyo (Tokyo's 1631), February 13, 1959, 294.9522.

37. The ROK-Japan Repatriation Problem, Memorandum of Conversation, Department of State, February 13, 1959, 294.9522.

38. Telegram from Embassy in Seoul to Secretary of State (No. 392): Memorandum of Conversation between ROK President Rhee and U.S. Ambassador Dowling, February 21, 1959, 294.9522.

39. "Hokusen kikokusen no bogai niwa jishin: Kaigunsanbosocho kataru [Korean Navy Chief of Staff Says Confidence of Blocking the Repatriation Vessel]," *Asahi Shimbun*, February 28, 1959.

40. Telegram from Embassy in Tokyo to Secretary of State (No. 1803), March 6, 1959, 294.9522.

41. Telegram from Mission in Geneva to Secretary of State (No. 1171), March 21, 1959, 294.9522.

42. Office Memorandum of Department of State from Parsons to Robertson: Your Meeting Today at 5:00 pm with Ambassador Yang, March 5, 1959, 294.9522.

43. "Ilbon jeongbueui jaeilhanin buksong gyehoeke daehan jochiwa gyosop gyeongwi [The Government's Measures and Negotiations Countering the Japanese Government's Project of the Repatriation of Korean Residents in Japan]," December 1959, in Jaeil hanin Bukhan songhwan mit Han-Il yangguk eokryuja sangho seokbang gwangyecheol, 1955–1960, Vol. 7, C1-0011, 393, MOFA, ROK.

44. Telegram from Embassy in Tokyo to Secretary of State (No. 170), July 19, 1959, 294.9522.

45. Telegram from Embassy in Tokyo to Secretary of State (No. 417), August 13, 1959, 294.9522.

46. Background of the Japanese Proposal to Repatriate Korean Residents in Japan Who Desire to Go to North Korea as Described by a Republic of Korea Government Official, Foreign Service Dispatch from Embassy in Seoul to Department of State (No. 463), March 3, 1959, 294.9522; Letter from ICRC President Leopold Boissier to Korean Red Cross President Chan Whan Sohn, July 16, 1956, 294.9522.

47. President's Far Eastern Trip, June 1960, Memorandum of Conversation (U.S. President, ROK Prime Minister, and seven others), June 20, 1960, FRUS 1958-1960, Japan, Korea, 668–72.

48. Background of the Japanese Proposal to Repatriate Korean Residents in Japan Who Desire to Go to North Korea as Described by a Republic of Korea Government Official, Foreign Service Dispatch from Embassy in Seoul to Department of State (No. 463), March 3, 1959, 294.9522.

49. Telegram from Embassy in Tokyo to Secretary of State (No. 1714), February 25, 1959, 294.9522.

50. Telegram from Mission in Geneva to Secretary of State (No. 1020), February 25, 1959; Outgoing Telegram from Department of State to Mission in Geneva (Geneva's 1020), same date, 294.9522.

51. Telegram from Mission in Geneva to Secretary of State (No. 1053), March 3, 1959, 294.9522.

52. Outgoing Telegram from Department of State to Embassy in Tokyo and Mission in Geneva (Tokyo's 1820), March 9, 1959; Telegram from Mission in Geneva to Secretary of State (No. 1149), March 18, 1959, 294.9522.

53. "Inoue Nisseki daihyo shuppatsu: Kokusaisekijyuji to hanashiai, Hokusen kikoku-yokuryugyohu kaiho [JRC Representative Inoue Departs: For Talks with ICRC on the Repatriation of Koreans to the North and the Return of Detained Japanese Fishermen]," Asahi Shimbun, February 20, 1959, evening.

54. Telegram from Embassy in Tokyo to Secretary of State (No. 2354), May 9, 1959, 294.9522.

55. Telegram from Embassy in Tokyo to Secretary of State (No. 2661), June 11, 1959, 294.9522.

56. Outgoing Telegram from Department of State to Geneva, Tokyo, and Seoul (Deptel 2774, Tokyo's 2645, 2661), June 11, 1959, 294.9522.

57. Telegram from Tokyo to Secretary of State (No. 2597), June 4, 1959, 294.9522.

58. The JRC-NKRC negotiations were conducted in strict secrecy, so even the U.S. government was unable to gather any information about them until four days later.

59. Telegram from Mission in Geneva to Department of State (No. 112), July 17, 1959, 294.9522.

60. Telegram from Mission in Geneva to Department of State (No. 188), July 24, 1959, 294.9522.

61. Outgoing Telegram from Department of State to Embassies in Tokyo and Seoul, and Mission in Geneva (Geneva's 149), July 21, 1959, 294.9522.

62. On the other hand, the United States warned that South Korea's willingness to accept Korean returnees should not be used as a tactic to delay the repatriation to the North. Outgoing Telegram from Department of State to Embassy in Tokyo (Seoul's 62), July 24, 1959, 294.9522.

63. Telegram from Mission in Geneva to Secretary of State (No. 240), July 31, 1959, 294.9522.

64. Report on Conversation with Ambassador Dowling from Vice Foreign Minister to Foreign Minister: "The Korea-Japan Relations," July 21, 1959, in Jaeil hanin Bukhan songhwan mit Han-Il yangguk eokryuja sangho seokbang gwangyecheol, 1955–1960, Vol. 2, Re-0003, 70–72, MOFA, ROK.

65. Informal Copy for Reference from Ambassador Dowling to Vice Foreign Minister Kim Dong-jo, July 17, 1959, in Jaeil hanin Bukhan songhwan mit Han-Il yangguk eokryuja sangho seokbang gwangyecheol, 1955–1960, Vol. 2, Re-0003, 63–67, MOFA, ROK.

66. Report from Vice Minister to Minister: Summary Record of Conversation with Ambassador Dowling, July 28, 1959, and Report from Vice Minister to Minister: Conversation with Ambassador Dowling on Korea-Japan Talks, July 30, 1959, in Jaeil hanin Bukhan songhwan mit Han-Il yangguk eokryuja sangho seokbang gwangyecheol, 1955–1960, Vol. 2, Re-0003, 99, 136–37, MOFA, ROK.

67. Foreign Minister Fujiyama reported to the cabinet on July 31 that he intended to accept the South Korean proposal; in response, the cabinet empowered him to do so without reservation. At the meeting, Fujiyama stated that his letter to Secretary of State Christian Herter requesting the good offices of the United States had contributed to the outcome. Incoming Telegram from Ambassador Yiu in Tokyo to the Office of the President and the Minister of Foreign Affairs, July 31, 1959, in Jaeil hanin Bukhan songhwan mit Han-Il

yangguk eokryuja sangho seokbang gwangyecheol, 1955–1960, Vol. 2, Re-0003, 149, MOFA, ROK.

68. Aide Note from Ambassador Yiu to Minister: "Reports on My Meeting with the Japanese Foreign Minister on July 30," August 3, 1959, in Jaeil hanin Bukhan songhwan mit Han-Il yangguk eokryuja sangho seokbang gwangyecheol, 1955–1960, Vol. 2, Re-0003, 189, MOFA, ROK.

69. For South Korea's forestalling tactic, see "Kaisetsu: mushikaeshi no kanosei mo [Commentary: Also Possibility of Backtracking]," *Yomiuri Shimbun*, July 31, 1959.

70. "Nikkan kaidan no mujyokensaikai [Unconditional Resumption of the Japan-ROK Talks]," *Asahi Shimbun*, July 31, 1959, editorial.

71. President's Far Eastern Trip, June 1960, Memorandum of Conversation (U.S. President, ROK Prime Minister, and seven others), June 20, 1960, *FRUS 1958–1960*, Japan, Korea, 668–72.

Chapter 4. Japan-ROK Normalization Talks and Institutionalization of the Security Triangle

1. Accordingly, the South Korean government considered the contentious claims issue to be related to Japan's understanding of the past. See Park Jin-hee, *Hanil hoedam: Je 1-gonghwagukeui daeiljeongchaek gwa Hail hoedam jeongae gwajeong* [Korea-Japan Normalization Talks: The First Republic's Japan Policy and the Development of the Normalization Talks] (Seoul: Sonin, 2008), 106, 178.

2. See Lee Jong-won, "Kannichi kaidan to Amerika: Hukainyu seisaku no seiritsu wo chushin ni [Korea-Japan Talks and the United States: With Special Reference to the Nonintervention Policy]," *Kokusai seizi* 105 (1994); Lee Won-deog, *Hanil gwageosa cheorieui wonjeom: Ilboneui jeonhucheori oegyowa Hanil hoedam* [Original Point of the Settlement of the Korea-Japan Past History: Japan's Diplomacy for Postwar Settlement and Korea-Japan Normalization Talks] (Seoul: Seoul National University Press, 1996); see also, Park Jin-hee, *Hanil hoedam* [Korea-Japan Normalization Talks].

3. Seikyuken mondai kaidan no shokidankai ni okeru kosho yoryo [Guiding Tactics for the Negotiation of the Claims Issue at Its Initial Stage], January 23 and February 12, 1952, Document No. 537, Sixth Declassification on Japan-Korea Normalization Talks, MOFA, Japan.

4. The U.S. State Department maintained a consistently ambivalent stance in the two documents issued on April 29, 1952 and December 7, 1957. Park Tae-gyun, "Hanil hoedam sigi cheonggugwon munjeeui giwon gwa Migukeui yokhwal [Origin of the Claims Issue in the Korea-Japan Normalization Talks and the U.S. Role]," *Hanguksa yeongu* 131 (December 2005): 35–59.

5. Documents attached to Je 5-cha Hanil hoedam yebihoedam: Miil pyonghwa joyak je 4-jo (cheonggugwon gwangye) eui haeseoke gwanhan

Migungmuseong gakseo gonggae, 1961 [Preliminary Talks of the Fifth Korea-Japan Normalization Talks: The Publicization of the U.S. Memorandum on the Interpretation of Article 4 of the Peace Treaty Pertaining to Property Claims], 723.1JA Chong 1961, Re-0005, MOFA, ROK.

6. Park Myung-rim, "Je 2-gongwaguk jeongchi gyunyeoleui gujowa byeonhwa [Structure and Its Transformation in the Political Division of the Second Republic]," in *Je 2-gongwagukgwa Hanguk minjujueui* [The Second Republic and Korean Democracy], ed. Paik Young-chul (Seoul: Nanam, 1996), 207–68.

7. Lee Won-deog, *Hanil gwageosa cheorieui wonjeom* [Original Point of the Settlement of the Korea-Japan Past History], 182.

8. Claude A. Buss, *The United States and the Republic of Korea: Background for Policy* (Stanford: Hoover Institution Press, 1982), 71–72.

9. Ibid., 75.

10. Tae-Gyun Park, "Change in U.S. Policy toward South Korea in the Early 1960s," *Korean Studies* 23 (1999): 94–120.

11. Lee Won-deog, *Hanil gwageosa cheorieui wonjeom* [Original Point of the Settlement of the Korea-Japan Past History], 184.

12. Donald Stone MacDonald, *U.S.-Korean Relations from Liberation to Self-Reliance: The Twenty-Year Record* (Boulder: Westview, 1992), 24–25.

13. Ibid., 286.

14. Telegram from the Commander in Chief, U.S. Forces Korea to the Chairman of the Joint Chiefs of Staff, Seoul, May 16, 1961; Telegram from the Chairman of the Joint Chiefs of Staff to the Commander in Chief, U.S. Forces Korea, Washington, May 16, 1961, *FRUS 1961–1963*, Korea.

15. A U.S. Special Intelligence Estimate later stated that the perpetrators of the coup had a "new sense of drive and discipline," although the coup was authoritarian and nationalistic in manner. Telegram from the Commander in Chief, United Nations Command to the Chairman of the Joint Chiefs of Staff, May 17, 1961, *FRUS 1961–1963*, Korea; Special National Intelligence Estimate, Washington, May 31, 1961, *FRUS 1961–1963*, Korea.

16. Notes of the 485th Meeting of the National Security Council, Washington, June 13, 1961, and Record of National Security Council Action No. 2430, Washington, June 13, 1961, *FRUS 1961–1963*, Korea.

17. Lee Won-deog, *Hanil gwageosa cheorieui wonjeom* [Original Point of the Settlement of the Korea-Japan Past History], 133–35.

18. Memorandum of Conversation between Kennedy and Ikeda, Washington, June 20, 1961, *FRUS 1961–1963*, Korea.

19. Kim Dong-jo, *Kan-nichi no wakai* [Korea-Japan Reconciliation] (Tokyo: Saimaru Shuppansha, 1993), 245.

20. Saikin no Kankoku josei to Nikankankei: Ikeda sori, Kim Yu-taek enjo kaidan shiryo [Recent Situation in Korea and Japan-Korea Relations: Reference Material for Prime Minister Ikeda for the Meeting with Kim Yu-taek], August 31, 1961, Document No. 361, Sixth Declassification on Japan-Korea Normalization Talks, MOFA, Japan.

21. Memorandum of Conversation, between Dean Rusk and Park Chung-hee, Seoul, November 5, 1961, *FRUS 1961–1963*, Korea.

22. Ibid.

23. Lee Jong-won, "Nikkan no shinkokai gaikobunsho ni miru Nikkan kaidan to Amerika, III [Japan-Korea Talks and the United States Analyzed from the Newly Declassified Diplomatic Archives, III]," *Rikkyo hogaku* 78 (2010), 158–59, 162–63.

24. Memorandum from Robert W. Komer of the National Security Council Staff to President Kennedy, Washington, April 23, 1962, *FRUS 1961–1963*, Korea.

25. See Memorandum from Robert W. Komer of the National Security Council Staff to President Johnson, Washington, January 23, 1964, *FRUS 1964–1968*, Korea.

26. When the Japanese representative Sugi Michisuke visited Seoul in 1960, the Chang Myon cabinet suggested a figure of US$500 million. Sugi suseokdaepyo banghan gwanryeon bogo [Report on Representative Sugi's Korea Visit], from Representative of Normalization Talks to Foreign Minister, November 1, 1961, JW-1110, in Kookmin University Institute of Japanese Studies, *Hanil hoedam oegyomunseo haejejip IV: Gowi jeongchi hoedam mit 7-cha hoedam* [Collected Interpretations of the Diplomatic Documents Related to the Korea-Japan Normalization Talks, IV: High Political Talks and the Seventh Talks] (Seoul: Northeast Asian History Foundation, 2008), 49.

27. Kim Dong-jo, *Kan-nichi no wakai* [Korea-Japan Reconciliation], 251.

28. Lee Jong-won, "Nikkan no shinkokai gaikobunsho ni miru Nikkan kaidan to Amerika, II [Japan-Korea Talks and the United States Analyzed from the Newly Declassified Diplomatic Archives, II]," *Rikkyo hogaku* 77 (2009), 128–40.

29. Lee Jong-won, "Nikkan no shinkokai gaikobunsho ni miru Nikkan kaidan to Amerika, III [Japan-Korea Talks and the United States Analyzed from the Newly Declassified Diplomatic Archives, III]," *Rikkyo hogaku* 78 (2010), 191.

30. Park euijangui neoesinmun gijahoegyeon [Park's Press Conference with Domestic and Foreign Reporters], from Minister in Tokyo to Foreign Minister, November 12, 1961, Konghan 11235; Kim Dong-jo, *Kan-nichi no wakai* [Korea-Japan Reconciliation], 261, 263.

31. Jungyo sinmun gisaeui gon [Report on Important News Coverage], from Minister in Tokyo to Foreign Minister, November 7, Konghan JW-11111; Jungyo sinmun gisaeui gon [Report on Important News Coverage], Minister in Tokyo to Foreign Minister, November 10, Konghan JW-11192, MOFA, ROK.

32. Park euijang-Ikeda susang hoedam hoeuiyorok songbu [Sending of the Memorandum of Chairman Park-Prime Minister Ikeda Meeting], from the Representative of the Korea-Japan Talks to Foreign Minister, November 14, 1961, Hoedam 6-20, 724.11JA 1961, Re-0013, MOFA, ROK.

33. U.S.-Korean Relations, Memorandum of Conversation between Kennedy and Park, Washington, November 14, 1961; Memorandum of Conversa-

tion between Dean Rusk and Park Chung-hee, Washington, November, 14, 1961; Memorandum of Conversation between Rusk and Park: U.S. Assistance to Korea, Washington, November 16, 1961, *FRUS 1961–1963, Korea*.

34. See Note No. 2 in Memorandum from Secretary of State Rusk to President Kennedy, Washington, May 17, 1961, *FRUS 1961–1963, Korea*.

35. Telegram from the Department of State to the Embassy in Japan, Washington, July 13, 1962, *FRUS 1961–1963, Korea*.

36. Memorandum Prepared in the Department of State: Korean-Japanese Relations, Washington, May 17, 1962, *FRUS 1961–1963, Korea*.

37. Ohira daijin, Rasuku choukan kaidanroku [Memorandum of Conversation between Ohira and Rusk], September 25, 1962, Document No. 1805, Sixth Declassification on Japan-Korea Normalization Talks, Ministry of Foreign Affairs, Japan.

38. Kim Dog-jo, *Kan-nichi no wakai* [Korea-Japan Reconciliation], 269.

39. For the Korean report on the meeting, see Kim Jong-pil bujang-Ohira oesang hoedam naeyong bogo [Report of the Conversation between Director Kim Jong-pil and Foreign Minister Ohira], from Ambassador Pae Ui-hwan to Minister of Foreign Affairs, October 21, 1962; and Kim Jong-pil bujang-Ikeda susang hoedam hoeuirok [Memorandum of Conversation between Director Kim Jong-pil and Prime Minister Ikeda], October 22, 1962, in Kim Jong-pil teuksa Ilbon bangmun, 1962. 10-11 [Kim Jong-pil's Visits to Japan in October and November 1962], 724.41 JA, File No. 07, Re-00130, MOFA, ROK.

40. Memorandum of Conversation between Rusk and Kim Jong-pil, Washington, October 29, 1962, *FRUS 1961–1963, Korea*.

41. Ohira used these terms in his talks with U.S. secretary of state Dean Rusk and with KCIA director Kim Jong-pil. See Ohira daijin, Rasuku choukan kaidanroku [Memorandum of Conversation between Ohira and Rusk], September 25, 1962, Document No. 1805, Sixth Declassification on Japan-Korea Normalization Talks, MOFA, Japan; Kim Jong-pil bujang-Ohira oesang hoedam naeyong bogo [Report of the Conversation between Director Kim Jong-pil and Foreign Minister Ohira], from Ambassador Pae Ui-hwan to Minister of Foreign Affairs, October 21, 1962, 724.41 JA, MOFA, ROK.

42. Originally Japan wanted a kind of give-and-take approach of exchanging item by item and issue by issue, rather than the Korean approach of sequential negotiations, with the claims issue first and the other issues later.

43. Bogoseo: Bundy chagwanbo banghan gwa Hanil hoedam [Report: Assistant Secretary Bundy's Visit to Korea and the Korea-Japan Normalization], from Presidential Secretarial Office to President, October 3, 1964, in Hanil hoedame daehan Mikukeui ipjang, 1961–1965 [The U.S. Viewpoint about the Korea-Japan Normalization Talks, 1961–1965], 723.1 JA, Mi 1961–1965, Re-0012, MOFA, ROK.

44. Telegram from the Embassy in Japan to the Department of State, Tokyo, January 3, 1964; Telegram from the Department of State to the Embassy in Korea, Washington, February 14, 1964; Telegram from the Department of

State to the Embassy in Korea, May 12, 1964, *FRUS 1964–1968, Korea*; Kim Dong-jo, *Kan-nichi no wakai* [Korea-Japan Reconciliation], 289.

45. Memorandum from Robert W. Komer of the National Security Council Staff to President Johnson, Washington, January 23, 1964, *FRUS 1964–1968, Korea*.

46. Nikkan gyogyo kosho no keika [Progress of the Japan-Korea Fishery Negotiation], January 14, 1965, Document No. 913, Sixth Declassification, MOFA, Japan.

47. Mark W. Janis, *An Introduction to International Law* (Boston: Little, Brown, 1988), 152–53.

48. Telegram from the Department of State to the Embassy in Korea, Washington, February 14, 1964, *FRUS 1964–1968, Korea*.

49. Telegram from the Embassy in Korea to the Department of State, Seoul, February 17, 1964, *FRUS 1964–1968, Korea*.

50. Nam Ki-jeong, "Hanil hoedam sigi Hanil yanggukeui gukjesahoe insik: Eoeop mit Pyonghwason ul dulleossan, gukjebopeul jungsimuro [Korean and Japanese Perception of International Society in the Era of Normalization Talks: With Special Reference to the Debates on International Law Regarding the Fishery Rights and the Peace Line]," *Segye jeongchi* 29, no. 2 (Fall-Winter 2008): 125–57.

51. Memorandum from Robert W. Komer of the National Security Council Staff to the President's Special Assistant for National Security Affairs Bundy, Washington, May 19, 1964, and Memorandum from Robert W. Komer of the National Security Council Staff to President Johnson, Washington, July 31, 1964, *FRUS 1964–1968, Korea*.

52. Korean officials were irritated by Ambassador Berger's heavy-handed approach on the normalization talks. See Edwin O. Reischauer, *My Life between Japan and America* (New York: Harper and Row, 1986), 207, 252.

53. Telegram from the Embassy in Korea to the Department of State, Seoul, August 19, 1964, and Letter from the Ambassador to Japan Reischauer to the President's Special Assistant for National Security Affairs Bundy, Tokyo, August 21, 1964, *FRUS 1964–1968, Korea*.

54. Bogoseo: Bundy chagwanbo banghan gwa Hanil hoedam [Report: Assistant Secretary Bundy's Visit to Korea and the Korea-Japan Normalization], from Presidential Secretarial Office to President, October 3, 1964, in Hanil hoedame daehan Mikukeui ipjang, 1961–1965 [The U.S. Viewpoint on the Korea-Japan Normalization Talks, 1961–1965], 723.1 JA, Mi 1961–1965, Re-0012, MOFA, ROK.

55. Memorandum of Conversation between Prime Minister Chong and Bundy, October 2, 1964, in *Documents on United States Policy toward Japan*, VIII, 62–68.

56. Yamada Eizo, *Seiden Sato Eisaku* [Biography of Sato Eisaku], Vol. 2 (Tokyo: Shinchosha, 1988), 15–16.

57. Ibid., Vol. 1, 391, 398.

58. Sato must have prioritized the Okinawa reversion above all other diplomatic tasks. He made an agreement in principle with President Richard Nixon on the reversion at their 1969 summit. Okinawa was eventually handed over to Japan under the Okinawa Reversion Agreement of May 15, 1972. The priority that Sato gave to the issue was reflected in the Japanese government's secret deposit of about US$60 million into the U.S. Federal Reserve Bank to finance the return of Okinawa. "Okinawa Reversion Account at Fed Found," *Japan Times*, March 6, 2010.

59. Telegram from the Department of State to the Embassy in Korea, Washington, November 11, 1964, *FRUS 1964–1968, Korea*.

60. Memorandum of Conversation between Sato and Rusk, January 12, 1965, *FRUS 1964–1968, Korea*.

61. Shiina gaimu daijin Kankoku homon [Foreign Minister Shiina's Korea Visit], February 17–20, 1965, Document No. 1329, Sixth Declassification, MOFA, Japan.

62. Kimiya Tadashi, "Ilhan kukkyo jeongsanghwa kyoseop eseoeui cheonggukwon munje jaego [Revisiting the Claims Issue in the Normalization negotiations]," in The Committee for Korea-Japan Collaborative History Research, *Je 2-gi Hanil yeoksa gongdong yeongu bogoseo* [Report of Korea-Japan Collaborative History Research], Section III (Seoul: The Committee for Korea-Japan Collaborative History Research, 2010), 77–128.

63. Memorandum of Conversation between Ohira and Bundy: Japan's Relations with Korea and Other Asian Neighbors, September 23, 1964, in Documents Related to Diplomatic and Military Matters 1964, Vol. 2 of *Documents on United States Policy toward Japan*, VIII (2001), 21–27.

64. Telegram from Embassy in Tokyo to the Department of State, Tokyo, September 8, 1964, *FRUS 1964–1968, Korea*.

65. Kim Dong-jo, *Kan-nichi no wakai* [Korea-Japan Reconciliation], 295.

66. Letter from Ambassador to Japan Reischauer to Assistant Secretary of State for Far Eastern Affairs Bundy, October 28, 1964, *FRUS 1964–1968, Korea*.

67. Wakamiya Yoshibumi, *Wakai to nashonarizumu* [Reconciliation and Nationalism] (Tokyo: Asahi Shimbunsha, 2006), 275.

68. Shiina's arrival speech, cited from Lee Won-deog, *Hanil gwageosa cheorieui wonjeom* [Original Point of the Settlement of the Korea-Japan Past History], 260.

69. Shiina gaimu daijin no hokan ni kansuru shimbun roncho [Tone of Newspaper Coverage about Foreign Minister Shiina's Korea Visit], February 17–23, 1965, Document No. 1332, Sixth Declassification, MOFA, Japan.

70. Shiina gaimu daijin Kankoku homon [Foreign Minister Shiina's Korea Visit], February 17–20, 1965, Document No. 1329, Sixth Declassification, MOFA, Japan.

71. Shiina made this clear in his answer to a question raised in the Diet after his return to Japan. Takasaki Sozi, *Kensho Nikkan kaidan* [Verification of Japan-Korea Talks] (Tokyo: Iwanami Shinsho, 1996), 166.

72. For discussion on the notions of intensity and distribution of power, see chapter 2.

73. Kim Dong-jo, *Kan-nichi no wakai* [Korea-Japan Reconciliation], 277.

74. Kim Ki-son, *Hanil hoedam bandae undong* [Movement against Korea-Japan Normalization Talks] (Seoul: Korea Democracy Foundation, 2005), 56.

75. Kim stepped down as KCIA director in January 1963 but then took part in the establishment of the Democratic Republican Party (DRP) the following month.

76. Memorandum from Michael V. Forrestal of the National Security Council Staff to Assistant Secretary of State for Far Eastern Affairs Harriman: ROK/Japan Settlement, Washington, February 12, 1963; Telegram from the Department of State to the Embassy in Korea, Washington, February 14, 1963, *FRUS 1961–1963, Korea*.

77. Memorandum from Michael V. Forrestal of the National Security Council Staff to President Kennedy: Korea, Washington, March 28, 1963, *FRUS 1961–1963, Korea*.

78. Office of Current Intelligence, CIA, "Special Report: The Future of Korean-Japanese Relations," March 18, 1966, *Japan and the United States: Diplomatic, Security and Economic Relations, 1960–1976* (Ann Arbor: Bell and Howell Information and Learning, 2000), No. 00554, microfiche.

79. Memorandum from President's Special Assistant for National Security Affairs Bundy to President Kennedy: Ambassador Berger's Call at 12:00 Noon Today, Washington, May 31, 1963, *FRUS 1961–1963, Korea*.

80. Telegram from the Department of State to the Embassy in Korea, Washington, March 28, 1963, *FRUS 1961–1963, Korea*.

81. President Park stated in February that the government was aiming to complete the negotiations in March, sign the treaty in April, and ratify it in May, but this schedule met with scorn among fishing organizations and opposition forces. Kim Ki-son, *Hanil hoedam bandae undong* [Movement against Korea-Japan Normalization Talks], 58.

82. Kim Jong-pil was depicted as the main perpetrator in the corruption scandals and the "humiliation diplomacy." He was likened to the traitor Lee Wan-yong who had worked for Japan's annexation of Korea in 1910. Kim Ki-son, *Hanil hoedam bandae undong* [Movement against Korea-Japan Normalization Talks], 59–66.

83. Kim Dong-jo, *Kan-nichi no wakai* [Korea-Japan Reconciliation], 286–87.

84. The anti-normalization demonstration had a nationalistic context. It was basically aimed at the Korean government's admission concerning the legacy of Japanese colonialism and the eventual restoration of national dignity. See Kim Song-sik, *Iljeha Hankuk haksaeng dongnip undongsa* [History of Student Movement in Korea during the Japanese Colonial Rule] (Seoul: Chongumsa, 1974), 226; Chi Myong-kuan, *Nikkan kankeishi kenyu: 1965nen taisei kara 2002 nen taisei e* [A Study on the History of Japan-Korea Relations] (Tokyo: Shingyo Shuppansha, 1999), 133–54.

85. Kim Ki-son, *Hanil hoedam bandae undong* [Movement against Korea-Japan Normalization Talks], 88–93.

86. Takasaki Sozi, *Kensho Nikkan kaidan* [Verification of Japan-Korea Talks], 172–74.

87. For the details of the Communist view on the normalization, see the argument of Terao Goro, the author of a sympathetic travelogue in 1959 entitled *38-dosen no kita* [North of the 38th Parallel]. He cautioned against the emergence of the U.S.-led regional military alliance, or so-called NEATO, the prolongation of the division of Korea, and the penetration of Japanese monopoly capitalism into South Korea. Terao Goro, "Shin anpo jouyaku to Nikkan kaidan [New Security Treaty and Japan-Korea Talks]," *Zenei* [Vanguard] 204, 1962-12: 118–26. See also The Executive Committee of the Central Committee, "Indoshina shinryaku hantai, Nikkan kaidan hunsai, gunkokushugi hukatsu to kenpo kaiaku hantai no daitoitsu kodo ni kekki shiyo [Let Us Take Unified Action to Protest the Indochina Invasion, to Smash the Japan-Korea Talks, and to Rally against the Resurrection of Militarism and the Revision of the Constitution]," February 12, 1965, *Zenei* [Vanguard] 235, 1965-04: 2–5.

88. Record of 42nd Lower House, Budget Committee, No. 1, December 11, 1962.

89. The Party Organ Bureau of the Central Headquarters, "Tokushu: Nikkan kaidan ni tsuite [Special Issue: About the Japan-Korea Talks]," *Gekkan Shakaito* [Monthly Socialist Party] 56, 1962-02: 2–35.

90. Jiminto nikkan mondai PR iinkai, "nikkan kaidan sokushin PR yoko [Guidelines for Expediting the Japan-Korea Normalization Talks]," *Seisaku geppo* [Policy Monthly] 83, 1962-12: 50–56.

91. While they were encouraged by the Franco-Chinese normalization on January 27, 1964—which signaled a crack in the U.S.-led alignment for containing Communist China—the Japanese Socialists considered blocking the establishment of NEATO as a strategic objective in their opposition to anticommunist military alliances. They believed that the normalization talks were part of a U.S.-initiated project to build such alliances.

92. Nihon shakaito chuohonbu kikanshi koho iinkai, *Nihon shakaito 50 nen* [Fifty Years of the Japan Socialist Party], (Tokyo: Shakaito, 1995), 301–302.

93. Editorial Board, "Nikkan kaidan to Nihon dokusen no doko [The Japan-Korea Talks and the Tendency of Japanese Monopoly]," *Gekkan Shakaito* [Monthly Socialist Party] 97, 1965-06: 23–28.

Chapter 5. Japan's Two Koreas Policy and Its Commitment to U.S.-Japan Alliance in the UN

This chapter is an extended and revised version of "Sino-Japanese Normalization and Japan's Korea Policy, 1972–75," in *The Koreas between China and Japan*, ed. Victor Teo and Lee Guen (Newcastle upon Tyne: Cambridge Scholars Publishing, 2014).

1. Chong-Sik Lee, *Japan and Korea: The Political Dimension* (Stanford: Hoover Institution Press, 1985).

2. Akira Iriye, "Chinese-Japanese Relations," *China Quarterly* 124 (December 1990): 631.

3. For the relaying of the issue, see Charles Armstrong, *Tyranny of the Weak: North Korea and the World, 1950–1992* (Ithaca and London: Cornell University Press, 2014), 159–61.

4. SSC VII: Korea, July 31, 1970, Microfiche No. 01306, in *Japan and the United States: Diplomatic, Security, and Economic Relations, 1960–1976* (Ann Arbor: Bell & Howell Information and Learning, 2000).

5. Japan Reacts Cautiously to US Troop Reduction in South Korea, Intelligence Note by Bureau of Intelligence and Research, Department of State, August 6, 1970, Microfiche No. 01307, in *Japan and the United States: Diplomatic, Security, and Economic Relations, 1960–1976*.

6. US Policy Concerning the Korean Peninsula (Reference NSSM 154), May 4, 1973, Appendix F, 5–6, *Digital National Security Archive: United States and the Two Koreas* (1969–2000), KO00143.

7. Intelligence Note, Bureau of Intelligence and Research, Department of State, August 6, 1970, Microfiche No. 01307, in *Japan and the United States: Diplomatic, Security, and Economic Relations, 1960–1976*.

8. NSSM 12: Policy toward Japan, June 1971, Microfiche No. 01391, in *Japan and the United States: Diplomatic, Security, and Economic Relations, 1960–1976*.

9. For the details of the U.S. approach before July 1971, see James Mann, *About Face: A History of America's Curious Relationship with China, from Nixon to Clinton* (New York: Vintage Books, 2000), 13–25.

10. Armin H. Meyer, *Assignment: Tokyo* (Indianapolis and New York: Bobbs-Merrill, 1974), 138.

11. Ibid., 142–43.

12. Christopher Howe, "China, Japan and Economic Interdependence in the Asia Pacific Region," *China Quarterly* 124 (December 1990): 678.

13. Tanaka Akihiko, *Nicchu kankei, 1949–1990* [Japan-China Relations, 1949–1990] (Tokyo: The University of Tokyo Press, 1991), 68–69.

14. For the Joint Statement of Japanese Prime Minister Eisaku Sato and U.S. President Richard Nixon, November 21, 1969, see http://www.ioc.u-tokyo.ac.jp/~worldjpn/documents/texts/docs/19691121.D1E.html; accessed December 1, 2014.

15. "72 nyeon 1 woleui Mi-Il jeongsang hoedame gwanhayeo [About the U.S.-Japan Summit in January 1972]," Report from Ministry of Foreign Affairs to President, Abuk 700-11, January 12, 1972, in Sato Eisaku Ilbon susang Miguk bangmun [Japanese Prime Minister Sato Eisaku's Visit to the United States], January 6–7, 1972, 722.12JA/US, 1971–72, C-0052, MOFA, ROK.

16. FONMIN Reportedly Questions Validity of Taiwan Clause, Telegram from Embassy in Tokyo to Secretary of State, June 2, 1972, in *Documents on*

United States Policy toward Japan, XVIII: Documents Related to Diplomatic and Military Matters 1972, POL JAPAN, Vol. 2 (Tokyo: Kashiwashobo, 2006).

17. See the Joint Statement of Japanese Prime Minister Eisaku Sato and U.S. President Richard Nixon.

18. Meyer, *Assignment*, 164.

19. Tanaka's China policy was well supported by the China-friendly group—composed of the Kochikai and his own faction. Interestingly, this group kept an overlapping interest in North Korea. As to the China-friendly associations at the popular level, see Franziska Seraphim, *War Memory and Social Politics in Japan, 1945–2005* (Cambridge: Harvard University Asia Center, 2006), ch. 4; Wakamiya Yoshibumi, *Wakai to nashonarizumu* [Reconciliation and Nationalism] (Tokyo: Asahi Shimbunsha, 2006), 206–207. As opposed to the China-friendly group, the pro-Taiwan faction supported the expansion of trade with China but opposed diplomatic relations. The politicians who belonged to this faction were anticommunist and supported Japan's defense capability.

20. Tanaka Cabinet's Policy Positions: Korea, Telegram from Embassy in Tokyo to Secretary of State, July 20, 1972, in *Documents on United States Policy toward Japan, XVIII: Documents Related to Diplomatic and Military Matters 1972*, POL JAPAN, Vol. 2.

21. Ikeda Naotaka, *Nichi-Bei kankei to hutatsu no chugoku* [Japan-U.S. Relations and Two Chinas] (Tokyo: Bokutakusha, 2004), 409.

22. Tanaka Cabinet's Policy Questions: Taiwan and Korea Causes, Telegram from Embassy in Tokyo to Secretary of State, July 19, 1972, in *Documents on United States Policy toward Japan, XVIII: Documents Related to Diplomatic and Military Matters 1972*, POL JAPAN, Vol. 2.

23. "Kissinger bojwagwan bangil jongryo [Completion of National Security Advisor Kissinger's Visit to Japan]," Telegram from Ambassador in Tokyo to Minister of Foreign Affairs, JAW-08369, August 21, 1972, in Tanaka Kakuei Ilbon susang Miguk bangmun, 1972.8.31-9.1 [Japanese Prime Minister Tanaka Kakuei's Visit to the United States], 722.12JA/US, C-0052, MOFA, ROK.

24. For the Joint Statement Following Meetings with Prime Minister Tanaka of Japan, September 1, 1972, see http://www.presidency.ucsb.edu/ws/?pid=3555; accessed March 26, 2015.

25. "Mi-Il sunoe hoedam eui pyeongga bogoseo [Analysis Report on U.S.-Japan Summit]," Telegram from Embassy in Tokyo to Minister of Foreign Affairs, Iljong 700-5157, September 18, 1972, in Tanaka Kakuei Ilbon susang Miguk bangmun [Japanese Prime Minister Tanaka Kakuei's Visit to the United States], August 31-September 1, 1972, 722.12JA/US, C-0052, MOFA, ROK.

26. Tanaka Statement upon Return from Honolulu, Telegram from Embassy in Tokyo to Secretary of State, September 5, 1972, in *Documents on United States Policy toward Japan, XVIII: Documents Related to Diplomatic and Military Matters 1972*, POL JAPAN, Vol. 2.

27. FM Ohira's Press Conference upon Return from Hawaii, Telegram from Embassy in Tokyo to Secretary of State, September 5, 1972, in *Documents*

on *United States Policy toward Japan, XIII: Documents Related to Diplomatic and Military Matters 1972*, POL JAPAN, Vol. 4.

28. The Joint Communiqué of the Government of Japan and the Government of the People's Republic of China, September 29, 1972. See http://www.mofa.go.jp/region/asia-paci/china/joint72.html; accessed March 24, 2015.

29. Tanaka Visit to Peking, Memorandum for the President from Department of State (by Marshall Green), October 2, 1972, in *Documents on United States Policy toward Japan, XVIII: Documents Related to Diplomatic and Military Matters 1972*, POL JAPAN, Vol. 5.

30. Initial Media Reaction to Tanaka-Chou Meetings and Joint Statement, Telegram from Embassy in Tokyo to Secretary of State, September 29, 1972; US Reactions to Sino-Japanese Communique, Outgoing Telegram from Department of State to Embassy in Tokyo, October 7, 1972, in *Documents on United States Policy toward Japan, XVIII: Documents Related to Diplomatic and Military Matters 1972*, POL JAPAN, Vol. 5.

31. For a political-economy explanation of the establishment of the Yushin regime, see Sang-jin Han, "Bureaucratic Authoritarianism and Economic Development in Korea during the Yushin Period: A Reexamination of O'Donnell's Theory," in *Dependency Issues in Korean Development: Comparative Perspectives*, ed. Kyong-dong Kim ed (Seoul: Seoul National University Press, 1987), 362–74; Hyug Baeg Im, "The Rise of Bureaucratic Authoritarianism in South Korea," *World Politics* 39, no. 2 (1987): 231–57.

32. Korean Peninsula, Background Paper, August 1972, Microfiche No. 01595, in *Japan and the United States: Diplomatic, Security and Economic Relations 1960–1976*.

33. Dietmen's Mission to North Korea, Telegram from Embassy in Tokyo to Secretary of State, January 17, 1972, in *Documents on United States Policy toward Japan, XVIII: Documents Related to Diplomatic and Military Matters 1972*, POL JAPAN, Vol. 2.

34. "Iljo euiryeon Bukgoe bangmun [The Japan-North Korea Friendship Promotion League's Visit to North Korea]," Telegram from Ambassador in Tokyo to Minister of Foreign Affairs, JAW-01266, January 20, 1972, in Ilbon Il-Jo uhochokjin euiwonyeonmaeng daepyodan Pukhan bangmun [Visit to North Korea by the Representatives of the Japan-North Korea Friendship Promotion League], 725.32JA, 1971–72, D-0021, MOFA, ROK.

35. Japan-North Korea Trade Agreement, Telegram from Embassy in Tokyo to Secretary of State, January 24, 1972, in *Documents on United States Policy toward Japan, XVIII: Documents Related to Diplomatic and Military Matters 1972*, POL JAPAN, Vol. 3.

36. "Iljo euiryeon Bukgoe bangmundan: Muyeokchokjine gwanhan hapeuiseo [The Japan-North Korea Friendship Promotion League's Visit to North Korea: Agreement on Japan-North Korea Trade Promotion]," Telegram from Ambassador in Tokyo to Minister of Foreign Affairs, JAW-01331, January 24, 1972, in Ilbon Il-Jo uhochokjin euiwonyonmaeng daepyodan Pukhan bang-

mun [Visit to North Korea by the Representatives of the Japan-North Korea Friendship Promotion League], 725.32JA, 1971–72, D-0021, MOFA, ROK.

37. Particularly see "Seifu wa Niccho boeki kakudai ni humidase [The Government Should Expand Japan-North Korea Trade]," *Asahi Shimbun*, January 25, 1972, editorial.

38. Kim Il Sung Interview by JSP Official, Telegram from Embassy in Tokyo to Secretary of State, February 8, 1972, in *Documents on United States Policy toward Japan, XVIII: Documents Related to Diplomatic and Military Matters 1972*, POL JAPAN, Vol. 6; "Kawasaki Sahoedang gukjegukjanggwa Kim Il Sung gwaeui hoegyeon [The Meeting between Kawasaki Kanji, the Director of the International Affairs Bureau in the Japan Socialist Party, and Kim Il Sung]," Telegram from Ambassador in Tokyo to Minister of Foreign Affairs, JAW-01309, January 24, 1972, in Ilbon Il-Jo uhochokjin euiwonyonmaeng daepyodan Pukhan bangmun [Visit to North Korea by the Representatives of the Japan-North Korea Friendship Promotion League], 725.32JA, 1971–72, MOFA, ROK.

39. "Bukgoe gwangye [About North Korea]," Telegram from Ambassador in Tokyo to Minister of Foreign Affairs, JAW-06068, June 5, 1972, in Ilbon juyo daepyodan Pukhan bangmun [Japanese Representatives' Visit to North Korea], 725.32JA, 1972, D-0012, MOFA, ROK.

40. "Nogyogyo demo koryu ni goi: Shatohochodan kikoku [Agreed on Agricultural and Fishery Exchanges Also: The Return of the North Korea Visiting Group of the Japan Socialist Party]," *Asahi Shimbun*, July 28, 1972; "Shatohochodan kikoku: Koryukakudai no seimei o happyo [The Return of the North Korea Visiting Group of the Japan Socialist Party: Publicization of the Statement for the Expansion of Exchanges]," *Yomiuri Shimbun*, July 29, 1972.

41. "Kang gongsa wa Sunobe asea gukjang kwaeui myeondamrok [Memorandum of Conversation between Minister at the ROK Embassy in Tokyo, Kang Young-kyu, and Director of Asian Affairs Bureau of the Ministry of Foreign Affairs of Japan, Sunobe]," JAW-01025, January 4, 1972, in Han-Il jeongmu ilban [Korea-Japan Political Affairs], 722.1JA, C-0051, MOFA, ROK.

42. "Myeondam yorok [Memorandum of Conversation]" (between ROK Ambassador and Japanese Foreign Minister), Telegram from Ambassador in Tokyo to Minister of Foreign Affairs, JAW-02406, February 23, 1972, in Han-Il jeongmu ilban [Korea-Japan Political Affairs], 722.1JA, C-0051, MOFA, ROK.

43. Telegram from Ambassador in Tokyo to Minister of Foreign Affairs (no title), JAW-03297, March 17, 1972, in Han-Il jeongmu ilban [Korea-Japan Political Affairs], 722.1JA, C-0051, MOFA, ROK.

44. U.S.-Japan Talks, Memorandum of Conversation between Yamazaki Toshio and Richard L. Sneider, May 9, 1973, Microfiche No. 01731, in *Japan and the United States: Diplomatic, Security and Economic Relations, 1960–1976*.

45. Yang Young-shik, *Tongil jeongchaekron* [A Study on Unification Policy] (Seoul: Bakyeongsa, 1997), 176–78.

46. "Daehanmingukeui Bukhan bulseungin bangchimgwa gukjesahoe isseoseoeui 'dugaeeui Hanguk' munjee daehan beobjeok mit jeongchijeok gochal

[A Legal and Political Analysis of the Relationship between ROK's Non-recognition of the DPRK and the 'Two Koreas' in the International Community]," June 22, 1973, in 6.23 pyeonghwa tongil oegyo seoneon, 1973–74 [June 23 Declaration of Peaceful Unification Diplomacy, 1973–74], 726.11, 1973–74, Vol. 1, D-0015, MOFA, ROK.

47. North Korea's opposition to the ROK proposal of simultaneous entry to the UN was a reversal of its previous position regarding UN membership. On February 9, 1949, North Korea submitted a membership application to the UN Secretary General; legally speaking, the application was still alive in 1973.

48. The U.S. media also welcomed the South Korean proposal, calling it a major foreign policy shift. See Don Oberdorfer, "Seoul Alters Stand on N. Korea in U.N.," *Washington Post*, June 23, 1973; and "Seoul, Shifting Policy on U.N. Entry, Won't Oppose Admission With North," *New York Times*, June 23, 1973.

49. Kim Dae Jung Case: ROK-Japan Relations, Telegram from Embassy in Seoul to Secretary of State, August 23, 1973. Microfiche No. 01796, in *Japan and the United States: Diplomatic, Security and Economic Relations, 1960–1976.*

50. Kim Dae Jung, Telegram from Embassy in Seoul to Secretary of State, August 24, Microfiche No. 01798, in *Japan and the United States: Diplomatic, Security, and Economic Relations, 1960–1976.*

51. The Kim Dae Jung Case: An Overview, Telegram from Embassy in Seoul to Secretary of State, October 10, 1973, Microfiche No. 01813, in *Japan and the United States: Diplomatic, Security, and Economic Relations, 1960–1976.*

52. The Committee for the Development through Truth Finding, National Intelligence Agency, ed., *Gwageowa daehwa, mirae eui seongchal: juyo euihok sageon pyeon* [Dialogue with the Past, Reflections for the Future: Main Mysterious Incidents], Vol. 2 (Seoul: National Intelligence Agency, 2007), 548–50.

53. Diet and Public Reactions to Kim Dae Jung Case, Telegram from Embassy in Tokyo to Secretary of State, August 27, 1973, Microfiche No. 01802, in *Japan and the United States: Diplomatic, Security, and Economic Relations, 1960–1976.*

54. Kim Dae Jung Affair, Telegram from Secretary of State to Embassy in Tokyo, September 14, 1973, Microfiche No. 01804, in *Japan and the United States: Diplomatic, Security, and Economic Relations, 1960–1976.*

55. FM Ohira Puzzled by PM Yamagata Statement on Kim Dae Jung Case, Telegram from Embassy in Tokyo to Secretary of State, October 17, 1973, Microfiche No. 01814, in *Japan and the United States: Diplomatic, Security, and Economic Relations, 1960–1976.*

56. Current Status of Kim Dae Jung (Allowing Travel), Telegram from Embassy in Seoul to Secretary of State, Microfiche No. 01853, in *Japan and the United States: Diplomatic, Security, and Economic Relations, 1960–1976.*

57. Discussion with GOJ on Kim Dae Jung, Telegram from Embassy in Seoul to Secretary of State, August 25, 1973, Microfiche No. 01800; Letter (no title) from Donald L. Ranard, Director for Korean Affairs, Department of State to Robert W. Duemling, Political Section of Embassy in Tokyo, May 10, 1974,

Microfiche No. 01858, in *Japan and the United States: Diplomatic, Security, and Economic Relations, 1960–1976.*

58. Kim Dae Jung Affair, Telegram from Secretary of State to Embassy in Tokyo, September 14, 1973, Microfiche No. 01804, in *Japan and the United States: Diplomatic, Security, and Economic Relations, 1960–1976.*

59. "Niccho kokko e go-mokuhyo: Shakaito chushin ni kokuminkaigi [Five Objectives of the Japan-DPRK Normalization: National People's Assembly Centered on Socialist Party]," *Asahi Shimbun*, September 9, 1973.

60. Telegram from Ambassador in Tokyo to Minister of Foreign Affairs (no title), JAW-09521, September 24, 1973, in Bukhan-Ilbon gwangye, 1973 [North Korea-Japan Relations, 1973], 725.1JA, D-0014, MOFA, ROK.

61. National Unification Board, *Bukhan choego inminhoeui jaryojip* [Collections of the Supreme People's Assembly Record], Vol. 3 (Seoul: National Unification Board, 1988), 657–59.

62. *Joseon jungang nyeongam 1976* [Korean Central Yearbook 1976] (Pyongyang: Joseon jungang tongsinsa, 1976), 134.

63. "Utsunomiya Ilbon Jamindang euiwon Bukhan bangmun, 1974.8.5–15 [LDP Diet member Utsunomiya's Visit to North Korea, August 5–15, 1974]," Analysis Report, 1974, 725.32JA, D-0018, MOFA, ROK.

64. The Joint Announcement to the Press Following Discussions with Prime Minister Miki of Japan, August 6, 1975. http://www.presidency.ucsb.edu/ws/index.php?pid=5155; accessed on March 24, 2015.

65. Shin Jong-hwa, *Ilbon eui daebuk jeongchaek* [Japan's North Korea Policy] (Seoul: Orum, 2003), 165.

66. "Gukoe Iril Jeongbo [Daily Foreign Information]," No. 159, July 11, 1974, in Ilbon eui dae Bukhan plant suchul mit suchurip eunhaeng jagum sayong seungin munje, 1974 [Japanese Export of Manufacturing Plants to North Korea and the Controversy over the Approval of the Use of Export-Import Bank Loans, 1974], 725.6JA, D-0018, MOFA, ROK.

67. Yoshihide Soeya, *Japan's Economic Diplomacy with China, 1945–1978* (Oxford: Clarendon Press, 1998), 98.

68. "Bukhan gisulja ipgukmunje, dae Bukgoe plant suchul mit sueunjagum sayong munje, 1966–1974 [Entry of North Korean Engineers, Japanese Plant Exports, and EXIM Bank Loans, 1966–1974]," Analysis Report, 1974, in Ilbon eui dae Bukhan plant suchul mit suchurip eunhaeng jagum sayong seungin munje [Japanese Export of Manufacturing Plants to North Korea and the Controversy over the Approval of the Use of Export-Import Bank Loans], 725.6JA, 1974, D-0018, MOFA, ROK.

69. "Ilbon eui dae Bukhan gyeongje gwangye juyo hyeonan muneui e daehan hoesin [Reply to the Inquiry into the Main Issues Related to Japan's Economic Relations with North Korea]," Letter from Korea Central Intelligence Agency to Minister of Foreign Affairs, Chungjaehaeng 150, in Ilbon-Bukhan gyeongje gwangye, 1972 [Japan-North Korea Economic Relations, 1972], 725.6JA, 1972, D-0012, MOFA, ROK.

70. "Bukgoe eui oechae hyeonhwang mit sanghwan gyosop hwaldong [North Korea's Debt and Its Negotiation Activities with Regard to Repayment]," Analysis Report, April 1974, in Bukhan eui dae seobang oechae munje, 1976–77 [North Korea's Debt to Western Countries, 1976–77], 725.6XG, Roll No. 2007-24, MOFA, ROK.

71. For details on the U.S.-China secret talks on the Korea question, see Hong Seuk-Ryule, "1970 nyeondae jeonban dongbuga detant wa Hanguk tongil munje [The Détente in Northeast Asia and the Korean Unification Issue in the Early 1970s]," *Yeoksawa hyeonsil* 42 (2001): 222–23.

72. Korean Peninsula, Background Paper, August 1972.

73. U.S.-Japan Talks on Korea, Memorandum of Conversation between Department of State Officials and Japanese Embassy Officials, May 8, 1973, Microfiche No. 01730, in *Japan and the United States: Diplomatic, Security, and Economic Relations, 1960–1976*.

74. Park Chi Young, "The United Nations and the Korean Problem," in *The United Nations: The Next Fifty Years*, ed. Han Sung-Joo (Seoul: Ilmin International Relations Institute, Korea University, 1996), 184–85, 188.

75. Korean Question in the UN: Seoul Moves for Compromise, Intelligence Note, November 6, 1973, Bureau of Intelligence and Research, Department of State, POL 32-4 KOR/UN, NARA.

76. Hong Seuk-Ryule, "1970 nyeondae jeonban dongbuga detant wa Hanguk tongil munje [The Détente in Northeast Asia and the Korean Problems in the Early 1970s]," 226.

77. For the Japanese position, see http://www.mofa.go.jp/mofaj/gaiko/bluebook/1974_1/s49-2-3-1.htm#a1; accessed March 24, 2015.

78. Choi Kyungwon, *Reisenki Nikkan anzenhosho kankei no keisei* [The Formation of the Japan-Korea Security Relations during the Cold War] (Tokyo: Keio University Press, 2013), 229.

79. General Assembly Resolution 3390: Question of Korea, A & B. See http://daccess-dds-ny.un.org/doc/RESOLUTION/GEN/NR0/001/03/IMG/NR000103.pdf?OpenElement; accessed November 27, 2014.

Chapter 6. Japan-ROK Security-Based Economic Cooperation

1. For the Address by President Gerald R Ford at the University of Hawaii, December 7, 1975, see http://www.fordlibrarymuseum.gov/library/speeches/750716.asp (accessed November 28, 2014).

2. Japan was a founding member of the Group of Six in 1975 and of its more official successor the G7 in 1976.

3. Muroyama Yoshimasa, *Nichibei anpo taisei* [Japan-U.S. Security System], vol. 2 (Tokyo: Yuhikaku, 1992), 458.

4. Zbigniew Brzezinski, "The Cold War and Its Aftermath," *Foreign Affairs* 71, no. 4 (Fall 1992): 40.

5. Michael T. Klare, "Superpower Rivalry at Sea," *Foreign Policy*, no. 21 (Winter 1975–76): 86–96, 161–67.

6. In exerting pressure on Japan to increase its defense expenditure in 1980, U.S. officials criticized Japan's defense expenditure ceiling of 1 percent of GNP. For the ceiling issue, see Don Oberdorfer, *Senator Mansfield: The Extraordinary Life of a Great American Statesman and Diplomat* (Washington: Smithsonian Books, 2003), 487–89, 494.

7. A Framework for Security Burden Sharing, Briefing Paper, Department of State, March 16, 1981, *Digital National Security Archive: Japan and the U.S., 1977–1992*, No. JA00836; Burden-Sharing, Telegram from Ambassador Michael Mansfield in Tokyo to Secretary of State, May 24, 1988, *Digital National Security Archive: Japan and the U.S., 1977–1992*, No. JA01540.

8. See G8 Information Centre, "Declaration," Bonn, Germany, July 17, 1978, http://www.g8.utoronto.ca/summit/1978bonn/communique.html; accessed December 5, 2014.

9. Robert M. Orr Jr., "The Aid Factor in U.S.-Japan Relations," *Asian Survey* 28, no. 7 (July 1988): 745.

10. Development Assistance, Briefing Paper, Department of State, September 15, 1978, *Digital National Security Archive: Japan and the U.S., 1977–1992*, No. JA00440.

11. Kent E. Calder, "Japanese Foreign Economic Policy Formation: Explaining the Reactive State," *World Politics* 40 (July 1988): 517–40; Akitoshi Miyashita, *Limits to Power: Asymmetric Dependence and Japanese Foreign Aid Policy* (Lanham, MD: Lexington Books, 2003), 190–96.

12. Michael Armacost, *Friends or Rivals? The Insider's Account of U.S.-Japan Relations* (New York: Columbia University Press, 1996), 25.

13. CODEL Solarz Meetings with GOJ Officials, January 2, 1981, *Digital National Security Archive: Japan and the U.S., 1977–1992*, No. JA00807.

14. For example, Japan's China-bound aid started as a multiyear program: a five-year program in 1980–85 followed by a seven-year program in 1984–90.

15. U.S. Policy toward Japan: Ambassador Togo's Call on Thursday, November 2, 11:00 a.m., Action Memorandum, November 1, 1978, *Digital National Security Archive: Japan and the U.S., 1977–1992*, No. JA00454.

16. With the Camp David Accords in September 1978 and the Egypt-Israel Peace Treaty in March 1979, the two adversaries moved toward normalized relations and came to an agreement on the Palestinian territories issue. In response to this rapid development, the Arab League Summit held in Baghdad on November 2, 1978, decided to impose sanctions on Egypt for the Palestine issue in particular. The Arab states regarded the issue as part of an overall Arab agenda, not a topic between Egypt and Israel. Avraham Sela, *The Decline of the Arab-Israeli Conflict: Middle East Politics and the Quest for Regional Order* (Albany: State University of New York Press, 1998), 206–207.

17. Economic Situation in Egypt and Israel, and Others, Memorandum of Conversation (Meeting of Richard Cooper and Kazuo Chiba), Department

of State, April 26, 1979, *Digital National Security Archive: Japan and the U.S., 1977–1992*, No. JA00524.

18. Security Burden Sharing: Aid to Strategic Countries, Briefing Paper, Department of State, March 13, 1981, *Digital National Security Archive: Japan and the U.S., 1977–1992*, No. JA00833; Security Burden Sharing: Refugee Assistance, Briefing paper, Department of State, March 14, 1981, *Digital National Security Archive: Japan and the U.S., 1977–1992*, No. JA00835.

19. Under this strategic consideration, Japan intended to expand economic interests and facilitated resource security. See Alan Rix, *Japan's Economic Aid: Policy-making and Politics* (New York: St. Martin's Press, 1980); Dennis T. Yasumoto, *The Manner of Giving: Strategic Aid and Japanese Foreign Policy* (Lexington, MA: Lexington Books, 1986); Robert M. Orr Jr., "The Aid Factor in U.S.-Japan Relations"; Robert M. Orr Jr., "Collaboration or Conflict? Foreign Aid and U.S.-Japan Relations," *Pacific Affairs* 62, no. 4 (Winter 1989–90): 476–89; Juichi Inada, "Japan's Aid Diplomacy: Economic, Political or Strategic?" *Millennium: Journal of International Studies* 18, no. 3 (1989): 399–414; Steve Chan, "Humanitarianism, Mercantilism, or Comprehensive Security? Disbursement Patterns of Japanese Foreign Aid," *Asian Affairs: An American Review* 19, no. 1 (1992): 3–17; Richard Grant and Jan Nijman, "Historical Changes in U.S. and Japanese Foreign Aid to the Asia-Pacific Region," *Annals of the Association of American Geographers* 87, no. 1 (1997): 32–51.

20. This has been true even after the Cold War thawed. See Akitoshi Miyashita, *Limits to Power: Asymmetric Dependence and Japanese Foreign Aid Policy* (Lanham, MD: Lexington Books, 2003).

21. Alberto Alesina and David Dollar, "Who Gives Foreign Aid to Whom and Why?" *Journal of Economic Growth* 5, no. 1 (March 2000): 33–63; David H. Bearce, Daniel C. Tirone, "Foreign Aid Effectiveness and the Strategic Goals of Donor Governments," *Journal of Politics* 72, no. 3 (July 2010): 837–51.

22. Japanese Aid to Pakistan, Memorandum for the Secretary of State and the Secretary of Defense, from Zbigniew Brzezinski, January 16, 1980, *Digital National Security Archive: Japan and the U.S., 1977–1992*, No. JA00626.

23. CODEL Solarz Meetings with GOJ Officials, Telegram from Ambassador in Tokyo to Secretary of State, January 2, 1981, *Digital National Security Archive: Japan and the U.S., 1977–1992*, No. JA00807.

24. Japan's Activist Foreign Policy, Issues Paper, Bureau of Intelligence and Research, Department of State, December 28, 1984, *Digital National Security Archive: Japan and the U.S., 1977–1992*, No. JA01258.

25. U.S. emphasis on Japan's air defense and antisubmarine capabilities may be traced back to the Carter presidency, specifically to 1977. Carter's national security advisor Brzezinski wanted Japan to enhance those capabilities and increase its contribution to the cost of U.S. troops in Japan. See Oberdorfer, *Senator Mansfield*, 487.

26. Letter to FM Sakurauchi on Japan Defense Efforts, from Secretary of State, Alexander Haig, February 10, 1982, *Digital National Security Archive: Japan and the U.S., 1977–1992*, No. JA00954.

27. "Ilboneui daehanguk gyeongjehyeomnyeok hwakdae [Expansion of Korea-Japan Economic Cooperation]," Economic Planning Board, 1981, in Hanil gyeongje heomnyeok silmuja hoedam, je8cha [The 8th Korea-Japan Economic Cooperation Working-Level Meeting], Tokyo, January 28–29, 1983, Roll 2013-0092, MOFA, ROK.

28. Japanese Foreign Aid, Briefing paper, Department of State, January 17, 1983, *Digital National Security Archive: Japan and the U.S., 1977–1992*, No. JA1077.

29. See "Japan-U.S. Summit Meetings," in The World and Japan Data Project, http://www.ioc.u-tokyo.ac.jp/~worldjpn/documents/indices/JPUS/index-ENG.html; accessed December 9, 2014.

30. George M. Guess, *The Politics of United States Foreign Aid* (London and New York: Routledge, 1987), 13–14.

31. Telling the Koreas Our Aid Plans, Action Memorandum, National Security Council, September 1974, *Digital National Security Archive: United States and the Two Koreas*, No. KO00170.

32. Ha Young-sun, "Hangukeui gunsabi jichuleui chusewa jeonmang [Trend and Prospects for Korea's Defense Expenditure]," *Nonmunjip* (Seoul National University Center for International Studies) 7 (1982): 289–306.

33. Immediately after his inauguration in January 1977, President Carter announced the three-stage withdrawal plan, to be carried out between the end of 1978 and July 1982. This withdrawal plan met with serious resistance from Congress and the ROK government; President Carter cancelled the plan on the occasion of his visit to Seoul in June 1979.

34. "Reagan Mihapjungguk daetongnyeonggwaeui dandok jongsangdtaehwa [The Talks with the President of the United States Reagan]," February 2, 1981, 10:45–11:00, in Chun Doo-hwan daetongnyeong Miguk bangmun [President Chun Doo-hwan's Visit to the United States], January 28–February 7, 1981, Vol. 6 of twelve volumes, Roll 2011-0014-0001, MOFA, ROK.

35. "Gungmuseong bangmusi hoedam girok [Record of Conversation of (President Chun's) Visit to the Department of State, February 2, 1981, 14:00–14:50,]" in Chun Doo-hwan daetongnyeong Miguk bangmun [President Chun Doo-hwan's Visit to the United States], January 28–February 7, 1981, Vol. 6 of twelve volumes, Roll 2011-0014-0001, MOFA, ROK.

36. Larry A. Niksch, "U.S. Troop Withdrawal from South Korea: Past Shortcomings and Future Prospect," *Asian Survey* 21, no. 3 (March 1981): 326–27.

37. The dispatch of part of the Seventh Fleet was in response to the two crises of December 1979: the Soviet invasion of Afghanistan and the Islamic Revolution in Iran. In order to fill the naval power vacuum, the Reagan administration wanted Japan to increase its defense capabilities not only in Japanese territory but in the surrounding seas and air space. Roger Buckley, *US-Japan Alliance Diplomacy, 1945–1990* (Cambridge: Cambridge University Press, 1992), 142.

38. "Hanmi jeongsang hoedam yorok [Memorandum of the Korea-U.S. Summit]," February 2, 1981, 11:00–12:00, in Chun Doo-hwan daetongnyeong

Miguk bangmun [President Chun Doo-hwan's Visit to the United States], January 28-February 7, 1981, Vol. 6 of twelve volumes, Roll 2011-0014-0001, MOFA, ROK.

39. Korea, Briefing Paper, Department of State, March 3, 16, 1981, *Digital National Security Archive: Japan and the U.S., 1977–1992*, No. JA00840.

40. Japanese Aid Policy toward the ROK, Telegram from Ambassador in Tokyo to Secretary of State, April 17, 1981, *Digital National Security Archive: Japan and the U.S., Part III, 1961–2000*, No. JT00345.

41. Ogura Kazuo, *Hanil gyeongjehyeopjageum 100eok dalleoeui bimil* [The Secret about the Ten Billion Dollars of the Korea-Japan Economic Cooperation Fund], trans. Cho Jin-gu and Kim Young-geun (Seoul: Dione, 2015), 10.

42. "Uyeogokjeol gyeonghyeopgyoseop 2nyon [Vicissitudes of the Two-Year Negotiations for Economic Cooperation]," *Donga Ilbo*, January 12, 1983.

43. ROKG's Request for GOJ Economic Assistance, Telegram from Embassy in Tokyo to Secretary of State, May 2, 1981, *Digital National Security Archive: Japan and the U.S., Part III, 1961–2000*, No. JT00347.

44. The Joint Communique of Japanese Prime Minister Zenko Suzuki and U.S. President Reagan, May 8, 1981. http://www.ioc.u-tokyo.ac.jp/~worldjpn/documents/texts/JPUS/19810508.D1E.html; accessed December 8, 2014.

45. Taketsugu Tsurutani, "Old Habits, New Times: Challenges to Japanese-American Security Relations," *International Security* 7, no. 2 (Fall 1982): 176.

46. Oberdorfer, *Senator Mansfield*, 474.

47. For example, "Kankoku, kyogaku no enjyo o Nihon ni yosei [Korea Requested Japan Large Amount of Aid]," *Nikkei Shimbun*, July 25, 1981, cited in Ogura, *Hanil gyeongjehyeopjageum*, 63.

48. "Uyeogokjeol gyeonghyeopgyoseop 2nyon [Vicissitudes of the Two-Year Negotiations for Economic Cooperation]," *Donga Ilbo*, January 12, 1983.

49. "Gukgyojeongsanghwa ihu Ilboneui daehan gyeongjehyeomnyeok hyeonhwang, 1966–1981 [The Trend of Korea-Japan Economic Cooperation after the Normalization, 1966–1981]," in Nakasone Yasuhiro Ilbon susang banghan [Japanese Prime Minister Nakasone Yasuhiro's Visit to Korea], January 11–12, Vol. 1 of three volumes, Roll 2013-0030, MOFA, ROK.

50. Japanese View of ROK-Japan Ministerial Conference, Telegram from Embassy in Tokyo to Secretary of State, September 18, 1981, *Digital National Security Archive: Japan and the U.S., Part III, 1961–2000*, No. JT00359.

51. "Chun Doo-hwan daetongnyeong gukjeong yeonseol [President Chun Doo-hwan's New Year Address on National Politics]," *Kyunghyang Shinmun*, January 22, 1982.

52. Intelligence Notes on East Asia, January 24–30, Report No. 1, Department of State, February 3, 1982, *Digital National Security Archive: United States and the Two Koreas*, No. KO00387; Japan-Republic of Korea Relations, Briefing Paper, Department of State, April 2, 1982, *Digital National Security Archive: United States and the Two Koreas*, No. KO00393.

53. "Gukgyojeongsanghwa ihu Ilboneui daehan gyeongjehyeomnyeok hyeonhwang, 1966–1981 [The Trend of Korea-Japan Economic Cooperation after the Normalization, 1966–1981]," in Nakasone Yasuhiro Ilbon susang banghan [Japanese Prime Minister Nakasone Yasuhiro's Visit to Korea], January 11–12, Vol. 1 of three volumes, Roll 2013-0030, MOFA, ROK.

54. Shin Yong-ha, "Nihon kyokasho waikyoku jojutsu no mondaiten [Problems of the Distorted Descriptions in the Japanese Textbooks]," *Toitsu hyoron* (October 1982): 38–39.

55. According to Shin's analysis, the five-year defense development plan was intended to strengthen the SDF's defense capability in line with the U.S. strategy of containing the Soviet military presence in the Far East; the plan would be developed into a rearmament plan in the event of revision of article 9 of the Japanese constitution that forbids Japan from maintaining forces with the potential to wage war. Shin Yong-ha, "Nihon kyokasho to shingunkokushugi [Japanese Textbooks and New Militarism]," *Toitsu hyorons* (November 1982): 29–30.

56. Nakasone was the first Japanese prime minister to pay an official visit to South Korea. Previous prime ministers had visited Seoul for ceremonial purposes only, including the inaugurations of President Park Chung-hee in 1967 and 1971, and the funeral of first lady Yuk Young-soo in 1974.

57. The Japanese text presented a watered down version, which read: "on the perception that close bilateral relations in various fields will contribute to peace and stability not only of the two countries but also of Asia." See "Hanil jeongsanghoedam gongdongseongmyeong [The Joint Statement of the Korea-Japan Summit]," in Nakasone Yasuhiro Ilbon susang banghan [Japanese Prime Minister Nakasone Yasuhiro's Visit to Korea], January 11–12, Vol. 1 of three volumes, Roll 2013-0030, MOFA, ROK.

58. Some observers have called U.S.-Japan-ROK ties a "triangular alliance." For example, see Cheol Hee Park, "Japanese Strategic Thinking toward Korea," in *Japanese Strategic Thought toward Asia*, ed. Gilbert Rozman, Kazuhiko Togo, and Joseph P. Ferguson (New York: Palgrave Macmillan, 2007), 186–87.

59. "Hanil jeongsang hoedam [The Korea-Japan Summit]," *Donga Ilbo*, January 12, 1983, editorial.

60. "Taito na Nikkan kankei no kochiku o [Expecting the Construction of Equal Japan-Korea Relations]," *Sankei Shimbun*, January 13, 1983, editorial.

61. "Nakasone susang banghan banung [Responses to Nakasone's Korea Visit]," Telegram from ROK Ambassador in Washington, D.C., to the Minister of Foreign Affairs, USW-50, January 7, 1983, in Nakasone Yasuhiro Ilbon susang banghan [Japanese Prime Minister Nakasone Yasuhiro's Visit to Korea], January 11–12, Vol. 3 of three volumes, Roll 2013-0030, MOFA, ROK.

62. Your First Meeting with Foreign Minister Abe, Briefing Memorandum, from Assistant Secretary of State Paul Wolfowitz to Secretary of State George Schultz, January 26, 1983, *Digital National Security Archive: Japan and the U.S., 1977–1992*, No. JA01100; Your Meeting the Minister of Finance Noboru

Takeshita, Briefing Memorandum, from Assistance Secretary Paul Wolfowitz to Secretary of State George Shultz, January 26, 1983, *Digital National Security Archive: Japan and the U.S., 1977–1992*, No. JA01102.

Chapter 7. Controversy over Historical Issues

1. It is fair to say that the troubling territorial disputes did not exist in East Asia before World War II, and those in the postwar period are in line with the Western tradition and norm of interstate relations. See David Kang, *East Asia before the West: Five Centuries of Trade and Tribute* (New York: Columbia University Press, 2010), 162–63.

2. "South Korea, Japan Agree to Irreversibly End 'Comfort Women' Row," *New York Times*, December 28, 2015.

3. For instance, Che-po Chan and Brian Bridges, "China, Japan, and the Clash of Nationalisms," *Asian Perspective* 30, no. 1 (2006): 127–56.

4. From a psychological perspective, as victims press perpetrators to admit their misdeeds, the latter attempt to defend them instead of admitting them. This was the case not only in Japan but also in Germany, particularly in the first decade after World War II. Jennifer Lind generalizes this phenomenon by saying that "backlash is a predictable response to efforts to apologize," and "contrition will spark domestic controversy featuring denials and justification of past misdeeds." Jennifer Lind, *Sorry States: Apologies in International Politics* (Ithaca and London: Cornell University Press, 2008), 6, 182.

5. From a cultural perspective, Japan's honor culture dominating interpersonal and international relations renders genuine apology and compensation impossible. James J. Orr, *The Victim as Hero: Ideologies of Peace and National Identity in Postwar Japan* (Honolulu: University of Hawai'i Press, 2001), 11; Kazuya Fukuoka and Barry Schwartz, "Responsibility, Regret, and Nationalism in Japanese Memory," 71–97, in *Northeast Asia's Difficult Past: Essays in Collective Memory*, ed. Mikyoung Kim and Barry Schwartz (New York: Palgrave Macmillan, 2010), 88.

6. For a similarly nuanced discussion of the sense of insecurity, crisis, and vulnerability arising in the mid-1990s and the resultant rise of centralized control and militarization in Japan, see David Leheny, *Think Global, Fear Local: Sex, Violence, and Anxiety in Contemporary Japan* (Ithaca and London: Cornell University Press, 2006), 27–47.

7. Michael Schaller, *Altered States: The United States and Japan since the Occupation* (New York and Oxford: Oxford University Press, 1997), 7–30.

8. Steven C. Clemons, "U.S. Role in Japan's Amnesia," *Far Eastern Economic Review*, October 25, 2001, 32.

9. Yuma Totani, *The Tokyo War Crimes Trial: The Pursuit of Justice in the Wake of World War II* (Cambridge: Harvard University Asia Center, 2008), 117.

10. Ibid., 177–78.

11. PPS 28: Recommendations with Respect to U.S. Policy toward Japan, Report by the Policy Planning Staff (Kennan), March 25, 1948, Northeast Asia: Japan, in Far East and Australasia, *FRUS 1948*, 691–96. This document was the basis of NSC 13/2: Recommendations with Respect to U.S. Policy toward Japan, October 7, 1948.

12. Higurashi Yoshinobu, *Tokyo saiban* [The Tokyo Tribunal] (Tokyo: Kodansha, 2008), 354.

13. Ibid., 358–66.

14. Ishikawa Masumi, *Sengo seijishi, shinpan* [The History of Postwar Politics, New Edition] (Tokyo: Iwanami Shinsho, 2004), ch. 9.

15. As the Cold War thawed, the leading politicians such as Ozawa Ichiro, Koizumi Junichiro, Abe Shinzo, and Ishiba Shigeru, in a revival of revisionism, began to push for Japan to become a "normal state." Richard J. Samuels, *Securing Japan: Tokyo's Grand Strategy and the Future of East Asia* (Ithaca and London: Cornell University Press, 2007), 112.

16. Other suspects who later became leading political and business leaders include Sasakawa Ryoichi, Ayukawa Yoshisuke, and Kuhara Fusanosuke. Maesaka Toshiyuki, "Tokyo saiban to so no go" [Tokyo Tribunal and Afterwards], see http://www.maesaka-toshiyuki.com/detail/314; accessed May 20, 2011.

17. Hara Yoshihisa, *Kishi Nobusuke: Keni no seijika* [Kishi Nobusuke: The Politician of Authority] (Tokyo: Iwanami Shinsho, 1995), 145–77.

18. See Abe Shinzo, *Utsukushii kuni* [The Beautiful Country] (Tokyo: Bungei Shunju, 2006); Norimitsu Onishi, "In Japan, a Historian Stands by Proof of Wartime Sex Slavery," *New York Times*, March 31, 2007, A4.

19. Kimie Hara, "50 Years from San Francisco: Re-Examination of the Peace Treaty and Japan's Territorial Problems," *Pacific Affairs* 74, no. 3 (Fall 2001): 361–82.

20. Seokwoo Lee and Jon M. Van Dyke, "The 1951 San Francisco Peace Treaty and Its Relevance to the Sovereignty over Dokdo," *Chinese Journal of International Law* 9, no. 4 (2010): 746.

21, Jung Byung Jun, *Dokdo 1947* (Seoul: Tolbegae, 2010), 727, 752.

22. Rusk Note of 1951, http://en.wikisource.org/wiki/Rusk_note_of_1951; accessed March 4, 2015.

23. The earlier drafts of the Peace Treaty, starting with the first draft on March 19, 1947, noted the islets as belonging to Korea; drafts from the sixth version in December 8, 1949, described the islets as belonging to Japan; later versions from the tenth, on August 7, 1950, to the final version did not identify the islets' provenance. See Seokwoo Lee, "The 1951 San Francisco Peace Treaty with Japan and the Territorial Disputes in East Asia," *Pacific Rim Law & Policy Journal* 11, no. 63 (2002), 96.

24. Van Fleet's mission, from April 26 to August 7, 1954, included trips to Korea, Taiwan, Japan, and the Philippines; the subsequent report was submitted to President Eisenhower. See Han Ho-sok, Dokdo munje milyak pagiga yuilhan haeogyeolchaek ida [Dokdo Dispute: Dissolution of the Secret Agreement Is the

Only Solution], *Tongil News Online*, August 4, 2008, http://www.tongilnews.com/news/articleView.html?idxno=79684; accessed April 12, 2015.

25. Fukuhara Yuji, "Takeshima kanren gensetsu no kento [Investigation of the Statements Related to Takeshima]," *Sogo seisaku ronso* (Shimane Prefectural University) 17 (March 2009): 69.

26. Jung Byung Jun, *Dokdo 1947*, 576–80.

27. Ibid., 577.

28. For the text, see http://www.ioc.u-tokyo.ac.jp/~worldjpn/documents/texts/docs/19510908.T1E.html; accessed April 16, 2015.

29. Hara, "50 Years from San Francisco," 373; Kent E. Calder, "Securing Security through Prosperity: The San Francisco System in Comparative Perspective," *Pacific Review* 17, no. 1 (March 2004): 139.

30. Wada Haruki, *Hopporyodo mondai: rekishi to mirai* [Problems of the Northern Territories: History and Future] (Tokyo: Asahi Shimbunsha, 1999), 235.

31. Japan incorporated these four islands into its territory under the Treaty of Commerce and Navigation with Russia in 1855.

32. Yoshimi Yoshiaki, *Jugun ianfu* [The Comfort Women] (Tokyo: Iwanami Shinsho, 1995), 72.

33. Ibid., 35–37, 78, 164.

34. Hayashi Hirofumi, "The Japanese Movement to Protest Wartime Sexual Violence: A Survey of Japanese and International Literature," *Critical Asian Studies* 33, no. 4 (2001): 575.

35. Wakamiya Yoshibumi, *Wakai to nashonarizumu* [Reconciliation and Nationalism] (Tokyo: Asahi Shimbunsha, 2006), 281.

36. For the statement, see http://www.mofa.go.jp/announce/press/pm/murayama/9508.html; accessed April 16, 2015.

37. Ryuji Mukae, "Japan's Diet Resolution on World War Two: Keeping History at Bay," *Asian Survey* 36, no. 10 (1996): 1011–30.

38. Yoshihiko Nozaki, *War Memory, Nationalism and Education in Postwar Japan, 1945–2007: The Japanese History Book Controversy and Ienaga Saburo's Court Challenges* (London and New York: Routledge, 2008), 141.

39. For further discussion of Japan's apology politics, see Seraphim, *War Memory and Social Politics in Japan, 1945–2005*; Jennifer Lind, *Sorry States: Apologies in International Politics* (Ithaca and London: Cornell University Press, 2008); James J. Orr, *The Victim as Hero: Ideologies of Peace and National Identity in Postwar Japan* (Honolulu: University of Hawai'i Press, 2001).

40. For the controversy over the terminology, see Wakamiya, *Wakai to nashonarizumu*, 254–58; Taku Tamaki, *Deconstructing Japan's Image of South Korea* (New York: Palgrave Macmillan, 2010), 132–37. For the resolution by the House of Representatives adopted on June 9, 1995, entitled "Resolution to Renew the Determination for Peace on the Basis of Lessons Learned from History," see http://www.mofa.go.jp/announce/press/pm/murayama/address9506.html; accessed June 4, 2015.

41. Yayori Matsui, "Women's International War Crimes Tribunal on Japan's Military Sexual Slavery: Memory, Identity, and Society," *East Asia* 19, no. 4 (December 2001): 119–42.

42. Christine M. Chinkin, "Editorial Comments: Women's International Tribunal on Japanese Military Sexual Slavery," *American Journal of International Law* 95, no. 2 (2001): 337.

43. Alex Dudden, "We Come to Tell the Truth: Reflections on the Tokyo Women's Tribunal," *Critical Asian Studies* 33, no. 4 (2001): 592–93.

44. Carol Gluck, "Operations of Memory: 'Comfort Women' and the World," in *Ruptured Histories: War, Memory, and the Post-Cold War in Asia*, ed. Sheila Miyoshi Jager and Rana Mitter (Cambridge: Harvard University Press, 2007), 49.

45. Sung-jae Choi, "The Politics of the Dokdo Issue," *Journal of East Asian Studies* 5 (2005): 475.

46. Paul Midford, "Challenging the Democratic Peace? Historical Memory and the Security Relationship between Japan and South Korea," *Pacific Focus* 23, no. 2 (August 2008): 189–211.

47. See Nozaki, *War Memory, Nationalism, and Education*, 150; Franziska Seraphim, *War Memory and Social Politics in Japan, 1945–2005* (Cambridge: Harvard University Asia Center, 2006), 159–67; Claude Schneider, "The Japanese History Textbook Controversy in East Asian Perspective," *Annals of the American Academy* 617 (May 2008): 113.

48. Fujioka Nobukatsu, *Jigyakushikan no byori* [The Pathology of the Masochistic Historical Perspective] (Tokyo: Bungei Shunju, 1997), 82–83.

49. Fujioka Nobukatsu, "Honsho 'Tsukurukai ga tou Nippon no bijon' wa nani o toou to shitaka [What Does *The Japanese Vision that New History Textbook Inquires Into* Aim to Inquire Into?]," in *Atarashii rekishi kyokasho o Tsukurukai ga tou Nippon no bijon* [The Japanese Vision that New History Textbook Inquires Into], ed. Tsukurukai (Tokyo: Fusosha, 2003), 5–7.

50. For a discussion of the concepts of honor, status, and prestige in the history of Japan, see Kenneth Pyle, *Japan Rising: The Resurgence of Japanese Power and Purpose* (New York: Public Affairs, 2007), 62–65, 77.

51. Tawara Yoshifumi, "Atarashii rekishi kyokasho o tsukurukai uha jin-myaku [The Rightwing Connection of Tsukurukai]," *Sekai*, June 2001, 124.

52. Fujioka Nobukatsu and Yoshida Yutaka, "Koko ga okashii! Rekishi kyokasho ronso [This Is Strange! Debate about the History Textbook]," *This Is Yomiuri*, March 1997, 48.

53. Narita Ryuichi, "Rekishi o kyokasho ni egaku to iukoto [To Describe History in a Textbook]," *Sekai*, June 2001, 69.

54. Besshi Yukio, "Nihon no rekishi ninshiki to higashi Ajia gaiko [Japanese Historical Understanding and Diplomacy in East Asia]," *Hokuto Ajia Kenkyu* 3 (March 2002): 144.

55. Fujioka and Yoshida, "Koko ga okashii! Rekishi kyokasho ronso," 37.

56. Fujioka, *Jigyakushikan no byori*, 80–81.

57. Besshi, "Nihon no rekishi ninshiki to higashi Ajia gaiko," 143.

58. Tawara, "Atarashii rekishi kyokasho o tsukurukai uha jinmyaku," 125.

59. Nozaki, *War Memory, Nationalism, and Education*, 149.

60. Tsukurukai was divided on the issue of textbook adoption. It originally set a target of getting 10 percent of its textbooks adopted in 2001, but the actual adoption rate was 0.39 percent for history textbooks and 0.19 percent for social studies textbooks as of April 2005. Fujioka was severely criticized for this.

61. Tawara Yoshifumi, *Tsukurukai bunretsu to rekishi gizo no shinso* [The Division of Tsukurukai and the Depths of the Falsification of History] (Tokyo: Kadensha, 2008), 3–4.

62. Tawara, *Tsukurukai Bunretsu*, 4.

63. Tawara Yoshifumi, "Nankin daigyakusatsu 70 nen to Nihon no kyokasho mondai [The 70th Anniversary of the Nanjing Massacre and the Japanese Textbook Issue]," *Kikan chugoku* 91, no. 12 (2007): 5–8.

64. J. Patrick Boyd and Richard J. Samuels, "Prosperity's Children: Generational Change and Japan's Future Leadership," *Asia Policy* 6 (July 2008): 25–28.

65. See the open letter sent to Abe Shinzo by VAWW-NET Japan. http://www1.jca.apc.org/vaww-net-japan/nhk/openletter050120.html; accessed June 16, 2011.

66. Martin Fackler, "No Apology for Sexual Slavery, Japan's Prime Minister Says," *New York Times*, March 6, 2007.

67. Hirofumi Hayashi, "Disputes in Japan over the Japanese Military 'Comfort Women' System and Its Perception in History," *Annals of the American Academy* 617 (May 2008): 129.

68. The four were published by Tokyo Shoseki, Osaka Shoseki, Fusosha, and Nihon Shoseki Shinsha. Fukuhara Yuji, "Takeshima kanren gensetsu no kento [Investigation of the Statements Related to Takeshima]," *Sogo seisaku ronso* (Shimane Prefectural University) 17 (March 2009): 63–65.

69. "Japan Textbooks Rekindle Old Disputes," *Korea Herald*, April 4, 2011; Mark Seldon, "Small Islets, Enduring Conflict: Dokdo, Korea-Japan Colonial Legacy and the United States," *Asia-Pacific Journal* 9 (April 25, 2011): 7.

70. On February 22, 2011, officials of the ruling DPJ for the first time attended Takeshima Day ceremonies held in Shimane prefecture. This is evidence that the issue had become part of a political struggle.

71. "Rival Parties Differ over President's Dokdo Visit," *Korea Herald*, August 11, 2012.

72. "Panel Concludes Japan, S. Korea Coordinated Wording of Kono Statement," *Asahi Shimbun*, June 21, 2014. http://ajw.asahi.com/article/behind_news/politics/AJ201406210040; accessed March 5, 2015.

73. Committee of the Historical Science Society of Japan, "Public Statement: A Critique of the Japanese Government's Stance on the Wartime 'Comfort Women' Issue and Its Coverage in the Media," October 15, 2014. http://rekiken.jp/english/appeals/appeal_20141205.html; accessed March 10, 2015.

74. Fifteen history textbooks published by six companies were approved in 2011 and 2012, thirteen of which contained descriptions of the comfort women issue. Since none of them directly cited the discredited Yoshida reports, the Ministry of Education said it had no plans to request their revision. "Il chulpansa, Asahi bodochwisoe gyogawseo gunwianbu naeyongbyeongyeong geomto [Japanese Publishers Examine Revision of the Content Regarding the Comfort Women after Asahi's Cancellation of the Previous Reports]," *Yonhap News*, September 14, 2014. http://www.yonhapnews.co.kr/politics/2014/09/14/0505000000 AKR20140914045100073.HTML; accessed March 5, 2015.

75. "Dokdoneun Il yeongto, wianbu imihaegyeol, Il ibeonen woegyeocheongseo dobal [Dokdo Is Japanese Territory, Comfort Women Issue Already Solved, Japan's Provocation in the Bluebook at This Time]," *Hangook Ilbo*, April 8, 2015.

76. For the idea of the logrolling coalition with reference to Japan in the runup to the Pacific War, see Jack Snyder, *Myths of Empire: Domestic Politics and International Ambition* (Ithaca and London: Cornell University Press, 1991), 142–50.

77. The effect of diplomatic efforts was short-lived. For instance, the reconciliation and future-oriented relations that Kim Dae-jung and Obuchi Keizo pledged to adhere to during their summit on October 8, 1998, did not last. South Koreans were frustrated in 2001 with the issue of Japan's official approval for the textbooks watering down the past history. As another rupture took place in 2005, South Korea and China opposed Japan's bid for a permanent seat on the UN Security Council.

78. The territorial dispute is unlikely to trigger a major conflict between the two states. One reason for this is that South Korea controls the islets, and another is that contested islets tend not to be used for delineating territorial waters. Zhang Tuosheng, "Disputes over Territories and Maritime Rights and Interests: Their Political Economic Implications," in *The Nexus of Economics, Security, and International Relations in East Asia*, ed. Avery Goldstein and Edward D. Mansfield (Stanford: Stanford University Press, 2012), 134; Min Gyo Koo, *Island Disputes and Maritime Regime Building in East Asia: Between a Rock and a Hard Place* (New York: Springer, 2009), 99.

79. Norimitsu Onishi, "Japan Court Rules Against Sex Slaves and Laborers," *New York Times*, April 28, 2007.

80. "Confirmation of [the ROK Government's] Violation of the Constitution in Regard to [Its] Nonfeasance on Article 3 of 'Agreement on the Settlement of Problems Concerning Property and Claims and the Economic Cooperation between the Republic of Korea and Japan,'" Constitutional Court Decision No. 2006 heon ma 788, August 30, 2011.

81. Emma Chanlett-Avery, Mark E. Manyin, Ian E. Rinehart, Rebecca M. Nelson, and Brock R. Williams, "Japan-U.S. Relations: Issues for Congress," CRS Report, January 13, 2015.

82. Gilbert Rozman, "Realism versus Revisionism in Abe's Foreign Policy in 2014," in *Asia's Alliance Triangle: US-Japan-South Korea Relations at a Tumultuous Time*, ed. Gilbert Rozman (New York: Palgrave Macmillan, 2015), 242.

83. Park Cheol Hee, "Korea-Japan Relations under Deep Stress," in *Asia's Alliance Triangle*, ed. Gilbert Rozman (New York: Palgrave Macmillan, 2015), 96–98.

84. "Group of U.S. Lawmakers Protest Japan's Review of Kono Statement," *Korea Times*, June 28, 2014.

85. See "Toward an Alliance of Hope," Address by Prime Minister Shinzo Abe to a Joint Meeting of the U.S. Congress, April 29, 2015. http://www.mofa.go.jp/na/na1/us/page4e_000241.html; accessed May 2, 2015.

86. Juliet Eilperin, "Agreement on 'Comfort Women' Offers Strategic Benefit to U.S. in Asia-Pacific," *Washington Post*, January 9, 2016.

87. Quoted in ibid.

88. Ibid.; Park, "Korea-Japan Relations under Deep Stress," 99.

89. Kang Seung-woo, "US Takes Sides with Japan on History Issue," *Korea Times*, March 1, 2015.

90. Many scholars, although for different reasons, have argued that the United States should play a role in alleviating tension focused on historical issues between Japan and its neighbors. Robert B. Zoellick, "Campaign 2000: A Republican Foreign Policy," *Foreign Affairs* 79, no. 1 (2000): 63–78; Gilbert Rozman, "U.S. Strategic Thinking on the Japanese-South Korean Historical Dispute," in *U.S. Leadership, History, and Bilateral Relations in Northeast Asia*, ed. Gilbert Rozman (New York: Cambridge University Press, 2011), 143–67; Gi-Wook Shin, "History, Textbooks, Divided Memories, and Reconciliation," in *History Textbooks and the Wars in Asia: Divided Memories*, ed. Gi-Wook Shin and Daniel C. Sneider (London and New York: Routledge, 2011), 12.

Chapter 8. North Korea Factor and the Persistence of the Security Triangle

1. For details on Japan's strategic thinking, see Tsuyoshi Hasegawa, "Japan's Strategic Thinking toward Asia in the First Half of the 1990s," in *Japanese Strategic Thought toward Asia*, ed. Gilbert Rozman, Kazuhiko Togo, and Joseph P. Ferguson (New York: Palgrave Macmillan, 2007), 57–78.

2. Don Oberdorfer, *The Two Koreas: A Contemporary History* (Reading, MA: Addison-Wesley, 1997), 266–67.

3. "U.S. Said to Give Deadline to North Korea," *New York Times*, January 24, 1992.

4. William J. Perry, *My Journey at the Nuclear Brink* (Stanford: Stanford University Press, 2015), 106–108.

5. For the development of the Korean standard model, see Lee Jong-hun, *Hangukui haekjugwon* [Korea's Nuclear Sovereignty] (Seoul: Gulmadang, 2009).

6. Nuclear Threat Initiative, "Korean Peninsula Energy Development Organization," http://www.nti.org/treaties-and-regimes/korean-peninsula-energy-development-organization-kedo/; accessed February 2, 2016.

7. The official name of the report was "Review of United States Policy toward North Korea: Findings and Recommendations (Unclassified Report)."

8. Sheryl WuDunn, "North Korea Fires Missile Over Japanese Territory," *New York Times*, September 1, 1998.

9. Park Jong-chul, *Perry Process wa Han-Mi-Il hyeomnyeok bangan* [The Perry Process and Search for Korea-U.S.-Japan Cooperation Measures] (Seoul: Korea Institute for National Unification, 2005), 5–9.

10. The TCOG operated until 2003 when the Six-Party Talks became the most important multilateral mechanism for the solution of North Korea's nuclear development.

11. Perry, *My Journey at the Nuclear Brink*, 162–65.

12. For the Joint Communique, see http://www.state.gov/1997-2001-NOP-DFS/regions/eap/001012_usdprk_jointcom.html; accessed February 1, 2015.

13. Perry, *My Journey at the Nuclear Brink*, 167–68.

14. Chinese believed that the revision of the Guidelines was intended to check Beijing's policy on the Taiwan Strait as well as to deter North Korean threat, in view of the fact that the revision occurred right after China's missile tests over the Strait. Thomas J. Christensen, "China, the U.S.-Japan Alliance, and the Security Dilemma in East Asia," in *International Relations Theory and the Asia-Pacific*, ed. G. John Ikenberry and Michael Mastanduno (New York: Columbia University Press, 2003), 34.

15. Peter J. Katzenstein and Nobuo Okawara, "Japan, Asia-Pacific Security, and the Case for Analytic Eclecticism," *International Security* 26, no. 3 (Winter 2001/02): 159.

16. The Japanese government eventually announced its decision to acquire MD capability on December 17, 2003. Hideaki Kaneda et al., "Japan's Missile Defense: Diplomatic and Security Policies in a Changing Strategic Environment," Report of the Japan Institute of International Affairs, March 2007.

17. Christensen, "China, the U.S.-Japan Alliance," 35–36.

18. "Nuclear Posture Review" (Excerpts), January 8, 2002. http://www.imi-online.de/download/Nuclear_Posture_Review.pdf; accessed February, 2016.

19. White House, "The National Security Strategy of the United States of America," Washington, DC: White House, September 2002, 6.

20. Korean Central News Agency, "Choseon oemuseong 8gaeguk sunoe-jahoweui seoneone choseonmunjega pohamdeonde dehayeo [Spokesperson for DPRK Foreign Ministry on Declaration Adopted at G8 Summit]," June 6, 2003.

21. See Lee Soo-hyuk, *Jeonhwanjeok sageon: Bukhaek munje jeongmil bunseok* [Transformative Incident: A Close Analysis of North Korean Nuclear Issue] (Seoul: Jungang Books, 2008), 51.

22. Jeremy Paltiel, "China and the North Korean Crisis: The Diplomacy of Great Power Transition," in *North Korea's Second Nuclear Crisis and Northeast*

Asian Security, ed. Seung-Ho and Tae-Hwan Kwak (Burlington, VT: Ashgate, 2013), 155.

23. The United States' engagement with North Korea at the multilateral talks ironically evidenced the failure of its policy to protect its ally through deterrence and pressure. Terence Roehrig, *From Deterrence to Engagement: The U.S. Defense Commitment to South Korea* (Lanham, MD: Lexington Books, 2006).

24. Larry A. Niksch, "North Korea: Terrorism List Removal," CRS Report for Congress, January 6, 2010.

25. Robert S. Litwak, "Living with Ambiguity: Nuclear Deals with Iran and North Korea," *Survival* 50, no. 1 (2008): 91–118; Patrick Disney, "Kicking the Hornets' Nest: Iran's Nuclear Ambivalence and the West's Counterproductive Nonproliferation Policies," *Nonproliferation Review* 19, no. 2 (2012): 159–75.

26. Testimony by Song Min-soon, the former ROK representative at the Six-Party Talks, at the conference held at Seoul National University, September 19, 2012.

27. For a full account of Koizumi's Pyongyang visit, see Tanaka Hitoshi, *Gaiko no chikara* [The Power of Diplomacy] (Tokyo: Nihon Keizai Shimbun Shuppansha, 2009), 99–139; Yoichi Funabashi, *The Peninsula Question: A Chronicle of the Second Korea Nuclear Crisis* (Washington, DC: Brookings Institution Press, 2007), 1–30.

28. The popularity of Koizumi and his North Korea policy, rose momentarily from 43 percent in August to 67 percent right after the summit. *Mainichi Shimbun*, September 23, 2002.

29. "Don't Haggle over Abduction Issue," *Japan Times*, November 1, 2002.

30. At the second summit, Koizumi offered US$100 million in assistance and 250,000 tons of rice aid. Victor D. Cha, *The Impossible State: North Korea, Past and Future* (New York: HarperCollins, 2012), 382.

31. "Pyongyang Summit Falls Short for Kin of Those Still Missing," *Japan Times*, May 23, 2004.

32. For the exploding impact of the abduction issue on Japan's North Korea policy, see Jung Ho Bae and Sung Chull Kim, "Japan's North Korea Policy: The Dilemma of Coercion," in *Engagement with North Korea: A Viable Alternative*, ed. Sung Chull Kim and David C. Kang (Albany: State University of New York Press, 2009), 73–98.

33. Mark E. Manyin, Emma Chanlett-Avery, and Helene Marchart, "North Korea: A Chronology of Events, October 2002-December 2004," CRS Report for Congress, January 24, 2005, 7; Hong Nack Kim, "Japanese-North Korean Relations under the Koizumi Government," in *North Korea: The Politics of Regime Survival*, ed. Young Whan Kihl and Hong Nack Kim (Armonk, NY: M. E. Sharpe, 2006), 170.

34. The impact of Japanese sanctions was limited, but subsequent South Korean punitive measures made North Korea even more reliant on the Chinese economy. Trade with China occupied 32.5 percent of the North's total trade in 2002, 67.1 percent in 2007, 88.3 percent in 2012, and 89.1 percent in 2013. Bang Ho-kyung and Hong Yi-kyung, "Choegeun Bukjung muyeogeui

juyo teukjinggwa sisajeom [Recent North Korea-China Trade, Main Points and Implications]," KIEP Regional Economic Focus 8, no. 29, June 2014.

35. " 'Indirect' Aid for N. Korea, Not Money: Aso," *Japan Times*, February 12, 2007.

36. "Japan's Missile Shield: Concerns Growing over Arms Race in East Asia," *Korea Times*, December 19, 2007.

37. "ASDF Now Giving Radar Info to U.S.," *Japan Times*, May 13, 2007.

38. "Upper House Panel Passes Bill on Space," *Japan Times*, May 21, 2008.

39. China demonstrated its assertiveness in the military use of space by destroying an old satellite. China became only the third country to succeed in carrying out such a test (the others were the United States and the Soviet Union). "China's Muscle Flex in Space," *New York Times*, January 20, 2007, editorial.

40. Jung Ho-Sub, "ROK-US-Japan Naval Cooperation in the Korean Peninsula Area: Prospects for Multilateral Security Cooperation," *International Journal of Korean Studies* 16, no. 1 (Spring 2012): 192–208.

41. In March 2011, the EDPC began analyzing North Korean threats and sharing information about them. The allies also carried out joint exercises and practiced decision-making procedures in preparation for a nuclear crisis. At the 45th SCM in October 2013, their defense ministers signed a tailored deterrence strategy. Ministry of Foreign Affairs, Republic of Korea, "Migukeui daehan bangwigongyak, hwakjangeokje [The U.S. Security Commitment to Korea, Extended Deterrence]," http://www.mofa.go.kr/trade/areaissue/noramerica/nuclear/index.jsp? menu=m_30_30_30&tabmenu=t_4; accessed April 20, 2015.

42. For the text, see http://www.state.gov/r/pa/prs/ps/2010/12/152431.htm; accessed February 10, 2015.

43. Kurt Campbell, Assistant Secretary of State for East Asian and Pacific Affairs, Hearing before the Committee on Foreign Relations, United States Senate, 112th Congress 1st Session, March 1, 2011.

44. "Korea, US, Japan Naval Exercise to Enhance Defensive Capabilities," *Korea Times*, June 16, 2012.

45. Bruce Klinger, "Washington Should Urge Greater South Korean-Japanese Military and Diplomatic Cooperation," Heritage Backgrounder 2734, September 24, 2012.

46. Ashley A. C. Hess and John K. Warden, "Japan and Korea: Opportunities for Cooperation," *National Interest*, March 19, 2014.

47. "Surely Japan and South Korea Can Patch Things Up," *Asahi Shimbun*, July 6, 2012, editorial.

48. Myoung-kyu Park, Philo Kim, Young-hoon Song, Yong-seok Chang, and Eun-mee Chung, *2013 Tongil euisikjosa* [Survey Analysis of Attitudes on Unification Issues, 2013], (Seoul: Seoul National University Institute for Peace and Unification, 2013), 67–68.

49. The Law of Nuclear Weapons State, adopted in April 2013, stated that North Korea "supports international arms control." Also, in his speech at the UN General Assembly in October, North Korea's vice foreign minister Park

Kil Yon proposed nuclear disarmament negotiations. See Press Release, Statement by Park Kil Yon, October 1, 2013. http://gadebate.un.org/sites/default/files/gastatements/68/KP_en.pdf; accessed February 15, 2016.

50. Bruce Klingner, "Washington Should Urge Greater South Korean-Japanese Military and Diplomatic Cooperation," Heritage Backgrounder 2734, September 24, 2012.

51. Kim Jiyoon, Karl Friedhoff, Kang Chungku, and Lee Euicheol, "Challenges and Opportunities for Korea-Japan Relations in 2014," Public Opinion Studies Program, Asan Institute for Policy Studies, March 17–19, 2014.

52. Xinhua, "Chinese President Delivers Speech at Seoul National University," July 4, 2014. http://en.people.cn/n/2014/0704/c90883-8751134.html; accessed February 1, 2016.

53. Cited in Kim Kyu-ryun, "Hanmi jeongsang hoedam gyeolgwa bunseok [An Analysis of the ROK-U.S. Summit Result]," Seoul: KINU, May 2014, 41.

54. "Han-mi-il Bukhan haek-missile jeongbo gongyu yakjong chegyeol ilji [Chronology of the Establishment of the Information Sharing Pact between Korea, U.S., and Japan]," *Yonhap News*, December 29, 2014.

55. Martin Fackler, "Japan and South Korea Vow to Share Intelligence about North via the U.S.," *New York Times*, December 30, 2014.

56. See Trilateral Information Sharing Arrangement Concerning the Nuclear and Missile Threats Posed by North Korea among the Ministry of National Defense of the Republic of Korea, the Ministry of Defense of Japan, and the Department of Defense of the United States of America, December 29, 2014.

57. "Intelligence-Sharing Deal," *Korea Times*, December 28, 2014, editorial.

58. Indeed, alongside the issue of trilateral information sharing, the possible deployment of a U.S. THAAD system on South Korean territory became a pressing and sensitive issue between South Korea, China, and the United States.

59. Sachiko Miwa, "Japan, U.S., S. Korea Sign Pact to Share Intelligence on North Korea," *Asahi Shimbun*, December 30, 2014.

60. Cited from "N. Korea Raps Seoul Allies' Military Info Sharing Pact," *Korea Herald*, January 15, 2015.

61. The most notable statement in the decision regarding collective self-defense is as follows: "The Government has reached a conclusion that not only when an armed attack against Japan occurs but also when an armed attack against a foreign country that is in a close relationship with Japan occurs and as a result threatens Japan's survival and poses a clear danger to fundamentally overturn the people's right to life, liberty, and the pursuit of happiness, and when there is no other appropriate means available to repel the attack and ensure Japan's survival and protect its people, use of force, to the minimum extent necessary, should be interpreted to be permitted under the Constitution as measures for self-defense in accordance with the basic logic of the Government's view to date."

62. For the extensive debate in Japan with regard to this armed attack issue, see Hosoya Yuichi, "Japanese Politics Concerning Collective Self-Defense," Asan Forum, August 11, 2014.

63. "The Guidelines for Japan-U.S. Defense Cooperation," April 27, 2015. http://www.mod.go.jp/e/d_act/anpo/pdf/shishin_20150427e.pdf; accessed April 30, 2015.

64. Some examples are Japan's MD operations in the name of protecting U.S. forces and the Japanese SDF escorting a convoy of U.S. ships transporting Japanese nationals from South Korea to Japan. "Jeongbu, yusasi Hanmi yonhap jakjeon guyeokseo Iljipdan jawigwon bulyong [The Government Would Not Allow Japan's Collective Self-Defense in the KTO]," Yonhap News, July 8, 2014.

65. "South Korea Urges Transparency in Japan's New Security Policy," Japan Times, September 29, 2015.

66. Lee Sung-eun, "Seoul Stays Tough on Japan's Security Laws," JoongAng Daily, September 21, 2015.

67. "China Voices Concern over Possible THAAD Deployment in S. Korea," Korea Times, May 31, 2015.

68. "South Korea, U.S., Japan to Set Up New Channel to Share Info on North Korea," Korea Times, January 22, 2016.

69. What makes the extended deterrence today distinctive is North Korea's nuclear weapons development. However, as Patrick Morgan aptly notes, deterrence has been woven into elements of foreign policy and national security strategy throughout the Cold War and the post–Cold War periods. In particular, deterrence against North Korea has long been the backbone of the U.S.-ROK alliance and one of the most important elements of their security cooperation. For the general discussion about the continued utility of deterrence both as a theory and as a strategy, see Deterrence Now (Cambridge: Cambridge University Press, 2003).

70. See Yuki Tatsumi, "Introduction," in US-Japan-Australia Security Cooperation: Prospects and Challenges, ed. Yuki Tatsumi (Washington, DC: Stimson Center, 2015), 15–16.

Chapter 9. Conclusions

1. James Mann, About Face: A History of America's Curious Relationship with China, from Nixon to Clinton (New York: Vintage, 2000), 65, 87.

2. Reinhard Drifte, "The Ending of Japan's ODA Loan Programme to China: All's Well That Ends Well?" Asia-Pacific Review 13, no. 1 (2006): 94–117.

3. Jae Ho Chung, Between Ally and Partner: Korea-China Relations and the United States (New York: Columbia University Press, 2007), 33.

4. See Joseph S. Nye Jr., Is the American Century Over? (Cambridge: Polity Press, 2015), 49–52.

5. John J. Mearsheimer, *The Tragedy of Great Power Politics* (New York: W. W. Norton, 2001).

6. See Christopher Coker, *The Improbable War: China, the United States, and Logic of Great Power Conflict* (Oxford: Oxford University Press, 2015); Jonathan Holslag, *China's Coming War with Asia* (Cambridge: Polity Press, 2015); Andrew F. Krepinevich Jr., "How to Deter China: The Case for Archipelagic Defense," *Foreign Affairs* 94, no. 2 (March-April 2015): 78–86.

7. Nye, *Is the American Century Over?*, 67; Michael D. Swaine, "The Real Challenge in the Pacific: A Response to 'How to Deter China,'" *Foreign Affairs* 94, no. 3 (May/June 2015): 145–53.

8. "Boeishishin to anpohosei 'senshu' honenuki no ayausa [Dangers of the Defense Guidelines and Security-related Legislation that Water Down the Defense-centered Policy]," *Tokyo Shimbun*, April 28, 2015, editorial.

9. "Aso, Il-junggwangye, 1,500 nyeongan budeureowoddeon jeok eopseotta [Aso Says There Has Been No Smooth Period in the Past One Thousand Five Hundred Years]," *Kyunghyang Shinmun*, May 5, 2013. http://news.khan.co.kr/kh_news/art_print.html?artid=201305052211575; accessed June 30, 2015.

10. The dual policy originates from the Chinese belief that North Korea has a certain degree of value in Beijing's strategy of reducing, resisting, and replacing (the so-called 3 Rs) U.S. influence in East Asia. North Korea apparently exploits this strategy and continues to carry out provocative actions. Scott Snyder, *China's Rise and the Two Koreas* (Boulder and London: Lynne Rienner, 2009), 130–32; Fei-Ling Wang, "Between the Bombs and the United States: China Faces the Nuclear North Korea," unpublished manuscript.

11. Evelyn Goh, *The Struggle for Order: Hegemony, Hierarchy, and Transition in Post–Cold War East Asia* (Oxford: Oxford University Press, 2013), 215–26.

12. Additionally, anti-Americanism that rose in the 2000s in South Korea contributed to the South Korean tilt toward China. See Gi-Wook Shin, *One Alliance, Two Lenses: U.S.-Korea Relations in a New Era* (Stanford: Stanford University Press, 2010), 11–18; David C. Kang, *China Rising: Peace, Power, and Order in East Asia* (New York: Columbia University Press, 2007), 104–25; Chung Min Lee, "Revamping the Korean-American Alliance: New Political Forces, Paradigms, and Roles and Missions," in *Korea Attitudes toward the United States: Changing Dynamics*, ed. David I. Steinberg (Armonk, NY: M. E. Sharpe, 2005), 155–79.

13. Ellen Hallams and Benjamin Schreer, "Towards a 'Post-American' Alliance? NATO Burden-sharing after Libya," *International Affairs* 88, no. 2 (2012): 313–27.

14. For details, see Lam Peng Er, "The Fukuda Doctrine: Origins, Ideas, and Praxis," in *Japan's Relations with Southeast Asia: The Fukuda Doctrine and Beyond*, ed. (Oxon: Routledge, 2013), 10–23.

15. Brad Glosserman and Scott A. Snyder, *The Japan-South Korea Identity Clash: East Asian Security and the United States* (New York: Columbia University Press, 2015), 11–17.

16. David Walton, "Australia and Japan: Toward a Full Security Partnership," in *Japan's Strategic Challenges in a Changing Regional Environment*, ed. Purnendra Jain and Lam Peng Er (London and Singapore: World Scientific, 2013), 149–73; Thomas S. Wilkins, "Toward a 'Trilateral Alliance? Understanding the Role of Expediency and Values in American-Japanese-Australian Relations," *Asian Security* 3, no. 3 (2007): 251–78.

17. See "Joint Statement of Japan-U.S.-Australia Defense Ministers," May 30, 2015. http://www.minister.defence.gov.au/2015/05/30/ministerfordefencejapanusaustraliadefenseministersmeetingjointstatement/; accessed July 12, 2015.

18. Mina Pollmann, "US-Japan-Australia Security Cooperation: Beyond Containment," *The Diplomat*, April 21, 2015.

19. Robert S. Ross, "US Grand Strategy, the Rise of China, and US National Security Strategy for East Asia," *Strategic Studies Quarterly* 7, no. 2 (Summer 2013), 29.

20. Michael McDevitt, "A Modest Proposal to Help ASEAN Reconcile Their Overlapping Claims in the Spratlys," *PacNet*, No. 40, July 9, 2015.

21. Ralf Emmers, "ASEAN's Search for Neutrality in the South China Sea," *Asian Journal of Peacebuilding* 2, no. 1 (2014): 61–77.

22. Ross, "US Grand Strategy," 34.

23. Richard J. Samuels, *Securing Japan: Tokyo's Grand Strategy and the Future of East Asia* (Ithaca and London: Cornell University Press, 2007), 77–80.

24. "SDF Observes Island Defense Exercise in Philippines, Aimed at Countering China," *Asahi Shimbun*, October 3, 2014. http://ajw.asahi.com/article/behind_news/politics/AJ201410030061; accessed July 7, 2015.

25. Prashanth Parameswaran, "Philippines to Hold Military Exercises with US, Japan," *The Diplomat*, June 19, 2015. http://thediplomat.com/2015/06/philippines-to-hold-military-exercises-with-us-japan/; accessed July 7, 2015.

26. "Philippines: US Lifts Restrictions on Military Aid," *Defense News*, January 22, 2015. http://www.defensenews.com/story/defense/international/asia-pacific/2015/01/22/philippines-military-aid-funds/22173719/; accessed July 7, 2015.

Bibliography

Archives

294.9522 in RG59, Central Decimal File 1955–1959, The U.S. National Archives and Records Administration.

Declassified Diplomatic Documents, 1959–1983 each year, Ministry of Foreign Affairs, Republic of Korea.

Digital National Security Archive: Japan and the U.S., 1960–1976. ProQuest, electronic resource.

Digital National Security Archive: Japan and the U.S., 1977–1992. ProQuest, electronic resource.

Digital National Security Archive: Japan and the U.S., Part III, 1961–2000. ProQuest, electronic resource.

Digital National Security Archive: United States and the Two Koreas, 1969–2000. ProQuest, electronic resource.

Documents on United States Policy toward Japan, XVIII: Documents Related to Diplomatic and Military Matters, Vols. 2–6. Tokyo: Kashiwashobo, 2006.

Foreign Relations of the United States (FRUS), 1948, Northeast Asia: Japan in Vol. VI, The Far East and Australasia; 1958–1960, Japan, Korea; 1961–1963, Korea; 1964–1968, Korea. Washington, DC: U.S. Government Printing Office.

Japan and the United States: Diplomatic, Security and Economic Relations, 1960–1976. Ann Arbor: Bell & Howell Information and Learning, 2000, microfiche.

National Institute of Korean History, ed. *Hanil hoedam gwangye migukmubu munseo* [The Department of State of the United States Documents Related to Korea-Japan Talks], Vol. 4 (1956–1958). Seoul: NIKH, 2008.

Sixth Declassification on Japan-Korea Normalization Talks, Ministry of Foreign Affairs, Japan.

Books and Articles

Abe Shinzo. *Utsukushii kuni* [The Beautiful Country]. Tokyo: Bungei Shunju, 2006.

Alesina, Alberto, and David Dollar. "Who Gives Foreign Aid to Whom and Why?" *Journal of Economic Growth* 5, no. 1 (March 2000): 33–63.

Armacost, Michael. *Friends or Rivals? The Insider's Account of U.S.-Japan Relations.* New York: Columbia University Press, 1996.

Armstrong, Charles. *Tyranny of the Weak: North Korea and the World, 1950–1992.* Ithaca and London: Cornell University Press, 2014.

Bailey, Kenneth D. *Sociology and the New Systems Theory: Toward a Theoretical Synthesis.* Albany: State University of New York Press, 1994.

Bang Ho-kyung and Hong Yi-kyung. "Choegeun Bukjung muyeogeui juyo teukjinggwa sisajeom [Recent North Korea-China Trade, Main Points and Implications]." *KIEP Regional Economic Focus* 8, no. 29, June 2014.

Bearce, David H., and Daniel C. Tirone. "Foreign Aid Effectiveness and the Strategic Goals of Donor Governments." *Journal of politics* 72, no. 3 (July 2010): 837–51.

Besshi Yukio. "Nihon no rekishi ninshiki to higashi Ajia gaiko [Japanese Historical Understanding and Diplomacy in East Asia]." *Hokuto Ajia Kenkyu* 3 (March 2002): 131–49.

Blaker, Michael, Paul Giarra, and Ezra Vogel. *Case Studies in Japanese Negotiating Behavior.* Washington, DC: United States Institute of Peace Press, 2002.

Boyd, J. Patrick, and Richard J. Samuels. "Prosperity's Children: Generational Change and Japan's Future Leadership." *Asia Policy* 6 (July 2008): 25–28.

Brzezinski, Zbigniew. "The Cold War and Its Aftermath." *Foreign Affairs* 71, no. 4 (Fall 1992): 31–49.

Buckley, Roger. *US-Japan Alliance Diplomacy, 1945–1990.* Cambridge: Cambridge University Press, 1992.

Buss, Claude A. *The United States and the Republic of Korea: Background for Policy.* Stanford: Hoover Institution Press, 1982.

Calder, Kent E. "Domestic Constraints and Japan's Foreign Economic Policy of the 1990s." *International Journal* 46, no. 4 (Autumn 1991): 607–22.

———. "Japanese Foreign Economic Policy Formation: Explaining the Reactive State." *World Politics* 40, no. 4 (July 1988): 517–40.

———. "Securing Security through Prosperity: The San Francisco System in Comparative Perspective." *Pacific Review* 17, no. 1 (March 2004): 135–57.

Cha, Victor D. *Alignment Despite Antagonism: The US-Korea-Japan Security Triangle.* Stanford: Stanford University Press, 1999.

———. *The Impossible State: North Korea, Past and Future.* New York: HarperCollins, 2012.

Chalmers, Malcolm. "The Atlantic Burden-sharing Debate: Widening or Fragmenting?" *International Affairs* 77, no. 3 (2001): 569–85.

Chan, Che-po, and Brian Bridges. "China, Japan, and the Clash of Nationalisms." *Asian Perspective* 30, no. 1 (2006): 127–56.

Chan, Steve. "Humanitarianism, Mercantilism, or Comprehensive Security? Disbursement Patterns of Japanese Foreign Aid." *Asian Affairs: An American Review* 19, no. 1 (1992): 3–17.

Chanlett-Avery, Emma, et al. "Japan-U.S. Relations: Issues for Congress." CRS Report, January 13, 2015.

Chi Myong-kuan. *Nikkan kankeishi kenyu: 1965nen taisei kara 2002 nen taisei e* [A Study on the History of Japan-Korea Relations]. Tokyo: Shingyo Shuppansha, 1999.

Chinkin, Christine M. "Women's International Tribunal on Japanese Military Sexual Slavery." *American Journal of International Law* 95, no. 2 (April 2001): 335–41.

Cho Ah Ra. "Hanilhoedam gwajeongeseoeu Migugeu yeokhal [The U.S. Role in Korea-Japan Normalization Talks: Focusing on the Claim Negotiation under the Kennedy Administration]." *Ilbon bipyeong* 10 (2014): 270–307.

Choi Kyungwon. *Reisenki Nikkan anzenhosho kankei no keisei* [The Formation of the Japan-Korea Security Relations during the Cold War]. Tokyo: Keio University Press, 2013.

Choi, Sung-jae. "The Politics of the Dokdo Issue." *Journal of East Asian Studies* 5, no. 3 (2005): 465–94.

Christensen, Thomas J. "China, the U.S.-Japan Alliance, and the Security Dilemma in East Asia." In *International Relations Theory and the Asia-Pacific*, edited by G. John Ikenberry and Michael Mastanduno. New York: Columbia University Press, 2003.

———. *Worse than a Monolith: Alliance Politics and Problems of Coercive Diplomacy in Asia.* Princeton: Princeton University Press, 2011.

Chung, Jae Ho. *Between Ally and Partner: Korea-China Relations and the United States.* New York: Columbia University Press, 2007.

Clemons, Steven C. "U.S. Role in Japan's Amnesia." *Far Eastern Economic Review.* October 25, 2001: 32.

Coker, Christopher. *The Improbable War: China, the United States, and Logic of Great Power Conflict.* Oxford: Oxford University Press, 2015.

Committee for the Development through Truth Finding, National Intelligence Agency, ed. *Gwageowa daehwa, mirae eui seongchal: juyo euihok sageon pyeon* [Dialogue with the Past, Reflections for the Future: Main Mysterious Incidents]. Vol. 2. Seoul: National Intelligence Agency, 2007.

Cossa, Ralph A. "Planning for the Future of the ROK-U.S. Alliance: A Joint Vision for Today and Post-Reunification." *Korean Journal of Defense Analysis* 25, no. 4 (2013): 519–29.

Disney, Patrick. "Kicking the Hornets' Nest: Iran's Nuclear Ambivalence and the West's Counterproductive Nonproliferation Policies." *Nonproliferation Review* 19, no. 2 (2012): 159–75.

Drifte, Reinhard. "The Ending of Japan's ODA Loan Programme to China: All's Well That Ends Well?" *Asia-Pacific Review* 13, no. 1 (2006): 94–117.

Dudden, Alex. "We Come to Tell the Truth: Reflections on the Tokyo Women's Tribunal." *Critical Asian Studies* 33, no. 4 (2001): 591–602.

Eilperin, Juliet. "Agreement on 'Comfort Women' Offers Strategic Benefit to U.S. in Asia-Pacific." *Washington Post*, January 9, 2016.

Emmers, Ralf. "ASEAN's Search for Neutrality in the South China Sea." *Asian Journal of Peacebuilding* 2, no. 1 (2014): 61–77.

Fioretos, Orfeo. "Historical Institutionalism in International Relations," *International Organization* 65 (Spring 2011): 367–99.

Fujioka Nobukatsu. *Jigyakushikan no byori* [The Pathology of the Masochistic Historical Perspective]. Tokyo: Bungeishunju, 1997.

——— and Yoshida Yutaka. "Koko ga okashii! Rekishi kyokasho ronso [This Is Strange! Debate about the History Textbook]." *This Is Yomiuri* (March 1997): 34–51.

Fukuhara Yuji. "Takeshima kanren gensetsu no kento [Investigation of the Statements Related to Takeshima]." *Sogo seisaku ronso* (Shimane Prefectural University) 17 (March 2009): 61–81.

Fukui, Haruhiro. *Party in Power: The Japanese Liberal-Democrats and Policy-making.* Berkeley: University of California Press, 1970.

Fukuoka, Kazuya, and Barry Schwartz. "Responsibility, Regret, and Nationalism in Japanese Memory." In *Northeast Asia's Difficult Past: Essays in Collective Memory*, edited by Mikyoung Kim and Barry Schwartz, 71–97. New York: Palgrave Macmillan, 2010.

Funabashi, Yoichi. *The Peninsula Question: A Chronicle of the Second Korea Nuclear Crisis.* Washington, DC: Brookings Institution Press, 2007.

Gaddis, John Lewis. *Strategies of Containment: A Critical Appraisal of American National Security Policy during the Cold War.* Revised edition. Oxford: Oxford University Press, 2005.

Glosserman, Brad. "Japan: from Muddle to Model." *Washington Quarterly* 37, no. 2 (2014): 39–53.

———, and Scott A. Snyder. *The Japan-South Korea Identity Clash: East Asian Security and the United States.* New York: Columbia University Press, 2015.

Gluck, Carol. "Operations of Memory: 'Comfort Women' and the World." In *Ruptured Histories: War, Memory, and the Post–Cold War in Asia*, edited by Sheila Miyoshi Jager and Rana Mitter, 47–77. Cambridge: Harvard University Press, 2007.

Goh, Evelyn. "How Japan Matters in the Evolving East Asian Security Order." *International Affairs* 87, no. 4 (2011): 887–902.

———. *The Struggle for Order: Hegemony, Hierarchy, and Transition in Post–Cold War East Asia.* Oxford: Oxford University Press, 2013.

Goldstein, Avery, and Edward D. Mansfield, eds. *The Nexus of Economics, Security, and International Relations in East Asia.* Stanford: Stanford University Press, 2012.

Gordon, Andrew. *A Modern History of Japan: From Tokugawa Times to the Present.* Oxford: Oxford University Press, 2003.

Grant, Richard, and Jan Nijman. "Historical Changes in U.S. and Japanese Foreign Aid to the Asia-Pacific Region." *Annals of the Association of American Geographers* 87, no. 1 (1997): 32–51.

Green, Michael J. *Arming Japan: Defense Production, Alliance Politics, and the Postwar Search for Autonomy.* New York: Columbia University Press, 1995.

Guess, George M. *The Politics of United States Foreign Aid*. London and New York: Routledge, 1987.

Ha Young-sun. "Hangukeui gunsabi jichuleui chusewa jeonmang [Trend and Prospects for Korea's Defense Expenditure]." *Nonmunjip* (Seoul National University Center for International Studies) 7 (1982): 289–306.

Hallams, Ellen, and Benjamin Schreer. "Towards a 'Post-American' Alliance? NATO Burden-sharing after Libya." *International Affairs* 88, no. 2 (2012): 313–27.

Han Sung-Joo. *The United Nations: The Next Fifty Years*. Seoul: Ilmin International Relations Institute, Korea University, 1996.

Han, Sang-jin. "Bureaucratic Authoritarianism and Economic Development in Korea during the Yushin Period: A Reexamination of O'Donnell's Theory." In *Dependency Issues in Korean Development: Comparative Perspectives*, edited by Kyong-dong Kim, 362–74. Seoul: Seoul National University Press, 1987.

Hara Yoshihisa. *Kishi Nobusuke: Keni no seijika* [Kishi Nobusuke: The Politician of Authority]. Tokyo: Iwanami Shinsho, 1995.

Hara, Kimie. "50 Years from San Francisco: Re-Examination of the Peace Treaty and Japan's Territorial Problems." *Pacific Affairs* 74, no. 3 (Fall 2001): 361–82.

Hasegawa, Tsuyoshi. "Japan's Strategic Thinking toward Asia in the First Half of the 1990s." In *Japanese Strategic Thought toward Asia*, edited by Gilbert Rozman, Kazuhiko Togo, and Joseph P. Ferguson, 57–78. New York: Palgrave Macmillan, 2007.

Hayashi, Hirofumi. "Disputes in Japan over the Japanese Military 'Comfort Women' System and Its Perception in History." *Annals of the American Academy* 617 (May 2008): 123–32.

———. "The Japanese Movement to Protest Wartime Sexual Violence: A Survey of Japanese and International Literature." *Critical Asian Studies* 33, no. 4 (2001): 572–80.

Hein, Laura E. "Growth versus Success: Japan's Economic Policy in Historical Perspective." In *Postwar Japan as History*, edited by Andrew Gordon, 99–122. Berkeley: University of California Press, 1993.

Hess, Ashley A. C., and John K. Warden, "Japan and Korea: Opportunities for Cooperation." *National Interest*, March 19, 2014.

Higurashi Yoshinobu. *Tokyo saiban* [The Tokyo Tribunal]. Tokyo: Kodansha, 2008.

Hirschman, Albert O. *National Power and the Structure of Foreign Trade*. Berkeley: University of California Press, 1980.

Holslag, Jonathan. *China's Coming War with Asia*. Cambridge: Polity Press, 2015.

Hong Seuk-Ryule. "1970 nyeondae jeonban dongbuga detant wa Hanguk tongil munje [The Détente in Northeast Asia and the Korean Unification Issue in the Early 1970s]." *Yeoksawa hyeonsil* 42 (2001): 207–41.

Horikane Yumi. "1970 nendai kankoku no jukagaku kogyoka to Nikkan keizai kyoryoku: Pohang Sogo Seitetsu to yondai kakukojou purojekuto o chushin to shite [South Korea's Heavy and Chemical Industrialization Push and Japan-Korea Economic Cooperation in the 1970s: The Cases of POSCO and the Four Core Projects]." *Meji daigaku shakai kagaku kenkyujo kiyo* 45, no. 1 (October 2006): 75–99.

Hosoya Yuichi. "Japanese Politics Concerning Collective Self-Defense." *Asan Forum*, August 11, 2014.

Howe, Christopher. "China, Japan, and Economic Interdependence in the Asia Pacific Region." *China Quarterly* 124 (December 1990): 662–93.

Ikeda Naotaka. *Nichi-Bei kankei to hutatsu no chugoku* [Japan-U.S. Relations and Two Chinas]. Tokyo: Bokutakusha, 2004.

Ikenberry, John. *After Victory: Institutions, Strategic Restraint, and the Rebuilding of Order after Major Wars*. Princeton: Princeton University Press, 2001.

Im, Hyug Baeg. "The Rise of Bureaucratic Authoritarianism in South Korea." *World Politics* 39, no. 2 (1987): 231–57.

Inada, Juichi. "Japan's Aid Diplomacy: Economic, Political, or Strategic?" *Millennium: Journal of International Studies* 18, no. 3 (1989): 399–414.

Iriye, Akira. "Chinese-Japanese Relations." *China Quarterly* 124 (December 1990): 624–38.

Ishikawa Masumi. *Sengo seijishi, shinpan* [The History of Postwar Politics, New Edition]. Tokyo: Iwanami Shinsho, 2004.

Jang Bak-jin. *Miwaneui cheongsan* [Incomplete Settlement]. Seoul: Yeoksa gonggan, 2014.

Janis, Mark W. *An Introduction to International Law*. Boston: Little, Brown, 1988.

Joseon jungang nyeongam 1976 [Korean Central Yearbook 1976]. Pyongyang: Joseon jungang tongsinsa, 1976.

Jung Byung Jun. *Dokdo 1947*. Seoul: Tolbegae, 2010.

Jung Ho-Sub. "ROK-US-Japan Naval Cooperation in the Korean Peninsula Area: Prospects for Multilateral Security Cooperation." *International Journal of Korean Studies* 16, no. 1 (Spring 2012): 192–208.

Kaneda, Hideaki, et al. "Japan's Missile Defense: Diplomatic and Security Policies in a Chaning Strategic Environment." Report of the Japan Institute of International Affairs, March 2007.

Kang, David. *China Rising: Peace, Power, and Order in East Asia*. New York: Columbia University Press, 2007.

———. *East Asia before the West: Five Centuries of Trade and Tribute*. New York: Columbia University Press, 2010.

———. "Getting Asia Wrong: The Need for New Analytic Frameworks." *International Security* 27, no. 4 (2003): 57–85.

Katsumata, Hiro. *ASEAN's Cooperative Security Enterprise: Norms and Interests in the ASEAN Regional Forum*. Basingstoke: Palgrave Macmillan, 2009.

Katzenstein, Peter J., and Nobuo Okawara. "Japan, Asia-Pacific Security, and the Case for Analytic Eclecticism." *International Security* 26, no. 3 (Winter 2001–02): 153–85.

Keohane, Robert O. *After Hegemony: Cooperation and Discord in the World Political Economy*. Princeton: Princeton University Press, 1984.

Kim Dong-jo. *Kan-nichi no wakai* [Korea-Japan Reconciliation]. Tokyo: Saimaru Shuppansha, 1993.

Kim, Hong Nack. "Japanese-North Korean Relations under the Koizumi Government." In *North Korea: The Politics of Regime Survival*, edited by Young Whan Kihl and Hong Nack Kim. Armonk, NY: M. E. Sharpe, 2006.

Kim, Min-hyung. "Why Provoke? The Sino-US Competition in East Asia and North Korea's Strategic Choice." *Journal of Strategic Studies* (May 2015): 1–20.

Kim, Sung Chull, and David Kang. eds., *Engagement with North Korea: A Viable Alternative*. Albany: State University of New York Press, 2009.

Kim Jiyoon, Karl Friedhoff, Kang Chungku, and Lee Euicheol. "Challenges and Opportunities for Korea-Japan Relations in 2014." Public Opinion Studies Program, Asan Institute for Policy Studies, March 17–19, 2014.

Kim Ki-son. *Hanil hoedam bandae undong* [Movement against Korea-Japan Normalization Talks]. Seoul: Korea Democracy Foundation, 2005.

Kim Kyu-ryun. "Hanmi jeongsang hoedam gyeolgwa bunseok [An Analysis of the ROK-U.S. Summit Result]." Seoul: KINU, 2014.

Kim Song-sik. *Iljeha Hankuk haksaeng dongnip undongsa* [History of Student Movement in Korea during the Japanese Colonial Rule]. Seoul: Chong-umsa, 1974.

Kim Yong-ho. *Nikkan kankei to Kankoku no tainichi kodo* [Japan-South Korea Relations and South Korea's Response to Japan]. Tokyo: Sairyusha, 2008.

Kimiya Tadashi. "Ilhan kukkyo jeongsanghwa kyoseop eseoeui cheonggukwon munje jaego [Revisiting the Claims Issue in the Normalization Negotiations]." In *Je 2-gi Hanil yeoksa gongdong yeongu bogoseo* [Report of Korea-Japan Collaborative History Research], Section III, edited by The Committee for Korea-Japan Collaborative History Research, 77–128. Seoul: The Committee for Korea-Japan Collaborative History Research, 2010.

Klare, Michael T. "Superpower Rivalry at Sea." *Foreign Policy* 21 (Winter 1975–76): 86–96, 161–67.

Klinger, Bruce. "Washington Should Urge Greater South Korean-Japanese Military and Diplomatic Cooperation." Heritage Backgrounder 2734. September 24, 2012.

Koh, B. C. "South Korea in 1996: Internal Strains and External Challenges." *Asian Survey* 37, no. 1 (January 1997): 1–9.

Koo, Min Gyo. *Island Disputes and Maritime Regime Building in East Asia: Between a Rock and a Hard Place*. New York: Springer, 2009.

Kookmin University Institute of Japanese Studies. *Hanil hoedam oegyomunseo haejejip IV: Gowi jeongchi hoedam mit 7-cha hoedam* [Collected Interpretations of the Diplomatic Documents Related to the Korea-Japan Normalization Talks: High Political Talks and the Seventh Talks]. Seoul: Northeast Asian History Foundation, 2008.

Krepinevich, Andrew F. Jr. "How to Deter China: The Case for Archipelagic Defense." *Foreign Affairs* 94, no. 2 (March-April 2015): 78–86.

Lake, David. *Hierarchy in International Relations*. Ithaca and London: Cornell University Press, 2009.

Lam Peng Er, ed. *Japan's Relations with Southeast Asia: The Fukuda Doctrine and Beyond*. Oxon: Routledge, 2013.

Lee, Chong-Sik. *Japan and Korea: The Political Dimension*. Stanford: Hoover Institution Press, 1985.

Lee, Chung Min. "Revamping the Korean-American Alliance: New Political Forces, Paradigms, and Roles and Missions." In *Korean Attitudes toward the United States: Changing Dynamics*, edited by David I. Steinberg, 155–79. Armonk: N.Y.: M. E. Sharpe, 2005.

Lee, Seokwoo. "Dokdo: The San Francisco Peace Treaty, International Law on Territorial Disputes, and Historical Criticism." *Asian Perspective* 35, no. 3 (July-September 2011): 361–80.

———. "The 1951 San Francisco Peace Treaty with Japan and the Territorial Disputes in East Asia," *Pacific Rim Law & Policy Journal* 11, no. 63 (2002), 65–146.

———, and Jon M. Van Dyke. "The 1951 San Francisco Peace Treaty and Its Relevance to the Sovereignty over Dokdo." *Chinese Journal of International Law* 9, no. 4 (December 2010): 741–62.

Lee Jong-hun. *Hangukui haekjugwon* [Korea's Nuclear Sovereignty]. Seoul: Gulmadang, 2009.

Lee Jong-won. "Kannichi kaidan to Amerika: Hukainyu seisaku no seiritsu wo chushin ni [Korea-Japan Talks and the United States: With Special Reference to the Nonintervention Policy]. *Kokusai seiji* 105 (1994): 163–81.

———. "Nikkan no shinkokai gaikobunsho ni miru Nikkan kaidan to Amerika, II [Japan-Korea Talks and the United States Analyzed from the Newly Declassified Diplomatic Archives, II]." *Rikkyo hogaku* 77 (2009): 109–40.

———. "Nikkan no shinkokai gaikobunsho ni miru Nikkan kaidan to Amerika, III [Japan-Korea Talks and the United States Analyzed from the Newly Declassified Diplomatic Archives, III]." *Rikkyo hogaku* 78 (2010): 155–205.

Lee Soo-hyuk. *Jeonhwanjeok sageon: Bukhaek munje jeongmil bunseok* [Transformative Incident: A Close Analysis of North Korean Nuclear Issue]. Seoul: Jungang Books, 2008.

Lee Won-deog. *Hanil gwageosa cheorieui wonjeom: Ilboneui jeonhucheori oegyowa Hanil hoedam* [Original Point of the Settlement of the Korea-Japan Past History: Japan's Diplomacy for Postwar Settlement and Korea-Japan Normalization Talks]. Seoul: Seoul National University Press, 1996.

Leheny, David. *Think Global, Fear Local: Sex, Violence, and Anxiety in Contemporary Japan*. Ithaca and London: Cornell University Press, 2006.

Lind, Jennifer. *Sorry States: Apologies in International Politics*. Ithaca and London: Cornell University Press, 2008.

Litwak, Robert S. "Living with Ambiguity: Nuclear Deals with Iran and North Korea." *Survival* 50, no. 1 (2008): 91–118.

Luhmann, Niklas. *Social Systems*. Stanford: Stanford University Press, 1996.

MacDonald, Donald Stone. *U.S.-Korean Relations from Liberation to Self-Reliance: The Twenty-Year Record.* Boulder: Westview, 1992.

Mahoney, James, and Kathleen Thelen, eds. *Explaining Institutional Change: Ambiguity, Agency, and Power.* Cambridge: Cambridge University Press, 2010.

Mann, James. *About Face: A History of America's Curious Relationship with China, from Nixon to Clinton.* New York: Vintage Books, 2000.

Manyin, Mark E., Emma Chanlett-Avery, and Helene Marchart. "North Korea: A Chronology of Events, October 2002-December 2004." CRS Report for Congress, January 24, 2005.

Martin, Lisa L., and Beth A. Simmons. "Theories and Empirical Studies of International Institutions." *International Organization* 52, no. 4 (Autumn 1988): 729–57.

Matsui, Yayori. "Women's International War Crimes Tribunal on Japan's Military Sexual Slavery: Memory, Identity, and Society." *East Asia* 19, no. 4 (December 2001): 119–42.

Mayer, Frederick W. "Managing Domestic Differences in International Negotiations: The Strategic Use of Internal Side-Payments." *International Organization* 46, no. 4 (September 1992): 793–818.

Mearsheimer, John J. *The Tragedy of Great Power Politics.* New York: W. W. Norton, 2001.

Meyer, Armin H. *Assignment: Tokyo.* Indianapolis and New York: Bobbs-Merrill, 1974.

Midford, Paul. "Challenging the Democratic Peace? Historical Memory and the Security Relationship between Japan and South Korea." *Pacific Focus* 23, no. 2 (August 2008): 189–211.

Miller, James G. *Living Systems.* New York: McGraw-Hill, 1978.

Milner, Helen. "The Assumption of Anarchy in International Relations Theory: A Critique." In *Neorealism and Neoliberalism: The Contemporary Debate,* edited by David A. Baldwin, 143–69. New York: Columbia University Press, 1993.

Miyashita, Akitoshi. "Gaiatsu and Japan's Foreign Aid: Rethinking the Reactive-Proactive Debate." *International Studies Quarterly* 43, no. 4 (December 1999): 695–731.

———. *Limits to Power: Asymmetric Dependence and Japanese Foreign Aid Policy.* Lanham, MD: Lexington Books, 2003.

Mo, Jongryn. "Domestic Institutions and International Bargaining: The Role of Agent Veto in Two-Level Games." *American Political Science Review* 89, no. 4 (December 1995): 914–24.

———. "The Logic of Two-Level Games with Endogenous Domestic Coalitions." *Journal of Conflict Resolution* 38, no. 3 (September 1994): 402–22.

Morgan, Patrick M. *Deterrence Now.* Cambridge: Cambridge University Press, 2003.

Morris-Suzuki, Tessa. *Exodus to North Korea: Shadows from Japan's Cold War.* Lanham, MD: Rowman and Littlefield, 2007.

Mukae, Ryuji. "Japan's Diet Resolution on World War Two: Keeping History at Bay." *Asian Survey* 36, no. 10 (1996): 1011–30.

Muroyama Yoshimasa. *Nichibei anpo taisei* [Japan-U.S. Security System]. Tokyo: Yuhikaku, 1998.

Nagano Shinichiro. *Sogoizon no Nikkan keizai kankei* [Japan-Korea Economic Relations of Interdependence]. Tokyo: Keisoshobo, 2008.

Nam Ki-jeong. "Hanil hoedam sigi Hanil yanggukeui gukjesahoe insik: Eoeop mit Pyonghwason ul dulleossan, gukjebopeul jungsimuro [Korean and Japanese Perception of International Society in the Era of Normalization Talks: With Special Reference to the Debates on International Law Regarding the Fishery Rights and the Peace Line]." *Segye jeongchi* 29, no. 2 (Fall-Winter 2008): 125–57.

Narita Ryuichi. "Rekishi o kyokasho ni egaku to iukoto [To Describe History in a Textbook]." *Sekai* (June 2001): 69–77.

National Unification Board. *Bukhan choego inminhoeui jaryojip* [Collections of the Supreme People's Assembly Record]. Vol. 3. Seoul: National Unification Board, 1988.

Nihon shakaito chuohonbu kikanshi koho iinkai. *Nihon shakaito 50 nen* [Fifty Years of the Japan Socialist Party]. Tokyo: Nihon shakaito, 1995.

Niksch, Larry A. "North Korea: Terrorism List Removal." CRS Report for Congress, January 6, 2010.

———. "U.S. Troop Withdrawal from South Korea: Past Shortcomings and Future Prospect." *Asian Survey* 21, no. 3 (March 1981): 325–41.

Nozaki, Yoshihiko. *War Memory, Nationalism and Education in Postwar Japan, 1945–2007: The Japanese History Book Controversy and Ienaga Saburo's Court Challenges*. London and New York: Routledge, 2008.

Nye, Joseph S. Jr. *Is the American Century Over?* Cambridge: Polity Press, 2015.

Oberdorfer, Don. *Senator Mansfield: The Extraordinary Life of a Great American Statesman and Diplomat*. Washington, DC: Smithsonian Books, 2003.

———. *The Two Koreas: A Contemporary History*. Reading, MA: Addison-Wesley, 1997.

Ogura Kazuo. *Hanil gyeongjehyeopjageum 100eok dalleoeui bimil* [The Secret about the Ten Billion Dollars of the Korea-Japan Economic Cooperation Fund]. Translated by Cho Jin-gu and Kim Young-geun. Seoul: Dione, 2015.

Oneal, John R. "The Theory of Collective Action and Burden Sharing in NATO." *International Organization* 44, no. 3 (Summer 1990): 379–402.

Orr, James J. *The Victim as Hero: Ideologies of Peace and National Identity in Postwar Japan*. Honolulu: University of Hawai'i Press, 2001.

Orr, Robert M. Jr. "Collaboration or Conflict? Foreign Aid and U.S.-Japan Relations." *Pacific Affairs* 62, no. 4 (Winter 1989–90): 476–89.

———. "The Aid Factor in U.S.-Japan Relations." *Asian Survey* 28, no. 7 (July 1988): 740–56.

Oshita Eiji. *Keiseikai Takeshita gakko* [The Keiseikai Takeshita School]. Tokyo: Kodansha, 1999.

Ota Masakatsu. *Meiyaku no yami: Kaku no kasa to Nichibei domei* [Dark Side of the Pact: The Nuclear Umbrella and Japan-U.S. Alliance]. Tokyo: Nippon hyoronsha, 2004.

Paltiel, Jeremy. "China and the North Korean Crisis: The Diplomacy of Great Power Transition." In *North Korea's Second Nuclear Crisis and Northeast Asian Security*, edited by Seung-Ho and Tae-Hwan Kwak, 95–110. Burlington, VT: Ashgate, 2013.

Park, Cheol Hee. "Japanese Strategic Thinking toward Korea." In *Japanese Strategic Thought toward Asia*, edited by Gilbert Rozman, Kazuhiko Togo, and Joseph P. Ferguson, 183–200. New York: Palgrave Macmillan, 2007.

———. "Korea-Japan Relations under Deep Stress." In *Asia's Alliance Triangle: US-Japan-South Korea Relations at a Tumultuous Time*, edited by Gilbert Rozman, 87–104. New York: Palgrave Macmillan, 2015.

Park, Myoung-kyu, Philo Kim, Young-hoon Song, Yong-seok Chang, and Eun-mee Chung. *2013 Tongil euisikjosa* [Survey Analysis of Attitudes on Unification Issues, 2013]. Seoul: Seoul National University Institute for Peace and Unification, 2013.

Park, Tae-gyun. "1950–60 nyondae Migukui Hangukgun kamchungnongwa Hanguk chongbuui Taeung [The U.S. Policy of Korean Troop Reduction and the Korean Government's Response in the 1950s and the 1960s]." *Kukje jiyok yongu* 9, no. 3 (Fall 2000): 31–53.

———. "Change in U.S. Policy toward South Korea in the Early 1960s." *Korean Studies* 23 (1999): 94–120.

———. "Hanil hoedam sigi cheonggugwon munjeeui giwon gwa Migukeui yokhwal [Origin of the Claims Issue in the Korea-Japan Normalization Talks and the U.S. Role]." *Hanguksa yeongu* 131 (December 2005): 35–59.

Park Jin-hee. *Hanil hoedam: Je 1-gonghwagukeui daeiljeongchaek gwa Hail hoedam jeongae gwajeong* [Korea-Japan Normalization Talks: The First Republic's Japan Policy and the Development of the Normalization Talks]. Seoul: Sonin, 2008.

Park Jong-chul. *Perry Process wa Han-Mi-Il hyeomnyeok bangan* [The Perry Process and Search for Korea-U.S.-Japan Cooperation Measures]. Seoul: Korea Institute for National Unification, 2005.

Park Myung-rim. "Je 2-gongwaguk jeongchi gyunyeoleui gujowa byeonhwa [Structure and Its Transformation in the Political Division of the Second Republic]." In *Je 2-gongwagukgwa Hanguk minjujueui* (*The Second Republic and Korean Democracy*), edited by Paik Young-chul, 207–68. Seoul: Nanam, 1996.

Pempel, T. J. "Structural Gaiatsu: International Finance and Political Change in Japan." *Comparative Political Studies* 32, no. 8 (December 1999): 907–32.

Perry, William J. *My Journey at the Nuclear Brink*. Stanford: Stanford University Press, 2015.

Purnendra, Jain, and Lam Peng Er, eds. *Japan's Strategic Challenges in a Changing Regional Environment*. London and Singapore: World Scientific, 2013.

Putnam, Robert. "Diplomacy and Domestic Politics: The Logic of Two-Level Games." *International Organization* 42, no. 3 (Summer 1988): 427–60.

Pyle, Kenneth B. *Japan Rising: The Resurgence of Japanese Power and Purpose.* New York: Public Affairs, 2007.

Reischauer, Edwin O. *My Life between Japan and America.* New York: Harper and Row, 1986.

Rhyu, Sang-young, and Seungjoo Lee. "Changing Dynamics in Korea-Japan Economic Relations: Policy Ideas and Development Strategy." *Asian Survey* 46, no. 2 (2006), 195–214.

Rix, Alan. *Japan's Economic Aid: Policy-making and Politics.* New York: St. Martin's Press, 1980.

Roehrig, Terence. *From Deterrence to Engagement: The U.S. Defense Commitment to South Korea.* Lanham, MD: Lexington Books, 2006.

———, Jungmin Seo, and Uk Heo, eds. *Korean Security in a Changing East Asia.* Santa Barbara: Praeger, 2007.

Ross, Robert S. "US Grand Strategy, the Rise of China, and US National Security Strategy for East Asia." *Strategic Studies Quarterly* 7, no. 2 (Summer 2013): 20–40.

Rozman, Gilbert. "Realism versus Revisionism in Abe's Foreign Policy in 2014." In *Asia's Alliance Triangle: US-Japan-South Korea Relations at a Tumultuous Time,* edited by Gilbert Rozman, 241–54. New York: Palgrave Macmillan, 2015.

———. "U.S. Strategic Thinking on the Japanese-South Korean Historical Dispute." In *U.S. Leadership, History, and Bilateral Relations in Northeast Asia,* edited by Gilbert Rozman, 143–67. New York: Cambridge University Press, 2011.

———. *Northeast Asia's Stunted Regionalism: Bilateral Distrust in the Shadow of Globalization.* Cambridge: Cambridge University Press, 2003.

Samuels, Richard J. *Securing Japan: Tokyo's Grand Strategy and the Future of East Asia.* Ithaca and London: Cornell University Press, 2007.

Sato Katsumi. *Waga taikenteki chosen mondai* [Korean Problem as We Experienced]. Tokyo: Toyo Keizai Shimposha, 1978.

Schaller, Michael. *Altered States: The United States and Japan since the Occupation.* New York and Oxford: Oxford University Press, 1997.

Schmidt Jr., Robert J. "International Negotiations Paralyzed by Domestic Politics: Two-Level Game Theory and the Problem of the Pacific Salmon Commission." *Environmental Law* 26, no. 1 (Spring 1996): 95–140.

Schneider, Claude. "The Japanese History Textbook Controversy in East Asian Perspective." *Annals of the American Academy* 617 (May 2008): 107–22.

Schoppa, Leonard J. "Two-Level Games and Bargaining Outcomes: Why Gaiatsu Succeeds in Japan in Some Cases but not Others." *International Organization* 47, no. 3 (Summer 1993): 353–86.

Sela, Avraham. *The Decline of the Arab-Israeli Conflict: Middle East Politics and the Quest for Regional Order.* Albany: State University of New York Press, 1998.

Seldon, Mark. "Small Islets, Enduring Conflict: Dokdo, Korea-Japan Colonial Legacy and the United States." *Asia-Pacific Journal* 9 (April 25, 2011): 1–10.

Seraphim, Franziska. *War Memory and Social Politics in Japan, 1945–2005*. Cambridge: Harvard University Asia Center, 2006.

Shin, Gi-Wook. *One Alliance, Two Lenses: U.S.-Korea Relations in a New Era*. Stanford: Stanford University Press, 2010.

———, and Daniel C. Sneider. eds. *History Textbooks and the Wars in Asia: Divided Memories*. London and New York: Routledge, 2011.

Shin Bongkil. *Hanjungil hyeomnyeogeu jinhwa: 3guk hyeomnyeogsamuguk seolipgwa hyeomnyeogeu jedohwa* [Evolution of the ROK-China-Japan Cooperation: The Establishment of the Trilateral Cooperation Secretariat and the Institutionalization of Cooperation]. Seoul: Korea University Asiatic Research Institute, 2015.

Shin Jong-hwa. *Ilbon eui daebuk jeongchaek* [Japan's North Korea Policy]. Seoul: Orum, 2003.

Shin Yong-ha. "Nihon kyokasho to shingunkokushugi [Japanese Textbooks and New Militarism]." *Toitsu hyoron* (November 1982): 26–43.

———. "Nihon kyokasho waikyoku jojutsu no mondaiten [Problems of the Distorted Descriptions in the Japanese Textbooks]." *Toitsu hyoron* (October 1982): 38–40.

Snyder, Glenn H. *Alliance Politics*. Ithaca and London: Cornell University Press, 1997.

———. "The Security Dilemma in Alliance Politics." *World Politics* 36, no. 4 (July 1984): 461–95.

Snyder, Jack. *Myths of Empire: Domestic Politics and International Ambition*. Ithaca and London: Cornell University Press, 1991.

Snyder, Scott. "The China-Japan Rivalry: Korea's Pivotal Position?" In *Cross Currents: Regionalism and Nationalism in Northeast Asia*, edited by Gi-Wook Shin and Daniel C. Sneider, 241–55. Stanford: The Walter H. Shorenstein Asia-Pacific Research Center at Stanford University, 2007.

———. *China's Rise and the Two Koreas*. Boulder and London: Lynne Rienner, 2009.

Soeya, Yoshihide. *Japan's Economic Diplomacy with China, 1945–1978*. Oxford: Clarendon Press, 1998.

Solingen, Etel. *Regional Orders at Century's Dawn: Global and Domestic Influences on Grand Strategy*. Princeton: Princeton University Press, 1998.

Solinger, Dorothy J. *China's Transition from Socialism*. Armonk, NY: M. E. Sharpe, 1993.

Solomon, Richard, and Nigel Quinney. *American Negotiating Behavior: Wheeler-Dealers, Legal Eagles, Bullies, and Preachers*. Washington, DC: United States Institute of Peace Press, 2010.

Son Kisup. "Hanil anbogyeonghyeop oegyo jengchaek [Policymaking of the Korea-Japan Security-Economic Cooperation: Japanese Governmental Loan to Korea, 1981–1983]." *Gukjejeongchi nonchong* 49, no. 1 (2009): 305–28.

———. "Ilbonui daechungguk wonjojeongchaekui pyonhwawa teukjing [The Change and Characteristics of Japan's Aid Policy to China: Compared with the Aid to Southeast Asia and Korea]." *Ilbonyeongu nonchong* 21 (2005): 63–103.

Suhrke, Astri. "Burden-sharing during Refugee Emergencies: The Logic of Collective versus National Action." *Journal of Refugee Studies* 11, no. 4 (1998): 396–415.

Swaine, Michael D. "The Real Challenge in the Pacific: A Response to 'How to Deter China.'" *Foreign Affairs* 94, no. 3 (May/June 2015): 145–53.

Takasaki Sozi, and Park Jung Jin, eds. *Kikokuundo towa nandattanoka* [What Was the Returning-to-Homeland Movement?]. Tokyo: Heibonsha, 2005.

Takasaki Sozi. *Kensho Nikkan kaidan* [Verification of Japan-Korea Talks]. Tokyo: Iwanami Shinsho, 1996.

Tamaki, Taku. *Deconstructing Japan's Image of South Korea: Identity in Foreign Policy.* New York: Palgrave Macmillan, 2010.

Tanaka Akihiko. *Nicchu kankei, 1949–1990* [Japan-China Relations, 1949–1990]. Tokyo: The University of Tokyo Press, 1991.

Tanaka Hitoshi. *Gaiko no chikara* [The Power of Diplomacy]. Tokyo: Nihon Keizai Shimbun Shuppansha, 2009.

Tatsumi, Yuki. "Introduction." In *US-Japan-Australia Security Cooperation: Prospects and Challenges*, edited by Yuki Tatsumi, 15–21. Washington, DC: Stimson Center, 2015.

Tawara Yoshifumi. "Atarashii rekishi kyokasho o tsukurukai uha jinmyaku [The Rightwing Connection of Tsukurukai]." *Sekai* (June 2001): 124–29.

———. "Nankin daigyakusatsu 70 nen to Nihon no kyokasho mondai [The 70th Anniversary of the Nanjing Massacre and the Japanese Textbook Issue]." *Kikan chugoku* 91, no. 12 (2007): 2–9.

———. *Tsukurukai bunretsu to rekishi gizo no shinso* [The Division of Tsukurukai and the Depths of the Falsification of History]. Tokyo: Kadensha, 2008.

Thompson, Kenneth W. ed., *Moral Dimensions in American Foreign Policy.* New Brunswick, NJ: Transaction Books, 1994.

Totani, Yuma. *The Tokyo War Crimes Trial: The Pursuit of Justice in the Wake of World War II.* Cambridge: Harvard University Asia Center, 2008.

Trumbore, Peter F. "Public Opinion as a Domestic Constraint in International Negotiations: Two-Level Games in the Anglo-Irish Peace Process." *International Studies Quarterly* 42, no. 3 (September 1998): 545–65.

Tsukurukai, ed. *Atarashii rekishi kyokasho o Tsukurukai ga tou Nippon no bijon* [The Japanese Vision that New History Textbook Inquires Into]. Tokyo: Fusosha, 2003.

Tsurutani, Taketsugu. "Old Habits, New Times: Challenges to Japanese-American Security Relations." *International Security* 7, no. 2 (Fall 1982): 175–87.

Wada Haruki. *Hopporyodo mondai: rekishi to mirai* [Problems of the Northern Territories: History and Future]. Tokyo: Asahi Shimbunsha, 1999.

Wakaizumi Kei. *Tasaku nakarishi wo shinzemu to hossu* [Wanting to Believe No Other Alternatives Available]. Tokyo: Bungei Shunju, 1994.

Wakamiya Yoshibumi. *Wakai to nashonarizumu* [Reconciliation and Nationalism]. Tokyo: Asahi Shimbunsha, 2006.

Walt, Stephen M. *The Origins of Alliances*. Ithaca and London: Cornell University Press, 1990.

Walton, David. "Australia and Japan: Toward a Full Security Partnership." In *Japan's Strategic Challenges in a Changing Regional Environment*, edited by Purnendra Jain and Lam Peng Er, 149–73. London and Singapore: World Scientific, 2013.

Wang, Fei-Ling. "Between the Bombs and the United States: China Faces the Nuclear North Korea." unpublished manuscript.

Wilkins, Thomas S. "Toward a 'Trilateral Alliance? Understanding the Role of Expediency and Values in American-Japanese-Australian Relations." *Asian Security* 3, no. 3 (2007): 251–78.

Yamada Eizo. *Seiden Sato Eisaku* [Biography of Sato Eisaku]. (Tokyo: Shinchosha, 1988).

Yang Ki-woong. *Ilbonui oegyo hyopsang* [Japanese Diplomatic Negotiation]. Seoul: Sohwa, 1998.

Yang Young-shik. *Tongil jeongchaekron* [A Study on Unification Policy]. Seoul: Bakyeongsa, 1997.

Yasumoto, Dennis T. *The Manner of Giving: Strategic Aid and Japanese Foreign Policy*. Lexington, MA: Lexington Books, 1986.

Yoon, Tae Ryong. "Making Peace: Learning to Cooperate Not to Cooperate, Bargaining for the 1965 Korea-Japan Normalization." *Asian Perspective* 32, no. 2 (2008): 59–91.

Yoshimi Yoshiaki. *Jugun ianfu* [The Comfort Women]. Tokyo: Iwanami Shinsho, 1995.

Zhao, Quansheng. *Japanese Policymaking: The Politics behind Politics*. Westport, CT: Praeger/Oxford: Oxford University Press, 1993.

Zoellick, Robert B. "Campaign 2000: A Republican Foreign Policy." *Foreign Affairs* 79, no. 1 (2000): 63–78.

Index

9/11, 2, 37, 173, 180, 187

abandonment, 4–5, 13, 19
Abe Shinzo, 37, 144, 156–157, 158, 159, 161–164, 183, 185–186, 196
Acquisition and Cross-Servicing Agreement, 182
Afghanistan, 117, 121
Agency for International Development, 85
Agreement on Japan-North Korea Trade Promotion, 98, 100, 107
aid. *See* burden sharing
Akagi Munenori, 74
Albanian Resolution, 92–93
Albright, Madeleine, 172
Algerian Resolution, 112
Armacost, Michael, 120
Association of Southeast Asian Nations, 14, 199–201

Bangladesh, 120
Berger, Samuel, 65, 71, 74–75
Blinken, Anthony J., 163
Boissier, Leopold, 54, 56
Brzezinski, Zbigniew, 117, 121
Bundy, William P., 75, 78
burden sharing, 1, 7, 9, 12, 13, 14, 15, 25, 128, 171, 189, 201; aid as, 4–6, 10, 11, 61–62, 63–65, 67–68, 123–127, 195, 200; connection with commitment (or partnership

commitment), 4, 11, 19–21, 25–37, 71, 86, 167, 190, 194, 195; in KEDO, 171, 188; two faces of, 194–196; U.S.-framed, 2, 6, 11, 24, 26, 36, 61, 69, 117–138, 194–195; U.S. pressure on Japan, 33, 35, 61, 67–68, 75, 127–129. *See also* U.S. intervention, Japan-South Korea relations, United States-Japan relations, United States-South Korea relations
Bush, George W., 173, 175, 180

Calcutta Agreement, 39, 52, 56, 58. *See also* repatriation
Cambodia, 117, 121, 200; Khmer Rouge, 121
Campbell, Kurt, 181
Carter-Kim meeting, 169
Carter-Ohira summit, 124, 135
Carter, Jimmy, 118, 121, 125, 127, 129
Chang Myon, 63, 64, 65
China: as reference of security, 191–194; assertive behavior, 14, 37, 180, 188, 192, 198–200; representation in UN, 89, 91–93, 95, 101, 114; rise of, 2, 3, 14, 22, 37, 140, 157, 167, 191, 192–193. *See also* Japan-China relations, United States-China relations
Cho Myong-rok, 172